Ⅱ0665717

SPIRITUALITIES:
PAST, PRESENT, AND FUTURE

AN INTRODUCTION

NATHAN R. KOLLAR

LORETTE WILMOT LIBRARY
NAZARETH COLLEGE

Copyright © 2012 Nathan R. Kollar
All Rights Reserved

ISBN: 147832032X
ISBN-13: 9781478320326
Library of Congress Control Number: 2012913938
Createspace, North Charleston, SC

DEDICATION

To Rudolph, Eleanor, Rudy, and Judy; to David, Carrie, Laura, Camille, Sharon, Todd, and Jean who share the spiritual journey with me: May your voices always bring joy, your tears the necessary water for love's growth, and your touch the warmth for needed compassion. You have helped me discover the promises of the future and urged me to fulfill them. Thank you!

ACKNOWLEDGEMENTS

This book has taken a lifetime to experience and research. It never would have been finished without the expertise and encouragement of Carol, Libby, Bonnie, Bill, Janet, and Mohammad—and, of course, Jean, whose love surrounded every thought and struggle I experienced to get the words just right.

An everlasting thanks to all those who participated in the retreats, seminars, classes of theology or religious studies, workshops, and hours of spiritual direction—your spirit enlivens everything that follows.

TABLE OF CONTENTS

Dedication iii

Acknowledgements iii

Table of Contents iv

Introduction vi

Part One: Spirituality 1

   1. Spiritualities: Where Do We Begin? .3

   2. Spiritual Connections: Culture, Religion, and Spirituality in a
      Liminal Age 19

   3. Spiritual Sources, Signposts, and a Compass for a Spiritual Life. . .50

Part Two: Classical Spiritualities: Past and Present 77

   4. God's People: The Classical Spiritualities of Judaism,
      Christianity, and Islam 81

   5. Seeking Eternity within and Harmony with All: The Classical
      Spiritualities of Hinduism, Buddhism, Taoism (Daoism),
      Confucianism, Shinto, and Indigenous Spiritualities. 130

Part Three: Liminal Spiritualities: Spiritual Offerings in a Time
      of Radical Change 176

   6. New Spiritualities: Modern Spiritualities in a Liminal Age 180

   7. Marginal Spiritualities: What's Old Is New Again 214

Part Four: Testing Spirits: Cultural and Personal **256**

    8. Spiritualities in Conversation: Death, Afterlife, Judgment,
       Suffering, and Evil. 258

    9. Hard Choices: Conversing with Self and Others to Discover
       Your Spirit. 294

Appendix: Dos and Don'ts of Spiritual Listening **324**

Glossary **326**

Glossary of Key Terms for Discussing Spiritualities **340**

Resources **346**

Notes. **350**

Index. **382**

INTRODUCTION

*The "here and now" never greets us. It is always present. Yet
we know we have lived and we hope we will continue to live.
Somehow, our past, present, and future are bound together. Do
we know, or care to know, what or who binds them together?
How do we become involved with this transforming force?
How exactly are we transformed? The way of life we call
"spirituality" offers us the vision, means, and community
to enable us to answer these questions.*

* * *

*Without loving and being loved, we die. Without speaking out
for justice and embracing life, we die. Without choosing the good
and avoiding evil, we die. Condemned to eternal life with a
dead soul is truly a daily hell.*

* * *

This book will help you understand what spirituality is, and it will
inform you of the various spiritualities available to you. Its emphasis is
upon factual descriptions of past and present spiritual ways of life so
that you can make the necessary choices to shape your future. Another book
I wrote, *Soul Searching: A Handbook for Discovering, Developing, and Talking
about Your Spirituality,* focuses on the practical ramifications of what is discussed here.

This book is about something very real: your spiritual life and the spiritual
life of others. You experience your spiritual life in the here and now, in the full
light of work, love, disagreements, cheering for your favorite team, and crawl-
ing into bed at night. This is real. You began it with your first breath. You have
lived it ever since. Your future spiritual life is what you are co-creating with
every choice you make. You may choose to deepen this spiritual life, abandon

it, or modify it in some way. With these choices, you create either an energized, alive soul or a soul without spirit—a dead soul.

This book describes the spiritualities of billions of others. Your life and theirs is connected because you cannot fully understand yourself without understanding others, and you cannot fully understand an "other" without understanding yourself. The "other" may be your own past, present, or future. It may be your neighbor. It may be someone in Asia, Africa, or South America. It may be nature. It may be God. The ability to know self and "other" as they really are is the ability to understand the uniqueness of each individual and the community within which she or he lives.

It's very difficult to recognize and understand spiritual realities in an age and culture in which illusion and trivia are admired and respected more than the people, ideas, actions, and communities that shape our future; when words change as quickly as a large corporation introduces a new product; when all opinions are of equal value, even when they are baseless and thus flawed; when professional experience and knowledge is distrusted; and when the discovery of a single personal flaw or the commission of a slight offense destroys a lifelong career. In this age of uncertainty, the hope of many who are seeking a deeper spirituality is simply to know what is rooted and real.

Most of the time our contemporary culture offers only the comfort of our niche and the security of the power that defends its borders. Your niche is the *here* and *now* of your life. *Where* are you right now? What are your eyes seeing, ears hearing, fingers touching? What do they connect you to? As you find answers to these questions, you discover your place. As you recognize where you draw the line in answering these questions, you recognize your "here"— your niche.[1] You are not only *here*; you are also *now*. You are present—not past, nor future. Certainly, clock time indicates your place in history. Personal time provides a consciousness of your "now." Does time seem to pass quickly for you or slowly? Do you fear the future and agonize about the past? Are you energetically and hopefully looking forward to what is coming next in your life? Would you rather stay in this moment? Are there moments in your past that you wish you could re-live? The answers to these questions slowly provide the shape of your present moment, your "now." You live in the here and now.

> *To transcend your niche is to become transformed into a new you.*

Even though your niche is comfortable, remaining in it is devastating to you physically, mentally, emotionally, and socially because it places you in a hall of mirrors reflecting only yourself and the multiplicity of your desires. Much like Narcissus in the Greek myth, you become absorbed with what you see; as a result, your growth is stunted. To transcend your niche is to become transformed into a new you.

Transcending the here and now is the opportunity offered by every form of spirituality. Some spiritualities transcend it by offering methods and reasons for making your niche disappear into an ever present "now"—beyond space-time and all individual identity. Some will transcend it by offering methods and reasons for creating a new future and place beyond all present struggles and uncertainty. All spiritualities offer an answer to the questions "Who am I?" "What should I do?" "What can I hope for?"

Those who live a spiritual life have four things in common: first, a conscious desire to go beyond their niche; second, a vision of how things will be when the desire is fulfilled; third, a means to fulfill this desire and arrive at this vision; and, fourth, a deep hope that it will be accomplished. All spiritualities provide sources for sustaining the desire and the vision of a spiritual life. All spiritualities offer signposts to help a person discern where he or she is on the road to transformation.

The sources of these spiritualities, such as a special book, a holy person, or a sacred place, provide the tangible means of transcending our here and now. The signposts of the various forms of spirituality offer a way of seeing and understanding our world and the possibilities of living in a future one. Examples of these signposts are the stories, songs, creeds, and compositions of various sorts that enable us to transform our present selves and transcend to this envisioned world. Spiritualities offer actions, both ritual and morally normative, to achieve this same transformation. While the emphasis may be on us as individuals, spiritualities offer traditions and a community of experience and fellowship that enables us to sustain the vision, the conversation about that vision, and the actions to achieve it. These signposts of spirituality become tangible in the diverse ways people live them throughout the world.

Therefore, spiritualities are real. They are lived by real people who effectively change themselves and their world

Though all spiritualities have in common the functions mentioned above, each is different in its vision of what is beyond our niche and in describing how we transform ourselves and transcend our niche. In the following chapters, we will find descriptions of what these spiritualities have in common as well as their unique differences. Two presuppositions form the basis of this book: one is that everyone has a spirituality and the other is that by learning about someone else's spirituality, we can perfect our own.

Too often in written literature, the history of spirituality seems to focus on spiritual geniuses. These are the gurus, spirit guides, priests, monks, shamans, nuns, imams, preachers, saints, rabbis, and others hailed as the sources of spiritual knowledge and spiritual experiences. As a result, some people think they can remain in their niche and let these spiritual leaders perform the necessary acts for social and spiritual betterment. Thus, the so-called "non-spiritual" people may remain comfortable in their niche while others do what is necessary for them to live transformed lives.

Instead of starting with a description of the spiritual life as extraordinary, unique, and deserved only by spiritual geniuses, this book starts by accepting the fact that to live you must grow by transcending the here and now in every way. Everyone has a spiritual life. A good one helps you grow. A bad one stunts or destroys you by making your life a daily hell.

This book also presupposes that you need to interact with other spiritualities to grow your own. Embracing your unique spirituality and going beyond it to embrace the spirituality of others is both an oft-told story and the only path to maturity. In doing so, you gain your future self by losing your present self. This paradox is confronted by the mystics of every religion and spirituality as they strive to join with their god and/or principle of existence. It is a paradox lived by shamans as they leave this world to defeat the evil spirits present in the other one so that good will come to this one. This paradox is expressed in religions across the globe as they challenge their followers to die to self so that others may live. This paradox was lived by Jesus, who died and went to hell, then to heaven, and then returned in his Holy Spirit to bring about the Kingdom of God. This paradox was lived by Buddha who, while breaking out of his present existence through enlightenment, had compassion on us and returned to aid in our enlightenment. To leave your niche to encounter the spirituality of others is to transform yourself and become a source of transformation to others.

With these presuppositions in mind, this book enables you to review the diverse spiritualities of the past, present, and future. It does this in four parts:

Part One—Spirituality, asks, "How spiritual are you?" It describes why spiritualities exist, what they are for, what they do and do not do, and how they have functioned in the religious traditions that have stood the test of time. It details how you are connected to the here and now of your daily life, and it describes how you can recognize and transcend your connections to the here and now. By the end of Part One, you will know what a spiritual life is and have a compass to direct you on your spiritual journey as you read the rest of the book.

Part Two—Classical Spiritualities, begins with the culture in which you exist. In knowing yourself, you begin to know where and when you are. Part of that knowing are the classical spiritualities of the West, such as Judaism, Christianity, and Islam. Once you have a sense of where you are, you are then offered a review of the classical spiritualities that are possibly quite different from the majority of those that surround you: Hinduism, Buddhism, Taoism, Confucianism, and Shinto. A description of survival spiritualities allows you to reflect on the basis of all spiritualities. At this point in the book, you should be able to understand how almost everyone, including you, lives a spiritual life.

Part Three—Liminal Spiritualities: Spiritual Offerings in a Time of Radical Change, reviews a distinction made in Part One between classical, modern, and contemporary, or liminal, spiritualities. It then describes modern spiritualities with an emphasis on those evolving out of the secular fundamentalism unique to the modern mentality. It demonstrates the link among diverse religious fundamentalisms and secular fundamentalisms, and it then describes three responses to the modern world that are found in most spiritualities. I have titled these responses traditionalist, contemporalist, and co-temporalist. A traditionalist approach rejects the modern and seeks the nostalgia of the remembered past. The contemporalist approach rejects contemporary forms of spirituality and replaces these ancient spiritual practices with modern methods of transcendence. The co-temporalist response presupposes the needs and truths present in both modern and ancient spiritualities. It seeks to build out of both of these a renewed vision and means of transcendence for contemporary spiritual living. Lastly, Part Three brings into the public forum those spiritualities, sometimes called occult or marginal, such as Wicca, Gnosticism, Satanism, Cabalism, and Tantric yoga that have existed for centuries alongside the classical spiritualities. These are explained under the rubric "Marginal Spiritualities." Part Three ends with the challenge to every spiritual life offered by the ecological, gender, and economic crises of the present era.

Part Four—Testing Spirits: Personal and Cultural, brings the diversity of spiritualities into a conversation about death, the afterlife, and suffering. Out of this conversation, you will discover the necessary means of choosing among spiritualities for a wholistic contemporary life. Moving beyond the here and now and outside the comfortable boundaries of your niche is difficult when done for personal growth. Your niche is not only a hall of mirrors but also a hall built out of a lifelong pattern of habits that make you who you are. To change these habits will take time and discipline. This is hinted at throughout the book, but the last chapter takes this as one of its major goals.

Our future spiritual life is created by the choices we make in the here and now that are good, true, and beautiful. One choice does not make a spiritual life. A pattern of choices does that. The beauty of someone whose life portrays this pattern is an awesome sight. Holy men and women are awe-inspiring, attractive, and a little scary because their beautiful lives challenge us. Their lives force us to ask, *Am I like them? Can I live as they do? Have I been like them? Do I want to be like them? Compared to them, am I beautiful or somewhat disfigured?*

The beauty of spiritual people is found in the goodness of the choices they make for themselves and their communities. Their choices are both responses to the desire for transcendence beyond the here and now of their lives and productive of the means to satisfy that desire. But feeling the desire for such deep change cannot guarantee that we will make good choices in life. Only choices based on truth can do that. The desire must be real. The means to satisfy the desire must be real. And what occurs in this real world as a result of this desire and the means to satisfy it must be real.

What this book offers you are the spiritual ways that this feeling and desire for deep change have been satisfied. It also describes how you can make productive choices in the present to create your future and have a positive impact on those who are close to you.

One last point before beginning: I will use the terms "wholistic" or "wholism" throughout the book. Many times dictionaries provide only one spelling for this word: holism. There are two reasons I retain the *w*. One is that we are whole. To sustain our wholeness we must pay equal attention to every part of our being: body, mind, soul, and spirit. To reduce us to only one of these manifestations of who we are deprives us of our humanity. The second reason is that the *w* in wholistic is like our arms stretching out to every living and nonliving being. We seek to touch, hear, see, taste, and smell. We are curious and thus we seek to know, understand, and connect with "the Other" and "others." We are all this and more. We are whole. With our arms outstretched wide and our palms open, we seek to engage in the dance of life with everything and everyone. That is what it is all about—we must grow in our understanding of others so that we can grow in our spirituality and assist others in their spiritual growth.

Let us begin.

PART ONE

SPIRITUALITY

"I've heard the spirit cry in children beaten by policemen's clubs. I've heard the spirit's shout in the proclaimed alleluias of a Pentecostal meeting. I've seen the spirit act in the calloused hands of a volunteer plumber fixing a poor woman's toilet. I've felt the spirit exit in the last breath of a dying child. I've felt the spirit calm a grieving teen stuttering about her friend's alcoholic death in a car accident. I've heard a spirit laugh at a comedians' joke. I've seen the spirit's steel hardened glint in the eye of a parent saying 'no.' I've drunk spirits in sorrow, joy, and comfort. I can get a spirit rebate at my local market!

Ah, a life of the spirit—whatever that may be."

Rudolph Roberts, January, 2008.

Webster's dictionary echoes Rudolph Robert's words by providing over fifteen meanings for the word *spirit*, and the *Encarta* thesaurus provides over seventy words or phrases to take its place. Google offers 41,800,000 sites for the word spirituality. This maze of meanings and offerings found on the Internet and in dictionaries requires you to discern what will aid you in your spiritual journey, and what will shunt you off onto a dead-end side road.

There are many eye-catching glittering ideas and sparkling methods that promise spiritual satisfaction. Celebrities, authors, motivational speakers, songs, movies, Internet sites, and so many other sources present their spiritualities for your acceptance. This book will offer ideas and consequences to consider before accepting and living whatever form of spirituality is best for you. Discernment is always necessary for healthy living.

Part One begins the journey by providing you with some critical tools of discernment. When you first start on a journey, you not only have to understand what the road looks like (which will be discussed in Chapter One), but also where to begin. Chapter Two describes the here and now of any beginning. The "here" is the physical spot upon which you stand; the "now" is the moment of consciousness when you begin your journey. But the paradoxes of life discussed in Chapter One reveal that your here and now is connected to the living environment within which you live. Chapter Two looks into some of those connections that condition the way you start your spiritual journey. Chapter Three provides you with a compass for your spiritual journey. To use the compass you need to have some sense of the sources and signposts of a spiritual life. By the end of Part One you will know the road you are to travel; you will have the means to recognize those who travel it with you; and you will have a compass to direct you on your journey in life and throughout the remainder of the book.

Chapter 1

Spiritualities: Where Do We Begin?

I'm not a good swimmer. I taught myself how to swim. I did it by watching others. At first, I tried to imitate them. It didn't work. Ultimately I figured out a way to do it myself which, hopefully, will save me if I'm ever in a boat that turns over (a hypothesis I hope I never have to test).

First, I watched people who were good swimmers. They would stand on the edge of the pool or dock. Some would dive straight in, cutting the water like a knife. Others seemed to hesitate as if waiting for the exact moment to dive. I remember watching one young lady who would stand on the edge of the pool, day after day, and contemplate her next move. She would stand there for a short while and then fall into the water with a large splash. Later she stood there and just dropped into the water with a smaller splash. The instructor tried to tell her how to do it, but she never seemed to be able to get her toes, knees, hands, and body together to dive into the water. Maybe she still drops in rather than dives. Diving in didn't work for me either.

Instead, I learned slowly at an old dam in Pennsylvania. There were no instructors; just a shore line and water. I usually tagged along with my teen uncles who were more interested in talking with the girls than teaching me how to swim.

I really had no idea what to do. Since I could hold my breath above water, I began to walk underwater holding my breath. As I did this, I realized how I could move underwater by imitating people I saw swimming above water. Then I tried to do the same thing above water. Eventually, and very slowly, I made myself swim from one shore to another. It was a very small cove. It took two or three years before I could do it without feeling like I was drowning. During those three years, I gradually established the habits of breathing and arm and body movements needed to swim. At the same time, of course, I got rid of those habits that prevented me from breathing and moving correctly. I am still afraid of diving off a boat and swimming in deep water.

My children learned from various instructors. They are totally at ease in the water and can stay in the deep water as long as they wish. I envy them.

It may seem strange to talk about swimming in a chapter titled "Where do we begin?" Sometimes the metaphor of the spiritual life as a journey leads us to believe that we answer this question by finding a clearly marked road with a starting point marked with an X. But discovering and deepening your spiritual life is more like swimming than following a map. It's a whole person exercise with devastating consequences if you do not get it right. If you don't swim when you are in the water, you drown. When you drown, you no longer breathe. Your spirit is gone. If you do breathe properly, you have the breathing-spirit. You may be alive, full of fun and energy and joy—very spirited. But if your energizing spirit points you in the wrong direction and you swim out to sea instead of toward the shore, onto the raft, or back to the boat, there will be devastating consequences. Even if you are breathing well and swimming in the right direction, the spirit of those around you influence what you do. All you need is one bully "accidentally" holding you under water or pushing you against the side of the boat to change your life forever. Such a malevolent spirit may hold serious consequences for all involved.

Spirituality Begins With the Recognition of Life's Mystery

Some look at spirituality as a way to escape this present life; others see it as a way to engage in it more deeply. In either case, the present is where and when life, as we know it, is lived. The past is done; the future is yet to be. This present is not only hemmed in by being neither past nor future, but also by place—we cannot be there when we are here. Yet even in the here and now we are severely limited to the boundaries of our sight, our hearing, our touching, our smelling, and our tasting. Our present consciousness, provided by our senses, is our glory and our limitation.[2] We know there is more time than the present and more space than here. We know there is more than our senses provide. And this "more to life" is the deep mystery of life itself. This mystery envelopes us and binds us all together in its unknowingness, in its all-inclusiveness—its boundary creating marking of our unique limitations. Every spirituality is born out of the realization of personal limitation and the desire to go into that mysterious unknown that exists beyond the present limits of the here (present place) and the now (present moment). It begins with the question more felt than spoken: "Is this it?" Is this place I stand upon, these people I'm connected to, this moment of remembrance and consciousness, these feelings of joy or of guilt, these sights, sounds, touches, tastes, and smells—are these it? Is this life?

> A spiritual life begins with our awareness of wanting "more" from our present life.

Each of us experiences these physical, mental, and social limits in unique ways. Maybe we cannot concentrate as well as we wish we could because we are easily distracted. Maybe we have a hard time making friends. Maybe we cannot walk. Maybe our life is boring. Maybe we are hungry and tired. Maybe we cannot find the correct words to express our selves. Maybe we hurt others easily, taking no thought of the consequences. All these maybes make us who we are.

Every human answers "no" to the question, "Is this all there is to life?" The "no" may be expressed by moving out of our niche and making our "maybes" real. The "no" may be found in the depths of uncontrolled pain and suffering. It may break into our lives in an exhilarating moment of joy and ecstasy that finds us gasping for breath at the awesomeness of moving beyond all limits. It may come suddenly and be called conversion or enlightenment. It may come slowly and be titled spiritual maturity. Its name may come spontaneously to our lips such as God, Tao, or Cosmic Compassion.

The first cry of a baby at birth is its way of shouting "no" to where it is and crying for "more." This striving for "more" is the beginning of every spirituality. To mistake the striving for "more" as the overcoming of mystery, however, is to mistake process for solution—walking the path for arriving at its destination. Life's mystery is always present.

Underlying and expressive of this foundational mystery of life are seven spiritual paradoxes that reinforce the mystery and stimulate the desire to transcend both the mystery and paradoxes. Every spirituality is a way of life that promises and promotes a unique way of dealing with both mystery and paradox. When our spiritual way of life loses its sense of mystery and paradox, it ceases to be a way of engaging life and, instead, becomes a way of satisfaction, certitude, and stasis—a present without a future. We no longer have a desire to become more than we are. Mystery and paradox no longer awaken a need to transcend our life. Both life's mystery and its inherent paradoxes must be brought to consciousness to know where to begin our journey.

What makes this "bringing to consciousness" process difficult are the habits we have formed over the years. Some have supported our desire and curiosity about the spiritual life; others distract us, and sometimes they even prevent us from beginning or deepening our spiritual life. What these habits are will slowly surface as we read and think about what we have done and what we intend to do with our lives.

Spirituality also Begins with Recognizing Our Habits

We are our habits. How we walk, speak, eat, think, pray, hate, love, hear, see, touch, and feel are the result of our habits. These, and so many more, were gradually initiated and learned by conscious choice, such as my learning to swim, or they were learned by subconscious imitation as we mimicked the habits of those closest to us in our formative years.

Our spiritual habits are formed in the same way that all habits are formed. We imitate our parents, our favorite aunt, our pastor, our teen leader, our best friend. We imitate how they speak, walk, and think. Some of these are chosen because of their attractiveness, such as adopting our favorite sociology or literature teacher's views about religion; some habits are rejected because they have caused us pain and/or embarrassment, such as not using electricity in the house on the Sabbath or having a small shrine at our home's entrance.

> **Spiritual habits enable us to transcend and grow our limited lives.**

Spiritual habits constitute the whole range of spirituality and religion: words, actions, community, doctrine, ritual, morality, and polity. Within this range of habits, we find two clear types: *worldly* and *other worldly*. The term *worldly*, in this usage, refers to everything we sense and the four dimensions of length, depth, width, and time.[3] Chapter Two deals with the importance of our here (place or length, depth, width) and now (time) for understanding our spirituality. A *worldly spirituality* is one that promises and promotes individual and social transformation to a clearly articulated way of life through a clearly designed process for getting there. For example, one may suffer from chronic depression. The clear goal is to rid one's self of its debilitating effects. The means of achieving this is a complex mix of medication and behavioral therapy. An *other worldly spirituality* promises and promotes individual and social transformation to a metaphorically described way of life through processes warranted by spiritual authorities based on this worldly but not otherworldly reason and experience.[4] An example of this is a type of Christian spirituality that offers heaven as its goal and the Bible as the sole authoritative means of thought, ritual, moral action, and community organization to achieve this goal. The authorities that provide the powerful metaphorical vision of the goal and the means to attaining it are usually recognized as tradition in what we will describe later in the book as signposts—rituals, beliefs, morals, and community;[5] someone else's or one's own transformative experience, such as a deep feeling of calm and an ability to foresee the future; and thoughtful reasoning about life's mystery.

These spiritual habits help name and interpret life's mystery. When we ask, "Is that all there is?" we learn to respond, "Of course not.". There is God, Brahman-Atman, Cosmic Compassion, Tao, Cosmic Order, Kami, Yahweh, Allah, Father, Son, Spirit, and other names and ideas explaining that which limits, binds, and draws us beyond ourselves. The worldly spirituality might title and explain the mystery differently by explaining the laws of nature as found in the various soft and hard sciences. In either instance, our habits constitute who we are, where we intend to go, and the questions we need to ask to get there.

Mature individuals examine their individual lives within the framework of life's mysteries and make their choices to retain or change their habits accordingly. They accept responsibility for their choices.[6] Our choices remain with us as long as we exist, for they result in who we are through the habits we form. Most spiritualities and religions

> *Human spirituality is paradoxical.*

accept the reality of our choices by suggesting that we will face consequences in this world and in the next. Heaven, hell, and Karma are suggestions as to the eternal consequences of choice. If we take the spiritual life seriously, there are consequences to our thoughts and actions that we should acknowledge as we begin describing, reviewing, acknowledging, and deepening our spirituality. Of course, any way of life is never entirely clear when making choices. There is always a great deal of grey in making them and living the consequences of those choices. All of life, in its own way, is a paradox.

Spirituality Begins and Ends in Paradox

Paradoxes are part of life. Recognizing the paradoxes inherent in life's mystery and our unrecognized habits is essential for making the choices necessary to live a healthy spiritual life.

Because paradoxes balance extremes, they often strike us as contradictory, and sometimes they sound silly to us. They are part of every spiritual life. You may have heard some of these paradoxical statements:[7] "Less is More." "Whatever I write is false." "I was born in 1960 and celebrated my fifth birthday in 1984." "Jesus is totally human and totally divine." "What is the sound of one hand clapping?" Most of the literature reserves the term paradox for written materials whether they are sentences, stories, or poems. Naturally, philosophers and others have divided them into various types depending on their truthfulness, falsehood, and other characteristics.

We tend to be uncomfortable with paradoxes. Consequently, individuals, cultures, and religions try to resolve them. We have established intellectual and cultural habits to avoid many paradoxes. Also, when living with some of the proposed solutions to a paradox, it is easy to forget the initial response to them. Contemporary Christians, for example, easily forget the eight hundred years of controversy over the paradox of Jesus being both human and divine.

What a paradox actually is, written or otherwise, is debatable. Common to the debate is an acceptance that while being filled with absurdity and, perhaps, contradiction, a paradox holds its various parts together in such a way that we sense something about it is true. It brings harmony and balance out of chaos and seeming contradiction. A paradoxical person is filled with contradictory qualities that should destroy her, but they do not. A paradoxical event is one that has no rational explanation while leaving us wondering how it happened. A paradoxical picture is both a rabbit and an old woman. Music is a paradox because it contains both silence and sound; it seems the two should cancel each other out, but instead the result is beautiful music. A paradoxical experience leaves us convinced that it really happened and yet filled with the mixed emotions of curiosity, avoidance, attraction, repulsion, and fear. It seems absurd to even think it's real because one part negates the other.[8] In some instances, especially of repeated paradoxical events demanding our response, we are left with a mixture of negative and positive feelings: negative feelings of frustration, anxiety, and sometimes psychologically dangerous impulses,[9] and positive feelings of curiosity, well-being, or amazement. Sometimes we are strongly inclined to favor one part of the paradox rather than the other. The negative feelings are too intense. The seeming irrationality fills us with too much fear. We abandon the stress-filled paradox for one of its parts. In doing so, we embrace the simplicity of clear and precise answers and reject the messiness of reality. The feeling of certitude becomes more important than the search for what is real.

Spiritual paradoxes produce the same effect as ordinary paradoxes by expanding our horizons and opening us up to the possibilities of new ways of living. These paradoxes have been part of living a spiritual life for thousands of years. The classical spiritualities presented in Part Two of this book are a history of people awakening after long periods of spiritual neglect to the reality of the paradoxes inherent in their spiritualities. During these periods of neglect, language, ritual, and moral imperatives develop, all of which adhere to one part of the paradox rather than another, thus providing certitude to the spiritual community enlivened by them. When we read about or live within one of these spiritualities, we do not recognize that which is seemingly paradoxical. For example, the first paradox is one of the experiences of life-death. The early Christians accepted the paradoxical nature of life-death by claiming that God was the source of life-death now and forever in our resurrected self. Slowly, through an acceptance of the body-soul language, people solved the paradox by arguing that human beings have an immortal soul. They claimed that the immortal soul lives forever with God after we die on this earth. There is no paradox to this. Each of us is a living being that lives forever. In our contemporary world, many people avoid the paradox by identifying the person with that which dies and decays: If there is no body, then there is no person and thus no paradox. I would like to suggest that both solutions to the paradox neglect a foundational experience of life. This mentality in the context of our conflicted society is dangerous. If this defines your thinking, see if you agree after reading the following paradoxes. Do you experience them as such, or does your spirituality offer a way to deal with them? To answer this question for each of the paradoxes is to begin to sketch your spirituality.

Here are the paradoxes that face us as we describe and interact with the spiritualities present in human society now and in the past:

- I am an immortal who dies.
- I need a "we" to be a "me."
- To be alive I must change and remain the same.
- I am one and many.
- My spiritual life is both free and earned; gift and purchased.
- I must fight to be in harmony with all.
- I am the same and different.

I Am an Immortal Who Dies

Ernest Becker in his Pulitzer Prize winning book *Denial of Death* describes the paradox inherent in all human spirituality. We are angels who defecate.[10] This "angelic" nature is a conviction that we are immortal heroes. Like a two-year-old, we tackle everything in life with a defiant "I can do it myself!" Like a teen, we feel deeply that we cannot be hurt no matter how we drive. Like a drunk, we sometimes sense that we can dive off a building and live. We can overcome all odds; even death. We can conquer illness, meet any challenge, and reign supreme over the earth. We can live forever. Becker, quoting Freud, suggests this foreverness of the personality when he says we can never imagine our own death. We might imagine seeing ourselves dead, but there is always the "me" seeing my dead body. I cannot imagine nothingness, which is death itself. Becker reminds us that no matter what our convictions are about our spiritual status, we always have to go to the bathroom; we bleed when cut, hurt when harmed, and die. As we mature, we realize we are the result of forces that surround and inhabit us: genes, society, atmosphere, water, food. And that is the paradox: How can we be limited (dead, done in by the forces that surround us) and unlimited (immortal, capable of overcoming these forces) at the same time? Our individual and social lives are spent dealing with the lived reality of this paradox. Our spiritual life is stimulated by it and, many times, seeks to resolve it.

Inherent to this paradox is a derivative of it: of being free and not free. Seemingly both these cannot be true at the same time—a paradox. Yet experience does not present the choice in such clear terms. Perhaps an example would help.

Many times when visiting San Diego, I would go to the beach and watch the surfers. You already know my experience with water, so this marvel of young people riding the waves is a deeply felt experience. I am awed at the large wave roaring in from the ocean to the shore, and at the sight of a person paddling out to meet it and then standing on a board to join the wave on its journey to shore. A surfer seems like the perfect example of California freedom! But here is the paradox: The wave is determined, and so is the surfer as she rides it to the shore. The freedom is in how she rides the wave. She is free and not free, just as we all are because we are limited and unlimited at the same time. Our freedom comes in shaping and providing direction to what limits us.[11]

Sometimes it seems that much contemporary discussion about and seeking for a spirituality is really a search for absolute certainty in life and thought. Such certainty avoids the tensions associated with freedom—and its consequent responsibility. Spirituality, in this reading, is associated with spirit, immortality, changelessness, faith, and the essence of who we really are. It avoids the paradox of being an immortal who dies, change and stability, and, from my perspective, the wholistic nature of a human being.

I Need a "We" to Be a "Me"

Caught up in the need to discover and enhance a life of our own, we slowly come to the realization that we need others to communicate with who will support us and share our seeking and our discoveries. We may need them to share our successes and failures. We may need them for approving or disapproving of our lifestyle. We may need them for food, warmth, and information. Our belly button proclaims we need others to be born. Our eyes and ears face outward demonstrating that we need the sight and sound of others to be who we are. Somehow, we grow in our unique spiritual life by a necessary sharing with others.

Caught within this same paradox is the claim I made in the introduction that anyone can lead a spiritual life. This is an important claim because it not only says that anyone can lead a spiritual life, but also that anyone can change the spiritual life he or she leads. The consequences of this presupposition may go against those models of a spiritual life that are found in publications and on the Internet, which favor literate adults who often have leisure time and adequate finances to wander the world eating and praying. Not everyone may be able to lead those types of spiritual lives, but everyone can lead some type of spiritual life.

This means that infants, children, teens, adults, elderly and the frail elderly can lead a spiritual life. One part of the life cycle is not favored over another. Historical and cultural diversity are also inherent to the spiritual life: people from diverse cultures, languages, and varying educational and economic backgrounds all lead some form of a spiritual life. Our "we" shapes our "me." The spiritual life of a medieval, literate Christian monk alone in his monastery and the spiritual life of the illiterate, third wife of an African herder are spiritual in quite different ways. Yet they do share the commonality of leading a spiritual life. Thus, spirituality is one common value with many manifestations.

This common value is a desire to make our lives better than they are here and now. We all wish to transcend the moment and transform our lives. Those seeking to lead a spiritual life often desire to become more than they are when they reach midlife; more than they are in this town at this time in history; more than they are at this moment in their spiritual life.

To Be Alive I Must Change and Remain the Same

When you look at pictures of yourself taken over the years, how can you be sure you are the same person in each of those pictures? Most people say you are the same person. Every form of spirituality agrees with them. Every form of spirituality also has a way of describing what there is about us that does and does not change. The practice of spirituality must do so because transcendence means change, and the transcendence known as death challenges spiritual authorities to explain how we remain the same as our body disintegrates.

Every spiritual life seeks to transcend to a new, better, life. In doing so, there is always a still point of identity that connects the past, present, and transformed future. How does one change and be still at the same time? In Part Two, you will read about some spiritualities that dissolve this paradox by describing all of life as illusory, and the still-point of identity as being much larger than our consciousness of individual identity. In fact, according to this view, we are all one—no individual consciousness exists. You will read about other spiritualities that claim we are an immortal self that has always existed. Our bodies are merely the temporary housing of that self in the continual process of change and disintegration as associated with a body. These and many other spiritualities explain the paradox. But no matter what explanation you accept, they all begin with the paradoxical fact that to be alive you must change and yet you remain the same.

I Am One and Many

The image, definition, and nature of a human being differs among spiritualities.[12] At the minimum they all accept that a human right now, at this place and time, is whole yet of many dimensions. We are body and soul. We are mind, will, and emotions. We are, as current research and academic divisions remind us, a combination of our psychology, sociology, physics, chemistry, anthropology, and politics. No matter what the parts or the dimensions we use to describe and analyze humans and their destiny, we are always a unique whole. We are one and many at the same time. We are something more than our individual dimensions. We are, as reminded in our first paradox, a reality that grows and disintegrates; in our second paradox, we are unique and interdependent; in our third paradox, we are static and yet changing.

A spiritual life demands that we attend to this moment to transcend this moment. Every form of spirituality provides methods tested by time for achieving this transcendence. Many of these methods emphasize one or another of our many dimensions. Some say that we are really our souls and not our bodies. Others say that we are none of these but an undisclosed spirit dimension that is beyond our consciousness. These methods dissolve the paradox by defining who the one is. Yet, the methods surrounding these definitions also start with the paradox of admitting that they seek to destroy this wholeness by condensing it into one of its parts. The awesomeness of the paradox is replaced by the spiritual certainty of the promised results.

My Spirituality Is both Free and Earned; Gift and Purchased

When talking about spiritualities in an American context, we sometimes are under the misapprehension that a spirituality is something we earn. "Work at it and you will get it." "Pull yourself up by your spiritual boot straps in ten simple spiritual steps." "If you believe strong enough, it will happen." Spirituality, though, as life itself, is part of the paradox of gift and purchase. Our future life is both deserved and undeserved; gift and merit. As the founder of an important Christian spirituality said, "Pray as if everything depended on God. Act as if everything depended on you."[13] As always with paradoxes, many spiritualities are uneasy with this saying and thus they dissolve the paradox through belief, action, or community.

This paradox merely condenses human experience. Each of us starts out life unearned. We are born of certain parents, at a certain time and place, with certain genes. We did nothing to be born. As we cry, eat, defecate, smile, talk, walk, work, and play, we enter into a world in which some things happen to us without expectation or explanation; others things happen because of our hard work and we can explain why they happened to us. In the eyes of some spiritualities, everything in our life is planned from all eternity. All is undeserved and a gift. It is, as they say, our destiny or the will of God. Their constant challenge is to motivate people to change if everything is planned. Other spiritualities claim that everything that happens to us is merited and deserved from what we have done in this or another life. We are born with certain genes to certain parents because of what we merited in the previous life. We must work to stop the wheel of rebirth. Their constant challenge is to explain how thousands and sometimes millions of people merited such events as Hiroshima, Auschwitz, and 9/11, or the Japanese earthquake and resultant tsunami of March 2011.

We will see what signposts these various spiritualities provide for living and advancing in the spiritual life. Most have quite detailed indicators for how to locate your present situation and how to move beyond it to achieve your spiritual goals. But they all begin with a foundational experience of getting something unexpected (gift) and being expected to be deserving of the gift (purchase).

I Must Fight to Be in Harmony with All

"Virtue stands in the middle" (*In medio stat virtus*) is an ancient saying that proclaims that the virtuous life is the moderate life, a life balanced between extremes. Faith itself may be seen as a continuous striving to keep one's balance between doubt and absolute truth. [14] Total doubt in one's way of life leads to personal anarchy. Total conviction of its absolute truth leads to a type of factual and experiential certitude, not faith. One loses one's balance in the extremes.

While seeking balance, every form of spirituality calls for a total concentration of life's energies to defeat the evils inside and outside ourselves—anything that prevents our transformation. These evils are seen by some as evil spirits, or as illusions that cause us to suffer. Still others view the threats to our life as self-defeating habits preventing personal and social maturation. In any case, there is the paradox of keeping things in balance while attending to the all-consuming necessity to fight whatever unbalances us. How do we do this? It is like trying to ride a bike while being attacked by a helicopter.

A possible suggestion is to get off the bike of paradoxes and onto the solid ground of clear, unambiguous principles for living. Such solidity and clarity, from this point of view, provides what is needed for an authentic spiritual life. It also provides the fundamentals upon which we can all agree and gives us a clear vision of what to reject.

These fundamentalist spiritualities, as we will see in Part Three, are strong and attractive in a pluralistic, global, tension-filled world. They provide a clear vision of what is wrong with our world and how to fix it. The only problem is that there are diverse sets of fundamentals and clear visions of the future. The only solutions provided, so far, to this diversity of vision and fundamentals is killing those who differ from our set of fundamentals or isolating each spirituality in its own niche to keep it separate from the others. Both choices seem untenable in our present world where the killing of some will become the killing of all, and where perfect isolation would demand total censorship to sustain an unambiguous way of life. It seems rather difficult to get off the bike of paradox.

Yet the challenge remains of fighting what will destroy us and being in harmony with our environment. How do we stand in the middle in harmonious balance when we necessarily have to focus on specific issues that threaten to take us away from our goal? How do we direct the multi-dimensional orchestra that we are when having to keep away the hornets of reality from stinging us?

Instead of being questions that simply need answering, we must live these are paradoxes within the mystery of life, since every spiritual life demands that we fight and be harmonious at the same time.

I Am the Same and Different

Deep within each of us is the need to belong, to join with others, to share what is common to all of us for the good of each of us. Deep within each of us is the need to be unique, to be "me," to be the hero. The paradox is that we are both at the same time. For our spirituality to abandon one part of the paradox for the other is fraught with inherent contradiction and psychological danger.

You will discover in subsequent chapters some spiritualities that focus on one part of this paradox to the near exclusion of the other in their stated beliefs and proposed spiritual methods. These descriptions are offered in those chapters for your review and your possible choice as a whole or in part. I would like to suggest, however, that a full, enabling, lifelong spirituality matures through faith responses to this paradox but it cannot be sustained over a lifetime with the contradiction inherent in choosing one part of the paradox over the other. One must look closely at the spiritualities that focus on the common identity of all spiritualities without admitting our differences and the spiritualities that demand that one's individual spirituality is the norm for everyone. Examine them to determine whether there are contradictions or the admission of the paradox that we are the same and different, and then choose.

What Is Spiritual?

Rudolph Robert's quote at the beginning of Part One hinted at the many ways the concept of "spirit" may be understood. Researchers have always been faced with the difficulty of describing what the word spiritual means. Late in the nineteenth century, the newly formed field of comparative religion faced a similar challenge surrounding the concept of religion. Because religion and spirituality have a great deal in common, what these experts did can help us understand what is meant when we talk about spirituality and being spiritual. Their difficulty and the choices that evolved surrounding it can be of great help in trying to discover what's spiritual in a spiritual life. What is it about the spiritual life that makes it stand out from the ordinariness of daily life?

The original investigators into what differentiates religion from other aspects of life suggested that certain experiences made it different. These were experiences of the *sacred*, the *mysterious*, the *holy*, and the *supernatural*. The first three were used to describe the same experience with a slightly different twist for each term. The last term, the supernatural, combined the experience

> **Spiritual emotions are important but diverse.**

described by the other three with a sense that the object of the supernatural was outside the physical (natural) realm, the here and now, this world or dimension of reality as defined by modern scientific methods. The explanation of the exact relationship between this supernatural side of life and the natural side varied among religions and researchers.

The experience of the sacred, mysterious, and holy was/is an experience of something that both attracted and repelled a person at the same time. It was awe-inspiring! It was a mystic's experience of being swept up into the being of God; it was the enlightenment described by Siddhartha; it was the cry of Muhammad in response to the angel shaking him and commanding him to recite. It was also the feeling you might have in realizing that someone loves you; the feeling you might have when alone skiing down a mountain, running a marathon, and getting into the "zone." If you have ever had the experience or feeling you are in the presence of something overwhelmingly powerful, wishing you could stay there and yet being frightened out of your wits at what would happen if you did, then you have had an intense sacred experience. This may be what you have in mind, say researchers, when speaking about the spiritual life. Most writers talking about the spiritual life take this experience of the holy as its distinguishing characteristic.

Seldom noted by the researchers were other experiences just as profound and common among the classical types of spiritualities and religions they researched. These too are deeply felt and may have been/are part of your life. A common spiritual feeling that is seldom mentioned is *duty and obedience* to a cause, a community, or a person. People are called followers and disciples because of this experience. Many times they are willing to sacrifice their life and fortune at the behest of their lord, master, king, general, or leader. *Justice*, as an experience and desired lifestyle for everyone, causes people and communities to sacrifice all for the experience of living with others who seek fairness in society and within themselves. Some spiritualities conceptualize life after death as an existence that satisfies this need for justice, honesty, and integrity. Belief in heaven, hell, and karma are examples of this experiential expectation. *Discipline,* as a consistent way of life, is seen by most spiritualities as constitutive to being spiritual. What use is it if we say one thing and do something else, or do something one day and its opposite the next? *Consistency* is essential to a spiritual life. It demonstrates character. So too is hope. *Optimism* is seen as the mark of a spiritual person because she expects life to be better than it is right now. Finally, many spiritualities are based on the conviction that there is a *power* or *energy* independent of everything and everyone we experience. This is expressed in stories of the creation of the world, daily miracles, and the power to destroy the world. This is found, too, in a deep fear some people have that a god will cause them suffering here or in the hereafter. These other experiences and convictions may be found in most spiritualities even though they are usually not attended to in as much detail as experiences of the sacred, the holy, and the supernatural by writers and researchers.

I would like to suggest that all of the experiences I have described have an underlying experience that comes from the depth of every human being and is inclusive of all those experiences. This is the experience of *transcendence,* of going beyond our selves. It is sensual even though it may originate in our minds, wills, and emotions.

Lived Transcendence

Our minds are curious. Our emotions seem never satisfied—each seeking to be the primary one attended to. Like a room full of hungry dogs, each wants to be fed NOW! And when that one emotion is satisfied, another one is right behind demanding the same satisfaction. Our will seeks to impose order on these emotions but even with the greatest discipline there is always the urge for "more," as anyone who has an addiction knows. We humans are always seeking "more"—seeking to transcend the moment and the place within which we swim.

The desire for transcendence is always present within each of us as we seek to move beyond the here and now to another reality. We see such desire in a small child spinning in a circle to experience a world beyond the ordinary and a person drinking or doing drugs to experience something different. We have thousands upon thousands of ways of entering into these other modes of existence: art, stories, music, work, play, and religion to name a few. Seeking transcendence is part of being human. Seeking and living transcendence is also the essential ingredient of a spiritual life. If we are fortunate, we may briefly enter into this other world of alternate reality promised by a spiritual life. Certainly each *spiritual life promises and promotes the vision and means to change the present into this other world in the near or distant future.* To live a spiritual life, we must be aware of what is promised to us, and the means that will bring us into its alternate reality.

This entrance into an alternate reality is a very difficult task since we can never be completely sure of what that new world is or will be. When we are totally transformed by living spiritually, we experience an ultimate transcendence—a world that is entirely different from the one we live in at this moment in time and space. Words in common usage such as heaven, hell, Nirvana, and enlightenment give us the impression that we know what ultimate transcendence is. Actually, all these words and stories are bumbling attempts to give us a sense of what this totally other existence is like.

> **A spiritual life seeks to transcend this life.**

The history of western spirituality has two terms to indicate the quandary of trying to describe what this other world is like and how to get there. These terms are used for both the difficulty of talking about this other world and the means of entering it through meditation or some other method. The *kataphatic* (which is sometimes spelled *cataphatic*) way of dealing with the totally transcendent is to use words, pictures, sounds, and images to express that world. For example, God (who is totally other/completely transcendent) is love (a word that describes a feeling we have had). Both "God" and "love" are words attempting to describe the totally transcendent. Another example of the kataphatic method is revealed when we worship an image of an elephant with several heads or another image of a woman with many arms. Our priest may sing and drop rose petals on the image. We may leave fruits in dedication to the image. A kataphatic meditation technique would be to use an image of God in praying to her as a mother or to concentrate on a statue representing a key figure in the spirituality such as Jesus or Buddha. The actual words we use to express our sense of what this mysterious world is both tell us something about that world and, at the same time, hide a great deal of what that world is like. An *apophatic* approach, sometimes called the negative way, begins by admitting that we can never know the totally transcendent reality as it is and thus we try to understand it by saying what it is not. So one would say that God is not evil (negative statement) but never say God is good (a positive statement). The apophatic methods of transcendence are also negative because they empty the person of all self-identity: memory, sense experience, images, words and ordinary ways of communicating. As one merges into nothingness, he or she merges into that totally other world that is incapable of ever being described or entered into while we are still in this one (i.e. you can never totally know or experience the supernatural world while in this one).

The attempts to describe what is inherent in the mystery that encompasses and penetrates us are cluttered with the same "messiness" of all human life. What keeps us moving forward is the essential human characteristics of curiosity, the desire for transcendence, and trust. Curiosity means we are never satisfied with the here and now. Desire for transcendence means we are always seeking to move beyond where we are. Trust means that we believe absolutely that life in general and our life in particular matters. Trust means that we are confident that no matter how paradoxical life seems, no matter how much uncertainty rattles our bones, no matter how alone we might feel, no matter what pain might shatter our consciousness, no matter how impossible it is to see justice and purpose in this life—despite any of this and more—we will transcend all these negative realities. We trust that essential to our present identity and our healthy living of it is our transcendence of it. We trust that there are ways we can become more transcendent in our everyday lives. We trust, in other words, that we will find a form of spirituality that will change the world and us.

Never forget, however, that no matter what the multiplicity of spiritual descriptions offered by resourceful people, you, I and others are alive right now. Reading this book. Thinking our thoughts and seeking for "more."

Part of being on a journey is seeing many things. This is just the beginning of the multiplicity of ideas and suggestions you will encounter. You encounter them because they offer you ways to think and act to become more than you are. A journey takes a while. Let's move on to some other introductory ideas.

Summary

We all have habits that make us spiritual. We recognize them as we bump into life's limits and want more than what we are experiencing here and now. Spiritual habits enable us to transcend our limits and experience our paradoxes. The spiritualities that enable us to transcend our limits offer us the promise of a life that has changed for the better. These spiritualities also provide the means for this promise to be fulfilled. The fulfillment of the promise and the means of fulfillment are accompanied with feelings of awe, mystery, duty, justice, optimism, power, and energy. The central spiritual experience is that of transcendence and change from our former life – our former "here and now."

Chapter Two

Spiritual Connections: Culture, Religion, and Spirituality in a Liminal Age

Etched in my memory is a scene from the Canadian Film Board movie La Guerre, Yes Sir! *It portrays the military funeral of a young Quebec soldier. Around the flag-draped coffin in a tight military parade stance were the dead soldier's British regimental peers. In the rest of the room were his Quebecois family and friends. The narrator voices the thoughts of both groups as they witness the young man's funeral. The British soldiers were disgusted. These people, they felt, showed no respect for their dead brother. They drank, sang, yelled, and screamed. The chaotic room smelled and tasted of whiskey, smoke, and sweat. The Quebecois, on the other hand, looked at these unsmiling, unblinking, foreign oppressors as machine-like robots who didn't give a damn for their military brother. They were doing this ceremony only because they had to. He had given his life for them, and they showed no emotion, no gratitude for what he had done.*

This scene depicts two views of the same reality: two identical feelings of grief and two radically different ways of demonstrating that grief for a loved one. Two communities, connected by grief for the dead and honor for a life, were unable to share both of these feelings because of geography, history, and religion. A common search among spiritualities easily leads not only to a sense of helpful knowledge but also to a sense of distain and rejection.

Our families are our connections. Our connections form our habits, and our habits express and shape our spirituality. Spiritual connections begin with the ground upon which we stand (geography), the belly button that centers us within a genealogy of family connections (history), and a conscious self that discovers patterns in both geography and history. It all begins with the culture within which we learn to live. It is within these cultural waters that we first meet the mystery of life's limits that entice us to transcend them. It is within these cultural waters that we first learn to swim spiritually and to write our spiritual story; to name the mystery and how to encounter and grow into it; to sense other stories and names that strike us as false to our reality. To know the difference between our spirituality and that of others is to know a fuller life.

Culture: Connecting the Here and Now; Habits of Interpretation

Life is a team sport. We share many of the values that make us who we are and the desire for transcendence that urges us forward to a mysterious time and place. "Culture" is used here to describe what happens to a group of people over time. Whenever people live and work together, they form patterns associated with their life and work. Their words, actions, and relationships become repetitious and patterned in such a way that words have a common meaning, actions are a common way of responding to the adventures of life, and the gathering, directing, and interacting of people in a community take on expected routines or habits. These patterns are expressive and formative of foundational attitudes that are necessary to live our lives. These foundational attitudes are those of meaning, belonging, purpose (justice, rightness), and well-being. Without some sense of meaning, belonging, purpose, and well-being, our individual and communal lives wither. Culture is the water within which we swim; the stage upon which we play out our individual and communal lives.

Unless you have made a conscious decision to live a "go-it-alone" spirituality, you are living a spirituality with deep cultural influences of place and time. Even if you are going it alone, others are interacting with you and you with them. A fourth century monk, Simeon Stylites (390-459 CE), began living a spiritual life with others in a monastery. Then he felt a need to be alone so he became a hermit. Finally, in 423 CE, he moved to the top of a series of high pillars (stylites) to be alone. The last one was fifty-five feet high. Was he alone? Not for long. Others began to imitate him and still others came to him for advice. And of course he needed food and water. Even when we choose a "go-it-alone" spirituality, we can't leave our connections with others.

Communal lives must be cultivated. If we do not take care of these patterns, they die. Culture must be cared for, argued about, attended to, and adapted to the changing environment. As communal life deepens through cultivation, the culture and the community deepen and enable people to adapt to the changes that threaten to destroy their present way of life. Most of the time, we are not aware of our culture. It is good that we do not attend to it because it is part of our being. Only when something threatens to disintegrate these cultural patterns do we notice them. When an individual or a group begins to have feelings that reflect patterns of pain, loss, ignorance, alienation, and purposelessness, they should examine their culture for the possible causes of those feelings. Many have those feelings today. They sense that something is threatening their local and global culture.

How many times, after a serious catastrophe happens, do we look back and see all the telltale signs of the forth-coming catastrophe that we either ignored or didn't notice. Those who are divorced describe the events that marked its coming. Hurricane victims describe the change in winds, waves, and temperature. Wars begin after the change in political climate, the propaganda of mutual distrust, and the popular demand for swift destruction of the now hated other. Today many people sense that deep change is coming on a global scale. They just do not wish to acknowledge and prepare for it. The last section of this chapter will discuss why many have these feelings of imminent catastrophe, and its consequences on our spiritual lives will be examined as well. Chapter Nine will present methods for changing our lives to adapt to such sweeping change. Right now we must look more deeply into what brings us to this present moment and the spirituality that enlivens us.

> *Spirituality begins at home.*

Connecting to "Here"—
Our Personal Geography: Our Home

Where are you reading this book? Have you always been there? How long have you lived there? Do you intend to remain in that general area as long as you can? The answer to these questions begins to sketch the spirituality of those you live with as well as your own. These answers indicate the place from which you experience the world. If you live in the mountains, a desert is extraordinary. If you live in a city, the forest is extraordinary. If you live on the equator, snow is extraordinary. The extraordinary, as already mentioned, usually fills us with attraction, repulsion, curiosity, and fear. This is especially so when the extraordinary breaks into our ordinary: when snow comes to the jungle, a mountain erupts in the desert, or an ancient city is discovered in the forest. Our sense of the extraordinary and transcendence starts from the ordinary place we are transcending.

"Home" is the name we give to a very special place. Certainly, it is one marker for our spiritual journey because it shapes many of our spiritual desires and the ways we expect to satisfy them. Home is where we may have had some of our first experiences of transcendence. Certainly modified transcendent experiences occur as we become more independent of our parental home. We may

> *Our spiritual home speaks a language and can be found on a map.*

still seek to reproduce those aspects of it that were most important to us. This experience of home is vital because it presents us with the ambivalence inherent in every spirituality: whether we gain more by leaving our "home" spirituality or "deepening" it. Feelings of nostalgia and solastalgia (the loss of environmental consistency) [15] indicate our loss of place and may be indicators of a need to refine our present spirituality. It seems that certain places have about them a spiritual energy and an ability to stimulate our transcendent desires and their satisfaction. These sacred places[16] have produced well-worn paths of pilgrimage for adherents to bathe in the River Ganges, to fulfill the religious need to go to Mecca, to visit the Temple Mount or the Dome of the Rock, to tread the Way of the Cross in Jerusalem, or to stand in awe of Uluru (Ayers Rock) in Australia. Many have discovered their spiritual way in pilgrimage to a sacred place as well as their presence at it. Closer to home, many have found their spiritual homes in local churches, synagogues, or temples. The sacredness of place and the consequent spiritualities that surround it are important to our reflections at both the personal and communal level.

Our personal geography is also our cultural geography. The fact that this book is written in the United States of America in the English language conditions our journey for searching, discovering, and deepening our spirituality. Two things should be mentioned at this point of our discussion: 1) our actual place sets us in a tradition of spiritual thought and action that determines our search; and 2) our language provides us with experiential dimensions of our present self that may determine our search.

Connecting to Here: Western or Eastern Spirituality

Within the geography of Western culture and the English language, a distinction developed based on where one stood in relation to the sun's rising (East) and setting (West). The terms East and West have been used variously throughout Western history. Today, the term *Western spirituality* generally refers to those spiritualities that originated in the eastern part of the Mediterranean (Middle East) and spread west from there, for the most part. These Western spiritualities found their origin in the religions of Judaism, Christianity, and Islam. *Eastern spiritualities* found their origins in the religions of India (Hinduism, Buddhism, Jainism, and Sikhism) and of East Asia (Taoism, Shinto, and Confucianism). Part Two of this book deals with these spiritualities in detail. We will refer to them as *classical spiritualities* because of their longevity, adaptability, and development. They differ significantly regarding their sense of time, deity, and humanity.

Connecting to Here: Body, Soul, and Spirit

It has often been said that the Eskimo language has a hundred words for snow while English has only one.[17] Each language and its culture determine how we understand things and what we expect when we see them. Where we stand at this moment in time is at the forefront of centuries of change—some good, some bad. It is difficult to evaluate which is good and which is bad.

Language change is always part of cultural change. The cultural change that resulted in the Middle Eastern religions of Judaism and Christianity becoming Western is one of those changes. Millennia ago the Greeks began to distinguish and then separate various dimensions of the human person: the bony, yet soft, external expression of the human began to be called a "body." The inner mental and emotional dimension began to be called the "soul" or "spirit." These linguistic distinctions that originated in the Greek culture and later became part of English speaking ones was so deep and comprehensive that we began to interpret everything around us using these terms. For example, while the Jewish Bible (Old Testament) had no words for our equivalent of body, soul, and spirit we translated certain Hebrew words and concepts into the Greek for body, soul, and spirit.[18] The rest, as it's said, is history. One explanation for why many people have a difficult time understanding any concept of a wholistic spirituality is because their present language, and thus their present spirituality, is based on dividing the human person into body, soul, and spirit.

Connecting to Here: Cosmic Placement

A friend of mine took her aged mother on her first plane trip to visit an uncle. As the mother looked down at the clouds, she leaned over and whispered to her daughter, "Where are the angels?" Her Bible-centered universe told her that God and the angels were above the heavens. She was now in the heavens. Where were the angels?

That friend had a slightly different view of the cosmos than her mother had. She read the newspaper every morning looking for what the astrology section told her was going to happen to her that day. Astrology with its mantra of "As above, so below" is based on an old scientific vision of the universe with the earth at its center and the stars and planets circling around it. Their movement determined what happened down on earth much like a puppeteer determines the movement of the puppets.[19]

Many spiritualities still presuppose the cosmos of the Bible, ancient Greece, India, or Egypt. Most educated people accept the current scientific vision of the universe as accurate. Our cultural place has changed even while some spiritualities retain their ancient roots. If you retain the ancient cosmological view of the universe in your spirituality and the modern view in your everyday life, does that mean that you, your spirituality, and your everyday practical living have no relationship? Or is it, instead, that your view of the cosmos is inconsequential to both spiritual and everyday life—something left to the scientists in their planetariums? Do you think science has anything to contribute to discussions about spirituality?

Connecting with One's National Culture

It's said that if you place a frog in cold water and gradually heat it to boiling, it will eventually die from the boiling water because it doesn't recognize the devastating consequences of the surrounding temperature change.[20] Cultural change is like that. It surrounds us. It influences our way of life and, at times, prevents us from seeing the real choices in life. Looked at from a spiritual point of view, modern American culture is shaped by what is described as American religion.[21] It has its roots in the Protestant Reformation and is a unique view of Christianity offered by those particular Protestants who founded the Massachusetts Bay Colony. It is still quite influential in how many people in the United States view the spiritual and religious world. It may determine what you seek in a spirituality either positively (you want things similar to this but better) or negatively (you abhor this way of life and want something else). Those who hold this view of religion and spirituality believe that every spirituality should focus on the individual rather than the community; should have easily understood beliefs; should have a clear separation between church and state; and should have a special book to follow, such as the Bible, as well as an experienced spiritual leader, prayer, a personal God, a special day of worship, and a set of laws to guide their moral lives. If you feel that all or a majority of these characteristics are necessary for someone to be religious, then you are influenced by American religion. Many of these characteristics, however, are not necessary to be spiritual. People have lived with only one or two of them throughout history. Most people throughout history, for example, could not read.

Breaking Connections, Transcending Place—Maybe

If you hold a child tight so she can't move, she struggles to get free. We're all like that: hold us too tightly for a long time and we struggle to free ourselves. Movement is part of who we are. We are connected to a place, but we need to be unconnected to live—a paradox perhaps?

> *Spirituality transcends place while we are in place.*

Spiritualities tend to move in two directions as they struggle to free us from the bonds of being held to our present place: They move inward and outward. The outward movement is demonstrated by the person standing with arms outstretched, palms facing up toward the heavens; the inward movement is depicted in the person sitting with legs folded, arms at his side, eyes shut, and head slightly bowed toward his body. One is an image of movement up and beyond the body-self toward the "more-beyond." The other is a symbol of moving beyond the body-self to deep within, toward the stillness that grounds the depth of our existence which is the "more-within." Both acknowledge life's mystery and face it. Both recognize the fact that spiritualities are not only determined by where we are but where we want to be and how to get there— being in our place and transcending it. What calls us beyond our place are the sources of transcendence that surround us and the signposts that place us on a sure spiritual path. For most people in the West, these sources have been the outward stretch to free ourselves of this place through the experience of an extraordinary-other that provided the means (sources) to break the connections of place such as a Bible, sacred bread and wine at Communion, joining with others in song, or through belief in God.

Yet these sources of transcendence have changed over time. An example of such change may be found in the foundational human experience of place itself. Most of the classical spiritualities originated when any movement into or out of a very restricted place was an extraordinary event. The mystery of life and its limitations were reflected in what they saw and how far they could travel. Their horizon was as far as they could see and their legs could take them. Their knowledge was restricted to what was learned from their elders and through experience. Their time and food was bound by the seasons and the necessity of struggling to survive. The fortunate few could read, write, add, and subtract; they could also travel beyond the horizon within which they were born. To individuals at these spiritual beginnings, whether able to read or not, the presence of a book was an extraordinary experience, as was the traveling minstrel and his songs, the entrance into a large cathedral, fierce storms, and sicknesses.

For example, upstate New York became known as the Burned Over District because of the extraordinary events witnessed there. From 1800 to 1850 as the snow melted and the new buds awakened every spring, many people would attend revival meetings and pray aloud in tongues, falling on the ground when they were "slain in the spirit," and in general being caught up in extraordinary happenings as they confessed their sins and were converted (or re-converted) by the preacher's call to a re-awakening of their spiritual life. With winter over, they could travel freely outside their cabins, see their neighbors, and eat fresh greens from the fields. Coinciding with their freedom from winter's bounds was their awakening to the movements of the spirit within them. Their movement from their winter place was indeed marked by extraordinary events and the beginnings of religions such as the Latter Day Saints (Mormons) and the Spiritualists.

The technologies that helped build the Erie Canal in upper New York brought more people to this place. New electronic technologies would take them out of it: the electronic telegraph (invented in 1833), radiotelegraphy (1895), and the thousands of inventions that resulted in human machines going beyond the earth and this galaxy. When, at the press of a button, we can hear and see people from around the world, our horizons are limited only by the technologies we can purchase. We seem to be freed of our place by our technologies.

Media provide us with the ability to see anywhere at any time. I can use a Google Map and see over every horizon. I can obtain video and audio of every sound and sight beyond my personal horizon. Just as the earth lost its centrality in modern cosmology and God moved beyond the heavens, the individual seems to lose her centrality in the ocean of sound and sight available at the touch of a button. The leveling of horizons results in the leveling of experience and expertise. Through the magic of contemporary technology, we can hear and see everywhere. What that does to a spirituality of place, home, neighborhood, pilgrimage, and sacred places, the peoples of the world will determine. We are certainly in a new spiritual situation with our capacity to be present anywhere in the world.

This omnipresence sometimes gives us a feeling that the best spirituality is one that is without a place. Our first paradox reminds us that this is not true. Even though you can taste the food of other cultures, hear their music, see their art and architecture, and share their ideas, you cannot experience their spirituality as they do without living it with all their connections and habits. All their sources of spirituality are different because of their place. A spirituality always has a here (place) as well as a when. To honor their spiritual place is to honor their uniqueness. If you choose to bring something into your spiritual way of living that is found in these other places, you are changing that spirituality by doing so. It is now yours, not theirs. As you read about other spiritualities, you will come to understand many of them and their various possibilities. You may choose to adapt some of them to who and where you are. In doing so, your spiritual life will change as you adapt to your place, connections, and habits.[22] The same may be said about your "now" and the history inherent to it.

Connecting with the Present Now: *When* are you?

If our "where" is determined by place, our "when" is determined by our personal and cultural history. Our experience of time begins with the present—this very moment. Right now may be calm or painful. Perhaps you seem to be experiencing nothing. But if someone snapped his fingers and commanded, "Who are you?" you would, in some fashion, begin to tell your story, your history. Your name alone begins to tell your history.

> *Every tick of a clock is a moment open to deepening our spiritual life.*

History is like that for individuals and cultures. It is a response to questions from the present to describe our past. It is looking for patterns told in stories about our past in response to questions in the present. These questions may be as simple as when someone was born or as complicated as why you changed occupations or never had children. Our stories of the past are directed by present motives and usually formulated as questions.

Some of these questions may never have existed in the past because there was no language for them, no experience to prompt them, or no curiosity to discover them. We cannot ask about the chemical composition of the moon's surface when we know nothing about chemistry or the moon. We cannot ask about religion until we have an idea of what "religion" is. We cannot ask about spirituality without the words to describe it. We cannot demand that we act in the past according to our present knowledge. Our past is a story told from the present with the questions, feelings, and ideas of the present.

A culture's history is also a story told from the present about the past. Until recently, spiritualities were embedded in religions. Their histories were part of the history of religions. A number of things have to happen before spiritualities may be talked about independently of a religion. Actually, as we will see, a number of things have to happen before the histories of religion can be talked about independently of cultural history.

This making of individual and communal history is important because what was done in the past is still part of who we are in the present.[23] This paradox lives within all of us. We have within ourselves (one) everything that has happened to us (the many). When we tell our story, we focus on an aspect of the many that exists within us.[24] The history of our culture is our history. To abandon the paradox for one part of our personal history is to abandon our self. It is the same with our culture. There was a time in Western culture,

> **Our history offers us choices for our spiritual life.**

when culture, religion, and spirituality were all the same. Today this is not true for most people in the West. We tend to forget, however, that the identity of culture, religion, and spirituality still exists in much of the world. We are pulling it apart by accepting our Western definitions of culture, religion, and spirituality. Keeping the concrete tension-filled paradox of the one (culture) and the many (religion and spirituality) may in the end be the best remedy for building a spiritual future. Then again, it may not be. That is why we are on our journey. We do not have all the answers.

Connecting with Personal Time and Historical (Cultural) Time

Most of us experience time and history in very different ways from how we mark it. We mark it with a watch and a calendar. We divide our days into seconds, minutes, and hours, and our lives into weeks, months, and years. What if there were no markers? We might experience the movement of time not so much as an arrow going somewhere but as we might taste a food, hear a sound, or smell a scent. We might say it is a slow or fast time, a light or dark time, an ordinary or extraordinary time. We might say it is a time to plant, to sleep, to marry, to eat. Our way of marking and "telling" personal time differs very much from one place to another. An examination of languages and cultures shows us the significant ways they differ in "telling" time.

There is a significant time difference among spiritualities of the East and the West. The classical Western spiritualities see time as going somewhere. Like an arrow that has direction, it begins and ends. Both personal and cultural history, from this perspective, is a story that has a beginning, middle, and end. Many Eastern spiritualities see history as a circle or a wheel: repeated, with no end in view. This basic difference in history is reflected in ways of understanding life after death. Western spiritualities usually see a person's or a nation's time ending on this earth with death, then continuing in heaven or on a newly made earth. Indian and Eastern spiritualities see life after death, for the vast majority of people, as a repetition of their life in some kind of reincarnation. Western spiritualities have an intense interest in time. Eastern spiritualities do not, since time does not exist as a significant marker of one's spiritual life. One's geographical spot marks more than where the body meets the ground but also where the mind encounters itself: past, present, and future.

Connections to the Past: Culture, Historical Time, and Our Present Spirituality

Human beings share similar events that are understood and experienced differently depending on their culture. The two views of the funeral that began this chapter demonstrated this. We have already seen how language as well as place helps determine what we may view as spiritual. Once we begin to have a word for and an understanding of what "spirit" is, then we may ask whether and how people have experienced "spirit" over the centuries. This is exactly what happened as Greek and subsequent Western philosophers began to ask whether animals had souls. In the nineteenth century, Sir Edward B. Taylor (1832-1917) continued this questioning as an anthropologist who viewed history as developmental and the modern scientific viewpoint as the apex of historical development. He described the origins of modern religion and spirituality as beginning when the first humans began to envision everything around them as having a conscious spirit. He spoke of this as animism. Recognizing that young children many times see their playthings as animistic, he saw this form of spirituality as infantile and primitive while he considered our present secular, scientific world as mature. The result was that many writers at that time accepted his views of religious development. We still see religious life portrayed in this way today. Some portray a growth from primitive religion to present Western religions.

28

Some authors would have the timeline end with no religion as humans evolve out of the dark world of superstition and religion to the modern world of truth and rationality. We live at a moment in time when such timelines and interpretations of development are being challenged. Nevertheless, the ideas and images of spirituality they gave birth to still exist in our literature, media, and many personal histories.

Connecting with Our Past Primitive Spirits: Spirituality before Crops, Livestock, and Strong Government (Animistic Spirituality)

Why did I marry you rather than her? Why did my child die? Why did his child kill a tiger? Why is it sunny today? Why did rain destroy the village? Why am I happy? I saw my father the other day, but now he's dead. I dreamt my dead mother told me where to look for food, and I found it! When we danced our night dance, I felt I was someone else. I saw my cousin speaking the way a wolf would speak.

How do all these experiences make sense? What's the pattern that connects them? How do things happen that have no cause to happen such as storms, being ill, catching a good fish to eat, giving birth to a male baby? How do we explain the sense that someone is present in a way that is unlike the way ordinary people are present, such as in dreams, trances, possessions, hallucinations, and feeling the presence of a dead person.

> **Does our spiritual history have spirits everywhere?**

An animistic culture finds answers to these questions by viewing everything we can see, and many things we cannot see, as animated by conscious, willful spirits. The answer to these questions is simply that there is a world beyond the mystery that encapsulates us. Everything that surrounds us is an animate, living being. That which animates us humans animates everything else in the universe. The mystery that surrounds us is actually a mirror of us without our everyday body. Our spirituality is a way to envision and enable this spiritual world. We envision the spiritual world through stories. We interact and manipulate it through ritual. Saying the right words and performing the correct actions provide the necessary balance among all things that exist. There is no hierarchy here. All are equal.

In some of these cultures, there exists a parallel spirit world. Death is the door to that world. In many instances, this is a world without pain and suffering and a world that influenced this world. The dream world and the world of the dead provide us with well-being, but also with pain and suffering. This other world must be appeased through worship, animal and human sacrifice, and daily communal and personal rituals. The worship of animals such as bears, whales, and coyotes are performed to better our ability to hunt and survive. Worship of the sun, moon, stars, rivers, and forests are performed for the same purpose. The stories describe the world beyond the senses present in this time and place. The rituals connect us to this world. The right ways of treating this world assure us of staying in harmony with it. This community of living things, no longer a mystery, results in the well-being of the humans within it.

Nothing is inanimate. Everything must be treated equally: rocks, vegetation, animals, fish, birds, stars, planets—everything. Our community consists of everything. Our well-being depends on treating everything that exists equally. How do we know how to treat our world fairly? The stories about them imprint the rules of what to do and not do. The stories tell us how to act. These stories told by parents, elders, healers, vision seekers, and others over the evening fire or while hunting or gathering berries and other foods tie together our present actions with our expected actions. They provide us with the way to understand our world and the mystery that encapsulates it. Why do we act and think the way we do? Because it is who we are! This is actually too abstract a question since it takes for granted that we can reflect on our actions and think about norms separate from what we encounter every day of our lives. While everyone is equal, everyone has to eat. These humans eat the food from the hunt and seasonable vegetation. Their challenge is to sustain equality among the spirits when they have to treat the living things that surround them differently in order to live.

This animistic interpretation of early religion begun by Taylor exists in our modern world as well as in the journals of anthropologists. Many cultures outside the West, and some still in the West, understand the world to be filled with spirits that must be dealt with daily. Certainly, our entertainment media are populated with talking animals, ghosts, vampires, and other worlds filled with wonder and human perfection. We tell our stories on giant screens and with music and sounds that leap from every corner of the room. Whether they still provide patterns of explanation for current experiences, as those stories did to "primitive" humanity, are evidenced in polls about the afterlife, ghosts, intelligence in animals, or life on other planets. The question, of course, is where does this truth fit into your spirituality?

Institutionalizing Our Connections: Farms, Family, and Centralized Government (Institutional Religion and Spirituality)

Out of the primitive, so the historical story goes, evolves another way of encountering and dealing with the mystery that shapes our realities and stimulates our spirituality.[25] People began to develop means of planting seeds and harvesting them, and domesticating certain animals and using them for labor and food. It became advantageous to stay in one place to care for their crops.

People gathered where there was fertile land and a constant supply of fresh water. They remained in those places to raise their families and work their farms. New ways of life developed and, consequently, new experiences were the result. Central to these experiences was the ability for large groups of people to work in a coordinated way to deal with enemies, natural disasters, and the necessary planning from season to season. Cultures developed resulting in people becoming more reflective, self-aware, and capable of thinking in abstract terms. With the necessity to coordinate common tasks among large groups of people, they also began to acknowledge normative moral claims outside their own families.[26]

Some began to write and read. These skills demanded an ability to not only reproduce markings, but also to control one's eyes and body to focus on the task. As these skills evolved, people learned to remember what they read in one part of the writing as they read another part along with acknowledging that they needed someone to teach them the skills of writing and formal, systematic, ways

> **Does our spiritual history include holy writings or books?**

of thinking. These technologies associated with reading and writing are with us today and are essential to the modern age. The linguistic symbols became an alphabet; something with which to write, such as a stylus or pen; something to write upon—in the West some type of paper—and a way to gather and reproduce the individual items upon which one writes, in the West what we now call a book. But the beginning technologies associated with reading and writing were reserved to specialists. Few people read or wrote because neither the need nor the technologies were present to permit everyone to be able to do so.

The dominant spirituality reflected this new culture. It was organized. It had specialists in ritual and knowledge who supported and enhanced the power of the ruling elite. Their writings (scriptures) contained the important stories and norms for the community. The core of these scriptures expressed a deep conviction that this present life was incomplete and could be perfected through the rituals that connected their religious lifestyle with this more perfect world. A religious community, in most cases identical to the political community, required obedience to its laws which, if deviated from, resulted in punishment in this and/or the next life. They included among their scriptures many of the stories found in the primitive religions of their place of origin. Naturally, these stories described how the people originated and the cosmology that was part of their origins. These "holy" writings or scriptures also contained elaborations upon these stories in codes of law, poetry, and other literary forms. In many cases, further story telling described how the cities and present cultures came about. In all the stories, gods, much like the spirits in animism, had a significant role.

An example of such development may be found in the early Greek religion that developed from the ninth century BCE to the second century BCE. This is one of the foundational religions and spiritualities to our Western approach to spirituality. By the end of its development in the second century BCE, there were three important religious expressions in Greek culture: the religion of the state, the religion of the philosophers, and the mystery religions.

State Religion

The state religion of ancient Greece was polytheistic. Reflecting its animistic origins, there were at least twelve gods each controlling different aspects of life. For example, Poseidon controlled earthquakes and the sea; Aphrodite dealt with love. Zeus was the King of the gods and had some control over all of them. These gods were immortal and more powerful than humans. They interacted with other gods, much like humans, expressing hate, love, and envy. They were always controlled by fate. These Olympians, so called because they live on Mt. Olympus, were the pantheon of Greek gods.[27] Lesser deities such as Dionysus (Bacchus) the god of ecstasy, Pan, the horned god of nature, Chaos, and Gaia are still heard of today and will be reviewed in Part Three when dealing with Wicca and Satanism. The written stories of the gods were passed on, adapted, and elaborated on from the days before writing. They are generally referred to as the Greek classics. Among these are Hesiod's *Theogony* (700 BCE) and Homer's *Iliad* and *Odyssey* (800 BCE). These were compilations of stories and songs offered by teachers and singers over the previous centuries. All described a virtuous life composed, for the most part, by temperance, fortitude, justice, and prudence. Vices too were prominent, especially those of excessive pride (hubris). Rituals were constitutive to daily life, but the rituals surrounding the altar were special in their devotion and sacrifices to the gods to whom the altar was dedicated. All these rituals, stories, and rules for behavior were performed not only because it was the tradition of the place but also because people expected the gods to guarantee their individual and communal well-being because of such actions.

> *Does our national identity strengthen our spiritual history?*

Philosophers' Religion

> *Does our spiritual history demand that our spirituality be reasonable?*

Not everyone accepted the reality of these gods. Many Greek philosophers argued that the gods did not provide well-being. Instead, they saw behind the mystery of life not the godly otherworld of polytheism with its imitation of the worst and best of human emotions, but instead the oneness of mind and reason. They believed there was one mind that reasoned, and that gave understanding and purpose to every human. This god (one mind) encompassed us. These stories of the gods were myths reflecting proper virtue but little truth. We should imitate the virtue but think reasonably about the truth portrayed there. The altars and the sacrifice were necessary for communal action, but the stories should be carefully reflected upon and not accepted just because they were considered classics.

Mystery Religions

The philosophers' thoughts and ideas were too abstract for most people. Many found other gods than those in the public arena. They worshiped them with secret rituals. These worship rituals were central to these mystery religions and their imbedded spiritualities. Names such as Eleusinian, Dionysian, Orphic, and Mithraicism clearly differentiated one cult from another. They were called mystery religions because they were secret. You became part of the community through a rite of initiation. In the initiatory rite, you learned the secrets of the group: secret rites, beliefs, and ways of action that would transform you into a new person.

Divinizing Our Connections: One Nation under One God—Judaism, Christianity, and Islam: everything is tightly connected

In our story of how our present is shaped by our past, it is important to keep in mind that the breaking of the cultural connections between religion, spirituality, and God or gods is a recent one. Depending on where you live, the connections may still be alive and well. In the United States, for example, many people strongly believe that God and country are bound together for eternity.[28] But as with all aspects of life, the current weakening or breaking up of such bonds by the dominant modern culture is filled with fear, threats, and disorientation that influence any spirituality. Remember, when a culture undergoes deep change, the religion and the spirituality undergo deep change.

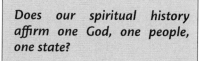

Does our spiritual history affirm one God, one people, one state?

A constant from the very beginning of our story is the unquestioned belief that every culture had its god or gods. Those deities, together with religion, spirituality, and culture, were one entity. Those who did not adhere to the religion (the culture; the accepted way of doing and saying things) were threats to the society, traitors best enslaved, or criminals to be imprisoned or killed. As today we might emotionally react to the sound of the national anthem and the flag waving in a stiff breeze, or the triumph of our teams at the Olympics, so many people in the present, as in the past, have a visceral reaction to religious holidays, religious music, and religious leaders. The outstretched hands of the fan at a music concert are easily seen reflected in the outstretched hands of one in prayer. To many, religion, nation, culture, and spirituality are one. They stand or fall together. The American experiment of separating church and state was, and is, an experiment not yet finished.

Two common ways that a culture changed its gods was when the leader changed gods and/or when the nation was defeated in battle. Many times this necessitated a change in gods because the role of the gods was to provide them with safety. Obviously, when they lost a battle, the gods had not done their work. The gods of the conqueror might do better.

The religions of Judaism, Christianity, and Islam believe in the same, one God. We will review their religious and spiritual lives in Part Two. This God becomes the God of Western culture in the ways just mentioned. The capitalization of the word God rather than god still indicates such dominance. It remained so for nearly two millennia resulting in cultural artifacts of literature, music, architecture, philosophy, and varied spiritualities that still shape discussions about and methods for living a spiritual life. During this time, several trends developed, which are of special importance for discovering and understanding our present time and place: the role of mystics and the development of a variety of ways of life called spiritualities.

Connecting to God: Mystics

To even begin to use the term mystic or mysticism in our postmodern world brings to mind what we said above about describing the past from the present. A dictionary such as *Encarta,* found in Microsoft's *Vista,* describes mysticism as "paranormal, belief in intuitive spiritual revelation, a spiritual system, confused and vague ideas"—a description very much from the modern age. Mystics were never viewed as confused and seldom offered their revelations as intuitive but, instead, as real as the ground they stood on and the God they believed in. What we call mystics today may be found in

> **Does our spiritual history demand a deep awareness of God?**

every culture, but their story in Western culture is important for spirituality and may be important for your spirituality. There are other types of mysticism than those presented in this chapter, but we are beginning this discussion with Western culture.

When we talked about an animistic culture, we noted that critical events open up new ways of interpreting the world for some people. The events of healing, possession, the presence of the dead, and trances provide them an opportunity to see their lives differently. We could have included some unique individuals that people have appealed to for help whom we, today, call shamans.[29] They explained their powers by describing how they went to non-earthly realms to bring healing and wholeness to those in need. While these are extraordinary events to us today, they were part of ordinary life before the scientific era. Simply put, the shaman was there—he had power; she healed us—just as today we might go to a doctor to be cured of an ailment. When belief in one God entered into these cultures, both animistic and otherwise, people sought patterns and ways of life to explain the relationships among all their experiences. Some people experienced God in such a way that made it all fit together. These were the Christian mystics. A personal God is central to this understanding of Western mysticism and spirituality because the culture and religions of the West took for granted that such a God existed. God is understood as the one who created and is creating this universe; directing it to its proper end. The mystic is someone who experiences a unique personal connection with God. Sometimes this is an experience of total absorption into God so that the person might say that she is God; sometimes the experience is one of such closeness to God that the only way the mystic has of describing it is by using the language of love and sexual intercourse. It's always a feeling of being embraced by God. Mystics may be professors of theol-

Medieval Culture	
Norm	That which we have done before that resulted in survival
Dominant mode of elites' reasoning	Deductive and a priori
Work	Farmer (hunter, gatherer)
Organization	Inherited or "ordained" status
Government	Feudal
Distrust	The new, the outsider, unbridled reason and analysis
Dominant Status	"Religious"—like God—speaker/actor; e.g., the pope, a king.
Core values	Sharing, work, loyalty
God	As king
Threat to status quo	Occult: dark and hidden works of the devil
Vision of Universe	The earth in the center surrounded by spheres of perfect circles which are the steppingstones to heaven, the farthermost sphere. Some retained a biblical view of the universe with the earth as the center and God in the clouds above the earth. Mountains were a means of touching the heavens and God.
Power	Coercive as local or transcendent. The transcendent is available to all, but many times is controlled by clergy.

ogy or housemaids. There is no hierarchy in who may or may not experience God in a mystical way. Many women, for example, have been recognized as mystics in the Christian tradition. There is no formal recognition, but rather it is whether the people surrounding the mystic recognize his or her description of their experience as authentic. These same people are also witnesses to the diverse happenings sometimes associated with the mystic as she leads her daily life as well as when she is in a mystic trance (the moment when connected with God). In our postmodern world, mystics always attract people's curiosity. Some mystics are described as being able to fly, heal people, read their thoughts, or foretell the future. These and many other unusual events are associated with their lives. The vast majority of mystics who have described their experiences in writing will warn people from paying too much attention to these paranormal events. Especially, they say, those who desire mystical experiences should never put any value in such events because they are serious distractions from getting close to God. From the mystic's perspective, it is the love of God and neighbor that is important, not some paranormal experience. Until the modern era, mystics were seen as unique among religious people, and theologians spoke of a special mystical grace given by God to some but not to all. Mystics are important to the history of spirituality because they place an emphasis on individual spirituality rather than communal, and because they speak from experience, not from knowledge gained from any book, including the Bible. Speaking from experience, they are also a threat to religious authorities who have not had this experience. They break the connection between institutional religion and individual spirituality while still being deeply imbued with the cultural religion.

They are also important to the history of spirituality because, when Westerners encountered other religions, the mystic experience and the writings associated with them provided a means of interpreting seemingly similar writings and experiences in other religions. Consequently, most research today will claim there are mystics in all religions. Those who do not have a personal, creator God will, instead, experience a deep connection with the god, energy, truth, self, nature, life, or nothingness that is the core of their religious transformation. They are at a loss as how to use their cultural language to describe precisely what they have experienced.

The mystic experience is usually described as a feeling of transcending the here and now and having a sense of being close to the origins of life. The depth and totality of the experience will determine its mystical nature. At the same time, the mystic strives to be in contact with the object of his/her experience. If one seeks to be a mystic for the experience of mysticism, one is not a mystic in the tradition we describe here.[30]

Methods for Connecting with God: The Holy Spirit, Ordered Spirituality, and Spiritualities

The language, idea, and experience of the spiritual was already well established by the time the concept of "spirit" and everything associated with it became associated with God in Western culture. Up to the time, for example, when Christianity began to be the institutional religion of the Roman Empire (313 CE, The Edict of Milan), people had a variety of experiences that pointed to realties beyond the five senses. I have already mentioned some of them, but there were others just as important that today we tend to forget. As people began to use abstractions to control their lives, they realized that these abstractions existed in a way that, while not of this immediate sensory world, certainly directly influenced it. Numbers and geometric shapes, for example, somehow existed in our minds. We were able to manipulate them in our minds, and the results could be used to manipulate the physical world around us. Using geometry and numbers, for example, we were able to predict the movement of the stars and the time for planting. The material reality experienced by our senses was in contact with our mental ability to manipulate it, and we somehow knew that it was important, practical, and real. Our minds could envision this reality and manipulate it using numbers and geometry. This essence, soul, or spirit, might be present in other, disembodied, ways. The stories handed down from previous generations gave us hints as to what these spirit ways might be. When the God of Christians and Jews entered into this world of spirits and the life built around them, things had to be re-thought in the light of this new God experience. In the West, the terminology and idea of a spiritual life, and the spiritualities associated with it, are rooted in the Christian notion of God as three in one. Using the language of the time, this would mean that God is Father, God is Son, and God is Holy Spirit, yet God is one God. This, of course, is a paradox that many Christian theologians have attempted to explain using philosophical language. Its importance here is that the idea of spirituality in the West is founded upon the doctrine that God's love (Spirit) is a gift (grace) to each Christian. God is present with and within each person enlivening and energizing that person, and providing a means for that person to not only live his life now but to transform this present life into a heavenly, grace-filled one in the future.[31] The means for receiving and encouraging this gift is through spirituality. Each of these methods becomes a way of life lived by thousands of people. These people support each other in developing their Spirit-filled lives, especially the men and women in what is known as religious orders or organizations. They

> **God is central to Western spiritualities.**

continue to exist today and, therefore, have long histories. These histories are filled with descriptions of mystics who were part of a particular spirituality—theologians attempting to understand the spiritual way of life rationally, and spiritual directors who helped people live the spiritual life. Some of these spiritualities are fifteen hundred years old. That is a great deal of experience living a spiritual life. The manuals and inspirational literature from the religious orders are easily available. These traditions live on for those who see this as their path in life either as a vowed member of the religious order or as one associated with it.

At the beginning of the age previous to ours, spirituality (*spiritualitas*) had two meanings:[32] a mode of being and a way of acting. As a mode of being, it was the opposite of corporality in much writing, and in legal tracts it reflected a division of life into the spiritual and the temporal realms. This latter, legal, application of *spiritualitas* easily gave way to talking about the spiritual in reference to the clergy and the temporal in reference to the laity. The second interpretation narrowed the meaning of the spiritual realm to refer to those who lead the contemplative (spiritual) life. Such a life was one more closely aligned with the life of the mind, the mystical life, and devotional life. The "active" life in this sense was one that took one away from being spiritual. It was one of work, family, sensuality, and the ordinary. Leading a spiritual life meant that one was separate from those who did not lead it. It meant a strict discipline of one's body in every way possible to enhance the person's mental, contemplative, spiritual existence. These distinctions between active and contemplative were challenged in subsequent centuries, but the spiritualities that embodied them continued.

Breaking Connections, Part One: The Modern Age in the West

"Is this all there is?" Up until this point in the history of spirituality in the West the response has been "no." There is more than we can ordinarily sense. We experience the extraordinary spirits and souls that surround us. We experience ourselves as distinct from our bodies. We are convinced that the mystery of life is a world beyond ours as well as our own that is created, ordered, and destined by God. It is all one world with one God. We can be in touch with God and the extraordinary world in all kinds of ways. One way in particular has been given to us by God to continually be present to and with God. That way is God's community, known as the church. Through God's church, we could know what to do and constantly "touch" God. The church and its saints, sacraments, sermons, savants, popes, bishops, priests, and monks act as primary intermediaries between this ordinary world and the one beyond our senses. We are part of one world, ordinary and extraordinary; the bridge is God's church.

The modern approach to answering the question of life is similar to the previous, medieval one, but with a slight difference. This slightly different approach began with the fracture of the whole that ultimately, by the end of the twentieth century, would break the connections built up over centuries. A group of well-educated monks said "no" to the role of the church officials as the sole bridge, or mediator, between the extraordinary world and this one. Lead by Martin Luther (1483-1576), they said that the whole artifice of Christianity was false since it did not reflect the cornerstone of the building itself: the Bible. Since medieval Christianity was not built on biblical principles, it should be destroyed and begun anew based on faith alone and the Bible that reflected and supported that faith. Most, if not all, sources of spirituality offered to the common person were superstitions, idol worship, and tools of the devil to take people away from the real biblical faith. To live an authentically Christian spirituality, the reformers said people had to break their connections to their medieval Christian religion and risk a return to the Bible to deepen both their religion and spirituality. In breaking their connection with institutional religion (Medieval Roman Catholicism), they began the disconnections that would result in what we today call the modern age.

Modern Culture	
Norm	That which is logical, scientifically proven, rational and results in economic security
Dominant mode of elites' reasoning	Inductive and a posteriori with an emphasis on the method to be used for both modes of reasoning.
Work	Industry
Organization	Rational bureaucratic authority
Government	Strong central bureaucracy
Distrust	The old, supernatural norms and experience
Dominant Status	Scientist (e.g. doctor) as objective discoverer of truth.
Core values	Individual accumulation, hard work, differentiation, choice, pluralism, relativity, reductionism, empirical (rational), this worldly. It is dominated by instrumental and pragmatic reasoning, and usually demeans tradition.
God	As machine
Threat to status quo	Parapsychology
Vision of Universe	The sun is the center of the solar system. Established upon the laws discovered by Kepler and Newton; seen by people like Galileo. The Copernican revolution changed how humans understood themselves in the universe.
Power	Coercive, usually associated with mechanical; elicitive, associated with professional knowledge; leaders.

The modern world had several essentials: the book able to be read by all, the mind capable of using science to discover a predictable world to manipulate through increased technologies, the individual as the center and arbiter of everything, an experimental method of reducing things to their essential parts and determining which one of those parts the whole depends upon. The focus was on a single connection proclaiming at times that it was the whole: book, mind, predictable world, technology, or "me.

The modern world began with the rejection of much that preceded it: the medieval church, untested tradition, clerical authority, superstition, and total dependency upon community. As it ended, it discovered that all of life could not be reduced to what the mind was capable of understanding, that other technologies beside the book could convey information and knowledge, and that the reduction of all of life to one person, idea, technology, or religion was destructive of all of life. Its dominant interpretative model became the machine and, in the end, the model began to destroy the organisms it was meant to enliven. The climate of war and the increasing environmental devastation of the twentieth century, which has continued unabated into the twenty-first, are symbols of the modern age at its worst. This is also an amazing age, in that we have extended the human life span and the human ability to connect with every other human everywhere and at any time. We can now gather information from across the globe and make it available to those who never would have had access to it before, but now they do through the simple technology of mobile phones with Internet capabilities. Food and other goods are available to many more people than ever before. Ultimately, however, modern culture is not able to sustain two paradoxes: "I need a 'we' to be a 'me'" and "I am one and many." The result has been a type of secular fundamentalism that reduces all mystery and paradox to one simple experience, one simple idea, and one simple truth. This fundamentalist mindset is overwhelmed by the multiplicity of life itself, which ultimately is unpredictable and diverse.

The spiritualities that have flourished during this time have unknowingly imitated the fundamentals of the culture. Thus the Bible (one book) has become the center of spirituality for many, the pope (one man) for many more, science (one source of knowledge) for yet others, and experienced transcendence for even more. We will review these spiritualities in depth in part three. Three things happened that resulted in how most people in the West look at religion and spirituality today. The concept known as organized religion developed. Religion became privatized. While the culture became secularized, the supernatural identified with the churches was conceptualized in opposition to the natural as promoted by the sciences. The result was the development of spiritualities unique to this age and the modification of previous spiritualities in the light of its presuppositions.

No More Religion and Culture

Before 1450 CE, religion referred to the type of life lived by the Religious— the communities of men and women who take vows of poverty, chastity, and obedience. By the middle of the seventeenth century, the word religion referred to a set of beliefs, rituals, and morals that people lived. Once this understanding of religion was established, we could do things like make laws dealing with religion. We could separate religion, culture, politics, and nation. With such a separation, we could think differently about our individual and communal lives. Religion could be seen to be separate from civil and state affairs, and as something to be chosen and dealt with as a vital, or not so vital, part of life.[33]

No More Religion, Faith, and Culture

Something else happened with the breakup of Christian Europe. When the medieval forms of church hierarchy, belief, and worship were changed, some began to see all ecclesial structures as fallible and lacking in their ability to be sources of a personal faith that emotionally moved one to a love of God. In the early American colonies, for example, during what became known as the First Great Awakening (1730-40), preachers went from town to town "awakening" churchgoers to their sinfulness and their need for a heartfelt yearning for redemption. It wasn't the Christian religious way of life (as it had come to be known) that counted, but rather the individual's feelings about central Christian truths and one's personal relationship with Jesus that determined one's spiritual life. If it couldn't be felt, it was not a faith capable of bringing one into the redemptive presence of God. The concept of faith was now understood as a necessarily personal, spontaneous, informal, and deeply felt emotion. One did not need culture or religion to have faith. One just needed to believe. "Just believe," however was not as disconnected as it may sound to contemporary individualists. Remember that this "belief" was understood as being connected to a book, the Bible; connected to other believers, especially on Sunday; connected to one called to preach to instill that belief. It is among these faith-filled believers that one's spirituality would grow and deepen.

Secularization: Institutional Religion Becomes Isolated

When those leading a religious way of life are convinced that God has told them how to act, how to celebrate, and what to believe, they view everything else as moving away from God. As the centuries move on from the founding of the religion, many of the cultural accretions easily become identified with God's revelation to the religion's founders. As the connections of medieval Christianity began to break apart, first with the divisions associated with the Reformation and then with the advancement of science evolving into what we know as the modern world, most everything apart from that previous medieval culture began to be seen as secular. As kingdoms fell and democracies arose, the new political systems were seen as secular. As music began to originate outside the confines of the religious belief, it was considered secular music. Anything that threatened those previous connections to God was to be feared. The word secularization was used on an ever-increasing basis to describe these threats.

Secularization has many meanings.[34] Today three dominate the scene: first, the Christian church has little influence on the direction of the culture (society is secularized); second, church members no longer hold to some or all of the beliefs of the church (norms of the secular world such as divorce are present in the church); third, sacred experiences are now also found outside the church. The sources of these sacred experiences are not always found inside the church ("Secular music in church, on Christmas!" "I felt God's presence among the homeless sleeping on the heat vents.") [35]

The term secularization reflects the diversity of contemporary spiritualities. Many people are finding the effects associated with experienced faith, as described by the mystics or claimed by the church, to exist outside rather than inside the churches.[36] The same can be said for contemporary adherents to Judaism and Islam. One reason for reading a book such as this is that one lives quite well in a secularized society, easily accepts ways of worship, beliefs, and norms rejected by the churches, and finds sacred experiences outside the churches. A search for a spiritual life sometimes reflects one's secular existence.

Building New Connections: Secular, Natural, Real, and True

We seek patterns. We do not allow our world to break apart without rebuilding it in some way. Rebuilding is always a challenge whether we do so with imagination alone or with the reality that surrounds us.

As we found new ways to think about cultural realities, we also found new ways to talk about reality. Until the modern age, entities known as spirits, gods, and souls, as well as other worlds, were real. They provided the patterns and language to explain people's experiences. Methods of dealing with the world of spirits, gods, and souls also developed to help people cope with the realities of life.

With the development of modern science, this world, its inhabitants, and the understandings that provided an interpretation of it were cast into a darkness that was unknowable, unnatural, and thus unreal. This happened because this once real world was no longer seen as such. It could not be demonstrated to be real. Now for something to be real it had to be sensed, measured, and replicated in diverse circumstances.[37] Mathematics and scientific experimentation were the eyes for seeing beyond imagination and myths, and were the means for providing us with a real world. The world of religion, spirits, and the sacred were the world of opinion and the supernatural—unknowable and dangerous for living in this secular, scientific, and modern world. [38] Besides this former world's inability to be proved, the scientific realm was able to provide explanations for the variety of experiences that gave rise to what people had called ghosts, spirits, souls, and gods. Angels no longer were seen as necessary for explaining the movement of planets; Newton's laws did that. People's sins were no longer seen as producing plagues: viruses and microbes were to blame. Possession, trance, visions of dead loved ones, and after-life experiences were explained by diverse psychological interpretations sometimes known as parapsychology. The older explanations of these experiences now had modern explanations. The entire provable reality of our present world could be explained without resorting to gods, souls, and other ethereal realities.

Many religious institutions, especially Christian ones, continued to evolve in this modern culture. These religions accepted the modern division into natural and supernatural. No doctrine said it, but many spiritual people came to believe that this natural, secular, world took us away from God. The spiritual was God. Anything that took us away from God took us away from the spiritual. The purpose of the church, its doctrine, rituals, community, and moral demands was to provide us with the means to live a supernatural life and to attain the fullness of that life in heaven, a supernatural place, where we, as a perfect soul, would live happily for all eternity. It was a life that needed no scientific proof to be true because our faith, instead of science, proved it instead. [39] The spiritual life, therefore, was beyond science, proof, and our ordinary life.

Such adaptation, however, did not mean total acceptance of the modern world. Institutional religions, and many spiritualities that reflected them, reacted to their perception of the modern world in three ways. First, they accepted the developing modern culture as good and normative to one's religious life; second, they rejected the developing modern culture as bad and destructive of one's religious life; third, they adapted to the modern culture by entering into dialogue with it and developing multiple norms

> *Many contemporary forms of spirituality advocate experiencing God outside the churches, synagogues, and mosques.*

or signposts from both the modern culture and religious traditions of the past. These three movements have been described in many ways: modernist, anti-modernist, main line, progressive, liberal, conservative, evangelical, and fundamentalist. [40]

In Chapter Six, we will review spiritualities that developed out of these reactions under the headings I have titled as traditionalist, co-temporalist, and contemporalist. The labels are not important because they are always shifting, and many times are determined by the label-creating media machine more centered on writing a particular emotion-catching story than a description of facts. What is important is that today we have a plurality of religions with various historical heritages that understand these heritages in vastly different ways depending on their response to their understanding of the surrounding environment and the questions they ask of both that environment and their tradition.[41]

Here and Now: Post Modern? Liminal!

Most historians divide our Western past as we have done in this book. Many would describe today's place and time as postmodern. But are we really *post-modern*? Geography as well as family usually trumps history, especially when dealing with spirituality. Where a person is born and with whom one lives her life—parents, peers, work, and family—greatly affects what she wishes to change and what she desires for herself, her friends, and her enemies. Historians are an infinitesimal part of the human family. Many, many people still view the world as modern. Many more are pre modern.[42] Yet many commentators describe our Western world as living in

> Spiritualities that reject history are challenged by their "here and now."

a postmodern epoch because, from their professional perspective, the modern world has disintegrated. Only you know how you look at things, what you accept as true for you, and what you value as necessary connections in your life. You will be able to compare your spirituality with others as we move into the rest of the book. Part One is to discover where you are here and now. In dialogue, in clarifying your spirituality, you will be able to build and grow.

One reason most commentators give for why the modern world is breaking apart is that which was once considered essential to the modern way of thinking and acting is no longer as absolute as it was. Modern reductionist analysis, dominance of objective reason, and norms needed for and resulting from such analysis began to fall apart in the face of intense historical research, archeological research, globalization, the consumer society, and the niche marketing associated with it. Postmodernism now offers, in the place of modernism's scientific certitudes, a way of life more like a raft than a home with a solid foundation. We live on a raft of data evidenced and held together by structures of power. The raft floats on a sea of uncertainty paddled in many ways by a type of Cartesian doubt (hermeneutic of suspicion) that provides little direction and results, many times, in conversations and stories about direction that somehow hold us in an existence that is equally directionless. But, as with the medieval and the modern perspectives, this postmodern view of power and truth has become part of the political and educational realms, and many religious ways of life.

Another reason that the modern world is seen as disintegrating is that it has not provided the benefits it promised. The First World War showed us how we could use reason to kill soldiers more efficiently. In the Second World War Adolf Hitler showed us how to kill our fellow citizens in a rational, efficient, and scientific way. The atomic bomb now offers the promise of destroying the earth. Between 1500 and 1900, there were about 589 wars and more than 141,901,000 deaths from those wars. Between 1900 and 1995, there were about 250 wars and 109,746,000 deaths.[43] In one hundred years we have caused as much death and suffering as the previous four hundred. When and how will it end? The beginning of the twenty-first century promises no less death and suffering as economic and environmental degradation increases along with nuclear proliferation. The modern habits we have established as individuals and cultures obviously

Liminal Culture	
Norm	That which provides an experience capable of being repeated and results in well-being.
Dominant mode of elites' reasoning	Dialectical and wholistic
Work	Technological, informational
Organization	Teams and transitional gatherings of professionals for immediate goals and objectives
Government	Democratic/populist, declining emphasis on authority, (church /state) for policy making but continually responsive to power groups capable of providing celebrity and populist experiences
Distrust	The boring and abstract, unbridled science; normative (religion) producing uniformity
Dominant Status	Celebrity providers of well-being
Core values	Leisure, individual self-expression, quality of life concerns
God	As love
Threat to status quo	Absolutes, norms, and acknowledged limits
Vision of Universe	No center demonstrated by the relativity of Einstein, the observations of Shapely, the Doppler Effect, and the Big Bang theory.
Power	Although the total destruction of the human universe is possible through human weapons, the day-to-day life of the liminal universe favors the elicitive power of choice over coercive power.

threaten to destroy us. Deep within each of us is the transcendent desire and the need to change the world we live in. Yet the habits of life that we, as a culture, formed in the modern world prevent us from making these changes individually or culturally. The postmodern world offers no clear measure of the spiritual goals involved in seeking new patterns and habits of life. No wonder so many wish it would all end and we could start again. Starting over, however, can never be done as if we haven't had a past. Our moment of starting over is actually an in-between moment[44] —a time of liminality.

The Liminality of the Present

Victor Turner used the term liminality to describe the in-betweenness of the puberty rites leading to adulthood for aboriginal peoples.[45] The children in a tribe live with the expectations associated with their role in society. They are comfortable with the mode of speaking, acting, and relating to those around them that are appropriate to the role of being a child. At a certain time, some children, the pubescent, are suddenly taken from the general group of children. Through ritual, they are transformed into adults. This "in between time" of the puberty rite is a time of liminality, of disorientation. All the former signposts of a child's way of life are gone. The children often have a sense that they have died.[46] The rites themselves many times include a portrayal of dying to one's old self and coming alive to one's new self. Once the children become aware, through ritual, of this new self, they re-enter society with new roles and the corresponding language, actions, and relationships inherent to those roles.

The concept of liminality has been used by many scholars to describe other struggles individuals have when facing difficult transition moments in the life cycle or movements within one's social hierarchy.

This concept can also be used to describe what happens in a culture, which, of course, is people. The people responding to postmodern change will experience individual liminality with a corresponding transition of identity and self. When they look back, they will be able to see the deep cultural changes that affected the way they believe, how they perceive right and wrong, and what they want to achieve in life.

These deep changes are found in pivotal marking events in politics, ideas, technology, and spirituality. Such a change in politics, for example, is first seen in a culture's inability to find common ground in the face of a common enemy—even to agree on who or what the enemy is. A revolution or an election marks the change. But the change is liminal because the revolution or election only serves as a brief interim before another revolution or election occurs that is as radical as the previous one. The same kind of deep change may be seen within religious institutions as people uncover deep disagreements with the central elements of the religions such as not attending to the leaders' commands, the interpretation of foundational writings, the inability to sense the fulfillment of the religion's promises in this life or the next, or of a fellow feeling. During these times, new religions begin to increase.

These signal events form a dialectical pattern in which the "new" breaks through at a certain moment in time to seemingly dominate the culture to only find, within a short time, that it was an illusion because the "old" returns with a vengeance. Conscious of what is happening, the old begins to exercise its power to destroy the new. This dialectic sometimes occurs quickly, and sometimes over centuries. The following is a way of illustrating this pattern:

OLD/OLD…NEW/old…new/OLD…New/Old…NEw/Old…NEW/old…NEW/NEW

The numerator indicates the culture of decreasing influence, the denominator the culture of increasing influence as visualized within the culture. The dialectic is such that there is a continual contest over the language spoken by the culture, the normative ethical and ritual actions of the culture, and the proper empowering modes of decision making in the culture. Gradually, what is new becomes part of the way people speak, act, and gather; these ways of speaking, acting, and gathering then provide a sense of meaning, belonging, rightness, and well-being to the change agents of the culture; then, through trial and error, the new way sustains peoples' lives, and slowly a new culture becomes THE way of life. Of course, we see this dialectic only from the rearview mirror of the now dominant culture.

What is going on among the various subcultures?[47] What is going on is a great deal of activity as people cross over from one way of living to another. The subcultures are composed of varying generations. As each new generation enters into the culture, the culture as a whole finds many of its members shifting from one way of thinking and acting to another. The older generations react to the younger generation by fighting, fleeing, adapting, or boredom. They quickly find that the children do not feel or react to what they thought was new. This is to be expected. The world has changed since the initial reaction of the parenting generations. This changed world is what the younger generation is reacting to, and it may easily see that the proper reaction is any of the four options we just mentioned.

A quick look at a recent example of generational difference in the United States as provided by R. Zemke, C. Raines, and B. Filipczak[48] in terms of how we view leaders demonstrates what I mean. From the beginning of the century to the end, it has flowed in this sequence from one generation to the next: the leader is the "boss" telling us what to do; the leader is all of us agreeing what to do; the leader is comprised of those who know what to do; the leader is a team working together to accomplish a goal, part of which is our mutual appreciation of each other. What we see here is an important part of any cultural life: its view of leaders. The same can be said of gender relationships, technological usage, economic expectations, and may other aspects of daily life. Such movement among these expectations of leadership, gender, technology, and economics within a culture is an example of what is happening within the subgroups because people are being socialized into various patterns and ways to react to larger shifts of words, actions, and social relations. This movement of subcultures and generations within them is the expression of the larger culture's liminality—the larger culture's attempt to stabilize itself in the face of "the new" of pivotal change.

Because we are talking about one dominant culture comprised of many subcultures, there must be something that brings the various cultures together. I would suggest that within each culture, there are transitional subcultures that act as agents of transition and translation of what is new and what is old; change agents that act as interlocutors between the old and new in a culture. Much like immigrant children who translate the language and actions of the new land to their parents from the old country, these transitory subcultures translate the old and new to each other[49]. Many experience this every day as they ask a younger person to help with a new technology. The "older" one may be eighteen and the "younger" may be six.[50]

The result of the dialectic from old to new is a culture that reflects, for a while, the stability of the recognized signposts that provide individuals and groups with the needed security for healthy living. A carefully chosen spiritual life is essential to living in a transitional culture. Such a spiritual life offers us a set of connections to where, when, and who we are and wish to be. We have reviewed our connections to our where and when in this chapter. It is necessary to describe and review our connections to others. It is only in being connected that we build a spiritual life. Yet in making and/or recognizing lasting connections in a liminal age is a monumental task.

Spirituality in the Here and Now: The Liminal Age

Here and now, we are between what was and what will come. We, as others before us, face the mystery of life and the spiritual paradoxes that are especially prevalent in a liminal time. Where do we find the spiritual resources and direction to live in these times?

At dinner the other night, a friend of ours from California handed us seven letters. They were old business envelopes with a small window in which her address was written by multiethnic immigrants learning to read and write English. They had sent them to her, their teacher, as a token of thanks for her work teaching them English. They had never held a pen until she taught them how. They had never written on paper until she taught them. They had never known what a mailbox was until she led them to the corner. These women, and the rest of the class, had come from abject poverty to a mysterious land in which they were now learning to live.

Many of the habits of their former lives still offered them a sense of security in this time of transition. All the Muslim women, for example, still wore the *hijab* and did not talk to men. A few younger women sometimes took their *hijab* off while in an all-female class. One day a man showed up at the door and just stood there and stared. The women immediately put on their *hijab*. The power of the past was obviously very much in the present through this man's stare. Their children were learning English, and their older children were working and associating with those outside their little enclave. Things were changing. Things were very difficult. The culture from which they came did not participate in any of the Western developments we just reviewed. Yet in many ways, they are caught in the tensions of liminality much like their Western counterparts. Words do not convey the same meaning as before. Previous ways of acting do not bring the same results. Ways to act between male and female are uncertain and serendipitous as to meaning and intent. The joy and spontaneity one sees in the lives of the very young who are conscious of neither time nor place is missing in those elders who do not know where they wish to go nor what their future will be. Liminality is like that—dispirited. Everyone is in a liminal time, and the spiritualities of the past face the imperviousness of the present.

But it does not have to be that way. The joy of creativity, the excitement of traveling a new path or renewing the one you have is here. We can face the future with fear that we do not know what is coming, or we can face the future with the conviction that we will be gifted with the energy and the conviction that we can treat this gift as an invitation to create a new, spirited life that will provide direction for ourselves and others. To do this we must be able to listen to the here and now and listen to those who live it with us in this liminal time. A new world awaits.

Summary:

In this liminal age, we stand alone with few permanent connections to other people, ideas, authorities, and ways of life. We are not meant to exist in such a liminal way – isolated in our own niche, our own here and now. Instead, we have seen how *I* is *we* when connected to a particular culture, a particular place, a particular history, and a particular language. A spirituality is always wholistic and interconnected. To ignore our connections in accepting the promise of a transcendent future is to forget the habits that form us and the mystery that envelopes us.

CHAPTER THREE

SPIRITUAL SOURCES, SIGNPOSTS, AND A COMPASS FOR A SPIRITUAL LIFE

The story is told of American marines traveling at night in their Humvee, lights off. Night vision glasses on, electronic jamming devices on, horseshoe attached to the front grille, they rode alert, searching for the bad guys. Night and day, they traveled this same road. They knew it well. They could tell if anything had changed along the route. They were alert, their hearts pumping and adrenaline passing quickly through their veins, somehow feeling unsafe even though everything indicated safety, including riding in a manufacturer-guaranteed safe armored vehicle.

They rode hoping they would once again make it to the end of their route. When a blinding flash of light, sound, and heat ripped them apart, the sure signs of safety were replaced with the scream of one of their own burning like a flare marking the spot of their destruction. The signs had changed. Their lives had changed. Now this apocalyptic flare from hell on earth marked their lives forever.

Where are you in this scenario? Safe and secure in the armored vehicle? Lying outside it seeing one of your own being destroyed? Enduring the screams and terror of a life going up in flames? Disinterested in all of this?

Our signposts tell us where we are. People without signposts are without identity, without place, without time. In some spiritualities, the disintegration of all signposts is a desirable resolution to the mystery of the here and now. In others, such disintegration is insanity. In either case, it is essential to know what your choices are. We will look at the signposts of transcendence in this chapter.

We will also review the various sources people have found for living a spiritual life over a prolonged period. Over the years we discover those places, times, beliefs, actions, and people who seem to infuse or awaken in us the desire to move forward and engage our inner and outer spirits. At particular times in our lives, we discover one of these to be more important than others. We will look at how these sources and signposts of the spiritual life change and provide a compass—a means of being aware of the direction of our spiritual lives. Where you are in the above scenario today may not be where you will be tomorrow.

Before moving on, I would like to review what we have said up to this point about the nature of spirituality. We have seen that the spiritual life is composed of two dynamic realities: one, our desire to become more and to transcend the present moment and place where we live; two, some method that transforms us, thus enabling us to transcend that moment and place. The first suggests that there is a satisfaction of this desire; there is a goal of living a spiritual life that will change us entirely from who we are right here and now. The second indicates a means or system for achieving this goal and satisfying this desire. The sources and signposts are part of the means to achieve the goal.

Both desire and means are part of daily life. As with all of life, we find ourselves at times overcome by some events and, for most of the time, just doing whatever it is that we do—the ordinariness of everyday life. The ordinary is what takes up ninety percent of our time: eating, drinking, working, sleeping, relating to those we like as well as those we dislike. Our hearts beat; our legs move; we live our lives. Death is the cessation of the here and now in the ordinary course of events. The extraordinary is also part of our lives as both time and space change as we become transformed beyond the ordinary. When our transformation is part of our spiritual life, our spiritual tradition has a way of describing both it and the means that brought it about. Thus, for example, in many Christian churches, the transformation into a spiritual life with God is described as grace and the means is faith and/or baptism. Our spiritual experiences, therefore, are both ordinary and extraordinary.

The spiritual sources provide us an opportunity to slowly or quickly become more than we are right now. Accompanying that "becoming" are what we have described as spiritual feelings in Chapter One under the heading "What's Spiritual?" Prominent among those feelings is that of the sacred. That

> *Our spiritual life is a mixture of a desire for transcendence and a way for the desire to be temporarily satiated.*

means that when we encounter a spiritual source, we also have a feeling of the sacred.

Sometimes we feel little in our encounter with a spiritual source, yet transformation is occurring; at other times we have intense feelings; here, too, transformation is occurring. Because we live in a liminal time, we easily retain our modern language and refer to the former as a secular moment and the latter as a spiritual one. Yet in both instances, transformation is occurring. We just have not had a deep experience of it. For example, within the context of God-believing spiritualities, that would mean that in a believer's ordinary or secular life she is minimally aware of God continually creating, keeping her alive. In the words of a familiar song, "He's got the whole world in his hands." Yet God is causing the significant transformation of life itself (without God there would be nothing).

At an extraordinary transformative moment and place, the mystical experience of someone caught up in God's overwhelming presence is evident to the eye and ear. It is scary and attractive at the same time. God the lover, yet God the destroyer is the one we are joined with. The person having the experience is overwhelmed by what it brings him in contact with. In the extreme transcendent experience, the transformation is witnessed in the changed physiology of the individual as well as changes in her manner of living: she looks and acts differently during and after the mystical moment. The transformative results of both the extraordinary and ordinary moments in life result in what we call character. Our character develops as our relationship to things, people, and the natural environmental changes from that first moment of awareness that transcendence is possible to the final moment of transcendence itself. Thus, using the same example, a person believing in God accepts God's gift of grace. Over time, the continual active acceptance of this gift offered through the sources of a spiritual life results in the development of character (following the signposts) and, ultimately, total life with God (transcendence) in what is described as heaven.

Sources of the Spiritual Life

Anything and everything has been found to be a source of spiritual life, touchstones of the sacred and transcendent. These times, places, persons, words, actions, things, and communities are believed to be a means though which you are in the presence of the power, energy, principle, or persona that sustains all existence. This presence may be a *remembered presence* such as seeing a picture or participating in a ritual, which results in your recalling the power, energy, principle, or persona. Much like going to a funeral and seeing a picture of the dead person might remind you of who this body was. This presence may

> *Every living and nonliving entity may become a means of satisfying transcendence—desire.*

also be an *embodied presence*. In this instance, you believe that you are in contact with the energy and can expect to feel it coursing through your body at any moment; or in contact with your god, expect to drink his blood or have your sins forgiven. What you see, feel, hear, touch, or taste is, for example, the words, the water, the music, or the red stone. What you encounter in memory or embodiment is the foundation of your spirituality, the means of transformation, and the goal of desired transcendence. What you encounter is a source of spirituality. This encounter expects and leaves these sources of the spiritual life with an aura of sacrality that demands care for the source, reverence for the source, and attentiveness to sustaining the originality of the source. Those sources believed to be the embodiment of a community's spiritual life are surrounded with architecture, precious metals, and jewels that demonstrate the source's importance. It is not an ordinary person who stimulates our spiritual life, just as it is not an ordinary piece of bread, mountain, or book that embodies what we believe. No, these sources of the spiritual life are extraordinary. They are sacred spiritual sources that can be seen as such because they reflect the surrounding light in the embedded jewels or are thrust high into the sky demonstrating in architecture the spirituality's ability to change an individual or a society's horizon.

Whether some time, place, belief, person, thing, vegetable, or animal is a touchstone of transcendence for you depends on which culture you were socialized into, as well as when and where the socialization occurred. For most people,[51] it also depends on the religion they were born into. It is not only the individual source of transcendence but the entire pattern or cultural signposts of transcendence that surround us and enable us to make the connection between the desire to transcend and transform and the source that enables that desire to be met. The pattern for most people is the when and where of the religious culture within which their spirituality dwells. For example, if you have been brought up in a culture that envisions a personal God as a central figure for every religion and spirituality, the means of contact with that God will be your obvious sources of transcendence. The Bible and preacher are such sources in North American culture. Pundits will become centers of controversy when they violently reject these sources and the God they represent. But note that there would be no controversy if there were not these particular sources of transcendence. If the concept of a personal God did not exist in this culture, the pundits' claims would not gain attention.

Another historical example is the bread and wine that Roman Catholics today accept as a significant focus of their spiritual life. They believe it is Jesus, whom they also believe is God. The context of the bread and the wine, in contemporary writing, is the Sunday celebration called "the Mass" or "the Holy Eucharist." These began as secular beliefs and practices, and outside of the Catholic Eucharistic contextual beliefs, they still are secular. The way the bread and wine are treated and their source of transcendence have changed over the nineteen or so centuries they have been part of Catholic ritual. According to the accounts in the Christian Bible,[52] Jesus had a meal with his special friends, the twelve disciples. There was a prayer that Jews usually said before meals. Jesus said it in a unique way that mentioned that this bread was his body and the wine in the cup was his blood. If this was a sacred Jewish Passover meal,

Jesus added a layer of sacrality to it by identifying the meal as a time of transcendence unique to his way of life. Certain items became further focus of transcendence (bread and wine) to the exclusion of others (e.g. lamb).

This ritual developed from a simple meal with friends to a church meal with persecuted members on the resurrection day (Sunday); then it became a sacred ceremony (without the meal) where the bread and wine were consumed only by a priest; later it transitioned to the bread being displayed for honor and worship by all members of the church, to a time when this sacred bread and wine were seldom eaten or drunk by ordinary Catholics. There came a time when the honored display of the bread was the central ritual that Roman Catholics used to come in contact with their God. Any religion, and the spiritualities embedded within it, has stories similar to that of Roman Catholics and the Eucharistic bread and wine. Most protestant Christians, for example, refer to their context of the sacred bread and wine as the "Last Supper," indicating a significantly different context from when this ceremony is called "celebrating Mass" or "the Eucharist." This contrast within the same religion, Christianity, emphasizes the fact that particular items of transcendence always fit within a set of signposts—all of which are part of a culture—that provide individuals and communities with sources of transcendence and sacrality. Descriptions of these sources will be part of the spiritualities we review in the following chapters.

The sources of spiritual life and their consequent signposts are in a unique situation of time and place. Today we live in a liminal time, thus both the sources and signposts are not as clear as when the culture was more stable. We in North America live in a pluralistic culture. Within North America reside all the religious and spiritual traditions of the contemporary world. All in their own way are shouting, "Here is the source of transcendence." Some of these have undergone the changes consequent upon modernization; others have not.

Various technologies enable an individual to participate in any of these spiritual traditions. Using these technologies, however, one encounters the sacred object and source of transcendence separate from the signposts provided by the particular religious culture. Such a non-contextual encounter suggests that an individual is capable of experiencing the transcendent without the culture. This would be similar to saying that a person could see a sentence printed in ancient Hebrew and understand it without knowing the Hebrew language. But no individual comes naked, without the dress of socialization, into a culture. As individual or as a religious spiritual tradition, we live today in a liminal time and in a pluralistic culture. The feelings associated with transcendence and transformation are undergoing change, as is the security of communal affirmation (socialization) associated with that change. Hopefully, this book will help you make sense of it all and make the choices necessary for a full life.

LORETTE WILMOT LIBRARY
NAZARETH COLLEGE

Signposts of a Spiritual Life

Markers on a road provide us with the security that we are traveling in the right direction. They also show us where to find the sustenance of food and drink, a place to sleep, a place for fuel, and whatever else we need for a good trip. This is a simple image of the spiritual life. If we follow the signposts, we will get where we want to go. At least that is the promise. As with our marines at the start of this chapter, there are always challenges along the way.

Here we need to be reminded that each of us is a whole person. Our paradoxes remind us of this fact. So too the signposts are both external, something we can engage with our five senses, and internal, something we can feel and think about. They are symbols because they link the tangible world with the non-tangible. The signposts, as with all symbols, are the result of communal experience. Whether it is the names given to street signs or speed limits on a major highway, these signposts reflect communal values and experience. Anyone who has traveled beyond his hometown knows, for example, that speed limits change from state to state.

The *inukshuk*, the signposts of those living in the Arctic, are essential to the life of these people. Lacking all natural markers of where they are, since everything is flat, lifeless, and covered with ice and snow, they have built *inukshuk* to enable them to move safely from one place to another. The *inukshuk* are sometimes used as places to store food, and they are places of experiencing the sacred.

> *Spiritual signposts are condensed sources for dealing with our transcendence-desire.*

Certainly, people have died, starved, or lost their minds in the process that resulted in choosing the correct place for an *inuksuk* to be built. In modern society, we often take for granted that signposts are purely technical items that have been placed to direct traffic. We sometimes forget that all of our signposts are more like the *inuksuk* than mere street signs. Anyone who has lived on a street where children have been killed because of improper speed limits, or anyone who has been lost because someone has destroyed the street signs realizes otherwise. Society constructs its *inuksuk* from its life experiences of how to travel safely from here and now to there and then.

Spiritual signposts as they exist today evolved out of the long development of religion from the beginnings of humankind.[53] They have been there since the beginning because, whether spiritual or not, they are part of being human. We speak. We act. We gather with others. We seek to move beyond our current situation and improve our lives. From the very foundation of our humanity, the spiritual signposts have evolved to where they are today in each of the spiritualities.

Five signposts are found in all spiritualities. They are essential to any spiritual life. No particular signpost is more important than the others, and each has relevance at various moments in our lives. Belief, for example, may be more important than community at one stage of the lifecycle, whereas ritual may be more important than the two at another point in the lifecycle. All, however, are always part of the set of signposts that provide direction for our lives. They are 1) *belief,* expressive of a desire for truth and trust; 2) *ritual,* expressive of a desire for harmony and predictability of formative actions; moral or 3) *ethical norms* (doing the right thing), expressive of a need for justice for self and others; and 4) *community,* reflective of a desire for togetherness and belonging. The 5)

> **The spiritual signposts are belief, ritual, ethical norms, community, and the inner desire for transcendence.**

inner desire for transcendence enlivens all these signposts. An understanding of them aids in our understanding of our self and the spiritual life we develop. They all are essential for a spiritual life. A spiritual life cannot be reduced to only one of these even though some advocates for contemporary spiritualities may wish to do so. As, for example, saying everything depends on one's belief and ability to project that belief into all of life thus enabling control of outer and inner desires. But more of that later as we engage the various spiritualities in this book. First we will look a little more deeply into each of these signposts.

The Signpost of Belief and Faith

The signpost of belief, as affirming what is both truthful and trustful, provides us with predictability in our personal and impersonal environments. When we believe that the water is free of harmful chemicals and germs, we can enjoy drinking it. When we believe the ground we walk on is firm, we can walk with certainty. When we believe the person we lean on will carry us, we can relax into her care. Belief is essential to living.

But in talking about the object of spiritual belief, we are talking about something more encompassing than water, food, drink, and help from others. We are talking about a mysterious reality that encompasses everything that exists. It is the context of all understanding and the horizon to all of life. It is our eternal presupposition—a reality that we become aware of through stories, creeds, words, songs, rituals, and all the sources of the spiritual life. Belief is our response to what we say is "there." To say we believe Jesus, Buddha, or any person who founded a religion or spirituality, we are saying that these individual persons existed and are trustworthy. The claim of belief is a claim that the descriptions we provide of the past, present, and future are true. It is a claim that the methods we claim will transform our present world are trustworthy and will result in the complete transformation of this world. Our belief provides us with the stability to travel our spiritual journey.

Devotees of the spiritualities we will examine developed ways of thinking about their belief and explaining it to non-believers. They developed methods of analysis concerning how this present world was to be transformed: how to celebrate life and death, how to deal justly with each other, how to relate to each other as comrade or stranger, and how to understand all the norms necessary to bring about a transformed world. They also developed ways of adjusting the belief as first stated to the various cultures its adherents emigrated to. As a result, followers of this way of life are present in our contemporary world with methods of handing down their belief and adapting their belief to present-day living.

However, many of these methods, as well as their resulting formulations of belief, pay little heed to what has happened over the last four hundred years in Western culture. Most spiritualities are still using methods of adaptation that provided them with survival over the past centuries. They do not attend to the completely new intellectual environment brought on by modern thought, politics, and education. Some of these spiritualities did respond positively or negatively to the modern mentality over the centuries; many did not. In either case, modernization challenges all the past spiritual statements and methods of adaptation by automatically placing them in the realm of opinion rather than truth. For someone who has based his or her entire life on certain religious beliefs to hear someone else say, "Believe what you want. It's just an opinion any-

> **Belief is a fact to a believer and an opinion to a non-believer.**

way," is a challenge not only to the belief itself but to the person's very life. It is equivalent to saying, "I don't really care who you are. You're just not relevant in the real world." The ancient spiritualities are dismissed out of hand as mere opinions. When these spiritualities demand that modern people repeat ancient beliefs using the spiritualities' ancient words, they are also rejecting modern people. The modern thinkers say, "It's all opinion." The ancient spiritualities say, "We teach both the truth and the only way to speak that truth." There is a possible conflict here between these two approaches to daily living. This conflict may be eased by reviewing what we mean by facts, faith, truth, and methods for knowing what's true.

Belief and Facts

Let's begin with facts. These are what we can point to and say: "there." And everyone agrees on what we are pointing to. Usually we have a word for what is there: page, man, flower, dog. It is a little harder when we have a feeling, because the only person feeling this is you. But we know that whether it is a dog, flower, man, or page, we may not have our facts straight. It may turn out to be something else. Even a pain for most may be a pleasure for some, and certainly intense pain varies from person to person. In general, however, facts are facts; the interpretation of them is what causes difficulty. *Interpretation* is an ability to see a pattern among the facts.

Because people often see patterns differently, interpretation is usually the source of difficulty when dealing with religious belief. A Christian Scientist prays and a leg heals. A medical doctor examines the leg and proclaims that it is the natural healing process of the body—a possible conflict of religious and scientific interpretation of the fact that the leg healed. A Christian fundamentalist walks into a museum housing dinosaurs and other fossils and proclaims the glory of God for designing such creatures and humans at the same time. The museum curator, while not dismissing God, views the entire collection as a demonstration of evolution. These are examples of conflicts of interpretation of the facts.

A way to think about this would be to see a fact as a puzzle piece—when dealing with living things it would be a living puzzle piece. The interpretation of many facts would be like making a picture or pattern out of the pieces. Thus, when various pieces (facts) are able to fit properly together, one can form an interpretation. Both facts and interpretation are intimately connected. The complete picture can be seen by those who recognize this pattern. The cosmic puzzle, however, is infinite. A pattern fits within a pattern within another pattern. As we live our daily lives, new facts become available as cultures change and new questions seek new facts as answers. The challenge is how to fit these new facts into the developing picture of what is happening around and within us. Belief in contemporary spirituality must deal with contemporary facts.

Belief and Faith

Spiritual faith is an ability to see unique patterns of facts that are sources of transcendence. All the signposts are aligned in a way coincident with the particular transcendent desire of the spirituality. Most of the spiritualities we deal with in this book reflect the faith of millions of people over millennia. Some faith perspectives are radically different from others; some perspectives, only slightly so. The resultant spiritual lifestyles that encompass these faith perspectives differ one from the other. Do these differences mean that all religion

> **Spirituality has everything to do with truth and reality.**

is mere opinion? Or does it mean that only one of these is true and the others are opinion? Or as some contemporary writers claim, that they are all superstitious distractions from the real challenge of living? Or does it mean that these faiths reflect humans who differ from each other sometimes radically and at others times slightly? All of these questions and answers, however, presuppose a modern way of spirituality with the scientific method at its foundation.[54]

Belief, Faith, and Truth

This scientific method demands that what we say is true. The method for discovering what is true has the characteristics of being sensed, logical consistency, agreement with other facts that provide its context, and repeatable (observed, experienced) anywhere in the world under the same conditions by anyone. That which is unique, unrepeatable, and not capable of being sensed by measurement is considered not demonstrable and thus not true. Religious and spiritual beliefs fit into the non-demonstrable claim for many who use this method for distinguishing between truth and opinion.[55] Within this modern scientific framework, several approaches can be helpful for clarifying your thoughts about what and why you hold certain spiritual beliefs.[56]

Reasons for Belief: Facts and Feelings

Do you believe in a certain form of spirituality because you feel it? Certainly, a dominant way of dealing with a religious belief is to say it is true because we feel it is. At one time, that would've been a denigration of belief, but not today when so many celebrities, books, and music offer "what feels good to you" as a magic wand to solve all problems: "Look into your heart, young man, and you will know what to do." Much of the pop culture tells us to solve our problems by going with our heart, not our head; depending on our feelings, not our minds. Any truth outside our hearts is not supposed to count for much. To the more serious thinkers among us, however, a life based on feelings alone is both frightening and disastrous. A few of these thinkers are declaring religion and its consequent spiritualities as dangerous for humanity because of religion's emotional support of war, gender, ethnic, and religious bias, and resistance to ideas foreign to their way of life.[57]

Spirituality, in this context, has nothing to do with truth and reality but with opinion and deeply felt feelings. We have ways of talking about and demonstrating what's real. Religion and spirituality do not fit into those modern ways. Our beliefs are certainly important because they are an expression of our feelings. You can believe all you want, but since it has nothing to do with reality or truth, as our culture sees it, do not expect your spiritual beliefs to affect any communal decision be it political, legal, or medical.

Another approach, beside feelings alone, for saying your spirituality is true adds something we all can see: what people do because of their spirituality. It says. "I can't tell you about your spiritual feelings. But I can tell you about any other claims you make that might support or result from those feelings." I believe because of what certain people said and did. I believe because those who follow these beliefs live good lives.

Once you go outside your feelings (religious belief), you are subject to the same rules of proof that everyone else is. If you say Siddhārtha Gautama, the Buddha, or Jesus, the Christ, lived at a certain time and said certain things, then it's not enough that you say this is so because you feel it is so. Where's the evidence that they lived and said what you claim? Why should your religious claims, no matter how long they have been spoken, be any different from the woman down the street who says she is Jesus's sister sent here by God their father? Who do you believe and why? If you say the world is created in six days, then according to this approach, I should be able to find scientific evidence of this creation. If you claim that human life begins at conception, then I should be able to find evidence of this. We have modern methods of demonstrating whether your beliefs are facts. Religious belief does not exonerate you from being scrutinized by those methods.

Between both of these approaches is another one that says, "Wait a minute. Your scientific methods of demonstrating something do not hold for religious and spiritual realities. These realities have a truth all their own. They are so different from the ways we live, think, and act in our modern world that it is impossible to hold them accountable to the rules of this world. There are two worlds, natural and supernatural, and thus two truths: religious/spiritual and scientific. Each world is subject to its own rules of interpretation. There is religious truth and scientific truth. The two never meet. But both are equally true even if one contradicts the other. "I believe because the way I live is true and you can't prove me false."

A final approach requires that, at the very least, when we proclaim our religious and spiritual beliefs, we keep the common rules of grammar and thought present in our culture. In other words, when spiritual people wish to become a serious part of a public conversation, they must keep the common rules we use in conversation. That means that if you claim something is true that you just said is false, you are contradicting yourself. You cannot say it is a spiritual way of talking. It isn't. Instead, it is a confused, spiritual person who does not respect the ordinary laws of grammar and logic. The evidence of confused language and logic indicate that you are not sure of what you say. In rejecting such confused talk, you accept that faith and belief can enter into our ordinary life and make sense to those who hear us talk about that spiritual life. "I believe because this way of life is true. It's coherent, consistent, and makes sense."

So, where do you stand and why? All these approaches, along with their opposites, are found in contemporary discussions about religions and spiritualities. If you are to have a conversation with those who live a spiritual life different from yours, what do you think is necessary to be taken seriously by your fellow conversants? Is there a common language you can use to discuss your spiritualities? This seriousness of speech and its consequences is sometimes dismissed in our opinionated culture as though words have no consequence. We find media pundits, politicians, and celebrities talking as if the rules of logic, speech, consistency, and coherence do not apply to them. Yet we all know words do have consequences. If they do not, community and society lose their bonds of trust and reality becomes illusory. It disintegrates. We cannot have a community unless we have common meanings for the words we use in our spiritual conversations. Furthermore, in having our conversations, are we willing to go beyond descriptions of our spiritualities to mutual affirmations of what the spiritual life is for all of us?

Before moving on to the other signposts, we need to consider three other issues that are intertwined with contemporary discussions about spiritual belief: illiteracy, doubt, and authority.

Illiteracy: Whose faith is it?

Our spiritual life in a liminal age is further conflicted by the documented religious and scientific illiteracy that surrounds us. People today know more about current movies, celebrities, music, and sports than about science and religion.[58] Scientific and religious facts are absent from most people's memories and lifestyles. It helps in any conversation that we have our facts straight in speaking about things that are important to us.

Know how to intelligently write about and discuss the faith that is the basis of your spiritual life.

As I write this, there are more bombings of schools in Pakistan. The reason given for these bombings is that the terrorists do not want such schools. Whether a school is blown up or the knowledge imbibed in the school is forgotten, the result is the same: illiteracy. In discussions about religion and spirituality, we cannot take for granted that all the conversants know what they are talking about. When they say "Christians" believe this, "Muslims" believe that, or any of the diverse spiritualities "believe" something else, we must always ask, in the back of our minds at least, "How do they know they believe this?" The conversation becomes very confusing when statements of belief become a Tower of Babel of contradictions. Even the statement "I believe" sometimes is also a claim that everyone does or should "believe" likewise.

Doubt: Doubting in the Face of Disbelief

Doubt and belief go hand in hand. We must remember, in light of the previous paragraph, that a great deal of doubt arises out of ignorance. Sometimes the presupposed doubt about a certain religion has nothing to do with the religion. For example, someone may doubt the Jewish belief that Jesus is Abraham reincarnated. Someone may doubt such a belief and consider Jews ignorant for holding it. But the truth is that Jews do not hold this belief! I made it up just now. Illiteracy may cause false doubts based on deeply felt or deeply imagined beliefs within one's own spirituality and religion as well as others.

There is also a necessary distrust, or doubt, when we are surrounded by those who wish us to trust them so they may sell us things. There are so many things people want us to buy, so much time they wish us to expend, and so many relationships they want us to form. We must be willing to doubt and ask, "Why should I believe? Why should I trust? What will be the consequences of this belief upon me and those I love?"

Our beliefs are many times questioned by those concerned with our health, our wealth, and our communal relationships. The motivation of questioners is always a matter of unease; some raise questions as a result of their scientific research, some do so to sell us products, and some to enlist our energy and perhaps our money. The possible motivations are infinite. These questions and motivations easily enliven our sense of doubt concerning our beliefs.

It may sometimes feel like we are bouncing back and forth between "believe this" and "don't believe this." Sometimes this feeling is so intense that we react to it as a threat since we cannot continue to live in such a random state of existence. Yet certain kinds of doubt may be an opportunity for growth in one's spirituality.

A few distinctions made by Paul Tillich, a famous Christian theologian, may be helpful at this point. He suggests there are several levels of doubt aside from what I have already mentioned: scientific, skeptical, existential, and redemptive.[59] Although these initially were developed in a Christian context, I have adapted them to our present discussion.

Scientific doubt is the foundation of our technological world and constructs our mathematical view of the universe. If Louis Pasteur (1822-1895) had not doubted the then current theories of disease, he never would have helped us overcome them. If Isaac Newton (1643-1727) had not doubted the explanations given for the motion of planets and the falling of apples, we never would have had his discovery of universal laws governing both. Scientific doubt is essential to our technological and scientific advancement.

Skeptical doubt is an attitude of total distrust in one's world and a deeply felt conviction that nothing is true and reliable. It results in a continual cycle of cynicism, despair, and indifference to everyone and everything. It is a dangerous attitude that sometimes leads to suicide since the doubter feels worthless and uncertain of self and the entire universe.

Existential doubt, for Tillich, is not as all-encompassing as skeptical doubt. While the individual has confidence in himself, he lacks total confidence in whether what he does has any worth and purpose. The daily actions and interactions are enjoyable, but the context of those actions, and life itself, is purposeless. He has no sense of what his life is all about and where it is going. The here and now are fine, but he has no sense that a there and then of any value and worthwhile dedication exists. He has no signposts.

Redemptive doubt occurs when a person has a sense of existential doubt, but, in the face of that doubt, says "yes" to her spiritual life, to a future, and to all that makes this future worthwhile. Redemptive doubt is a dynamic of trust that the universe, and your role in it, has a purpose even while tainted with an existential despair that this desire may remain unfulfilled. The doubter realizes that all signposts in a changing world are relative when placed in an infinite horizon. With this realization, the redemptive doubter says "yes" to life in the face of doubt.

The signpost of belief, therefore, always has about it a tinge of doubt: redemptive doubt. The signpost is also part of spiritual transcendence: there is always more life than what we have here and now. But it does provide direction and is a vital part of every spiritual life.

That means that in our daily spiritual lives, we will face challenges regarding what to believe. The stories, the conversation, the creeds, the books, and the songs that may be the sources of our belief seem fragile, not only when compared to the unlimited choices available to us, but also in comparison to spiritualities that enliven other people's lives. But many find that the moments of fragility are also the moments of deepening courage. Caught in this paradox of fragile mortality and deeply felt immortality, the most rational act is to step forward on our spiritual journey, first slowly, then more quickly until we reach the pace needed for our unique journeying. The journey, in this instance, brings the courage, the belief, and the trust that enlivens our daily, courageous passage into transcendence.

Belief and Authority

Even though you ultimately choose to believe something, such belief is within the context of the spiritual paradoxes, especially that of "I need a 'we' to be a 'me.'" This recognition of the importance of others for our spirituality is also an acknowledgement of the role of diverse authorities in our spirituality. An authority is someone or something that provides a basis for belief and the acknowledgement that all our signposts are true. Many authorities provide a basis for our belief;

> **Doubt is okay. Learn from it!**

these could be a person, an experience, a book, a tradition, or the rules of logic. What is important for us to remember is that some authority is always involved in our believing. In turn, our belief is only as certain as our authority for it.

The Signpost of Ritual

The signpost of ritual is expressive of a desire for harmony and predictability of formative actions. Ultimately, when we change our habits, we change our lives. Rituals are essential for affirming the changes of the past and initiating those of the future. Spiritual rituals such as prayer, meditation, celebrations of birth, marriage death, and the worship of God, gods, and spirits are central to any spirituality.

We cannot live without rituals. Rituals are also a key signpost. They are comforting in their familiarity, just like the habitual rituals of brushing our teeth, signing our name, cheering for our team, or celebrating a birthday, a wedding, or a funeral. Spiritual rituals are those habitual actions that pull us forward beyond the here and now and provide, in various degrees, a sense of the sacredness of life and our purpose in it.

> **Spirituality is kept alive with daily spiritual rituals.**

As I am writing this, we are preparing for the winter holidays, or Christmas as many of us still call it. This ritual is both religious and non-religious: spiritual for some and purely materialistic for others. Yet it is a ritual with significantly different meanings for its celebrants. As a ritual, it is repeated each year with variations depending on individual religious and ethnic backgrounds as well as finances. This repetition mainly involves giving gifts, gathering with family members, reminiscing about holidays past, and discussions of the future in general and, perhaps, next holiday season in particular. When it begins and ends varies. Commercial interests keep expanding the buying season, which is part of the holidays. Certainly, it extends from at least Thanksgiving to the week after New Year's Day. Some may wish it to extend to the Super Bowl, which in itself is an intense ritual. The time is filled with numerable religious holidays, among which are St. Nicholas, Hanukkah, Christmas, Kwanzaa, Yule, Hijra, Muharram, Eid al-Adha, Gantan-sai and Three Kings Day. What has come to be known as the winter holidays is THE ritual time in North American culture.

The winter holiday season is also a significant time for religious rituals. Is it a spiritual time? The answer to this question lies in the characteristics and purpose of a spiritual ritual within its cultural context. We presuppose that a spiritual ritual offers a visible, tangible, repeatable pattern of words and actions through which one senses the presence of the source of spiritual transformation. One's response to this presence varies depending on where one is at in one's life and the innate dynamic of the ritual itself. Four possible purposes for spiritual rituals are usually given: seeking expiation of guilt for some wrong, supplication for help in overcoming some difficulty, praise and thanksgiving for what one has received, and immediate personal engagement with the source of life. These responses usually are a response to what has happened in the past or present or what is expected in the future. So, if somewhere during the winter holidays you have an awesome yet scary sense of thanks, of dealing with your guilt, of seeking help for significant issues in your life, or of expressing happiness with your life—a realization that your search for more to life, for transcendence, is happening—this is indeed a time of spiritual rituals.

Of course, such feelings can be had though out the year. Ritual opportunities abound to focus eventful happenings in our lives. There are *lifecycle rituals* around birth, marriage, and death. There are *seasonal rituals* associated with spring, summer, fall, and winter. There are rituals that call attention to our change in status in a community, such as becoming an adult or graduating. As we review the diverse spiritualities, we will highlight some rituals that are unique to them. For many people rituals rather than belief are their central signpost.

Our culture is still highly influenced by the critique of the early Protestant reformers of medieval-era Roman Catholicism. The reformers saw in the medieval ritual magical superstition and, in its place, presented a gospel of Bible-based faith as directed through the integrity of their preachers. They seemed to feel that in religious and spiritual ritual, there was always something that should be feared because it touched a realm beyond the mind. The central reformers such as Martin Luther (1483-1546) and John Calvin (1509-1564) were learned writers and scholars. Their immediate inclination in everything was to appeal to their listeners' minds through their words and books to deal with any issue, religious or otherwise. The spoken word and belief, therefore, were central to their approach to religion and spirituality. The illiterate peasants needed not only the Bible but also the means to read the Bible, which eventually sparked the rise of public education. The holy ointments, waters, places, sounds, people, bones, and clothes that had helped constitute the world of the non-literate Christians, along with the rituals that focused on them, were condemned as superstitious. This absolute vilification of most religious rituals left a mark on Western culture that remains to this day. This mark was an attitude that favored words and belief over ritual and action as true sources of the transcendent. After four hundred years, it may be time to look again at the importance of rituals in developing a spiritual life. After all, if we can't live without habits in our daily lives, I doubt we can live without the spiritual habits found in ritual in our daily lives.

The Signpost of Ethical or Moral Norms

The signpost of ethical or moral norms expresses a need for justice for self and others. Every religion and spirituality has norms for what is right and wrong, good and bad. It seems that deep within us there is a need to be treated fairly. The mixture of feelings and reasoning that have produced the codes of conduct associated with various religions and spiritual practices have long histories that have produced complex debates. But not matter how complex, they leave us with the fact that spirituality and morals, as with belief and ritual, are essential to living a spiritual life. In the West, the two standards for millennia have been the Ten Commandments and the Seven Deadly Sins. Each religion and spirituality, as we will see, has its own list. Every religion has its reason why this signpost is not consistently followed by everyone in the religion. Sin, ignorance, deep uncontrollable cravings, and desire are a few reasons. We will see these later in the text.

The social sciences suggest two other reasons why the majority of people do not live up to their moral ideals: social relativism and necessary personal growth. Social relativism is conveyed in the oft-heard remark, "They don't do that everywhere, so why should I do it here?" The speaker usually is talking about sex, but it also may be about cheating, lying, killing, and anything else. When you are thinking about leading a spiritual life, no matter what

> *Spiritual words without spiritual deeds lead to ill spirits.*

you hold philosophically about universal moral norms, to which this question alludes, the fact is that you cannot lead a spiritual life unless you have moral norms. The fulfillment of moral norms is a marker of an authentic spirituality. It is what you do that makes you spiritual; not what you say. This signpost keeps you on the road. Your reasons for choosing what is good, as we will see in a moment, may vary. It is not necessarily moral relativism to have diverse reasons for doing right or wrong. Changing your moral norms, as in changing your beliefs, may result from a thorough reasoning process arising from your life experiences. Change does not necessarily equal relativism. The tree outside my window is losing its leaves. During spring and summer, the norm for this maple tree is to have leaves; during fall and winter, the norm is to have no leaves. It has changed significantly. Yet the tree is still the tree. Because a human changes his or her moral norms under certain circumstances does not mean he or she is no longer a moral human. You do not abandon your spiritual life when you abandon old norms for new ones. Instead, you are changing your spiritual life when you do so. You abandon spiritual living only when you abandon moral living. Such change is easily seen in one's personal development.[60]

Over the years, I have noticed that some people have great difficulty in distinguishing between what is legal and what is moral, and what is the law of social and religious organizations and how they should act according to their own system of values. The latter is what is necessary for a spiritual life. The following story may help you discover your approach to law and morality.

> Helen's mother was very ill. The doctors indicated that she would die in the next few weeks. Helen had been caring for her for the last week when, quite to her surprise, her mother called her to her bedroom. "There," she said, pointing to a dresser. "There beneath the sheets in the drawer, there's a bag. Take it. It's yours."
>
> "But what is it, Mother?" Helen asked.
>
> "Those old coins your brother collected when he was young. He gave them to me a long while ago. Take them. Give them to your children for their education."
>
> Helen paused. She could use the money. But she knew he had not given the coins to her mother. It was her brother's money. Yet no one would know. What *should* she do? What would *you* do? *Why* would you do it?

A review of the research of ethical decision-making, such as Helen's, should help clarify what you would do in her situation. These are not normative descriptions of actions; in other words, their application to the Ten Commandments. Rather, they are descriptions of people's motivations for their actions and why they think this is the right thing to do.

One of the principal researchers in this field was Lawrence Kohlberg.[61] He suggested that we should look at the reasons why we *think* an action is wrong rather than examining our behavior or talking about what is right and wrong. To know a person's reasons for action is to know the direction of his way of life. For example, upon observing a child named Billy, you notice that he never does anything unless it makes him feel good. You suspect that Billy does things only for pleasure. That is his way. Let us look at some of the other reasons why people see some acts as good and others as bad.

Who or What Determines What Is Right?

The first way is what Kohlberg calls *pre-conventional*. Here the concern is for "me" as the center of all action. There is generally a lack of identity with anyone beyond our self. There is no feeling of identity with society or a group. To move out of this type of egoism, we must be able to put ourselves in the place of another. To be a part of society, we must understand that rules have a purpose. Those who act for a pre-conventional motive do so because they are afraid of punishment. Reward and punishment are the basic motivators for their actions. Everything is viewed in terms of what makes them feel good or what will hurt them. A good action, from this perspective, is that which gives us pleasure.

Another way is the *conventional*. Here we see that meeting the expectations of our family, group, or nation is perceived as valuable in its own right regardless of immediate and obvious consequences. Here the attitude is not only one of conformity to the social order and to others' expectations of us, but of loyalty to it, of actively maintaining, supporting, and satisfying the order, and of identifying with the persons or group involved in it. To do something good, in this instance, is to do that which pleases, helps, or is approved by others. We do it because we want others to think well of us. Right behavior is doing one's duty and showing respect for authority. We must be able to think abstractly to act upon these motivations. To appreciate the existence of a group requires an ability to think in an abstract way and to be able to see ourselves as a member of a group. We realize that an ordered society and membership in this society demands that we give up immediate pleasures for social order and security.

The *post-conventional* approach to moral action makes a clear effort to define moral values and principles that have validity and application apart from the groups or persons holding these principles. Here we see ourselves as good if we act independently of our own egocentrism and the society in which we live. "Good" transcends society and us. All of us must match our behavior to that which is beyond us. The "beyond" may be, for example, a set of rational principles or a set of norms implicit in all human action. It is upon these transcendent principles or norms that we base our actions. This is the ideal goal in any spiritual life.[62]

People, obviously, have various reasons and motivations for doing good. They may act for immediate pleasure or pain, to meet the expectations of others, or to adhere to principles. We see, in other words, that there may be one way of acting, but many reasons for us to act the way we do. Our spiritual life will reflect these motives. The norms of our spiritual life will favor one of these motives above the others.

A brief summary can be seen by asking a Christian why he goes to church on Sunday. His answer shows you where he is in Kohlberg's developmental theory.

- I go because someone will punish me if I don't, or I'll go to hell.
- I go because God or someone will be good to me.
- I go because everyone goes.
- I go because it is my duty.

- I go because a person should recognize his or her relationship to God.
- I go because this is the best expression of love to God and neighbor.

It's All Relative: Truth, Right, and Religion

A great deal of writing, many times under the heading "Spiritual Development," occurred toward the end of the twentieth and the beginning of the twenty-first centuries, which expanded on the ideas of Kohlberg and Piaget.

> **Doing right builds a spiritual world.**

This writing was in response to many deep changes in the culture, especially the experience of school counselors in secondary and postsecondary education who reported a significant increase in the number of students searching for meaning and purpose in life. Most of these writings used William Perry as a jumping-off point for their reflections.

Intellectual Development And Core Values (W. Perry)[63]

The following description begins with those entering into their late teens.

1. *Dualism.* What is important and true is given to us by authorities who know more about these things than we do. Our task is to make them part of us. They teach us these things because they are true and, consequently, we should expect no conflicts. *The teacher knows what's correct. I'll learn it and use it.*

2. *Multiplicity.* There are a plurality of values and truths, but there seem to be no established criteria for evaluating them, or for establishing that a certain set is better or more appropriate than another. The critical reasoning we apply to these values and truths seems to provide only limited sense that there are solid norms for anything. *Teachers don't know what they are talking about. They constantly contradict each other. I'll tell them what they want to hear, but I'll never use that stuff.*

3._ *Relativism.* There is no right way of living because everything is relative to the context and people who are living them. We live in a confusing world with little mutual support for the way of life we were taught and value. I live my way. You live your way. That's it! It seems that the best way to live with others is to accept everything as relative. *Nothing is certain. It's all opinion. Their word is as good as mine. I'll give them what they want to pass the test.*

4. *Commitment in relativism (no cheap relativism).* Indeed, there are many systems of values, but some are more appropriate than others; some provide a better way of life than others in specific situations. We must strive to discover these for ourselves and for those with whom we live. We must discover, strive for, and build common

> **Spiritual development requires spiritual change.**

truths and values to enable us to live together in acceptance of our differences. *It seems that things may not be absolutely certain always and everywhere. But some things are, and I have to base my life on these. If a teacher can show me why something is true and I understand it, especially compared to other claims, I'll do it.*

Once again, we see various levels of development. Certainly, there will be some tension in those advocating a certain form of spirituality as to whether these developmental theories are of any significance in light of that spirituality's doctrinal explanation of why people act right or wrong, good or bad. In such a context, we must remember that these developmental theories are a description of how we change over time. They are not normative; in other words, they are not stating emphatically, "This is the way we must change to be spiritual." Authorities disagree over whether the last developmental stage of Erikson, Piaget, Kohlberg, or Perry should be thought of as "best." We do not have to get into the argument here. If we accept developmental theory as describing the different ways people change, we realize that every spiritual way of life is made up of many individuals at various stages of living their changing lives. We should not presuppose that an ecclesiastical position or a certain number of birthdays necessarily includes emotional, conceptual, or ethical maturity. Within our signpost of moral/ethical norms for the spiritual life the important thing is that we have the norms and know what they are. Why we have them will many times be unique to the individual.

The Signpost of Community

The signpost of community indicates that every person's spirituality comes out of a spiritual tradition and adds to a spiritual tradition. We are not traveling a spiritual journey alone. Spiritualities seldom come full blown out of the mystery of transcendence. As we have seen in dealing with the history of spirituality, many times they originate with one person or group of persons. As with any living thing, they grow and adapt. Thus in encountering most contemporary spiritual traditions, we must remember that they are the result of centuries of experience, change, and positive results within a community of people. When one is socialized into a community, one is socialized into its traditions. Returning to the image of a puzzle used in the signpost of belief, we can say that we are socialized into a pattern of putting all the pieces of our puzzle together: beliefs, rituals, moral norms. We are socialized into the expected feelings associated with both the pieces of the puzzle and the puzzle itself. That is what tradition provides every individual: the pattern. With time, however, as new pieces, experiences, enter into your, and the community's, way of life, that pattern now must adapt to a new situation. A living tradition will gradually adapt. A dead tradition will gradually wither away. All the spiritual traditions you read about in this book have significantly adapted to the historical changes they encountered over the centuries. The Christmas tradition today is appreciably different from when it began over two thousand years ago and the centuries in between. A thousand years from now, it will have traditioned radically to a new form. Dynamic communities have a dynamic tradition, which results in dynamic individuals.

The Signpost of Desiring Transcendence

The desire for transcendence is the core energizing force within belief, ritual, moral norms, and community. Certainly, it is a constant presence seeking "more" out of the totality of inner and outer life and seeking to change our present lives for the better. This seeking finds, through socialization, some satiation in our religious culture's words, actions, and human relationships. But for many in today's liminal times this initial taste from our first sources of transcendence are insufficient. They desire to transcend these sources. In doing so, however, they will have to reinvigorate their first sources or find others. They are seeking a clearer path for invigorating their spiritual lives.

A Compass for Use in the Ocean of Paradoxes and Spiritualities

For a compass to be effective, it must have a piece of iron or steel that points north. This pointing needle enables us to know which way to direct our journey relative to the four directions: north, south, west, and east. A spiritual compass also has a needle made up not of iron but of our transcendent experiences coalescing around one root value. This "needle" enables us to direct our spiritual journey relative to the spiritual signposts (directions) embodied as root values: truth, harmony, justice, and community. Contrary to an ordinary compass, the spiritual compass's true north varies throughout one's life while the necessary directions, or signposts as we have called them, remain constant. Each of the points on the compass is capable of taking us in the correct direction, but we need a true north for comparison in order to know the direction we're taking at this time in our life. This true north is our pivotal root value, usually found embedded in one of the four signposts. We recognize this root value by discovering where and how we are experiencing significant transcendence in our lives.

This experience of transcendence is usually stimulated and encouraged by the spiritual sources that make up the signposts of a spirituality. In an individual's spiritual life, these sources congeal around the four values that intensify the transcendent experience: truth, harmony, justice, and community. The desire for transcendence provides us with a spiritual direction; it usually expresses itself most intensely and continually experienced in one of these values. The remaining values, while present, serve to support this enabling experience. While these root values are not of equal importance at each moment of our spiritual lives, all must be present in a healthy spirituality. Truth, for example, may be more important than the need for community at one stage of the life cycle, whereas harmony may be more important than these two at another point in the life cycle. All, however, are always part of the signposts that provide direction for our lives. All fit together, but our primary "pointer" value takes priority and gives direction to the rest. In providing such direction, we usually see the others in the light of the pointer value. For example, when the pointer value is truth, the others (harmony, community, and justice) will be seen in the light of truth. Thus, in any of the revealed religions, that would mean no ritual is accepted unless it reflects the truth advocated by the revelation. Therefore, in evangelical Christianity, for example, which accepts the Bible as the source of God's revelation and truth, if it's not in the Bible, it cannot be in the ritual.

The following chart is a visualization of the compass and how it acts in our life through positive and negative emotions.

Root Value	Root Positive Experience	Root Negative Experience
Truth: Belief that things are the way they should be, and amazement that they are so beautiful and attractive.	It's real! I can depend on it.	Ignorance; repulsiveness
Harmony: ritual, many times resulting in a sense of well-being	A place for everything and everything in its place	Chaos; loss of self-control in body, mind, or spirit
Justice: morality; doing the right thing in a fair and purposeful manner.	Action; getting things done properly	Stasis; inertia

Community: between two individuals, it is expressed as love and/or friendship; among a group, it is a sense of fellow feeling and togetherness.	"We:" a sense of belonging	Alienation; grieving for the loss of a significant other or others

The use of the compass in our spiritual lives enables us to do three things: to solidify our present sources of transcendence, to recognize the role past sources play in our present lives, and to discover those necessary sources of transcendence as we continue to grow in our spiritual lives. Many times the negative root experiences are more telling than the positive ones. We might easily be able to cope with being alone and alienated, yet find ourselves in a state of near total panic when we cannot understand something or satisfy our curiosity about it. Our compass more than likely is pointing to truth as the primary root value. Sometimes we find that the only reason we continue to practice a religion that gave birth to our spirituality is because we feel a deep sense of joy and well-being as we celebrate the holidays or repeat prayers we were taught in our youth. Thus, harmony is the value.

Our ability to know where our spiritual true north is today enables us to recognize more easily what it was that provided us with a sense of identity and spiritual security in the past. If our socialization process was successful, we experienced the elation associated with the approval of authority figures as we did the right things, thought the right thoughts, and celebrated in approved ways. With time, we usually abandoned some of these practices. Knowing where we are today enables us to recognize some possible sources for guilt associated with this abandonment as well as to remember the sense of well-being associated with successfully following our true north.

As we grow older, we discover that one of these directions is the dominant force in our lives. We respond to the positive experience of this root value in a stronger way than we do the others. Perhaps it is our sense of truth and belief that provides us with a strong sense of transcendence and becomes in our lives a means of transforming our world. We like to think and figure things out. We don't like the unknown. But then it may be a feeling of being together with others, or together with one special person in married love. We don't like feeling alone and isolated from everyone else (alienation), and we fear deeply the loss of a relationship to an idea, things, or a person (grief). Our compass needle points to our present course in relationship to possible other courses. We should take advantage of this present awareness and, realizing that the past experiences of transcendence are truly in the past, we should take the means to deepen the experiences our pointer value indicates while seeking to discover its presence in the other root values.

False Readings, Spiritual Idols

Where I live, it is not unusual to find a street sign turned around—some late night reveler enjoying the power of misdirecting people. Stories abound of how one's trusted GPS system leads one astray, such as into a lake, perhaps. Likewise, spiritual signposts can lead us off course in two ways: one, by providing us with sources of transcendence that are destructive to the individual and/or society; two, by allowing the signpost in its many tangible forms to become identified with the final transformative reality.

Judaism, Christianity, and Islam have a word for this misplacement of our transcendent desires and adopting inadequate sources and signposts to fulfill authentic ones: idolatry. An idol, in those traditions, is allowing something or someone to take the place of God. Work, race, patriotism, church, and religion itself may easily be seen as idols.[64] We can see this same image of idol worship applied to contemporary adherence to ideas, culture, education, religion, classical texts, and other sources of transcendence. One does not have to believe in God to recognize the necessity to be constantly aware of how we can turn something or someone into a guaranteed source of transcendence, and ignore its inherent fragility of meaning and purpose .[65]

Americans worship two obvious idols that keep getting them into trouble. One is thinking of faith as a mental attitude or power of the mind capable of controlling the self or things. The other is thinking that everything can and must be done quickly. This way of thinking places people struggling to develop a healthy spiritual life in a psychological double bind. On the one hand, it is their will (mind) power that makes things happen; on the other, when things do not happen, it is due to their lack of faith/ belief/ mental power. In this approach, nothing happens beyond our control. The paradox of "the spiritual life is both free and earned; gift and purchased" is rejected. People are placed in an impossible situation that suggests that they can control everything about their lives as long as they have a strong and proper belief. Such an emphasis upon total faith proclaims the person as an all-powerful god. After all, it is the person's faith that is in control, not God. Suffering is always a challenge to such proclamations, and death is the argument against it. This type of belief is many times linked with the conviction that the spiritual life is, like instant oatmeal, capable of being produced in five minutes: just mix properly and stir. Certainly sudden conversions happen. Certainly, an unexpected happening at a spiritual source may provide a physical, psychological, and/or mental thrill that awakens spiritual realities that bubble up from our subconscious. These are real to the person experiencing them. But just as real are the necessary lifelong tasks of embracing this experience, unencumbering ourselves from the old habits that prevent us from being aware of spiritual realties, and developing new ones based on the appropriate authorities. The spiritual masters of all religions warn us repeatedly that the spiritual life is not developed in a day or a moment. It is a lifetime's joy, realization, and development.

The signposts and sources themselves may become idols. When the spiritual source stops being the source but the sacred reality itself for us, we have a classic Western description of an idol. In this instance, for example, the statue, song, church, or book becomes God to those who come to find God present in them. Everything and anyone may become an idol, except God in those religions that believe in God.

> **Don't make your spirituality a god.**

The signposts can easily become idols when they are seen as magic—providing an automatic entry into the world of the transcendent if the beliefs, morals, and rituals are done precisely as indicated. Thus, if the words of belief are repeated over and over, transcendence is guaranteed no matter what desire is in the heart of the one repeating those words. If one acts the way the sacred person, book, or other source says one is to act, one's transformation will occur. Only true believers are good. Only true adherents to the spirituality are seen as worthy of life. Others, their beliefs and actions, are believed to be roadblocks to the advent of the newly transformed world.

Words and actions, of course, are essential for any ritual. Rituals that become ritualistic—that is, done without attention to what is being said and done; without attention to the life from which the ritual comes—are idols that take one away from living a full spiritual life. A sense of community can too easily become an idol when it develops into an enclave into which those who differ from the spiritual person(s) cannot enter. It is easy to see how the signposts of the spiritual life can become signposts of dysfunction and death for an individual or a culture. Idols are like that. They make us feel good for a moment but bring suffering for a lifetime.

Not all change is good. The current economic and environmental crises bear witness to that. Quick growth based on false formulas, short-term profits, and imaginary capital resources were causes of the great recession of 2008.

Transformation and transcendence is a form of change. Unless these are appropriate to the individual, the society, and the ultimate possibilities of change, both the transformation and the experienced transcendence will be destructive rather than constructive of humankind. Spiritual masters are constantly warning us about being deceived by false readings of our feelings and of those means that promise and promote transcendence. To adhere to a tangible manifestation of any one signpost as the *only* way to adhere to a spiritual tradition—without leaving that manifestation open to a traditioning, or development, of that tradition—is to make an idol of that tradition.[66] This is why mystics in any religious tradition are always a challenge to the authorities in that tradition. This is why having a complete understanding of the various spiritualities discussed in this book is so important to realizing one's spiritual life.

Summary

Our faith and belief paint the picture of our spirituality's promise. Our rituals, ethical behavior, and fellowship promote the fulfillment of that promise while giving detail to that picture. These signposts direct our transcendent desires to our spirituality's promised end. To touch the spiritual sources that constitute the signposts is to touch the energy and power that stimulates the deeply felt experiences of truth, harmony, justice, and community. The negative experiences of ignorance, repulsiveness, chaos, loss of self-control, stasis, or alienation tell us where we are right here and right now in our spiritual life.

Schema for Understanding any Form of Spirituality

SPIRITUALITY & RELIGION	PLACE OF ORIGIN	MEM-BERSHIP	KEY DATES	CENTRAL PERSON	BOOKS
CORE ISSUE	**BELIEFS**	**RITUALS**	**MORALS**	**ORGANIZATION**	**PROMISE**
Foundational evil that prevents the fulfillment of the promise	Descriptive stories, beliefs, songs, and words that are normative for describing and bringing about the promise	Repeated words and actions that help fulfill the promise	What is considered right or wrong; who is good, and thus will help to fulfill the promise.	Polity, how the spiritual community comes together or is divided. Those who help the individual fulfill the promise.	Complete transcendence for the individual.

PART TWO

CLASSICAL SPIRITUALITIES: PAST AND PRESENT

Before we were born, nature's mystery was.
After we die, it will still be.
Before humans were, it was.
After humans, it will be.

Steady our senses; meet it; seek it; live with it.
Compass in hand we swim within it.

Our compass is worn.
Its directions followed over thousands of centuries.
Survival at least; abundance at most.
Time worn, life tested, culture- and person-sustaining.
These spiritualities are many.

Throughout time
Across the globe
Spiritual classics they are.
A classical compass they provide.

Ways of Life never exhausted nor limited
Able to leap over centuries, cultures, and continents
To live in each, enliven all, and bring benefit to most.

***

M
ost of the people you know live a classical spirituality. In our popular media culture, as an increasing number of people are in need
of a quick high or a spontaneous solution to sudden or perennial

problems, the religious institutionalization of these spiritualities is portrayed as boring, restrictive, and many times destructive of a true spiritual life. These spiritualities are embedded within the classical religions of Hinduism, Buddhism, Tao (Dao), Confucianism, Shinto, Judaism, Christianity, and Islam. You may recognize your values and lifestyle in one of these religions. It may easily happen, too, that you recognize aspects of these religions that are distasteful and/or incomprehensible.

Classics of all kinds seem to resonate with deep convictions, habits, and ways of living. Classical spiritualities have embedded within them other classics such as texts, music, dress, art, and architecture. Classics are symbols. As we've stated previously, symbols, either slowly or suddenly, empower our lives with a sense of meaning, community, purpose, and well-being. As symbols, such classics are spiritual sources and signposts because they place us in the presence of those agents that transform us.

We will describe and review some of these classical spiritualities. Because of the enormity of our task, I will select those generally recognized as of central importance to contemporary spiritual living. A classic truly encountered reshapes our world. As a continual part of that world, it shapes it by the habits it supports and continues to reinforce. Spiritual classics always have the capacity to re-energize our lives and move us in a deeper or newer direction. Classical religious texts, for example, slowly shape an adherent's life yet may suddenly be read and/or heard anew resulting in a sudden change and direction to one's life. For example, a man named Giovanni Francesco di Bernardone had frequently heard the gospel's demand to sell all and follow Jesus, yet within a certain personal and social context Giovanni stripped naked and began a new life of poverty and dedication to the poor. Today, many know him as St. Francis of Assisi. Siddhartha Gautama sat quietly many times underneath a Bodhi tree repeating a classical meditation ritual, yet at one particular moment, he broke into enlightenment, and has been recognized as the Buddha ever since.

Classics shape us and awaken us. At the moment, you may not feel affected by a spiritual classic. But the nature of a spiritual classic is to weave itself into who you are; to offer you an opportunity to become more by transcending this place and time. Then, all at once, like Francis and Buddha, you awaken to its call and begin to live life anew.

Your reading and reflecting on the classics, as presented here, are not how Francis and Buddha were exposed to the spiritual classics of their time. The classical religions and their spiritualities, as presented in the following, are artificial constructs drawn from the lives and writings of real people, but they are not the classics themselves. We know that these ways of life have enabled people to live by constantly adapting to new situations. At times, these spiritualities enable individuals and cultures to survive; at other times, they enable people to grow creatively and thereby alter the future in surprising ways. History demonstrates that this has happened many times and is still happening. Yet to convey what it is that causes these things to happen is a guess—a construct of students of the social sciences and experts in the respective religions seeking to convey the essence of a way of life in a few sentences when it takes a lifetime to fully embrace and live a spirituality. It also takes the spirituality and the religion in which it is embedded, forever, if even then, to discover exactly what it is about a classical spirituality that enables us to live life to its fullest. This process of discovery is also a process of re-invigorating and reforming the classical religion.

Religions begin as movements. If they continue to exist beyond the first generation of founders, they become more stable, thus providing further clarity and security to their adherents. Consequently, a larger number of people can live their entire lives according to the tenets of this particular religion. As time passes and society changes, the religion and its spiritualities may seem unable to meet the challenges of the day. There is a sense that something is wrong with how people are living their religious lives. This inchoate, yet deeply felt "something wrong" grows into a movement of reform that challenges the "traditional" (meaning the most recent) way of living the religion. The reform movement clearly senses what is wrong with the religion but does not know how to reinvigorate it. There is unity in the movement about what is wrong with the current practice of the religion, but there are diverse opinions about how to correct it.

The reform movement usually causes the "traditional" religion to change in reaction to the movement and, at the same time, new ways of living the religion are initiated. The constant challenge for those writing and reading about the religion is to understand which of the reformers offer true expressions of the classical religion.

I take the position that they all are authentic as long as they exist over several centuries, thus enlivening many generations. In what follows, I present a set of core signposts that seem consistent among the diverse interpretations of the core. What is the same is the symbol- fact; what is different are the symbol and the symbol- event. Thus, everyone may believe in G-O-D (symbol- fact), but the symbol (Yahweh, Trinity, Allah) provides a different interpretation and source of life to the diverse manifestations of the classical spirituality and religion. You will be reading interpretations of these spiritualities and what they have to offer using the categories we discussed in Part One. Hopefully, what we offer in this discussion will stimulate your interest in these diverse spiritualities. I know it has done so for others, I hope it will do so for you.

These offerings will be provided in two chapters. "Knowing oneself is the beginning of wisdom," said the philosopher Aristotle. Lao-Tzu offered the same idea when he said, "Knowing others is intelligence; knowing yourself is true wisdom."[67] The beginning of spiritual wisdom begins with the knowledge of self; that knowledge, and our unique place within our culture, are essential to understanding who we are. Jewish, Christian, and Muslim spiritualities helped create the culture expressed through the English language.

Chapter Four is titled *God's People* based on the central conviction that within each of these spiritualities, those who belong to this religion and its consequent spiritualities have a special relationship with God: different from those who do not belong.

Chapter Five demands that you move out of your cultural ways of thinking about religion, about time (now), about place (here), and about your very self. Originally, it had no title. The intent was to leave the page blank, hoping that the empty page would act as a koan to make you aware that your world may not be as it seems. On reflection, however, I realized that would result in too much confusion, which is the natural result of a koan, but not appropriate to an introduction to spiritual living. Instead, Chapter Five is titled *Seeking Eternity within and Harmony with All*. In it we will discuss the spiritualities of Hinduism, Jainism, Buddhism, Taoism (Daoism), Confucianism, and Shintoism. A short discussion of aboriginal spirituality will set the scene for Part Three.

CHAPTER FOUR

GOD'S PEOPLE:
THE CLASSICAL SPIRITUALITIES OF
JUDAISM, CHRISTIANITY, AND ISLAM

The English word "god" has a long history. "God" with a capital "G" has been part of the English language for centuries. The word, as well as the idea it expresses, has developed over these centuries in relationship to other cultures, ideas, experiences, and time itself. Just as the English language didn't always have a word for "God," so other languages and cultures did not, and some still do not. The process of accepting a new religious or secular word and idea into a culture is similar.[68] What must be understood, for our purposes, is that god becomes **God** in the English language to signify the Christian god. In doing so God becomes part of our language and the way we think. With all the development surrounding the word over the centuries, the central idea is that God is unique: there is no other god, person, thing, being, or idea like God. God is totally other. God is responsible for our existence. God is creator; and, continues to create everything that exists. God wishes creation to grow to perfection and, thus, God guides this growth. God is savior. God alone is the one we should worship. God alone should be the pivotal relationship in our life.

While God is completely different from us, we can still use human language and images to describe who God is, what God does and how God interacts with us. Thus, we say that God communicates with us through God's word. Most Western classical spiritualities will look back to the original meaning of "word" in Hebrew, where this concept of God began, and see it as more than sounds coming from a mouth or presented in written form. Instead, "word," especially as God's word, is a psychodynamic reality that creates, possesses, demands, and shapes the intent of its speaker. One of the first things God does in the Bible is speak. "In the beginning of creation, God *said*, 'Let there be light.'" (Genesis 1:1-3). In this instance God's word created light. God's word is especially found among the prophets who convey God's "word" to his people.[69] As God's means of communication, it is also God's revelation of who God is, what God expects, and what God intends for us and for all of creation.

Although God's word may be found among many people, God's unique revelation is found among God's chosen people.[70] The three classical spiritualities, and the religions that provide their home, each claim to be God's people. Jews refer to God as Yahweh, Lord, or G-d. Muslims use the word Allah to refer to God. Christians use the word for God or deity in whatever language is available in their culture; the words they first used were the Hebrew (Yahweh), Aramaic (elahi / Elah)), Greek (Theos), and Latin (Deus). The words for God may differ because of differing languages and cultures, but who God is remains the same, as do the central ideas associated with that word as it has developed in the English language.

Not all classical spiritualities believe in God as a separate, unique entity. But who God is, what God expects, and what God intends for us is central to understanding the core spiritualities of the West. These expectations and intentions can only be fulfilled as intended among God's people. These spiritualities also believe that God is so deeply related to them that everyone who shares their spirituality may be called God's people. They are such because God shows, or reveals to them, that God wishes to be bound (covenanted) to them differently than to others. They are chosen. Notice that what is central here is that first God chooses his people, and the people respond to this choice by acknowledging and accepting the consequences of it by making a covenant with God. Notice, also, that the covenant is between the people and God. The individual who is part of this people is covenanted because he or she belongs to the chosen people. Covenant, in its own way, says that none of us is alone on our quest for spiritual fulfillment. Our spiritual fulfillment is found in God and is directed by God among God's people. This spiritual way of life results in our transformation, our total change for the better.

The consequences of covenant are many but easily summarized by saying that certain rituals are required, certain ways of treating self, others, neighbors, and God are required, and certain ways of organizing our lives are required. Following these requirements is the means through which this spiritual way of life transforms the individual and society. Each of these religions sees these requirements through its own spiritual lens, but they all accept that God creates them, cares and watches over them, and is to be worshiped. God is theirs and they are God's.

The first people of the covenant were the Jews. Christianity and Islam recognize this and re-interpret it in terms of their own spirituality.

Judaism originated around 1200 BCE; Christianity, in 30 CE; Islam, in 609 CE. Among the classical religions, these are not the oldest. They represent 53.7 percent of the world's population (Christianity, 33.1 percent, Islam, 20.4 percent, Judaism, .2 percent). They are the majority in one hundred fifty-four nations (Christianity in one hundred six, Islam in forty-seven, Judaism in one). [71] Commentators describe them as monotheistic religions, religions of the book, Western religions, and Abrahamic religions.[72] They are a formative influence on Western civilization. Many of the ideas, language, and expectations associated with spirituality of those who read and speak English as their primary language are found here.

We begin our discussion of classical religions and spiritualities with Judaism because it is the first historically. The other Western spiritualities see themselves as somehow a clearer or more complete fulfillment of God's original covenant with the Jews. One cannot understand Christianity and Islam without first understanding Judaism.

Jewish Spirituality

Shema Yisrael Adonai Eloheinu Adonai Echad.
Hear, O Israel: the Lord is our God, one Lord,
and you must love the Lord your God with all your heart and
soul and strength (Deuteronomy 6:4-6).

Prayer is our response to God's word. The prayer quoted above, considered by most Jews as central to their spiritual life, is also a proclamation of God's uniqueness and centrality. The full prayer (Deuteronomy 6:4-9) demands that we respond to God with our whole being—our body, mind, and soul. How to do this is clearly laid out in the *Torah* God reveals to us. Torah is a word many times translated into English by our word "law." It means more than that, however. It also means instruction, teaching, the first five books of the Hebrew Bible, and a way of life. To break Torah is to break one's covenant with God. To break an ordinary covenant between king and people may result in a justifiable punishment upon those who do the breaking. The word we use in English to designate such an offense is "sin." The entire Hebrew sacred writings (*Tanakh*) is a delineation of what covenant life requires: the history, stories, and poems of those who lived it, as well as those who broke it; those who spoke out to interpret it during difficult times and predicted the consequences of not following it (the prophets); and the laws (*mitzvoth*) themselves—all 613 of them according to most accounts.[73] The core of Jewish spirituality, then, is doing mitzvoth, which are the means by which one transcends this life and follows God's will.

Contemporary Jewish Spirituality: One Speaker, Diverse Listeners

Today Jewish spirituality is multifaceted and the result of a unique interplay between its origins and consequent historical realities—especially "modernity," the Holocaust, and anti-Semitism. The Shoah, or Holocaust (1938-1945), murdered six million Jews. Nations within the German empire condemned, sought out, and killed them. The atmosphere of anti-Semitism that pervaded Europe before and during the Holocaust determined that those who saw themselves as having this unique relationship to God must be isolated from ordinary people because they were dangerous.[74] Living within an atmosphere of anti-Semitism and the recent history of the Holocaust leaves many Jews with a subconscious fear that sooner or later history will repeat itself.[75] It has also left many Jewish thinkers wondering how God is keeping covenant with the Jews when so many of them were murdered. But argument (Genesis 18:16-33) and anger (Psalm 44:22-26), even with God, over the meaning and consequence of covenant is not new.

Jewish ghettos were established in Europe as early as 1084, which is when the ghetto in Speyer, Germany, was first documented by Bishop Rüdiger Huzmann. Most ghettos gradually dissolved after the French Revolution (1789-1799). The freedom from ghetto life meant that Jews were able to move beyond the traditions that bound the ghetto together. Many began to use their minds, wills, and bodies to transition from a culture dominated by traditions of all sorts to a new one dominated by unfettered wonder, search, experiment, discovery, and implementation. Because of these modern experiences and thought, some Jews moved away from traditional Jewish spirituality.[76] They abandoned dietary laws (*mitzvoth*/kosher) that were unnecessary in an age aware of the causes of disease and the means to prevent them. They read the Torah (the holy books) using the historical and literary tools developed for interpreting other ancient classics. They celebrated traditional weekly and seasonal rituals using their everyday language, not Hebrew.

This reform movement responded in these and many other ways to the basic question of how to live Jewish spirituality in the modern world. Their initial response in the nineteenth century resulted in two counter responses and the basic question of how to be Jewish in the modern world: the Orthodox Movement, which was the mirrored reflection of the Reform Movement, and the Conservative Movement, which attempted to live between these two ideologically opposed ways of dealing with modernity.[77] Of course, there are other more vocal and media-attractive ways of living Jewish spirituality today that focus on varieties of Jewish mysticism such as Hasidism, the Kabbalah, and Zohar. We will review the Kabbalah and Zohar in Part Three in our discussion of religions on the edge of modernity. The Hassidism, however, should be mentioned here because of its presence in Western culture and the important insight it gives into a spirituality too easily seen by many as bound to the legal minutiae of living *mitzvoth*.

Hassidic Judaism began as an eighteenth-century ultra-orthodox movement among Jews in several Slavic nations, such as Poland, Lithuania, and the Ukraine. The dress of those who follow this spirituality clearly states that they are different. The men usually wear large black fedoras, black suits of diverse styles with what looks like a square white shirt (*tallit katan*), with fringes hanging out of the corners (*tzitzit*), and full-growth beards. On Sabbath, the fedora is exchanged for a large, round, fur hat (*kolpik*). The women wear the modest dress of all orthodox Jews. Beneath this sober looking dress lurks a spontaneous, joyful, spirituality filled with miracles, future telling, healing, heartfelt prayer, and the charismatic leadership of a rabbi (*Rebbe*). The *Rebbe* who began Hassidic Judaism was Israel ben Eliezer (1698–1760). Central to this spirituality is a conscious, enthusiastic awareness of God's presence in us and ours in God.

Ecstatic prayer is the means for discovering God. Such prayer sends one's soul out of the body toward the God who is in all and is all. Ecstatic prayer is never a cold, analytical repetition of sound but rather a deeply felt encounter with The One who is the beginning, middle, and end of all life. This prayer uses techniques passed on and developed among the Hassidic group, or court, as it is called. One unique development among the Hassidim is a form of music called *nigunim* or *niggunim*. Usually composed by a Rebbe, *nigunim* is a type of humming that anyone can do, and it is used to set the context for ecstatic prayer.

The spirituality of Hassidic Judaism is marked by prayer, the centrality of the Rebbe, a spirituality open to all, a tight-knit community, and dedication to those in need. God and the believer are mutually present and influential to each other (*devekus*). They share many of the signposts of Orthodox Judaism, but their spiritual compass holds steady, marking the centrality of ritual prayers that leads to a type of transcendence that has kept their community alive over the last three centuries.

Signposts of Jewish Spirituality

The signposts of Judaism slowly and continually evolved within the context of communal and personal historical experience founded upon God's word as manifested in the Tanakh and interpreted in the Talmud, which is a collection of commentaries on that word. Out of these steady signs of God's will for humanity came the diverse sub-spiritualities such as the Hassidic, which we have already seen, and the current contemporary ones such as the Reformed, Conservative, and Orthodox, which we will see. Jewish spirituality has always sustained itself with strong, vocal arguments about what God has said and what we should do in response to what God has said. So it has been; so it will be.

Here is where things stand in Jewish spirituality at the beginning of the twenty-first century.

Belief

Judaism may be seen as a religious belief system and/or a claim to a cultural heritage.[78] In the past, for example, we could presuppose that all those who were Jewish also belonged to the Jewish religion. That is not so today as is reflected in the statistic that 42 percent of Jews living in Israel see themselves as secular.[79] Thus, there are Jews for whom the traditional Jewish view of God is not part of their spirituality. They may easily have one of the spiritualities we will review in the following chapters. Jewish spirituality, however, must have, as the *Shema* proclaims, a belief in one God.

This is the God they trust to bring them to a just end of life individually and communally. In God they find the origin of truth as found in God's creation and revelation. The specifics of that truth have been the source of continual argument over the centuries. To Christians, so accustomed to the cry of "heretic" among those with differing beliefs, it seems strange that specific beliefs are not as divisive among Jews as they are among Christians. There are deep differences about afterlife, suffering, evil, the end of this world, and the nature of humanity itself. These differences are part of any understanding of and participation in Jewish spirituality. A quick review demonstrates this diversity and, at the same time, allows us to see why it is not in belief that Jewish spirituality finds its strength, but in action; not in saying what is right, but doing what is right.

How is one to know what to do or believe? "Find out what God says" is the most obvious answer in Judaism. But there has never been a unanimous answer to that question among Jews. Looking back at the development of the Jewish religion, we realize that it took over 1500 years to write, gather, and agree upon their holiest writings known as the Tanakh (the Jewish Bible).[80] The same can be said about those who were acknowledged as interpreters of these writings. The prophets, Sanhedrin, priests, and rabbis all claimed to have a knowledgeable interpretation of the texts. By the sixth century CE, however, only the rabbis remained. All other claimants, including the Temple itself, were gone. Rabbinic Judaism was and is the result. For over fifteen hundred years, in other words, the Rabbis have been the learned interpreters of God's word.

By the twenty-first century, three clear approaches are evident in interpreting that word. First, the written word contains the solution to all the problems one may encounter in living a spiritual life, and the most learned rabbis can tell us what those solutions are. Second, these texts contain specific problems and some solutions for our spiritual lives but not all the problems and solutions we will face. Knowledgeable rabbis have the methods for applying the word of God to these problems. Ask them to do it for you. Third, these texts reveal general directions and principles for living. Rabbinic authorities can determine general lines of how to deal with them in everyday living, but it is left up to the individual to decide exactly what is to be done.[81]

Once we see how God's revelation or word may be understood, the plurality of interpretations of this revelation is more understandable. There are some Jewish spiritualities that believe that afterlife is the remembrance of us by our relatives from generation to generation; others, that we live as an immortal soul; others, of a resurrection of the dead at the end of time; and still others of a survival in a nether world. This is just a taste of the diversity of belief within Judaism.

Ritual

Jewish spirituality may be filled with diverse rituals dealing with eating, sleeping, defecating, washing, marrying, being born, dying, and communal celebrations. Jewish family rituals are especially prominent in most Jewish spiritualities. Orthodox Jews follow the rituals mandated by the *mitvoth*. Reformed Jews do not follow as many mitzvoth as Orthodox Jews do, especially those pertaining to kosher; Conservative Jews follow those that deepen Jewish identity. One can see, especially in Orthodox Judaism, how sacred rituals shape and

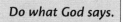

Do what God says.

form one's spirituality. Doing and saying the same thing day after day forms us physically, mentally, and spiritually according to the spiritual path designed by God and provided in the Torah.

Thus prayer said three times a day helps us realize the deep presence of God throughout the day. Food eaten only as commanded by God (kosher) becomes part of our very heart, bowels, and body. Sacred days and sets of days such as the High Holy Days (*Rosh Hashanah*, New Year; *Yom Kippur*, Day of Atonement) focus our attention for an entire week on judgment for our sins and the necessary repentance to atone for them. The holiest time of all is Sabbath (*Shabbat*), a day even God observed (Genesis 2:2-3). Stated as one of the Ten Commandments of God (Exodus 20:2-17; Deuteronomy 5:6-21), it begins on Friday at sunset and ends on Saturday at sunset. A Jewish family comes together at the Sabbath meal to remember its past, reinvigorate its present, and prepare for its future. A day set aside every week for rest, prayer, and study sets a weekly pattern reminiscent of our creation and the direction of it by God. Many Jews consider this to be the holiest time in the Jewish calendar.

Celebrations of life cycle events condense what is an ordinary human activity into a transcending-making ritual of words and actions proclaiming our relationship to God. Circumcision of an eight-day-old male child marks the covenant between God and all Jews (Genesis 17:1-14). *Bar* and *Bat Mitzvah* proclaim to the world that this thirteen-year-old young man (*Bar Mitzvah*) and this twelve-year-old young woman (*Bat Mitzvah*) are responsible for keeping the *mitzvoth*. The proclamation is made through their taking a central religious role at *shul* (Orthodox), synagogue (Conservative), or temple (Reform), and a special meal is usually held to mark the occasion, which often is a celebratory and gift-giving occasion. Bat Mitzvah is not done in all synagogues. The diversity of Jewish experiences scattered throughout the globe are reflected in their marriage and funeral rites. Each, as with all the major celebrations, reflects a blend of key ingredients from the Torah and the culture of the religious community.

Doing the Right Things: Ethics

We have seen that Judaism is quite clear as to what "the right thing" is. Obeying Torah as reflected in the *mitzvoth* marks a clear path to doing what is right and fair to self and others. Because Judaism is so foundational to Western culture, much of what we expect as correct ethical action is found here starting with what is known as the Ten Commandments (Exodus 20:2-17; Deuteronomy 5:6-21). These commands, though listed and translated differently among the different monotheistic religions, are accepted by all. The explanations and application, as we know so well, are also significantly different among religions and derivative spiritualities. The Orthodox, Conservative, and Reformed ways of living the mitzvoth direct their eating, dressing, and celebration of the Sabbath. The same can be said when dealing with the hot button issues of today such as abortion, capital punishment, environment, gender, war, and business ethics. But do not mistake diversity for anarchy. The commonality of the Ten Commandments is also found in the common acceptance of the ancient Jewish prophets such as Elijah, Amos, Hosea, and Jeremiah, who proclaimed that true spirituality must be based upon individual and communal justice and mercy shown to all people.[82]

> **Do everything God says.**

Community

If you grow up in a nuclear family and live in a competitive individualistic culture, your sense of togetherness is one thing. If you grow up in an extended family surrounded day and night by those you are forever identified with, togetherness is something else. Jewish spirituality began within the context of tribal life and continued, until quite recently, within a tight knit community oppressed by a surrounding culture. When you and those you live with are seen as dangers to the larger society, your personal and communal identity is different from what it would be if you were accepted easily into that same society. The killing of over six million Jews in the Holocaust and the continual presence of anti-Semitism are constant reminders to those seeking or living a Jewish spiritual life that they are "other"

> **Your fellow Jews will always help you hear and listen to God.**

to those who surround them.[83] To the majority of those living a Jewish spirituality, their identification with Jews begins with their first breath and offers a lasting awareness that at any time they can once again become the scapegoat for the cultural failures of those who see them as "the others." Community is a realization that these are my people and I am theirs. I may not have sought them, but I am them.

The Jewish communal spiritual life begins at home and extends to the *shul*, synagogue, or temple. The Jewish Community Center (JCC) has become a focus for many Jews, especially those in a pluralistic culture such as the United States and Canada. While JCCs are open to everyone in the local community, their main focus is on Jewish culture, education, and celebrations.

Inner Desire for Transcendence

The Torah both stimulates and directs our desire to move beyond the here and now to fulfill the wishes of the one who created, creates, and, with loving mercy, covenants us with each other and with our God. God's Torah is both clear and mysterious, but we can always be sure that if we follow the path laid out there, we will co-create with God the present that brings the future. Indeed, thinking is invigorating; willing is directive; but, it is doing that imitates the creator God. God first acted, and then said it was good (Genesis 1:1-19). So, in living the Torah, we do, and in so doing, we are assured that God will also say of our works, "It is good."

There are always those who seek a deeper meaning in life beyond the principle thrust of the tradition. Judaism is no different. Reading Torah and seeing God talking, walking, and being close to people, they too want to share in such an experience. They sense that they too are special and seek God's presence and, to their mind, personal directives to experience what few have. The Jewish mystical tradition has gained a great deal of media attention recently with much of that attention focusing on the *Kabbalah* and *Zohar*. Because of this recent revival it, is best to deal with it in the context of postmodern spirituality. Aside from these important medieval aspects

The future is yours.

of Jewish mysticism, there is much more. The Hasidic movement is an excellent example of going beyond, but not excluding, the *mitzvoth*. This "going beyond" is found in their *rebb* who is a source of the sacred because of his holiness and contact with God. It is found, too, in the tight-knit community of seekers (and discovers) of a deep life with God. Finally, it is found in the renewal of the experiences of those who walked with God: Adam and Eve in the garden; Noah after the flood; Abraham as he brought the sacrificial knife down to kill his son; Jacob as he wrestled with the angel; Moses on the mountain; and the prophets in the wind and fire, and even in the shade of a castor bush. Jewish spirituality is a way of living that has been tested by many and found fruitful. As you consider what you have read, you might want to compare it with your spirituality.

Key Facts for Jewish Spirituality

SPIRITUALITY and RELIGION	PLACE OF ORIGIN	MEMBERSHIP	KEY DATES	CENTRAL PERSON	BOOKS
JUDAISM	MESOPOTA-MIA/ PALESTINE	World membership is one of the small-est; North America, second largest.	+/- 1700—Origins 1200—Exo-dus 597-538—Exile 70 CE—Jerusalem destroyed 1948—for-mation on the State of Israel	Abraham—eigh-teenth century BCE Moses—twelfth century David—tenth century	The Tanakh Compila-tion begins in twelfth century BCE; finalized first century CE. Talmud as a commentary on the Tanakh.
CORE ISSUE	BELIEFS	RITUALS	MORALS	ORGANIZA-TION.	PROMISE
How can we live a good life? Acts contrary to the covenant	Torah YAHWEH (YHWH) People of God Kingdom of God	Seasonal and life-cycle rites Sabbath Circumcision	Mitzvah (613 for men) Torah Ten Com-mandments	Synagogue Orthodox Conservative Reformed	Kingdom of God. Remain God's people forever.

Christian Spirituality

Pater noster, qui es in cælis: sanctificétur nomen tuum; advéniat regnum tuum; fiat volúntas tua, sicut in cælo et in terra. Panem nostrum cotidiá-num da nobis hódie; et dimítte nobis débita nostra, sicut et nos dimít-timus debitóribus nostris; et ne nos indúcas in tentatiónem; sed líbera nos a malo. Amen.

Western Christians prayed this Latin prayer for over twelve hundred years.[84] The ancient and influential description of first century Christianity,

The Teaching of the Twelve Apostles (*Didache*), said Christians should pray it three times a day. Monks chanted it at least six times a day until the middle of the twentieth century.[85] Over two billion people pray it today. One can imagine, for example, all of them, each in her or his own language, praying it aloud as one on Easter Sunday. What a sound. It is known in English as both the Our Father (*Pater Noster*) and the Lord's Prayer. It is understood to be the prayer of Jesus, the Christ, and the center of Christian spirituality. It, as Christianity itself, is prayed in many versions. Here are some typical English ones.

King James Version[86] Matthew 6:9-13	Roman Catholic Mass	American Bible Society[87] Matthew 6:9-13	The New English Bible[88] Luke 11:2-4
Our Father	Our Father,	Our Father	Father,
Which art in heaven	who art in heaven	in heaven:	
Hallowed be thy name.	hallowed be thy name		Thy name be hallowed;
Thy Kingdom come,	Thy kingdom come	May your Kingdom come;	Thy kingdom come.
Thy will be done, In earth as in heaven	Thy will be Done On earth as it is in heaven	May your will be done on earth as it is in heaven.	
Give us this day our daily bread.	Give us this day Our daily bread	Give us today the food we need.	Give us each day our daily bread.
And forgive us our debts As we forgive our debtors.	and forgive us our trespasses as we forgive those who trespass against us.	Forgive us the wrongs that we have done, As we forgive the wrongs that others have done us.	And forgive us our sins For we too forgive all who have done us wrong
And lead us not into temptation,	And lead us not into temptation	Do not bring us to hard testing,	And do not bring us to the test.
But deliver us from evil.	But deliver us from evil. Amen.	But keep us safe from the Evil One.	
[For thine is the kingdom, and the power, and the glory, forever. Amen.]			

It is indeed the "Lord's" (Jesus's) prayer, for it summarizes his teaching and is an utterance of togetherness both with the teaching and the teacher. The key elements of his teaching are that God is our loving Father (*abba* / daddy); this relationship with God is ever deepening and will be finalized in the future kingdom; God, our Father, will care for us with food, with forgiveness, with deliverance from evil; we must act like our Father and forgive others. Some parts of the prayer are easy to understand today; others are not.[89] What was first prayed by Jesus is continually prayed by Christians because, indeed, God is also their Father. The ritual repetition of Jesus's words places one in fellowship with all those who prayed them in the past and in the future.

The Christian spirituality voiced in the Lord's Prayer is a spiritual way of life deeply involved with Jesus's thoughts, words, and deeds. Those who follow this way of life are called Christians. The internal disposition and empowerment to recognize and live it is called faith.[90] Trust and truth are the two feelings associated with faith in who Jesus is and what he asks of us. To know and understand Jesus's thoughts, words, and deeds as an individual and as a community has led to the formation of many Christian

> **Jesus is alive.**

churches which are communities of shared ways of living and understanding: Jesus's teachings, beliefs, ways of celebration, following God's laws, and bringing to life his vision of a just and peaceful universe. [91] Each signpost is a joining with Jesus not only in prayer but also in belief, fellowship (community), ritual, and doing and being good (ethics).

The Origins of Christianity

The origins of Christianity are many. To an African Pentecostal Christian, it is when she is filled with the Spirit. In the light of that experience, she looks at her tribal brothers and sisters in a new way, hears the prayers of her fellow Christians as never before and listens to the biblical Good News as the Word of God. For an American fundamentalist Christian, his Christianity stands solid on that rock of his faith, which is the Bible, and the translation overseen by King James I of England. It is in this book that he finds the source of his faith and his spirituality. It is within this book, and from his present faith in it being God's word, that he continually rediscovers the origins of Christianity. A Roman Catholic bishop, while being deeply socialized into his church's reading of its long history, looks to the understanding of Christianity's origins to the contemporary teacher of those origins, the pope. An academic historian looks to encompass all the experiences just mentioned and place them in contact with those first moments of time when the word "Christian" was first spoken and when Jesus, the Christ, was first talked about.

How It All Began Historically: Naming Jesus's Followers

The word "Christian" is derived from the Greek *christos* (the anointed one / messiah) and *ianus* (belonging to). Thus a Christian was one who belonged to Jesus, the Christ. Early Christians also called themselves many other names such as brethren, disciples, believers, and those of the way.[92] But it was Christian, a term first used by outsiders, that gradually became the term both they and others used to describe them.

Originally, they were a small group of Jews who kept talking about this Jesus who said, did, and promised amazing things. The group itself certainly was close knit and showed a deep concern for helping those in need. This early group of Christians originated from the disciples and apostles of Jesus who had spread his message and way of living because they were convinced it was the only way the world could be a better place. From these early Jewish followers, other people became interested and began to live Jesus's way of life. After a while, particularly after the destruction of Jerusalem in 70 CE, Christianity spread throughout the Roman Empire. Two thousand years later, Christians are found throughout the world.

As mentioned above, the word "Christ" is derived from the Greek word *Christos*, which is a translation of the Hebrew word Messiah or anointed one. When Jesus is called the Christ, he is being recognized by Christians as the Jewish Messiah.[93] At the center of the Jewish understanding of the Messiah is the conviction that God will send someone to save the Jews from suffering and injustice and begin God's Kingdom. That person is the Messiah. According to one Jewish tradition, the Kingdom begins with the Messiah's resurrection.

All the early Christians were Jews, and thus all the religious images and expectations of Judaism were theirs. They expanded the dominant view of the time that saw the Messiah as a conquering king and added, from images in the Tanakh, the Messiah as priest, prophet, and suffering servant who, through his suffering and death, would bring about the Kingdom of God. Jesus's resurrection demonstrated this expanded view of the Messiah. Resurrection marked the end of the old world and the beginning of the new world, the Kingdom of God. Jesus, the Christ, brought about the world described in his teachings and shaped by his miracles. He preached and brought about the advent of the Kingdom of God.[94] A Christian spirituality enables one to respond to Jesus's message that the Father's kingdom come; the Father's will be done on earth as it is in heaven. The challenge and the historical controversy is how to balance the Jesus of the past with the Jesus of the present and the future. Every classical form of spirituality has diverse interpretations of what it is, what such balance requires, and where it will lead us. Christianity is no different. Is Jesus the humble carpenter going about serving the needs of others without fanfare— even dying for others? Is Jesus the prophet speaking out to right the wrongs present in society? Is Jesus the priest who sacrifices himself for others? Is Jesus the conquering Messiah coming to rule his selected few while destroying their enemies? Who was this Jesus? Was he the Messiah, the Christ, the one who began Christianity—or all three?

The Present

Today Christianity has 2.1 billion members.[95] It is the world's largest religion and is found everywhere. Most of its members are in the Third World, with a significant number still in North America and Europe. It has some members in Jerusalem and its environs where it began.

Most Christians designate themselves by the denomination with which they're affiliated and whether they are Catholic or Protestant: Catholic / Roman Catholic (1 billion), Pentecostal / Charismatic (500 million), Protestant (Lutheran, Anglican, Presbyterian, Baptist, Methodist, etc.) (438 million), and Greek Orthodox (200 million). There are at least four hundred denominational designations of Christians in the United States.[96] These would reach into the thousands if we included groups with no institutional affiliation. In North America, Roman Catholicism is the largest religion, whereas in the United States, Protestantism is the largest and Catholicism is second. Christians are over 75 percent of the North American Population,[97] although this is rapidly changing with 15 percent confessing no religious affiliation. Worldwide, Christian Pentecostals are growing the fastest.

One way of distinguishing Christians among themselves is by describing them as *traditional Christians* or *Bible-believing Christians*.[98] This distinction in no way is meant to say that Traditional Christians do not believe in the Bible; they do. Nor is it meant to suggest that Bible-believing Christians reject Christian tradition; they do not. But it is meant to describe how most contemporary Christian churches may be grouped.

The *traditional Christian churches* emphasize that Christianity has existed over the last two thousand years in a continuous manner as the presence of Jesus in the world. They emphasize Bible, creed, and reason as ways of discovering God in our midst. They continue many of the same Christian rituals, feasts, and fasts that became part of the Christian church as it grew in numbers and importance over the centuries. Their priests, pastors, ministers, and bishops usually wear some of the ancient dress of times past in their ceremonies. When a person is baptized, he or she becomes part of Jesus's church that has existed over the centuries. What is important for them is to provide a time-tested, well-worn home for one to live in her whole life.

On the other hand, *Bible-believing Christians* read the Bible literally and accept it as the only creed and norm of all reason and science. The Bible is God's word revealing Jesus as personal savior, destroyer of sin, and teacher for life. It is through faith in God as revealed in the Bible that one is saved and joins with others—who are also alive with the grace of God—to become Jesus's church. The ancient Christian rituals are not as important as the Bible and the preaching that is based upon it. That is why most preachers of God's word do not wear the dress of ancient Christians but the more modern dress of academic robes or a modest dress or suit. What is important to them is to tell others (evangelize) about what God has done to save those who ask for salvation and to experience Jesus's salvific response to them. The gathering of the saved enables them to support each other in deepening their lives in Jesus and gathering into this life as a Christian church. Bible-believing Christians dominate the media image of Christianity in the United States.

There is no way of providing a clear, comprehensive enumeration of the total membership among all the Christian churches in the world because the definition of "membership" is neither clear nor agreed upon. Some Christians only recognize as members of their church those who have had a certain experience, such as being saved or being filled with the Holy Spirit. Others recognize as members those who have been baptized and confirmed. Some have no record-keeping mechanism for membership beyond the local level; others keep local, national, and international records. Some drop people from membership when they cease financial support; others do not. Some baptize babies and therefore count them as members; others do not baptize babies and do not count them. The above numbers are not as solid as they seem. But they are generally correct even though actual counting seldom occurs and a universal agreement as to what membership in a Christian church means does not exist.

However, within the question of membership are also the questions of identity. Who is a Christian? What is Christianity? The cultural bias mentioned above influences our acceptance of answers to these questions. Two particular biases that may shape our acceptance are belief that religious membership should be voluntary and the almost universal acceptance of media usage of the term "Christian."

When the United States was founded, the vast majority of Christians in the world baptized infants. All the baptized were members of the church. Many of those who founded the United States did not agree with this practice. Instead, they believed that one could only be a member of a church when he or she freely chose to do so as an adult. Consequently, they baptized only adults. As a result, the numbers representing church membership will vary depending on one's definition of what makes someone a church member. Demographers usually accept the numbers given to them by the respective churches. In other instances, where such information is not freely available, they will accept citizenship as equal to membership in a religious group. In countries where Christianity is the dominant religion, church membership numbers are easy to determine. This is not as easily obtained in those countries that demand everyone be of the same religion, such as in Saudi Arabia, for example.

Many times when American media outlets use the word Christian, they are referring to just one of the groups who call themselves Christian. The media accept this self-designated name and therefore, without clarification, they make blanket statements that "all" Christians are against abortion or in favor of a president's policies, to give a few examples. Other writings, such as textbooks, encyclopedias, and sources outside the United States, use the term to refer to those churches that demonstrate historical roots in the Christian way of life.

The word "Christian" typically refers to three types of religious organizations: those who have originated in the last few decades and claim to be Christian without any clear linkage to traditional historical Christian beliefs, ways of celebration, moral imperatives, and organizations; those who have originated in the last five hundred years as attempts to change the previous Christian churches to what they consider the correct form of Christianity; and those who claim to be in succession to the original Christian communities as their rightful heirs and living in accordance with Jesus's words and actions. For the purposes of the following discussion, the second and third descriptions of Christianity will be used to describe the signposts of Christianity.

> **Jesus is God's word.**

The Signpost of Belief: Revelation, Bible, and Creeds

Billions of people do not believe in the Christian God. Obviously, the two billion people who call themselves Christian must have a reason for saying God is real. The reason many give is God's self-revelation. In other words, they are convinced that God gives them a "gift" called faith so they can know who God is and what God wants of them and the entire world. Having said this, there is disagreement as to how God goes about revealing these things. Some Christians say we can know some things about God by just using our mind and its reasoning powers. Some Christians say our mind is inherently blinded from seeing God, and thus we can only know God through the Bible. Other Christians say God becomes known through the mind and through the other ways God has chosen to come into our lives: encountering other people, reading the Bible, participating in special rituals called the sacraments, nature, holy people, and history itself. Once God becomes part of our lives, we use all the tools we have to discover more about God. This faith-seeking understanding is known as practicing *theology*. Theology, then, is a way of taking what God shows us and expanding and deepening that revelation using our reasoning power. In general, Traditional Christians acknowledge the use of our reasoning powers in dealing with God's words and actions. The Roman Catholic natural law ethics is an example of this.[99] Bible believing Christians, especially fundamentalist evangelical Christians, will hesitate to acknowledge the mind's natural reasoning powers as an avenue to God or as a supportive role in relation to faith.

The use of the Bible in individual and communal prayer and in directing our thought processes is a good example of how revelation is viewed among all Christians. First let us look at what the Christian Bible is, and then we will examine how it is used in the various Christian ways of life.

The Christian Bible

Christians believe that a book, the Bible (Holy Scriptures, Word of God) shows us how God wants us to live. As a whole, it took over three thousand years to write, roughly agree upon its contents, and label its chapters and verses. Many authors suggest it should be seen as a library of books rather than one book. It contains both some writings of the early Christian church, called the New Testament,[100] as well as the sacred writings of the ancient Jews (Tanakh/Hebrew Scriptures/Torah), which is called the Old Testament. The word "testament" is another word for "covenant."

Christians believe that God speaks through the Bible whether in its original languages (Hebrew, Aramaic, and Greek) or in the many translations of those languages. Some Christian churches favor certain translations of the Bible (King James) while others favor others (Revised Standard, Vulgate). Three different translations of the Lord's Prayer were used to introduce this section as examples of these translations. Translations differ one from another not only because of the interpretation from the original languages but also because not all translators, or their churches, accept the same number of books in the Bible or the authenticity of the same ancient texts.[101] The various renditions of the Lord's Prayer that introduced Christian spirituality had one that is found in the King James translation. It ends with the statement "For Thine is the kingdom, the power, and the glory…." Many Protestants Christians believe this sentence is part of the actual prayer Jesus said. Yet contemporary scholars say it is not present in the original manuscript. No original copy of the books of the Bible exists today. Translations are not the original written word, although many times Christians forget that.

The general listing of the books (Canon) was done by the Ecumenical Council of Nicaea (325 CE). It was not until the thirteenth century that the chapters were designed and the sixteenth century that the sentences were numbered (verses given). How the books should be arranged has always been a matter of controversy. For example, Mark's Gospel is older than Matthew's, but Matthew's is always first in the New Testament. Another controversy surrounds when the books were written. Certainly, no one wrote down what

The Bible is God's word.

Jesus said and did as he was saying it. Nor was anyone present when the world was created even though the first book of the Bible describes God's creation of this world. The earliest writings in the New Testament began sometime around 60 CE and ended around 110 CE, although some would place the last writings earlier. Not everything Christians wrote during that time was included in the

New Testament. As mentioned earlier in this chapter, *The Teaching of the Twelve Apostles* (Didache) was written earlier than some of the New Testament books. The reason why some were included and others are not is a controversy not yet settled. Only those books accepted by the apostolic churches became the current Bible. Others were not.

The Bible and Jesus

Most of what we know about Jesus is from the four Gospels. They were not written to provide an exact history of Jesus's life but rather to tell us what he said and did. This is considered the good news (gospel /*evangelion*) of Jesus. However, we can glean some facts that provide a common picture of him. Jesus was a Jew who worked as a carpenter. At a certain time, either a year or three years before his execution, he was baptized by John the Baptizer. After his baptism, he began to teach about the coming of God's Kingdom: what it was, what was expected of those who were part of it, its proximity in time and place, and his role in its arrival. He is also described as helping people through what we now call miracles. Central to these Gospels, and the oldest core of the material used to write them, is that Jesus was arrested for breaking the law, judged guilty, beaten, executed by crucifixion, and then resurrected. According to these accounts, a small group of terrified followers discovered on the Sunday after his execution and burial that he was alive—resurrected. Resurrection means that the same Jesus who was born of Mary, his mother, is alive today. He is alive in a different form because he now has a new, eternal kind of body. These beliefs (resurrection, God's title as *Abba* /Father/Daddy, Jesus's teaching about the Kingdom of God) and Jesus's actions (helping those in need, living a simple life, and suffering for others) are the ideological origins of Christianity. His resurrection is also a reason that he is called Jesus the Christ, shortened to Jesus Christ.

Most Christians agree on these key points. Where they differ is in their interpretation of it. Bible Believing Christians will say that the Bible in its common sense meaning is the sole norm of revelation. The Traditional Christian churches (Roman Catholic, Orthodox, Anglican/Episcopal, and many Protestants) place the Bible as the first source of revelation, but they quickly add that how it is interpreted, and how people lived their lives in the past consequent upon their interpretation of it, are also significant for its reading today. Pentecostal Christians favor the Holy Spirit's actions within themselves as the lens through which they read the Bible.

The actual printed pages and book that is the Bible is handled with care and honor by all Christians. Especially in Traditional churches, the Bible is given a special place in the church and in the community's ceremonies. Selections of scripture verses are read in all of the principal rituals, and the book itself is usually covered in many ornate ways as well as kissed and incensed. It may be found in many of these churches in an honored place at any time of the day. In the Bible Believing churches, it is usually found within the hands of the preacher and the people as the authoritative text for learning and discovering God's will for the individual and the entire world.

Creeds and Bible

Many Christians proclaim each Sunday what they believe when the say or sing the Creed. Some books refer to these as *creedal Christians*. They are also the Traditional Christians we have been talking about. They are the majority. Many of those who call themselves Bible Believing Christians, while not explicitly rejecting what the creed says, do not accept its formulation of belief, the process through which it came about, and some of the words used in its construction.

Jesus is God.

They say we should not use words other than those God gave us in the Bible to declare who God is. This creed, and others that followed it over the centuries, do just that.

The Creed on the following page is the proclamation of belief that Christians have voiced aloud in one form or another, first at the Ecumenical Council of Nicaea in 325 CE and then the Ecumenical Council of Constantinople in 381 CE. It is divided into three parts, each expanding on Christians' understanding of God who is Father, who is Jesus, who is the Holy Spirit—or God as Creator, Redeemer, and Sanctifier. This Trinitarian concept of God is identified with Christianity by most Traditional Christian churches. [102]

Community: The Council of Nicaea (325 CE), Its Creed, and How Churches Determine Belief Today

A council, and in particular an Ecumenical Council, was, and is, the way the Traditional Churches decide affairs that pertain to Christianity. A Council gathers all the local decision makers at some place where they can make decisions for everyone in the churches. This means that for those churches with bishops, the bishops are the principal decision makers. The Council of Nicaea (325 CE) was the first ecumenical council. Most of the Christian leaders of the world at that time attended. Although there were several minor issues—such as the date of Easter, the sinfulness of taking interest on loans, and whether once a person was made a bishop of one diocese he could become a bishop of another—the main issue was whether Jesus was totally God and totally human. Nicaea, and then Constantinople (680 CE), used and created a new Greek word (*homoousios*) to declare that he was God. "One in being" is the English translation or, as many Christians say, one person (Jesus) with two natures

The Creed [103]	A modern commentary on the Creed [104]
We believe in one God, the Father, the Almighty, maker of heaven and earth, of all that is, seen and unseen	Those at the Council clearly state they believe in Yahweh God, the God confessed by all Jews as creator of the world. This God creates and is creating all that exists. Of course, "God" has no sex since only creatures possess sex.
We believe in one Lord, Jesus Christ, the only Son of God, eternally begotten of the Father, God from God, light from light, true God from true God, begotten, not made, of one Being with the Father; through him all things were made.	Jesus is God. God the Father did not "make" Jesus or give birth to Jesus in such a way that the Father is first in time and then Jesus. No. Jesus, the Son, and God the Father are together for eternity—one.
For us and for our salvation he came down from heaven, was incarnate of the Holy Spirit and the Virgin Mary and became truly human.	God creates everything that exists. Jesus is the eternal God here on earth. Jesus is totally human and totally God. God incarnated as human: born of a virgin (virgin birth), i.e. without a human biological father.
For our sake he was crucified under Pontius Pilate;	The God-Man suffered and died.
he suffered death and was buried.	Dead! Like any human who dies.
On the third day, he rose again in accordance with the Scriptures; he ascended into heaven and is seated at the right hand of the Father.	He rose from the dead (resurrected). He lives. Using older cosmology, Jesus is alive in the heaven, above the heavens; also alive on earth as his Spirit.
He will come again in glory to judge the living and the dead, and his kingdom will have no end.	He will come again to this earth as judge and as king of a new way of living (his kingdom)
We believe in the Holy Spirit, the Lord, the giver of life, who proceeds from the Father [and the Son], who with the Father and the Son is worshiped and glorified, who has spoken through the prophets. We believe in one holy catholic and apostolic Church.	The Holy Spirit is God, God with us now, directing us in all ways to lead this kingdom life, the life found in the prophets and the Church Jesus's church is one church: a church of holy people; a church founded by the Apostles and living in the manner the apostles designated; a church meant to be in every part of this earth (catholic).
We acknowledge one baptism for the forgiveness of sins.	Baptism takes away all our sins.
We look for the resurrection of the dead,	Like Jesus, we will live forever as a resurrected person.
and the life of the world to come.	This world will end like Jesus said when he was preaching and performing miracles.
Amen	So be it. We believe it. (Amen[105])

(human and divine).[106] The difficulty at that time was to believe that Jesus is God. Several early ecumenical councils repeatedly affirmed that he was God in every way possible—even to say that his mother, Mary, gave birth to God (*theotokos*). Today it seems many Christians have difficulty believing that Jesus was totally human. [107]

Christian decision making, as at Nicaea, is an important concern among all the Christian churches. Today, with our emphasis upon the individual, we generally think, "How can **I** make a decision that's right for me?" For Christians throughout the centuries, this question was always conditioned upon the church leaders asking, "How do **we** decide what to do?" For it is only in the framework of defining what constitutes the Christian way of life that an individual Christian can decide her Christian way of life.

> **Jesus is our brother.**

To make this determination, early Christians looked to what other Christians were doing, but for more certitude, to those chosen by Jesus as one of the twelve apostles. These twelve, along with Paul, were accepted as having a special role in the early church. When the apostles died, the churches where they taught were looked to as preserving Jesus's message. Any of their writings were also looked to for understanding Jesus's way of life. It was only natural that their churches were seen as having a special insight into what those writings meant since those churches possessed, in a way, "the mind of the apostle." Those who were prophets, and sometimes the martyrs, were also seen as witnessing to Jesus's life and message.

Acts 15 and Galatians 2 in the New Testament, tell us about a gathering in Jerusalem (+/- 62 CE) that settled the important early Christian question of whether the non-Jews that were joining Christianity (remember, Christianity was an offshoot of Judaism at that time) had to keep all the Jewish laws. The decision that split the early Church was when that gathering said Christians did not have to keep Kosher, be circumcised, and keep other *mitzvoth*.[108] This shows how the first Christians solved problems among themselves: They gathered the leaders and decided for all. How they decided is not clear. Certainly one of the first decisions (Acts 1:16-20) dealing with the replacement of one of the apostles (Judas) was done by lot, a traditional Jewish way to know the will of God. The Jerusalem Council suggests discussion among the apostles was how they decided what to do. Subsequent councils, and certainly from Nicaea on, decided what to believe, what to celebrate, what to hold as right or wrong, and how to organize the churches by a vote of those so chosen by their respective churches. Voting was also the way people elected their bishops, including the pope, as leaders of their church. This is still the dominant way decisions are made in most Christian churches, especially Traditional ones.

How Churches Decide What They Believe

Today there are three major ways Christian churches are organized and how they make decisions: the hierarchical, the congregational, and the connectional. The hierarchical places the final decision-making in the hands of one individual be it pastor, bishop, or pope. In ordinary circumstances, the Traditional churches' decisions are usually the result of some sort of councilor action. Many Bible based churches, while congregational in format, emphasize the role of pastor as one with a unique calling of God to lead. Consequently, once the pastor makes a decision, it is usually seen as final. Ordinarily the term hierarchical refers to such churches as the Roman Catholic, Eastern Orthodox, and Episcopal, although it may also be applicable to some Lutheran and Methodist churches. The bishops in each of these churches are the ultimate decision-making body. Most of the churches also have lay councils and advisory boards from the local church up to the national level and international levels. The pastor of each individual church is usually chosen by the bishop with consultation of the members of the local church, or the local church chooses who they want for their pastor with the approval of the bishop. The bishop is the spokesperson for his or her local area, usually called a diocese. Some hierarchical models have the bishops gathered together as spokespersons for the national church; some do not, with each bishop and his or her diocese only joined together at the international level as a synod of bishops or some other institution.

> *Our brothers and sisters help us hear God's word.*

The congregational style is at the other end of the organizational chart. Each local congregation is independent of the other. Some make their decisions based on the voting or consensus of the local community (parish, congregation). That decision is binding upon that church and only that church. Each congregation also hires its own pastor. The connectional, or sometimes called the Presbyterian form, is between the hierarchical and the congregational. Here, each congregation is linked to another congregation not by one person such as a bishop but by a representative group or committee. For example, representatives from each local church are elected to be part of a state committee that speaks for the church at the state level; in turn, representatives from each of the states are elected to be part of a national committee that speaks for the church at a national level. Each of these levels has its own area of responsibility. For the most part, Bible Believing churches use the congregational model of governance and the Traditional churches use the other models.

The purpose of a religious organization is not organization for organization's sake, nor is it for professing common beliefs just to have uniformity of belief and action. Instead, it is to provide our spirituality with a secure signpost of belief and mutual support for those seeking to follow Jesus's way of life.

Christians have used the word "church" to describe this organization. It is derived from the Greek *kyriakon* (belonging to the Lord) or *ecclesia* (assembly). There have always been a multitude of churches reflecting the diverse ways people seek and respond to God's revelation. The term "church" in the first centuries of Christianity referred to individual churches and the Christian church as a whole.

Others who have wanted to imitate Jesus's way of life have had names for their communities besides "Christian." They have used such phrases as Body of Christ (1 Corinthians 12:27), People of God (Ephesians 2:17-22), and Temple of the Holy Spirit (1 Corinthians 6:19-20). But it was the word we translate as "church" that came to be the most frequently used. This Greek word, *ecclesia*, also meant assembly, synagogue, people of God. Today most Christians simply say "church."

When the deadly persecutions ended in the fourth century, Christians began to build separate public structures dedicated to worship. Slowly the word that initially meant the Christian community began to be used to refer to the building where they worshiped. One cannot emphasize enough, however, that in Christian spirituality, it is the community that constitutes the sign-post, not the building. And "community" in both form and substance differs throughout time as the experience

> **Christianity is organized as hierarchical, congregational or connectional.**

and expectation necessary to energize the individual spirituality of its members develops. We have just seen this in the three different ways the Christian church is organized and reaches decisions.

One particular form of community we have not talked about is that formed by men or women who spend their lives together in order to enhance their spiritual lives. It was and is a central part of Christian communal living among the Traditional churches. It has existed from the early centuries of Christianity until the present. It began with some Christians going into the desert to be alone with God, striving to follow God's will in total dedication to God and God alone. They discovered that they could not do it alone. They needed others in order to be alone with God and respond to Jesus's commands: to share one's goods with others (Matthew 25), to be perfect as God is perfect (Matthew 5:48), to leave all for Jesus's sake (Matthew 19:16-26), and to not marry for the kingdom's sake (Matthew 19:10-12; Mark 18:28-30). This dedication is publicly witnessed to by their vowing poverty, chastity, and obedience. The vow of stability (staying within their community their entire lives) is also part of this lifestyle. Ordinary Christians looked up to those living this style of life as holy and close to God. They were the "religious" we mentioned in Part One. They were the monks, nuns, sisters, brothers, and mendicants who lived lives in the footsteps of Jesus and their founder, hoping to transcend this life and everything about it to live with God forever. For centuries, they were the dominant model of what a Christian community should be. Their spirituality is instructive for many Christians struggling for ways to control the diverse desires that lead them away from God's call. In the past, monastic communities were the guardians of knowledge as they hand-copied ancient books, taught people to read and write, and developed the necessary technologies for a better urban and rural life. Western culture and the Christian religion would be radically different without them. Their ancient lifestyle continues as it was first founded, but some Christians are attempting to adapt it to contemporary life and its demands.[109]

Signpost of Ritual: Celebrations of the Christian Way of Life— Sacraments, Ordinances, Feasts, and Fast

As we have said, we all gather with other people to celebrate and/or commemorate special community events such as the Fourth of July, the Super Bowl, presidential elections, and individual events such as births, weddings, deaths, and birthdays. We usually celebrate them in the same way: with special food, drink, songs, and people. This repeated way of celebrating is a ritual. When a group of people has existed for over two thousand years, these rituals and celebrations are ingrained in the culture. Christianity is part of Western culture with special days that, while the meaning has changed over time, still give witness to significant events in Christian spirituality and in cultural tradition. Jesus's birth (Christmas), death (Good Friday), and resurrection (Easter) are the most noteworthy. Many of these days became public holidays because so many people celebrated them as part of their spirituality.

> **When we celebrate Jesus is there with us.**

As countries become more pluralistic, we can expect that these Christian rituals will not be provided the same reverence as in the past. Good Friday, in most places, has lost its public recognition. The meaning of religious celebrations shifts radically over time. They usually retain their public acknowledgment as long as the religion dominates the culture. Christmas is a good example of changing cultural significance as it has become part of the contemporary holiday season, which today includes Kwanzaa, Yule, Al-Hijra/Muharram, Eid al Adha, Gantan-sain and Three Kings Day.

A number of pivotal events for both the individual Christian and the Christian community are usually called sacraments by the Traditional Churches and ordinances by some of the Bible Believing Churches, and are not given a general title by other Bible Believing churches but are simply called by their individual name, such as baptism. Whenever a celebration is called an ordinance, the church is emphasizing the fact that it was commanded to be done by Jesus. These churches will refer to Baptism (Matthew 28:16-20) and the Lord's Supper (Eucharist; Luke 22: 19) as ordinances. Some will also celebrate foot washing (John 13) as an ordinance.

The current idea of a sacrament is that it is a ritual celebrated by the individual, the community, and God. This celebration has a real effect on all those involved, especially as it pertains to the focus of the ritual (water, oil, bread, wine, persons). By the end of the second millennium, there were seven sacraments: Baptism, Confirmation, Eucharist, Holy Orders, Marriage, Anointing of the Sick, and Reconciliation. The Eastern Orthodox tradition calls these Mysteries (*mysterion*) in the sense that they convey God's saving presence to those celebrating them. We use the Roman Catholic listing since it represents the vast majority of Christians. Their number and titles vary among the other churches.

Some Christians refer to the first three as *Sacraments of Initiation* because their purpose is to bring a person into full unity with God and God's church. These are essential for living a Christian spirituality from a Traditional church's standpoint.

Baptism makes one a member of the Church by taking away all former sin(s) to enliven one with the life of the Spirit and enable her to follow Jesus's way. Aside from prayer and song, three ways of performing the water ritual have developed over time: sprinkling, pouring, or immersing the person to be baptized in water while invoking a Trinitarian formula. Most Christian churches baptize infants, but some do not, preferring to baptize only adults who can witness to their experience of being saved and freely accepting their baptism.

Confirmation celebrates one's life in the Spirit by enabling him to witness to the Word and enter more deeply into the life of the Church and Jesus's presence in the world. Some Christian churches do not believe Confirmation is a sacrament. Among those who do, some offer it as a separate sacrament usually for early teens, while most have it as part of the ceremony (for infants or adults) who are baptized and will immediately celebrate Eucharist and receive communion.

Eucharist (Mass, Lord's Supper, Liturgy, Communion), on the one hand, is doing again what Jesus asked his followers to do (Lord's Supper, Luke 22:19; John 6:53-58), and, on the other hand, celebrating and reinforcing the unity of those gathered (communion) by praising and thanking God for all God has done (Eucharist). Various Christian churches have different names for this ritual, which is celebrated every Sunday by the Traditional churches and less frequently by the Bible Believing churches (usually on the first Sunday of each month). The celebration consists of two parts: one focuses on readings from the

Bible and a short sermon or homily based on the Bible readings; the other, on Eucharist, a prayer of praise and thanks over the bread and wine, along with the eating and drinking of the bread and wine (communion). This is a very special celebration. Most Christian churches believe that Jesus is present in a special way during these celebrations. The Roman Catholic Church's name for this special presence is *real presence*, which occurs through the process of transubstantiation, which states that Jesus is substantially present in the bread and in the wine. Because of this, Roman Catholics "reserve" or keep the bread in a special container, in many of their churches called a tabernacle, until it is eaten. Some other Traditional churches do this also, in imitation of the early church, to take and share with those who are sick in the hospital or at home. There are various ways of practicing communion, which are better witnessed by attending a service. Roman Catholics have developed many rituals surrounding the bread that occur outside of their Sunday Eucharist.

The rituals surrounding *Marriage* and Ordination (*Holy Orders*) are clearly seen as sacraments by some of the Traditional churches (Roman Catholicism and Eastern Orthodox). All Christians see marriage as a special ritual that calls for God's blessing upon the two people marrying. The same could be said about the ritual of ordination to leadership in the Christian community. Both of these rituals have recently caused much controversy surrounding both the sexual orientation and the gender of those to be married or ordained. Some Christian churches marry and ordain gay couples. Some do not. The same can be said of women in the priesthood. While most Christian churches allow those who are ordained to be married, the Latin Rite of the Roman Catholic Church has not done so for the last thousand years. There have been some recent exceptions to this law in Roman Catholicism. The arguments for such exceptions are very convoluted and are best explained by those enjoying such exceptions—married Christian clergy converting to Roman Catholicism.

The rituals surrounding sickness and forgiveness of sin are not recognized as sacraments by many Christians, but most Christians have rituals dealing with the sick. The sacramental rituals for healing are called *Anointing of the Sick*, and for the forgiveness of sins, there is the ritual of *Reconciliation / Confession / Penance*. Both of these rituals, as with the others, involve prayers of various sorts plus reading from the scriptures. The person who is sick is anointed with blessed oils while the priest, pastor, or church elder asks for their healing and forgiveness of sins in imitation of various statements in the New Testament, but especially in James 5:11-15.

Many rituals are unique to a local community of Christians; some of these have a long history. For example, the raising of hands and shouting "praising the Lord" during worship services, or responding to the "altar call," where individuals come to the altar to be prayed over. Among all these rituals, of course, are those surrounding Christmas (the crèche), Easter (eggs), Three Kings Day, also known as Epiphany (giving gifts), Pentecost (wearing red), and many other days of feasting and fasting (Lent, Advent).

After thousands of years of doing things over and over, they are part of the culture in ways people seldom recognize in their ordinary lives. Sunday, for example, is an important day for Christians. Currently it has diminished significantly as a day of worship in Western culture, but it still holds primacy of place as part of a weekend dedicated to something outside one's ordinary work. Just as Sunday is a remnant, and a constant reminder of the influence of Christianity upon the culture, the same can be said of much of the legal systems, moral expectations, and character ideals within that same culture.

Signpost of Ethics: Christian Morals—Doing Right, Being Good

Our sense of being good and doing the right thing varies throughout our lifetimes. Psychologists have examined how we develop our sense of right and wrong, and how we determine what is good and bad. All the various investigations and schemas of development end with what is described as the mature individual's source of right/wrong and good/bad. This "source" is always transcendent to the individual's selfish motives and/or the impulse to follow the crowd. Christianity calls its transcendent "God" and offers the wisdom of ages in models of living by holy people, in practiced ways of wholistic living, and in various models of what is right and what makes us good. There are some lists summarizing what it is to do right (commandments, virtues) and how to avoid evil (sins, vices). Those from the Bible would be the Ten Commandments (Exodus 20:2-17; Deuteronomy 5:6-21), Jesus's command to love everyone (John 15:12), and his Beatitudes (Matthew 5:3-10).

The list of Seven Deadly Sins was developed by the early church. It draws from the entire Bible. This list was the one most frequently used during the first fifteen hundred years of Christianity. These sins are Lust, Pride, Gluttony, Sloth, Envy, Anger, and Avarice. Contemporary Christians are most familiar with the Ten Commandments, though most commentators claim few Christians can name all ten.[111] How the ten

> *Jesus's way is the right way. Care for those in need. Love God and love neighbor.*

are numbered differ among the churches. If you are a Christian, you might attempt to name the ten before reading them here: (1) I am the Lord your God; you shall not have strange gods before me. (2) You shall not take the name of the Lord your God in vain. (3) Remember to keep holy the Lord's Day. (4) Honor your father and your mother. (5) You shall not kill. (6) You shall not commit adultery. (7) You shall not steal. (8) You shall not bear false witness against your neighbor. (9) You shall not covet your neighbor's wife. (10) You shall not covet your neighbor's goods.

Lists of good ways to act are also found among many Christians. There are the theological virtues (faith, hope, and love/charity) as well as the cardinal virtues (prudence, justice, temperance, and fortitude). Many Roman Catholics learn the importance of the corporal works of mercy: Feed the hungry. Give drink to the thirsty. Shelter the homeless. Clothe the naked. Visit the sick. Visit the imprisoned. Bury the dead.

These lists are summaries of centuries of advice and practice of trying to live a good life. Yet memorizing a list of commandments, virtues, and sins is easy compared to living them.

God, for example, commands that I do not kill. But does that mean I never kill anything, or that I never kill another human? Do I kill only those humans that want to kill me? Am I theoretically killing someone if, when they need something like a job or food to live, I do nothing? Does it make a difference if I kill someone, even if I do not want to and it is purely accidental, such as if I run over a child who ran between parked cars and darted into the street? Many times it is difficult to know what God wants me to do here and now. The commandments are not always clear. As a consequence, spiritual leaders develop diverse means for helping their followers know exactly what God wants of them right now.

The Roman Catholic Church, for example, shows how it clarifies the commandment not to kill in its *Catholic Catechism*.[112] The official position is both clear and nuanced. To deliberately, consciously, and directly kill a human is intrinsically evil and a sin. The application of this clear elaboration on the Fifth Commandment is then applied to abortion, euthanasia, stem cell research, war, and capital punishment. At present, the official Catholic position is that doing certain things with the intent to do them is immoral. Let's consider this using the example of the child running between the cars and into the street. Your level of responsibility for hitting and killing that child is dependent upon many things: Were your car's brakes defective? Did you hit the child because the weather was rainy and your car slid when you put on the brakes? Had you been drinking alcohol before driving? Were you trying to avoid killing a squirrel and lost control of your car and hit the child instead? Circumstances modify human responsibility for an action. What you intend to do may also influence your responsibility for the action. The famous distinction between killing and letting die is one of those distinctions, as well as that between ordinary and extraordinary means of sustaining life. Nuance in morality is as important as nuance in life; it may be the difference between prison and/or sin. Official Catholic policy, for example, supports hospice as a way of making the last moments of a person's life physically, mentally, and spiritually comfortable. It does so because it does not advocate using every means possible to sustain life.

But should the killing of another result in your own death, capital punishment, or in the death of many others, such as in war? These two moral dilemmas have undergone, and are still undergoing, significant modifications in contemporary Catholicism. Perhaps the following quote from the *Catholic Catechism* summarizes best the current state of affairs.

> *If bloodless means are sufficient to defend human lives against an aggressor and to protect public order and the safety of persons, public authority should limit itself to such means because they better correspond to the concrete conditions of the common good and are more in conformity to the dignity of the human person. (#2267)*

The Catholic response to contemporary life reflects its struggle to adhere to the gospel of Jesus as it has been preached through the centuries. It shares with many people of good will and many Christians the general principles of compassion for one's neighbor necessary to live in a global environment, while supporting specific means to bring those principles into action. The support of those means shapes the identity of the Roman Catholic Church today.

Yet many Christians, including some Catholics, do not agree with the Catholic Church's official position on abortion, capital punishment, war, and social issues. To understand Christianity is to understand both the agreement on the commandment as well as the disagreement with its interpretation. To

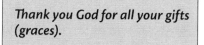

Thank you God for all your gifts (graces).

live a Christian spirituality is to make an informed choice among the disagreements and to live that choice.

Signpost of the Inner Desire for Transcendence

In Christianity, the inner desire for transcendence cannot be satisfied by the person herself. It is like having a deep thirst for water but needing someone else to provide the water. The reasons for this are twofold: One, God, the transcendent, is completely different from us; and, God is free to do what God wishes. God can never be controlled by humans—God would not be God if humans could control God.

God's total difference is impossible to describe because we are creatures and God is not. A feeble example might be that God is as different from us as an oil painting (us) is from the artist (God) who created it. That painting can never become like the painter unless something happens to it. If we are to become totally transcendent from the person we are here and now, we need God's help. God helps us by being constantly with us and enabling us to begin living this transcendent life here and now. This help and presence is called grace. This graceful presence is all encompassing within the world we see, touch, and hear.

This grace is freely given and is expressed in many ways. Some are easily seen and accepted; others are not so easily recognized and thus are unknowingly rejected. Still others are sometimes initially rejected because they are counterintuitive to our expectations of who and where God is. The previous signposts described the generally recognized ways Christians expect to transcend their present lives. The unexpected, however, are sources of major tensions within the Christian churches.

In the New Testament, Acts chapter ten describes a vision of the Apostle Peter in which God offers him non-kosher food to eat. Peter rejects God's gift because he was brought up to see anything that was not kosher as unholy and thus lacking in God's goodness. God commands him to eat it! The story goes on to describe Peter's encounter with those he does not think should be loved by God, but he finds God's powerful presence among them. All Peter can do is recognize God's mysterious ways and God's presence. Another story in Matthew's gospel expresses the same theme. This is the story of Jesus's judging who is good and bad at the end of the world. The people being judged gasp in disbelief as they are condemned because they did not recognize Jesus as those who were poor, hungry, thirsty, and without clothes (Matthew 25:31-36). Their inability to recognize God's graceful, real presence in the poor resulted in their eternal condemnation. At least Peter was able to learn his lesson in time. The common theme of both these scenes is that we cannot expect to know where God is all the time. The doors to transcendence present in life's mystery are there. We may not always be able to recognize them.

The tension between those easily recognized means of transcendence and those counterintuitive means have been part of Christianity from its very beginning. The two selections mentioned above are part of many stories repeating the same freedom of God to be present to whomever God wishes and however God wishes. These tensions are present today in at least four ways: mystics, Pentecostals, cultural adaptation by the churches, and the easy availability of other religions and their spiritualities.

Christian Mystics As Challenging Expected Means of Transcendence

In Chapter Two we saw how mystics often lived on the edge of the established churches because their experiences and writings challenged the usual signposts of Christianity.[113] Many Christian mystics' descriptions of these experiences are a particular challenge to the traditional acceptance of a deep distinction between God and humans. The mystics frequently claim a deep, abiding unity with God that destroys this necessary distinction between Creator and created. In doing so, they convey the image of us as God rather than creatures of God. If such a claim were literally true, it would void the basis of all monotheistic religions. The challenge for Christians is to explain this experience in light of Christian origins and developments since then.

Contemporary Pentecostalism as a Challenge to Expected Means of Transcendence

Contemporary Pentecostal experiences and beliefs also challenge established views of God. Christian Pentecostalism is an awakening of a strong expression of seeking, discovering, and expressing transcendence in our contemporary world. Remember that the typical Christian in these early decades of the twenty-first century is poor, of black or brown skin color, living in a Third World country, and Roman Catholic and/or Pentecostal.[114] The signposts are present in Pentecostalism in their diversity of traditional and Bible-based expressions. Yet it is the expected, very visible, and intensely felt Spiritual gifts for all Christians that distinguish Pentecostals from other Christians past and present. Roman Catholics expected their saints to evidence some of these gifts. Bible-based Christians rejoiced in the presence of these gifts among the early Christians as evidence that God acted among them.

Contemporary Pentecostalism's claim, however, is that today's Christians have the same gifts that were present at the origins of Christianity. Some of these gifts, especially talking in tongues, are evidence of their lives with God, the Holy Spirit, indwelling them. These gifts of healing, miraculous powers, prophecy, discerning true and false spirits, and talking in tongues (ecstatic utterances) are easily seen and evidenced.[115] The mark of Christian spirituality are the gifts of the Spirit (Galatians 5:22). This Pentecostal expectation was a challenge to the general practice of Christian spirituality up to the beginning of the twenty-first century because it democratizes God's extraordinary presence. These gifts, which Pentecostals claim are available for every Christian who asks God for them, can be found not only at Christianity's origins (this is what most Bible-believing Christians believe), but according to traditional Christianity, only among certain saints. How does one reconcile these diverse Christian claims?

Secularism as a Challenge to Expected Means of Transcendnce

Another challenge is the absorption of contemporary secular ways into Christian spirituality. Such absorption happened frequently for the first thousand

> *Does any language spoken two thousand years ago sound the same today?*

years of Christianity. The bread and wine of ordinary people became the Lord's Supper. The Roman celebration of the Winter Solstice became Christmas. The organization of the Roman Empire was modeled in the division of Western church into dioceses. From the same standpoint, most Christians are subject to or benefit from interest on loans (usury), yet the Bible condemns it,[116] and ecumenical councils repeated this condemnation.[117] When the medieval world of clerics and kings collapsed and democracy and pluralism grew, the churches became less inclined to adapt secular ways of any kind. Yet Peter's quandary still stands. Where is the Spirit acting outside the accepted ways of the churches? Is God acting in modern society on gender issues, the environment, peace and justice, and democracy? These and many more may be the Spirit's invitation to Christian spirituality to develop into a fruitful future.

Pluralism: Living With and Recognizing Other Religions

Pluralism seems destined to be a part of the future. People are moving across national borders at an unprecedented rate. This book represents a response to such movement. Daily, in person or through the electronic media, we meet individuals representing diverse spiritualities that have enlivened the lives of billions, yet until recently, have been titled pagan, of the devil, or considered secular philosophies by most Christians. Yet the questions asked of Peter by God still have to be answered: are they clean, meaning of God, or unclean—opposed to God. Or, should the people we encounter every day be recognized as our "neighbors" and thus included in Jesus's command to love one's neighbor as oneself.[118] More and more Christians recognize God's presence among these religions and spiritualities. Both Bible based Christians and church authorities in the Traditional religions are hesitant to follow them. As with the other issues just presented, there is great tension among Christians as to where the means of transcendence may be found outside the currently recognized churches.[119]

Certainly, Christian spirituality will retain the signposts mentioned above. Yet for some Christians, their spiritual journey will be one of creative tension as they seek to discover where the Spirit is present among those who do not recognize or diminish these signposts. For now, in the context of Christian spirituality, it might be well to remember the evidence of the Spirit's life: "But the harvest of the Spirit is love, joy, peace, patience, kindness, goodness, fidelity, gentleness, and self-control" (Galatians 5:22). The greatest gift of the Spirit is love (1 Corinthians 13) because God is love (1 John 4:8-9). The core of a Christian spirituality is love.

Key Facts for Christian Spirituality

SPIRITUAL-ITY and RELIGION	PLACE OF ORIGIN	MEMBER-SHIP	KEY DATES	CENTRAL PERSON	BOOKS
CHRISTIANITY	PALESTINE (Jerusalem, Nazareth)	Largest in the world and in the United States	25 Origins 1054: Division of Catholics and Orthodox 1517: Division of Catholics and Protestants 19th century evangelical movement 20th century Pentecostal movement	JESUS (4 BCE–30 CE)	The Bible: Old Testament (Tanakh); New Testament; Apocrypha. N.T. begins compilation by 50 CE and canon complete by 4th century
CORE ISSUE	**BELIEFS**	**RITUALS**	**MORALS**	**ORGANIZATION**	**PROMISE**
Following Jesus's way of life Sin and free will	God: Creator, Redeemer, and Sanctifier Jesus Grace People of God	Life cycle and seasonal rites Sacraments or Ordinances Saints Sabbath is on Sunday.	Sermon on the Mount Ten Commandments Prayer, fasting, almsgiving	Eastern Orthodox Roman Catholic. Protestant Church Monasteries	Kingdom of God Heaven

Muslim Spirituality

Allaahu Akbar, Allaahu Akbar, Allaahu Akbar, Allaahu Akbar. Ashhadu Allah ilaaha illa-Lah. Ashhadu Allah ilaaha illa-Lah, Ash Hadu anna Muhamadar rasuulullah, Ash Hadu anna Muhamadar rasuulullah. Hayya' alas Salaah, Hayya' alas Salaah. Hayya' ala Falaah , Hayya' ala Falaah. Allaahu Akbar, Allaahu Akbar. Laa ilaaha illa-Lah.

God is great, God is great, God is great, God is great. I bear witness that there is none worthy of worship except God. I bear witness that there is none worthy of worship except God. I bear witness that Muhammad is the Messenger of God. I bear witness that Muhammad is the Messenger of God. Come to prayer. Come to prayer. Come to felicity. Come to felicity. God is great. God is great. There is none worthy of worship except God.[120]

Five times a day this call to prayer echoes among the buildings of the rich and the poor, among shepherds and fishermen, and scientists and politicians. Over a billion people throughout the world respond to it with deep devotion by arranging their hands, head, feet, and whole body in ritual word and action repeating the main themes of the prayer (*salaah*) and the book that is its source, the Quran. They stand, kneel, and prostrate with their body pointed to Mecca, their head touching the floor, chanting in Arabic that God is Great (*Allaahu Akbar)* and the most holy words (here translated) of the first verse of the first chapter of the Quran.

Praise be to God, Lord of all the worlds. The Compassionate, the Merciful. Ruler on the Day of Reckoning. You alone do we worship, and You alone do we ask for help. Guide us on the straight path, the path of those who have received your grace; not the path of those who have brought down wrath, nor of those who wander astray. Amen[121]

These people believe that it is God (Allah) who is the center and director of our lives. We must submit (Muslim[122]) to God in body, mind, and soul, for God is our creator and absolute Lord. Hear God's very words of guidance provided in the Quran (the recitation).[123] God has given us direction for all aspects of our lives. Life is whole, as our spirituality should be, and thus there is no distinction between religion and politics or religion and culture. All of life is governed, guided, and judged by the one God (Allah) whose governance and guidance are given in the holy Quran and explicated by the *sharia*. The *sharia* is our law, our spiritual path, our way of life.

Why do we pray? How do we know these things? Because Mohammad (570 CE-632 CE), God's last prophet, has recited God's word placed in the Quran and explained God's will to us through his actions and words (*hadith*[124]).

God is great, is lord, compassionate, and merciful.

Until the time that Mohammad, God's prophet, spoke, many other prophets told us what God wanted of us, such as Adam, Noah, Moses, Abraham, and Jesus, all of whom are revered in Judaism and Christianity.[125] What they recited of God's word was ultimately transmitted to us, but the transmission was flawed in many ways. That is why God (Allah) sent his angel to give Mohammad the final and last words of God. We are all Muslims since we all must submit to God's will. Islam means surrender. When one recognizes the reality and necessity of surrender to Allah, one is a Muslim. To say with total confidence, out of the very depths of your being, *La ilaha illa Allah! Muhammad rasul Alla* (There is no god but God. Muhammad is the Messenger of God)[126] is to officially proclaim what you are by birth. It is your entry into the spirituality of Islam and the path that leads to Allah.

The Present as Enlivened by the Past

Islam is Arabian in its origins, prayers, and holy book. Yet most Muslims today are not Arabians. The clear picture presented by the media is one of Muslim women covered from head to foot and men screaming in Arabic. Yet Muslims, who represent one fifth of the world's population and belong to one of the fastest growing religions, are from all over the world. Only 18 percent of the world's Muslims live in Middle Eastern countries.[127] As a global religion and spirituality, Islam is shaped by the local culture while keeping its central core of the Arabic language for the Quran and for prayer. Two examples of such cultural diversity are helpful for their ability to highlight the diversity of exemplars of perfect Muslim living.[128]

Sunan Kalidjaga, born Raden Mas Said (1460-?), is one of the founders of Indonesian Islam. The story is told that he was the son of a high official in the Hindu-Buddhist kingdom of Madjapahit that dominated Eastern Java. In his teens, Said moved to the new province of Djapara where, free from parental control, he spent lavishly to satisfy his many desires. After he spent his inheritance, he became a notorious bandit. One day he encountered a well-dressed man covered with jewels and carrying a gold cane. He threatened to kill the man if he did not give him his jewels, cane, and clothes. The man laughed and called Said by his full name, and told him that he was acting like a child who has no control over his desires when, in reality, we live only for a moment. "Look," he said, there is a tree full of money." When Said looked to where the man pointed he saw a tree filled with gold and jewels. At that moment, he realized that what the man said was true. His life was worthless in comparison to what the man was able to do. He begged the man to teach him this spiritual power. The man warned him that such a lesson would be extremely difficult to learn. Said promised that he would dedicate his life to learning that lesson. "Okay," said the man, "stay here by the river until I return."

While the world around him changed, Said remained by the river for forty years. When the man returned, he was amazed that Said was still there. He proceeded to ask him many questions about life and the spirituality that invigorated it. With those responses, the man commanded that he go forth to spread Islam. And Said, now Sunan Kalidja, did so with great effectiveness. The man with the miraculous touch was Sunan Bonang, another great founder of Indonesian Islam. Notice there is no mention of the Quran or even Mohammad. This model of holiness seeks reality within the meditative process where, much like Buddha, Sunan Kalidja finds reality—in this instance, Allah. The story is closer to those of the Hindu and Buddhist holy men we will discuss in the next chapter.

Sidi Lahsen Lyusi (1631-1691) began his life as a Moroccan shepherd. He was born into a time of turmoil and crisis. Since religion and politics were one, diverse holy men supported or founded groups that attempted to destroy the others and dominate the Moroccan way of life. A certain restlessness characterized Lyusi's life that drove him to leave the shepherds of his birth. He wandered from group to group until one day, upon arriving at Tamgrut, he met a famous holy man called Ben Nasir who was sick with smallpox. Ben Nasir was lying there covered with sores and seeking some relief from them by trying to get someone to wash his pus-soaked clothes. Lyusi took the clothes to a spring, washed them, wrung them out in a bucket, and drank the water! When he brought the clothes back to Ben Nasir, his eyes were filled with *baraka*, Allah's presence for good and supernatural powers given to a holy man (marabout) in West Africa. With this single act of moral courage, God gave Sidi Lahsen Lyusi the power to teach Islam and perform miracles. His subsequent life was filled with both. Notice how his Islam was more external, active, and demonstrated in the many acts of power and moral persuasion that lead him to be honored among the Berbers and others in North Africa as a model of Muslim living.

Within the diversity of global cultures represented by these two holy men is the permanency of ancient divisions and ideologies represented by the Sunni, Shiite, and Sufi perspectives on the signposts of Islam. Remember the origins of Islam. Mohammad, a shepherd, merchant, and manager of his wife's holdings, took time from those occupations to pray and meditate in a cave near his home in Mecca. In prayer, he experienced the presence of an angel who told him to remember the words of God, which he spoke to him. These words clearly stated how to live our lives—the creator, through one of his messengers, an angel, told the created, through Mohammad, what their lives should be. While Mohammad lived, there was a living witness to how we were to live in submission (Islam) to Allah. After his death, how do we know what God wants? How can we know what Islam (submission) is? First there is what Mohammad recited and had others memorize. These words of God were written down (644-656 CE) during Mohammad's life. After his death, they were put together in the book form that became the Quran.[129] Then there was how Mohammad explained what God said, managed his growing community of believers, and lived his life. The one worthy of bearing God's word to humanity certainly is the primary example of how that word should be heard and responded to. His response in word and act, in time, was written down and became the *Hadith*.[130]

For a religion that has existed over fifteen hundred years and expanded over the globe, the question of how do I give, or submit, my life to God had to be asked repeatedly. That leaves us in the present where most Muslims do not ask questions such as these but live their spiritual lives within their birth communities or with those who accept them as a Muslim. There are three generally recognized Muslim responses to the question of hearing and living in response to God's word today. The Sunni look to those who, trained in methods refined over the centuries, use the Quran and the recognized Hadith to answer the question. You might say tradition is their tool for contemporary living. The Shiites, while accepting the Quran as central and their recognized Hadith as auxiliary, look to individuals chosen by God to lead them to authentic living. You might say leadership is their key to authentic Islam. The Sufi look to mystical experience flowing forth from the Quran and devotional practices to discover the question that goes beyond law, interpretation, and daily life. Modeled on Mohammad's time of deep meditation awaiting the angel, they seek God alone who is both the question and the answer to human existence. The questions of the present are only dealt with by being overwhelmed by God alone. A brief review of the origins of these perspectives on Islamic life might be helpful in further understanding the dynamics of their spirituality and present tensions with modernity in both culture and religion.

Sunni and Shiite Muslims

Sunni and Shiite Muslims have been distinct since the beginning of Islam. The acceptance or non-acceptance of certain hadith will support the position of one or the other of these perspectives. When Mohammad died (632 CE), he was the supreme leader of the Muslim community with its headquarters at Medina. In contemporary language, he was the head of both church and state. Two ways of choosing successors (caliphs) existed among the tribes under Mohammad's leadership: heredity and election. The Shia reading of Muslim history follows

> **Mohammad is God's prophet and messenger.**

the first type; the Sunni reading follows the second. The Shia (short for: *Shi'atu 'Ali,* followers of Ali) say that Ali, the husband of Fatima, Mohammad's daughter, was designated by Mohammad to lead the Muslim community. Such a designation was of God and thus Ali was the successor to Mohammad. The Sunni reading considers the first caliph and the four successors the God-given leaders of Islam.

As a matter of historical fact the first caliph, Abu Baker, was elected, but he appointed the next caliph. Ali was chosen as fourth caliph. Ali was murdered by the Kharijite *Ibn Muljam*. The Kharijites believed that no matter who the caliph was, he must be a follower of God in mind and body, leading an exemplary life as Mohammad himself had done. If the leader's lifestyle did not indicate he was a true believer, then he should be deposed. Ali did not lead such a life, and thus was deserving of death. This division in Islam never changed the signposts that we describe below but they do show how a devout Muslim (Sunni/Shia) recognizes the law (Sharia) that reveals how we are to live our lives today.

Sunni Muslims

Sunni represent approximately 85 percent of Islam. It follows the tradition as found in the Quran, the Hadith, the consensus of the Muslim community (*ummah*), and reasonable analogies between what happened in the past and the present situation. The description of how to live this way of life is Sharia. It has the role of being the absolute authority for everything in one's life. Since one usually lives Sharia from birth, most Muslims are not conscious of it as an "authority," just as many Americans are not conscious of the authoritative regulation of voltage in their electrical systems. The Quran, of course, is the word that all must submit to. The Hadith, as already indicated, are many. The process of winnowing out the authentic from the inauthentic rules took many centuries, but today we can say that the Sunni agree upon those directives that they claim represent the thought and deeds of the Prophet Mohammad. The consensus of the community (ummah) has been gathered over time. It must be recognized, however, that once the ummah make a decision, it is final, not to be revisited centuries later. Such revisiting would be heresy and put one outside the community. Most Sunnis see everything else as opinion. At the same time, there is no central authority in Islam. Consequently, some individuals have questioned what might seem to be accepted opinion and provide their own. Many contemporary ultra-conservative movements in Islam originated in this way.[131]

According to the Sunnis, aside from Mohammad, only the first four caliphs were able to provide authoritative Sharia for the universal ummah. That leaves us with those who have a specialized knowledge of Sharia and therefore provide necessary *fatwa*, or opinions, about how Sharia should be lived today. As with any legal opinion, it may be accepted by the ummah but certainly will be debated by other scholars. A Sunni spirituality, therefore, is a wholistic one embodied in Sharia providing direction for how to dress, eat, interact with others, pray, fast, carry on business and all the other necessary aspects of living one's life. To live this spirituality is to submit to God's will as found in the Sharia.

Shia Muslims

The Shia perspective is one of high hopes dashed by the realities of death at the hand of one's enemies. Their spirituality is imbued with a sense of sorrow and suffering in a world that awaits the true leader (Imam) who will once again stand in the spirit of Mohammad to bring us all to God's submissive design. Until then, they survive persecution and martyrdom as they look forward to his coming when they will be vindicated and peace will be achieved. This is when the entire world recognizes God (Allah) with true submission (Islam).[132] Ashura (tenth) is a day commemorating the death of the third imam and the grandson of Mohammad, *Husayn ibn Ali*, at the battle of Karbala (680 CE). It is a national holiday in countries such as Iran where Shiites are the majority. It is a major day of commemoration in other places such as India with a population of approximately 50 million Shia. This is a day of mourning and sadness at what happened to Husayn. In many places, men will beat themselves with chains to share in the suffering of Husayn. Drums, poetry recitations, cries of mourning, and preaching about the injustice of life without a true imam can be heard from the Shiite mosques throughout the world. Even more, it is seen as a martyrdom of one who faced up to oppression and injustice caused by traitors to the ideas and ideals of Mohammad. The town of Karbala in Iraq is of special importance because this is the place where it all happened.

Sufi and Wahhabi (Salafi) Muslims

La ilaha illa Allah! Muhammad rasul Alla (There is no god but God. Muhammad is the Messenger of God). It is easy to worship things other than God. Tribe, nation, learning, ease of living, power through armaments, position, inheritance, influence, or money are all capable of being worshiped, becoming a god to us. It is easy, too, as the years and centuries pass to see other learned and exemplary teachers as God's messengers. Every monotheistic religion faces the overwhelming attraction of idols. Islam was and is no different. Two movements of the past that are very much present today are Sufism and Wahhabism. Each are responses to the perceived worship of idols in their midst.

Sufism arose during what is referred to as Islam's Golden Age (approximately 750-1250 CE), a time of great intellectual, military, political, and cultural achievements. As the Islamic community (ummah) grew, there was unease among some Muslims that all this growth threatened to distract people from God. They considered the construction of beautiful mosques and the various teachers of the law as distractions from who really counted: Allah.

The Sufi movement offered a way of looking beyond appearances and provided spiritual methods for traveling into the depths of God. One learns Sufi methods from a Sufi master, who has learned those methods from other masters and is recognized as one who lives the Sufi way. The word Sufi is derived from the Arabic word for wool, thus expressing an easy way to distinguish the Sufi from others in the ummah. They wore wool as a gesture of simplicity.[133]

Two methods in particular have caught many people's attention: *Dhikr* (remembering/supplication) and whirling. *Dhikr* has many forms, but essentially it is living the presence of God brought on by repeating the names of God or verses of the Quran or *Hadith*.[134] The ritual dance of the Whirling Dervishes has the same objective as the *Dhikr*—to place one in the presence of God. This "placement of one in God's presence" is many times understood among both adherents and critics as being one with God. If it is true that Sufi spirituality claims oneness with or being the same as God, then it seems opposed to the Muslim understanding of God as creator and humans as the created. Humans cannot be the creator.[135]

Sufi spirituality is alive and well, however, especially in India and Pakistan where it has a long history. Followers of the theosophist Gurdjieff will find some Sufi ideas and methods present in his works. Their music and ideas may also be found among some contemporary bands and vocalists such as Madonna.

Wahhabism began with Muhammad Ibn Abd-al-Wahhab (1703-1792 CE). He reflected upon Islam after its golden age, just before the age of colonialism and modernism, and was disgusted at what he saw. The ummah, he said, was filled with idolatry. The changes since Mohammad's time had taken people away from God, not brought them closer. People go to shrines, seemingly worshiping people just as Christians worship their

> **The Quran is Allah's word.**

saints. No one or place should be holy except God. Abd-al-Wahhab believed they should destroy the graves and shrines that people were attracted to. He taught that those who practice idolatry or interpretations other than the Quran and *Hadith*, such as the Sufi, should be condemned to death. Those who disagree should be killed. A strict adherence to Sharia is considered the only way to be truly submissive to Allah. The house of Saud took up the cause of what came to be called Wahhabism, but was titled Salafism by the Saudis. They saw it as the basis for gathering all Muslims, no matter what country, into one visible and political ummah.

Today the King of Saudi Arabia is from the house of Saud and promotes Whabbism (Salafism) throughout the world using his oil money. Whabbism is the Muslim spirituality preached in the mosques and schools supported by the King. Saudi Arabia is the model of how it should be lived.

The diversity of tribal, national, and spiritual perspectives just described is always in tension with the bedrock foundational practices that are essential to Muslim identity. How they are practiced has varied over time and throughout the Muslim world. But these five are usually recognized by all as common obligations among all Muslims: *Shahada* (profess faith), *Salat* (prayer), *Sawm* (fasting), *Zakat* (almsgiving), and *Hajj* (pilgrimage to Mecca).[136] These common obligations are intertwined with other obligations particular to an individual's and a community's total religious culture. A review of Muslim signposts lets us see more of how one may lead a spiritual life in Islam.

Belief

La ilaha illa Allah! (There is no god but God/Allah) is the keystone of belief. All that is Islam depends on it. Belief does not exist alone in a culture or an individual: there can be no keystone without the other stones. The other "stones" in this instance are further understandings of who "Allah" is in practice and in other beliefs. The signposts described below

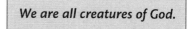
We are all creatures of God.

present Allah's wishes for Muslims and elaborate on who God is. There are four beliefs that provide some detail of the nature of Allah and Allah's creation: the nature of God's uniqueness; the unseen world that surrounds us; the essential goodness of every human person; the end of this world.

Tawhid

Tawhid refers to the creator God's oneness and uniqueness. All the monotheistic religions hold firm to this belief. Islam expresses *tawhid* constantly, publicly, and eternally. As created beings, we are born submissive to Allah because we are created by God. Allah shares himself with us through his Prophet Mohammed and the Quran, which is the word of Allah in our midst. We are also bound together as part of God's creation. We are one as creatures. To reject our creaturehood and/or to follow and dedicate our lives to anyone or thing other than God is to follow an idol. To act in such a way is to deny our very humanity and place ourselves outside Allah's dedicated community. God is one. We must be one in following Allah's commands.[137]

Malāʾikah and Jinn

Allah's creatures are both visible and invisible: angels (*Malāʾikah*) as well as spirit beings (*jinn*) called genies in English. Angels have no free will and therefore are good, but genies have a free will and therefore they are both good and bad. For example, Gabriel (*Jibril*), God's special messenger, is good. We find Gabriel and others like him actively communicating Allah's wishes to humans.

Gabriel is the one who delivered God's word to Mohammed; this became the Quran. *Iblis* is from the genies, an evil one, initially lived among the good angels until he rebelled. After being rejected by the other angels, he now lives among humans turning them away from God until the time of judgment. Jinn (Anglicized as genie) live in both the visible and invisible world at the same time. Some of these help humans follow Allah's will; others do not.[138]

Fitra

Humans are essentially good (*fitra*). We are born with an innate sense of God's *Tawhid* called *Fitra*. Fitra is everything it takes to be human. Fitra makes each of us a perfect human, beautiful in our own right. Yet, we need all the help we can get to remain perfect and beautiful. That help is found among Allah's prophets, the Quran, and the Sharia that describe in detail how to sustain the fitra we are.[139]

Judgment and Afterlife

Allah is the creator of our present lives and our lives after everyone and everything is dead. Life comes from God. Without it we do not exist now or hereafter. We do not have a right to life since it is Allah's gift to us. We are creatures. Every night when we sleep we enter into Allah's world, the world we might call afterlife. Our dreams sometimes describe this world. When the angel *Israfil* blows his trumpet, the dead will resurrect (*Qiyamah*) and be judged by Allah. Based on that judgment, our afterlives are lived in heaven or in hell. The signposts that follow, if lived according to Sharia, with God's mercy and grace, secure our lives in heaven after the judgment.

Ritual

Our understanding of Islamic ritual depends upon our experience of holy ritual. Chapter Three described how holy ritual gradually transforms us to a holy person. If these are spiritual rituals, they help transform us into a spiritual person. Much like the ritual of smoking tobacco gradually makes one addicted to tobacco, we might say the rituals of God makes us addicted to God. Certainly, the central ritual of a Muslim's life, *salat*, if performed according to the Sharia, evidences our devotion to God and enhances God's centrality in our lives. Commanded by God, it leads us to God.

We bow to God alone.

The Salat Ritual

Discussing only one aspect of ritual, such as its words, without paying attention to everything else easily leads to misunderstanding. Rituals are wholistic: word,

122

act, mind, heart, and will. Certainly, this is true of *salat*, which is a mixture of body action and words in the context of a purified life and focused attention on God alone.[140] We have already commented on and described the call to salat at the beginning of this section. That section on Muslim spirituality repeated the important words of the ritual.

The salat itself is, to the outsider, a ritual with many minor rituals: the call to prayer, purification, opening supplication (*niyyat*), and the prayer itself. The prayer may be and is said without the call to prayer. The prayer should happen five times a day: dawn, noon, mid-afternoon, after sunset, and in the evening. In Muslim countries one can hear the call to prayer from the minaret attached to a mosque (place of prostration). In many non-Muslim countries, Muslims will pray together or individually, usually on a rug; always directed to Mecca (*qibla*). Any male may lead the prayer. When someone does lead it, he performs the actions of the salat in front of everyone who follow his lead. Men and women pray separately except at home where all may pray together. If praying in a mosque, you remove your shoes and purify your body. In most instances, this consists of a ritual washing of hands, arms to elbows, face, ears, feet, ankles, hair, mouth, and nostrils.[141] Once purified, you face Mecca and make the proper intention for prayer (*Niyyat*) and begin the Salat ritual by standing with hands in a ritual posture saying *Allahu Akbar* (God is great). in a cycle of standing, bowing, kneeling sitting, and prostration and chanting the prayers we mentioned above is called one Raka (unit).. The amount and vocalization of the Salat vary according to the times of day or the occasion of the prayer. For example, the noon Friday salat at a mosque usually has a sermon. The rest of the day continues with the ordinary pursuits of life. Whereas the Jewish Sabbath and its later Christian imitators see their weekly holy day as one of rest, Muslims do not. Three other common Muslim obligations are also rituals: *Zakat* (almsgiving), *Sawm* (fasting), and *Hajj* (pilgrimage to Mecca).

The Zakat Ritual

Zakat (growth/purification) is not an act of kindness or charity towards those in need. Indeed one is urged to do that throughout the year. Zakat is an obligation of every Muslim who has the minimum amount of wealth needed to share some of it with those in need. It is also the right of one in need to receive their fair share of *zahat*. Depending on where you live and the legal interpretation associated with various types of wealth, you must give between 2.5 and 10 percent of your net savings each year to the Muslim community. Like salat, it is commanded by God and is an obligation of every Muslim.

> **Allah tells us to share our wealth.**

The Ritual of Sawm and Ramadan

Fasting (*sawm*) is part of Muslim spirituality—especially the fasting that occurs during the month of Ramadan. Muslim spirituality follows the lunar calendar and the natural marking of the day. Thus, the day begins at dawn and ends with sunset. The month begins and ends with the sighting of the crescent moon. Such sighting will, naturally, differ because of location and weather. Ramadan is the ninth month of the Muslim calendar. It is dedicated to fasting, temperance, community, and celebration. Various days are dedicated to each of these. Fasting is essential throughout the month. Fasting is defined as no food, sex, sensual pleasures, anger, or unkind remarks from dawn to sunset. Many spiritualities have holy days. As with Lent in Christianity (which is actually forty days), this is a holy month with an emphasis on that holiness experienced as dedication, loyalty, and duty.

The Ritual of Hajj

A pilgrimage to Mecca (*Hajj*) is essentially a complex of rituals imitative of Mohammad's life. The Quran says it is obligatory for every Muslim.[142] Mecca is the center of the Muslim universe. It is here that Mohammad lived, where the Quran was given, and where the new world revealed in the Quran was born. Every time you pray *salat* prostrated toward Mecca, you remember it and what happened there. Mecca and Medina are known as the *Al-Haramayn*, the Two Sanctuaries. To enter these sanctuaries, you must be purified by fasting and dressed in ritual dress. The dress for men (white *ihram*) is very closely ritualized. The result is an overwhelming experience of community as people from all over the globe and from different cultures and languages become one as they come into Mecca and circling the *Ka'aba* seven times, offering sacrifice, and drinking *Zamzam* water.[143] There are other rituals found in Sharia associated with birth, marriage, and death, but Hajj is the most important and fulfilling.

We have used the word "ritual" to describe this signpost because it has already been described in Part One. Some Muslims do not like the word ritual. From their perspective, it is equal to ritualistic. Our use of the term certainly does not reflect this interpretation but rather the sociological sense that we introduced in part one. The same possibility of misinterpretation might be part of our next signpost of "ethics" or "morals." Muslim thinking will make no distinction between ethics, morals, and civil law. There is no secular neutrality in the face of God's commands. God's will for our lives includes every hair on our head, every action of our being, every thought in our mind, every stimulus of our spirit. Sharia is comprehensive and detailed because it is God's will for us. What some might say is custom, Islam says is God's will.

Ethics

Allah tells us that life is sacred.

When it comes to a general understanding of God's will for us as to how we should live our lives, a common thread runs through the Quran, Bible, and Torah. Consider the following quote from the Quran in light of the listing of Ten Commandments often used by Christians and Jews.[144]

> *17.023 Thy Lord hath decreed that ye worship none but Him, and that ye be kind to parents. Whether one or both of them attain old age in thy life, say not to them a word of contempt, nor repel them, but address them in terms of honor. 017.033 Nor take life—which God has made sacred—except for just cause. And if anyone is slain wrongfully, we have given his heir authority (to demand qisas or to forgive): but let him not exceed bounds in the matter of taking life; for he is helped (by the Law).*

> *017.034 Come not nigh to the orphan's property except to improve it, until he attains the age of full strength; and fulfill (every) engagement, for (every) engagement will be enquired into (on the Day of Reckoning).*

> *017.035 Give full measure when ye measure, and weigh with a balance that is straight: that is the most fitting and the most advantageous in the final determination.*

> *017.039 These are among the (precepts of) wisdom, which thy Lord has revealed to thee. Take not another god apart from God lest thou shouldst be thrown into Hell, blameworthy and rejected.*

The challenge is, as often said, not in the general ethical principles but in the details of how to apply them. This is especially true with some of the most contentious moral issues of our time: war, abortion, euthanasia, capital punishment, the ecological crisis, gender roles, homosexuality, and social justice. In these issues one will discover significant inter- and intra-religious differences. Two examples will suffice: war and social justice.

Muslim Ethics and War

The Quran affirmatively provides two views regarding war. In surah 002.190 it states that only defensive warfare is allowed; excessiveness is strictly forbidden, but in the next set of surah (2.191-3), it supports the destruction of those who fight against them. The Quran commands, however, that if they stop fighting, then you must stop, and indeed, God is forgiving and merciful (2:192). The Quran position is understandable. If someone is going to kill you, you should have a right to self-defense. The modern quandary, of course, is that in a nuclear war both good and evil are usually destroyed together. Muslim, Jewish, and Christian scholars continue to argue the morality of waging war in our modern world. Hopefully all will come to a forceful conclusion that enables a full spiritual life.

Muslim Ethics and Social Justice

Social justice asks the basic question "How should we share the goods of this earth?" The response begins with the declaration that God created the world. This world is God's, not humans'. Humans, however, are to be stewards of God's creation. Up to this point all three monotheistic religions agree. The answer to the question of how to best exercise this stewardship gives rise to both inter- and intra-religious conflict; many times, those of a common perspective within the religion feel more in common with those in another religion than with their own co-religionists. A good example of this is the common political and economic response to property. Do I have absolute control of the property I own? Does my use of my property depend on others, as represented by the state? The answers to these questions usually take the form of either a capitalist or a socialist world view. These are moral questions—questions of justice and fairness among peoples within one religion and amongst religions. These questions are part of the moral signposts of all forms of spirituality. These broader questions may be particularized by asking one question: May I accept or pay interest on loans? More particularly, may I accept accrued interest on my savings? May the bank demand interest on my mortgage? We have already seen that the Christian and Jewish Bible condemn it, and how it took centuries for these two religions, and economic theory, to develop to where no one even considers the intense moral debate over these issues in the past as relevant.[145] All Muslims agree that it is immoral to practice usury (*Riba*). The Quran is very clear.

> *002.275 Those who live on interest will not rise (on Doomsday) but like a man possessed of the devil and demented. This because they say that trading is like usury. But trade has been sanctioned and usury forbidden by God....*

> *002.276 God will deprive usury of all blessing, but will give increase for deeds of charity: For He loveth not creatures ungrateful and wicked.*

Of course, moral commands are always not as clear as they seem—remember what we saw with the commandment not to kill. So too the above words of God in the Quran must be clarified. In the clarification, Muslim economics may have developed a middle ground between capitalism and socialism. On the one hand, it affirms private property and the right of people to earn a living from it; on the other hand, it embraces the moral imperative of distribution of some of that wealth by recognizing the poor's right to it (*zakat*) and outlawing the accumulation of wealth without labor (see usury above).

Community

Because Islam recognizes the coherence and unity of culture, the notion of community is one where everyone is recognized as equal before God and the law (Sharia) The Muslim ummah (community) is comprised of those who can say with confidence and submit with their whole being to its absolute truth: *La ilaha illa Allah! Muhammad rasul Alla* (There is no god but God.

> **God's people must follow God's laws- always.**

Muhammad is the Messenger of God). The submission is demonstrated in its laws and lived by those who speak this truth. The signposts are present for their pilgrimage to God and heaven. The result is a community of social justice and respect for God's creation both animate and inanimate. Individuals are to be brothers and sisters to each other, protecting each other from harm. When the Muslim life is fully lived, life is fully enjoyed (Quran, 9:71). The goal of the ummah is to extend itself to every land and person in the world.

The ummah gathers regularly at the mosque. The word mosque, if translated into English, means place of prostration. It is here that the ummah worship by praying salat. The mosque is also a center for many other activities, such as study, political discussions, health clinics, and gyms. Usually it reflects the architecture of the local culture. It can be a small shack, large room, or a grand architectural wonder. The original mosques were simple open spaces where the people gathered for salat. Today, obviously, they have become the center of life for the Muslim community where they gather to celebrate feast days as well as to pray.

Today every mosque will usually have a place for the ablutions (*wudu*) necessary to perform salat: washing their hands, forearms, face, and feet. Also they will usually have a place to put one's shoes since one enters into prayer without shoes. The place where salat is performed (*musalla*) usually has opposite to the entrance a *qiblah* wall that is oriented to the *Kaaba* in Mecca. Led by the imam, the congregants will line up in rows, facing Mecca, and pray salat. Together, praying to Allah/God, the community expresses its fundamental faith in what the Prophet Mohammad experienced: God alone is God.

Inner Desire for Transcendence

Our inner desire for transcendence many times mistakes idols for God. Expecting the desire to be satisfied, we instead discover it intensified. The desire is not some abstract, unembodied, experience but instead an expectation we are socialized into. As our desire for food is satisfied by those items we are socialized into as being food, so our transcendent desire is one shaped by the society we live in. Many people in the United States, for example, look to fast foods to satisfy their hunger-desire; to God to satisfy their transcendent-desire. How does one feel when encountering God? If you feel submissive, obedient, law abiding, and loyal when you are doing what you think you are supposed to do, are you encountering God? Most Muslims would say yes. One's daily life lived obeying Sharia is a life lived in and for God. It is satisfying to our inner desire for transcendence.

Yet, some want more than that satisfactory experience. They believe that God calls them to a deeply felt personal relationship, much like one has with her or his lover. Here, then, the God experience is that of close personal attraction and togetherness. Like a deep discussion with a friend, an exhilarating argument with a colleague, a deep embrace of skin on skin with one's lover, or being taken up into the spirit of a piece of music. Some might even say the experience is like loving sexual intercourse. We have seen those seeking such an experience among many mystics of other religions. Here we have seen it among the Sufi. Yet even the Sufi would warn us to never concentrate on the experience but on the object of the experience who is God alone. We cannot make an idol of our experience when we worship only God. As with Christianity and Judaism, in Muslim spirituality there is no god but God. Faith can so easily look to idols of reason, experience, visions, and miracles instead of to God. But the one who submits, the true Muslim, always proclaims in the face of all idols: *La ilaha illa Allah!* This must always be at the center of Muslim spirituality.

Key Facts For Muslim Spirituality

SPIRITUAL-ITY and RELIGION	PLACE OF ORIGIN	MEMBERSHIP	KEY DATES	CENTRAL PERSON	BOOKS
ISLAM	ARABIAN PENINSULA	Second largest in the world and third largest in North America.	570-632 CE—Origins 630-1492 CE—Growth 18th century: beginning of colonization	MUHAM-MAD 570-632	The Quran was begun in 610 CE and finalized in 632 CE Hadith.
CORE ISSUE	**BELIEFS**	**RITUALS**	**MORALS**	**ORGANIZA-TION.**	**PROMISE**
Primacy of God and obeying God's will as in the Quran.	Allah Quran Universal Brotherhood	Friday Lifecycle and season rituals Ramadan	Five Pillars Hajj	Mosque Shiite Sunni Sufis	Heaven

God's People?

After reading about these three spiritualties, are you attracted to one of them? Perhaps, by birth, you currently live one of them. Are you comfortable knowing that you are one of God's people and all that entails?

Summary

When you look at the key facts at the end of each section you find that the promise of transcendence for each of these spiritualities differs: Judaism looks to the fulfillment of the covenant promise for all Jews and the coming of God's Kingdom; Christians, to heaven and the final creation of God's Kingdom together with resurrection; Muslims to heaven and/or the resurrection. The means to total transcendence differs as you look at their signposts. One thing that does not differ is acknowledgement and dedication to God and the use of ancient images, stories, rituals, and laws as means to express this acknowledgement and dedication. As classical spiritualties they bring the past into the present. Whether in doing so they are truthful to their origins or not is a matter for their theologians to argue and their authorities to decide. Whether they stimulate and respond to your inner desire for transcendence only you can decide.

CHAPTER FIVE

SEEKING ETERNITY WITHIN AND HARMONY WITH ALL: THE CLASSICAL SPIRITUALITIES OF HINDUISM, BUDDHISM, TAOISM (DAOISM), CONFUCIANISM, SHINTO, AND INDIGENOUS SPIRITUALITIES

Who seeks? You do! You seek to go beyond yourself; to fulfill the heroic, transcendent desires within you. But yours is not to go beyond the here and now of sensory life but to go deep within the here and now of your existence. You are convinced that what you see, feel, touch, smell, and hear is not real; it is illusory—false to what you feel is really necessary; what will really bring you peace; what will ultimately fulfill your heroic need to be complete, at peace, and permanent. If this is what you seek, the Hindu and Buddhist signposts provide a time-tested road to walk.

Who seeks? You do. You are part of this ever flowing path that you see, feel, hear and touch that surrounds you. You are enmeshed in it. This here and now, the path itself, is constituted by plants, animals, rocks, streams, people, power, feelings, and energies—in a word, by nature both seen and unseen. When all this is in harmony with the way we are to live, our lives are fulfilled. Your spirituality is complete when you, with your recognized uniqueness, become one with the harmonious commonality that is the path of all life. Taoism and Confucianism provide the necessary signposts to enable this harmonious spiritual life.

These short paragraphs condense the wisdom of centuries and the insight of individual spiritual masters since the beginning of written history. These religions, and the spiritualities embedded in them, are among the oldest classical religions in the world: Shinto (2000 BCE), Hinduism (1500 BCE), Buddhism (531 BCE), Confucianism (551 BCE), and Taoism (350

130

BCE).[146] They represent 26 percent of the world's population: Shinto, 3 million; Hinduism, 870 million (13 percent), Buddhism 380 million (5.9 percent), Confucianism, 6 million (.1 percent) and Taoism, 3 million.[147] They differ in many ways from the classical spiritualities reviewed in the last chapter.

"Creation" as something that begins out of nothing and is sustained by a "personal creator God" does not exist. With no creation of a purposeful universe there is no time and the directional history it weaves. Instead, in Hinduism, for example, time is cyclical like the seasons, not linear like a calendar with its succession of days, weeks, months, and years. With no creation and no time, there is only the eternal. Where and when we are right now is forever. Time is a myth. We are part of the eternal here and now.

We are one. The dualism of creator and created; past and future; body and soul are not as clear as in the monotheistic religions. As a result, the classical spiritualities we will discuss in this chapter are sometimes referred to as monistic religions. We are this one. We, and all that exists, are eternal. It is not belief and words that are important but the ability to discover the truth of this eternal existence which is beyond words and logic. But essential to the sense of difference is the realization of how deep that difference is. For example, when I said "we" are one, you probably thought of your conscious self, the one reading these words, thinking, reflecting—seeking. But that is not the "we" or the "I" or the "you" of this religious and spiritual perspective. This is a radically different perspective from the last chapter. A realization of this difference is essential to sensing the classical spiritualities associated with it.

When English speakers from Western cultures study Eastern spiritualities, they do so with categories of language, culture, and history that bias them in their understanding of these other cultures. Central to that bias is colonialism and its consequences upon the West, the colonizers.

When one conquers another people through war or commerce, the conqueror has the immediate task of managing the conquered. Management means bureaucracy. Bureaucracy means unification. One immediate means of unification is to have a common language of commerce. English, naturally, was that language for England. When the English arrived in South East Asia, the home of Hinduism and Buddhism; China, the home of Confucianism and Taoism; and, Japan, the home of Shinto, they saw or imposed unity where there was great disparity.

Religion was one of those areas of disparity which, when viewed through colonial bureaucracy and linguistic necessities, resulted in a perspective that many times distorted the reality of people's actual religiosity. This is reflected in the choice of words to describe what I am calling religion and spirituality. When traders and conquerors first encountered these people, they viewed them as pagans and unbelievers. The first category was an easy one: they are not like us. They do not worship God. Since there is only one God, and we are God's people, they must worship the devil. So looking at the people and what they did in their shrines and daily lives the colonizers saw evil, ignorance, superstition. As they gained more knowledge about and from these people, especially in contact with those who thought deeply about many of the things that intellectuals thought about in the West, they learned about another, more abstract, and seemingly deeper layer to what they had first seen as superstition. Through the distortion of translations and the diversity of ancient cultures, Western intellectuals saw these deep thoughts and the actions resulting from them as profound philosophies that must be studied for their originality and profundity.

Naturally, written materials became the conduit for sharing these thoughts from one culture to the other, especially when one of these cultures saw a book, the Bible, as essential to their religious life. This gathering of writings, thoughts, and descriptions by the colonizers gained coherence from the necessity of study and bureaucracy. They also gained the titles we use today such as the word Hinduism, which initially was a word describing all the religious and philosophical activity in South East Asia, or Shinto, describing the national religion of Japan.

It was these titles, then, that provided our vision of the beliefs of these peoples and our understanding of what we now call Eastern religions and/or spiritualities. Even today we find remnants of these ways of understanding Eastern spiritualities. Some Christians call them pagans, and some bookstores or libraries place books about Eastern religions in the Philosophy category.

I always remember a famous Hindu scholar describing his first encounter with the realities of the Hindu religion. After years of study in the United States he finally was able to go to India. As he got off the plane it was not the abstractions of *atman*, *samsara*, *Brahman*, and *Karma* that he had spent years studying but the smell of decaying vegetables, stale incense, human sweat, and the noise of thousands and thousands of people as they fought to survive in this culture so different from what he had become accustomed to.

Are these Eastern spiritualities Pagan worship? Philosophy? Religion? Spirituality? Belief in gods or God? Atheists? Our look at these religions and spiritualities is caught up in the history of words, ideas, and translations as they have come down to us over the centuries. If we want to know them as they are, not as we wish them to be, we must be aware of our own spirituality in

> **You are not who you think you are.**

order to enter into conversation with theirs. Stretch your mind, your spirit, and your soul to become aware of them, and in doing so you may come to realize none of these (mind, spirit, or soul) exist as you know them.

Seeking Eternity Within:
Hinduism, Jainism, Buddhism

OM (AUM)

The goal, which all Vedas declare, which all austerities aim at, and which humans desire when they live a life of conscience, I will tell you briefly it is aum. This one syllable is indeed Brahman. This one syllable is the highest. Whosoever knows this one syllable obtains all that he desires (Katha Upanishad).[148]

The Vedas (2000-800 BCE) are a set of basic texts of Indian culture. The Upanishads are found toward the end of the Vedic collection and were probably first written down around 1000 BCE. These scriptures are accepted literally by some of the religions coming from this culture (Hinduism), re-interpreted by others (the *Bhakti* movement),[149] and rejected by still others (Buddhism and Jainism). *Om* as part of this text is part of this same acceptance and modification but not rejection. And just as *Om* is part of all of the Hindu religions and their derivatives, so are some essential words and the ideas associated with them such as *atman, Brahman, samsara, karma, dharma,* and *moksha.* Just as in Christianity, the historical reality of Jesus was significantly modified over time,[150] so the meaning and consequences of these terms were modified over the three thousand year written history of Indian culture. The brief outline of Western spirituality we reviewed in Chapter Two comes to play here as we move from the Iron Age to the present within Hinduism.

Hinduism began with the reality of war, the conquered and the conquerors. This reality left the beginning of Indian culture stratified into a warrior class, a priestly class, and everyone else. This division gradually developed into what was accepted as "natural" by the *Vedas* and, with time, confirmed as necessary religious reality in what the first Portuguese traders in the sixteenth century called *casta.* As we will see, this complex division of society has spiritual and religious ramifications. This order of society is reflected, and dependent upon, the order of the cosmos. *Dharma* was the term first used to describe the proper order of both universe and society. This order must be sustained. Initially it was sustained by the power of the warriors and the priests. The priests sustained this order by chants and sacrifice.[151] *Aum (om)*is one of the primitive chants that, when sounded by the righteous in the proper manner, aligns both earth and heavens. All the earths and the heavens, both seen and unseen, are connected in a never-ending flow of life; like the seasons, life and death are in an everlasting cycle of birth and rebirth. *Samsara* is the term used to describe this never-ending cycle of life and death. Many in the English-speaking world have used the term reincarnation as a translation of *samsara* when applied to humans, but notice this is a cycle of both life and death. It applies to all of nature.

For most believers of *samsara* such a cycle was a condemnation to another life of suffering and death after death in this life. To some recent moderns, born into an economy that benefits them, reincarnation and new life seems opposite to such suffering and death but as an opportunity for more pleasure and happiness. These moderns are fortunate in their present life but forgetful of what might become of them if reincarnation is a fact of life. They could end up as a dog picking through the garbage in India. We are bound to this cycle by our individual *karma*, and what we have done, thought, and felt in the past and are doing now determines our personal *samsara*. Our *karma* may cause us to be reborn as a dog, a flea, a soldier, a priest, or some other living thing.

Indians see *samsara* as something to escape rather than to attain. They seek *moksha*: freedom or liberation from this wheel of death and suffering. Such freedom is brought about through various means of liberation such as *karma yoga* (the way of action), *bhakti yoga* (the way of devotion), and *jnana yoga* (the way of knowledge). And just what or who is freed from *samsara*? *Atman*, your essence, who you really are, is freed. Sometimes *atman* is translated soul and sometimes spirit. It originates as a term in association with cremation by the priests. One of the hymns chanted by the priests at the cremation asks the god Agni not to destroy everything that makes up the human being but to allow these various physical elements to continue on. One of these is the person's *atman* or breath. With time, as reflected in subsequent hymns, this atman becomes a reality (spiritual body?) that is sustained and perfected by the sacrifices so the person may go to the heavenly realms (*loka* / sacred place) after death with a body already prepared for life there.[152] We will see different views of what the *atman* is in the Indian religions. But no matter what the view, both *atman* and *Brahman* are connected. *Brahman* is ultimate reality. Some see the Brahman as having some personal characteristics, especially those who follow *bhakti yoga*; others see Brahman as impersonal, especially those who follow *jnana yoga*. We will see more of this in the following signposts of Hinduism.

> **Keep trying until you know who you really are.**

The Spirituality of Hinduism

oṃ pūrṇamadaḥ pūrṇamidam pūrṇāt pūrṇamudacyate
pūrṇasya pūrṇamādāya pūrṇamevāvaśiṣyate
oṃ śāntiḥ śāntiḥ śāntiḥ

Om ! That is infinite, and this is infinite.
The infinite proceeds from the infinite.

taking the infinitude of the infinite,
It remains as the infinite alone.
Om ! Peace ! Peace ! Peace[153]

Om trayambakam yajaamahe sugandhim pushtivardhanam
Urvaarukamiva bandhanaan mrityor muksheeya maamritaat

We worship the three-eyed One (Lord Siva) Who is fragrant and Who
nourishes well all beings; may He liberate us from death
for the sake of immortality even as the cucumber is
severed from its bondage (to the creeper).

Vakratunda Mahakaya
Surya Koti Samaprabha
Neervigna Kurume Deva
Sarva Karyeshu Sarvada

O Lord Ganesha possessing a large body
curved trunk, with the brilliance
of a million suns, please make all
my work free of obstacles—always.[154]

These prayers are a miniscule representation of the enormous diversity of
the Hinduism that must be described, reviewed, and brought into conversation
with all the spiritualities in this book.[155] Remember that Hinduism is a collection of religions with a few common ideas, geography, and scriptures. With
that in mind let us begin by seeking a commonality in its signposts.

Hindu Community

India is an ancient culture with Hinduism as a sustaining influence throughout the millennia. It encompasses every form of community, both rural and
urban. The extended family is central to this culture, although recently a
greater focus on the nuclear family is becoming common in urban areas.[156]
These extended families trace themselves back through their departed ancestors.[157] It is within these families that the basic sense of community occurs and
an essential view of the entire Hindu
approach to existence is revealed:
people's families determine their present ways of life. The term *jati* is used
to express this essential ingredient in

> *Try Karma yoga:*
> *Keep your proper place and do*
> *what is expected of you.*

Hindu spirituality. The English term for jati is caste. Each jati has its set of acceptable foods, occupations, marriages, and associations with other jati.[158] The caste system is consecrated in the Rig-Veda (10:90). Although *Varna* is often translated as caste, the original meaning may be color.[159] The Rig-Veda describes the Varna as cosmically ordained when it describes three divinely ordered castes: priests, nobles/warriors, commoners/farmers/merchants. The fourth caste of servants is added in the *Manu Smriti,* or Hindu law code. These Laws of Manu were composed between 200 BCE and 200 CE.[160] Herein is found the dharma of each caste.

What is delineated in the Manu Smriti must be done in order to be reincarnated to a higher caste. As the castes are ordered so is the universe. What one does in this life as described by one's dharma (caste-obligations) results in one's karma. It is this never-ending cycle (samsara) that one seeks to escape (moksha) and transcend. Our family, in other words, is essential to our spirituality, for it is here that we learn, live, and determine our future. But, ideally, we are not bound to our families for our entire life—at least if we are males of the first three castes. According to the Laws of Manu, the dharma of these men, aside from that required by their caste, was to be first students, then to marry, then to have children, and once the children were grown, to live a simple life, and, finally, to become a *sannyasin* (renunciant)—living alone without possessions and without any desires.[161] In doing so one is prepared for the final transcendence. One's spirituality, for males of the first three castes, is dependent not only on birth but also on age. Living the proper dharma for both these assures a better reincarnation in the next life.

Hindu Ethics

What is right and wrong, or good and bad, then, is determined by one's dharma. As we have seen with many cultures, there is no clear distinction in Hinduism between religion and culture, spirituality and societal expectations. Nor is it crystal clear what my exact path is to moksha. How do I discover my path and clear dharma? A personal *guru* is the best way. This Indian word has been overburdened with meanings as Hindu ideas have come into Western culture. Yet within Hinduism, the guru is one who teaches us special things about

> *Try Bhakti yoga:* Love of god is all of life.

ourselves, our moksha, and how to achieve it. Our guru gives us our personal *mantra.* We have already seen the most basic mantra, *om.* Mantras are seen by many gurus as thought forms of reality, and by chanting them we control the reality expressed by them. Thus when our guru gives us our mantra, he or she is providing us with the essence of who we are and the means to become who we are through the perfect chanting of our mantra.[162] Yet, for most Hindus, it is not the blessed ability to have the time, interest, and, perhaps, money to seek a guru, follow the guru, and chant one's mantra but rather the everyday seeking to survive from hour to hour that they, and their spirituality, are challenged by. In India, the home of Hinduism, the 2001 Census states that the overall literacy rate was 65.38 percent (Male: 75.96 percent, Female: 54.28 percent).[163] Such statistics underline the necessity for a spirituality of survival that provides individuals with a sense of control over their lives and their futures. This spirituality must be found primarily in one's family (jati), one's household shrine, and one's gods.

Hindu Ritual

Every religion has embedded within it a spirituality of survival. Those within Hinduism are examples of what is present in all religions. A spirituality of survival consists of those signposts that provide the means of entering into, coping with, and coming out of the transformative life events that challenge all of us: birth, suffering, marriage, death, job, personal relationships, and what we call self-image today. The signpost of ritual, especially magical ritual, is central to a spirituality of survival. Magical ritual has the repetition that is part of all rituals, but added to this repetition is a conviction that if the ritual is done perfectly, the end of the ritual will be achieved. "Done perfectly" includes not only the ritual combination of words and actions but also the interior disposition described as faith by some, intention by others, and devotion by still others. In many instances the ritual is one of accommodating the gods, saints, angels, or spirits whom we wish to care for us. The accommodation usually takes the form of sacrifices of various kinds as well as devotional prayer and action. Hinduism includes all these. We will review four: *bhakti yoga* (*bhakti marga*), the home altar, temple sacrifice, and tantric meditative practices.

The way of devotion (*bhakti yoga/ bhakti marga)* is designated in the Bhagavad Gita as one of the major ways of transcending this life. A shrine to some deity in one's home is one of the best expressions of this affection. *Puja*[164] is the term used when speaking about the diverse means of expressing one's relationship to the deity. Every Hindu home has its shrine. These are diverse in construction, placement, and expansiveness. They are the core of the spiritual life, for it is here that we are in contact with our god or gods, with our desires, and our interaction with both gods and desires. Fruits, food, and burning incense are all types of sacrifice daily offered to the god for individual and family benefit. In turn, the family shares the food and drink after offering it to the deity. A common practice is also to touch the image of the deity in some way. On some occasions the entire family may gather for a more intricate ritual where the head of the family chants prayers while others bathe the image of the deity and offer sacrifices of some sort.

As puja is carried out at home, so it is carried out in temples by priests dedicated to a god who will fulfill the particular needs of the petitioners. The priest's role is both to care for the image of the deity as well as carry out rituals required by the deity and/or by those who come with their requests for the deity. *Yajna* is an ancient ritual whose central focus is the sacred fire. In rituals performed by Vedic priests, a fire or fires are present in which one priest casts the sacrifices into the fire while he and others chant ancient Vedic prayers.[165]

A typical Hindu marriage ceremony is a *yajna*. The belief is that anything cast into the fire as sacrifice goes to the gods. Animal sacrifices are also found among some Hindus, especially in Northeastern India and Nepal. The most famous animal sacrifices are those that occur every five years at the Gadhimai festival in Nepal where they sacrifice thousands of animals over several days. Most animal sacrifice is to the mother goddess, *Shakti*. Shakti has many and diverse names and functions in the Hindu pantheon. These sacrifices take place because she is seen as the source of all good things, and the sacrifice to her is seen as a means of eliciting her favor to meet our present needs.

These sacrifices to her reflect her powerful presence among Hindus. This all began between 400 CE and 1500 CE as part of the larger bhakti (devotional) yoga movement. The gods Vishnu and Shiva are also part of this movement with all the devotional practices associated with them. Shakti, however, is worthy of our attention because of both her presence in art of every sort and a communicable energy present in her; Shakti means power or might. Shakti is the power of creation, the power of transcendence, the power of change. To participate in that power in some way, one must learn the rituals appropriate to doing so.[166]

An aspect of Shakti that has gained a great deal of attention in the West is *Tantrism*, which has been translated into a ritual that is a type of muscle-mind-spirit control of sexual activity. Translations of this type are common in Hindu spirituality. Most scholars refer to this interpretation of Tantrism as pop Tantrism or California Tantrism.[167] The reason they do so is because many of its Western practitioners confuse Tantric bliss with orgasmic pleasure. Tantrism is a yoga and as such it requires traditional Hindu rules of conduct, extensive meditation, and, usually, the guidance of a guru. That being said, the conviction of all practitioners is that with preparation and the proper ritual action, the power of Shakti can be used for all the necessities of survival spirituality and an ultimate transformation from samsara.[168]

This same focus of god-like energies is found through forms of meditation such as that practiced by *siddhars*, holy men, who claim they can read minds, transmit themselves over long distances, go without food and drink, and perform many other wonders. The focus of these otherworldly energies through a variety of meditative practices results in their wonderful perfections (*saddhis*) to achieve this-worldly wonders. Siddha medicine and the *varmam* art of self-defense are found in parts of India as a result of the siddhars' activities.[169] Before the advent of modern beliefs, the siddhars played an important role in the development of the Hindu rituals considered necessary in survival spirituality.

Hindu Belief and the Inner Desire for Transcendence

If belief is founded in a conviction that there is more to life than we experience, then *Jnana yoga* is belief par excellence. It distrusts everything. It says that we must believe nothing that we hear, feel, see, or touch. We must go beyond belief and beyond understanding to perfect our spirituality, to realize we are Brahman. This is true belief. This is the *Jnâna yoga* (Gnana yoga) the way of knowledge.

> **Try Jnana yoga:**
> - *Believe nothing.*
> - *Control your senses.*
> - *Control your mind.*
> - *Concentrate.*
> - *Renounce all that is not dharma.*

We have seen karma yoga, the way of action, when we reviewed the signpost of community, and bhakti yoga, the way of devotion, when looking at ritual. Here we must re-examine those essential principles of Hindu belief in light of *Jnana yoga*. According to Adi Sankara (788 CE to 821 CE) in his *Crest Jewel of Wisdom*,[170] we begin this way by sustaining a deep desire to escape all time and place through the practice of the six virtues: control of one's mind, control of one's senses, endurance, faith, perfect concentration, and renouncing everything that is not part of dharma. Such practice will result in perfect detachment from the here and now, resulting in the ability to distinguish between what is real (Brahman) and what is not real (everything else). Note that the reading, thinking, and reflecting you are doing right now is part of that which is not real because you are Brahman, the eternal; everything else is illusion. You, *atman*, are Brahman. With such a realization, you break free from the wheel of karma and experience moksha. Just as a drop of water falling into the ocean becomes ocean water, so our atman, upon attaining moksha, becomes Brahman. Such a realization is not a reasoning process but an experiential one.

Bhakti yoga, of course, does not see moksha in such impersonal terms but rather as a state of eternal bliss filled with the devotional pleasure from the sight of our god. This eternal presence with our god is the culmination of a lifetime of darshan, the affective, sight-filled embracing of our god.

Every touch, every darshan, every sacrifice throughout life gradually breaks the karma of past life to enable our eternal future with god in his or her heavenly loka.

This brief description of *Jnana yoga* brings to an end our review of the diverse ways Hinduism deals with the mystery of life. We are limited because we accept the illusion (*maya*) of limitation, and the mystery is intensified by our negative actions (karma) that reinforce this illusion. Things are mysterious only when you don't understand what they really are. Just as someone who doesn't understand what a television is may see it as a window into someone's home, we sometimes see mysteries in life when there are none. We can break out of this cycle of illusion and limitation in three ways: the way of action, the way of devotion, and the way of knowledge. This is not easy, but it can be done. It is up to you to choose, to act, to be who you really are.

Key Facts For Hindu Spirituality

SPIRITUAL-ITY and RELIGION	PLACE OF ORIGIN	MEMBER-SHIP	KEY DATES	CENTRAL PERSON	BOOKS
HINDUISM	INDIA	Fourth in the world. Among the smallest in North America	2750 BCE, 1175, 1690, 1947 CE		Rig Veda(Vedas) 1500;Upanishads 800-400 BCE; The Bhagavad-Gita 500-200 CE
CORE ISSUE	**BELIEFS**	**RITUALS**	**MORALS**	**ORGANIZA-TION.**	**PROMISE**
Desire as formative of the conscious self (ignorance and illusion)	Karma, Rebirth, Liberation/ escape (Moksha) One eternal self— who we are. Atman is Brahman.	Home altar and Puja Devotion to gods and goddesses Life cycle Meditation Chants Mantra	Kama (plea-sure), Artha (wealth) Duty (Dharma) to the proper order of things. Mosha (libera-tion) Caste. No meat, fish, eggs, alcohol, gambling, or illicit sex	Caste (Jati) Temples	Liberation; escape from this Illusionary life

Reform of Ancient Hinduism

Hinduism does not have a central authority. As a religious tradition, however, it does have its signposts, which have acted as such throughout the centuries. As an ancient culture, many of its most ancient texts, the Vedas, became sacred touchstones of religious authenticity. Naturally there are diverse understandings and ways of putting them into practice. The signposts presented above reflect the dominant interpretation of these texts and the way most Hindus practice their religion. The reforms and interpretations of the past were part of that presentation. Historically, however, some of the understanding of these texts and their resultant signposts gave rise to not only reforms of Hinduism but also new religions. For our purposes, three particular reform movements help us understand more of Hinduism as well as offer significant differences from it. Two of these are generally recognized as religions: Jainism (567 BCE) and Buddhism (551 BCE). Another reform movement is many times offered as a contemporary summary of Hinduism, for it is the first to offer a clear delineation of ways to break samsara. This movement is expressed in the *Bhagavad Gita* (*Song of God*: 200-300 CE[171]). Let us begin with it.

The Bhagavad Gita as an Instrument of Reform: Love in the Vedas

The Vedas' origins go back at least a thousand years before the Common Era. They are a touchstone of Hindu orthodoxy even while Hindus claim to be inclusive of all views. They contain hymns and formulas to be used by the priests in their sacrifices. In addition to the Vedas are the Upanishads.[172] These are the scholarly reflections on the rituals portrayed in the Vedas. Particularly the earlier part of the Upanishads, the *Mukhaya Upanishads*, are part of that same primitive foundation of orthodoxy.

Death is of no consequence.

The *Bhagavad Gita* summarizes and provides a pivotal perspective on these ancient writings. The yogas we reviewed above are the summary provided in the *Gita* of the ancient writings. The pivotal perspective is at times a challenge to the impersonal view of the universe found in the sacred writings and a strong affirmative thrust into the future for Bhakti yoga.

The Gita, as the *Bhagavad Gita* is often called, centers around the story of a warrior, *Arjuna*, and his chariot driver, *Krishna*. In the midst of a battle Arjuna refuses to fight when he sees all the death it will cause. Krishna argues that death does not matter; only duty (dharma) does. A warrior's dharma is to fight. To do so, the warrior will be liberated from samsara. Knowledge does the same thing. But even more, love and devotion are above all these other yogas. Krishna reveals himself to be the supreme god, Vishnu. Here in the human form of the charioteer is the impersonal force and power that underlines the universe. Krishna proclaims, "Take refuge in devotion to me" (XII.11); "Love me" (IX.33); "If you love me, you will not perish" (IX.33).

What the Gita does is continue the advocacy of the past found in the Vedas and the early Upanishads while affirming the myriad devotions expressed in the rituals that had grown up over time as ways to break from samsara. If the love Arjuna displayed for Krishna was the love that was expressed in these devotions, then everyone could stop the terror

> **Love of Krishna is everything.**

of karma and realize what the early Upanishads taught and the Vedas sought through sacrifice: Atman is Brahman—the end of life as we know it.

Jainist Reform: Do Not Kill Anything or Anyone

Historians consider Nataputta Vardhamana (597-527 BCE), called Mahavira, the founder of Jainism. Jains see him as the last *tirthankara*. A tirthankara is someone who has found a way to cross over the river of rebirth (samsara). He is seen as the twenty-fourth, and last, tirthankara in this cosmic cycle. He was a warrior, married, with one young daughter. He abandoned this life and wandered naked through-out India seeking to live a life of self-denial and

> **Kill no living being.**

to avoid attachments at all costs. He never stayed more than a day in any one place. He lived a life of *ahimsa* (non injury; non-violence) to such an extent that he strained the water he drank through a cloth so anything living in the water would not be destroyed in his drinking. He swept where he walked with a broom for the same purpose. Thirteen years after he began, he reached the point of complete detachment.

The movement that evolved from his life and teaching rejected the sacrifices and chanting of the priests expressed in the Vedas as a way of breaking samsara and replaced it with a life of total asceticism condensed in the Five Great Vows (*mahavratas*): non-violence, truth, non-stealing, chastity, and detachment. The *Namokār Mantra* is a ritual summarizing both the history and commitment of the movement:

> *Namo Arihantânam. Namo Siddhânam. Namo Âyariyânam.*
> *Namo Uvajjhâyanam. Namo Loe Savva Sahûnam. Eso Panch*
> *Namokkaro, Savva Pâvappanâsano Mangalanam Cha Savvesim,*
> *Padhamam Havai Mangalam.*

> *I bow to the Arihantâs (Prophets). I bow to the Siddhâs (Liberated*
> *Souls). I bow to the Âchâryas (Preceptors or Spiritual Leaders). I*
> *bow to the Upadhyâya (Teachers). I bow to all the Sadhûs (Saints).*

This fivefold bow destroys all sins and obstacles and of all auspicious mantras, is the first and foremost one.[173]

Behind these signposts of ritual and ethics is a deep and challenging belief system that uses the words of the Hindu tradition but understands them differently. It is not so much atman that is the self but the *jiva*, which we might translate as spirit or soul.[174] There are an infinite number of eternal jiva, each with pure knowledge, goodness and perfect happiness; each with a certain number of senses—for example, humans with five, plants with one (touch). The jiva, however, is weighed down by karma. When we do anything it results in karma. And karma is not spiritual but material. It weighs down the soul, thus limiting it. For example, our karma results in limited knowledge. If we did nothing then we would not have karma. The purpose of rituals, ethical behavior, vows, and asceticism in general is to free us from karma and become, once again, the jiva we truly are.

Jainism does not look to the Vedas for its source of inspiration. When it does look to written materials, it looks to those called the *agamas* (tradition), which are a compilation of the teachings of important holy men throughout time including Mahavira. It takes the nonviolence inherent in Hinduism and makes it the central theme of its spirituality. One might say that it sees the nonviolence offered to cows and asks us to do the same to all living creatures; it sees the sacred Ganges not only as the water of purification and the place of many sacred shrines but also as a seemingly unending power of karma and its consequent samsara.[175] It sees these and proclaims that you are eternal; beyond your karma is a "you" of eternal bliss and knowledge; a "you" that can be discovered by nonviolence, truth, non-stealing, chastity, and detachment..

> **Control of body-mind relationships makes you free.**

Buddhist Reform: The Middle Way

The Buddhist movement begins with Siddhartha Gautama (563-483 BCE) in India and expands throughout Asia. Together with Islam and Christianity, it is one of the world's largest, as well as oldest, religions. It began in India but is a minor force there today, whereas it has deep and continual influence throughout the rest of Asia.

There are many stories about its founder, Siddhartha Gautama. Most are filled with great miracles and awe-inspiring constellations of heaven and earth. The core of the story, or at least the one most repeated, is that he was born into the warrior class. He lived a protected life in which he encountered neither suffering nor death. He married and had one child. He possessed, however, a deep, unsatisfied yearning that his upper class life never satisfied. This unfulfilled desire led him to look for fulfillment. He began to venture beyond the family compound. In his adventures, he witnessed suffering, the pain of old age, and death: a stumbling old man, a sick man wracked with pain, and the body of a dead man being carried to be cremated. Such suffering and death overwhelmed him until, in one of his travels, he saw a monk in his yellow robe walking calmly along the road. These are called the "four passing sights."

With the sight of the monk, he returned home feeling that he had to do something about his life. One night he left home, shaved his head, clothed himself in the robe of a monk, and began to seek how to end suffering and death. This is known as "the great renunciation." With this he began his search. First he went to the priests (the Brahmins), then he tried the meditative techniques found in writings such as the *Upanishads*, and finally he lived the life of intense asceticism much like that found among the Jains.

None of these succeeded in helping him calm his desires. A turning point came in his ascetical life when, after five years of fasting, he fainted in the company of five ascetical companions. It seemed he was dead. He was revived and given food and drink. He ate it, and in eating it resolved that the way of asceticism was also unsuccessful. What to do? Rejected by his companions who saw his eating and drinking as heretical, and realizing that all the usual spiritual paths were useless, he determined to continue his search.

He sat down under a fig tree, now called a *bodhi,* or enlightenment, tree, and began to meditate with the purpose of discovering the answer to his quest. Two descriptions of what happened from diverse Buddhist scriptures are helpful to understand both his possible experiences and the foundation of Buddhism.

The first description centers on temptation. Mara, the god of death, overwhelmed him with the pleasures of his old life, but this did not stop Siddhartha's meditation. Mara tried again by sending his three daughters Discontent, Delight, and Desire. Siddhartha called the earth to aid: his left hand was in his lap facing upward; his right hand was on his knee with its fingers touching the earth. With this Mara-defying act, Siddhartha realized that it was desire that kept him trapped in samsara. With this realization he was enlightened—he broke the cycle of life and death; he entered Nirvana. He was now Buddha, the enlightened one, awake to the way of ordering one's life. These hand gestures are embedded in many statues of Buddha.[176]

The second description marks the progress of his meditation through the night. In the evening he realized all the lives he had lived in the past; at midnight he saw (with the divine eye) the cyclical life and death of all beings and how karma effected each of them; late at night he stopped his desire for everything and grasped the essence of how to do that, which is comprised in the Four Noble Truths. He was now Buddha.

Both stories do not end with his becoming enlightened. They go on to describe how he had to make a decision of whether to tell others how to become enlightened or continue in Nirvana. He decided to return and tell everyone how to become enlightened. When the sun rose, he returned to discover gathered around him the five ascetics who had rejected him. He then proceeded to give what has come to be known as the Deer Park Sermon. He described the Middle Way as being that which falls between that of the self-denial of ascetics and the self-indulgence of the hedonists. His proclaimed Middle Way of ordering life (dhamma/dharma) became known as Buddhism.

This Middle Way of spirituality is summarized in the Four Noble Truths: all life is suffering (dukkha); the cause of suffering is desire; stopping desire will stop suffering; the Eightfold Path is the best way to stop desire. The Eightfold Path consists of the following: right views, right intention, right speech, right action, right livelihood, right effort, right mindfulness, and right concentration.

Siddhartha Gautama lived forty-five years after his awakening and being accepted as Buddha. With his death, never to be reborn again, Buddhism began. Hinduism and the Vedas were reformed.

Buddhist Spirituality

Buddham saranam gacchami
Dhammam saranam gacchami
Sangham saranam gacchami

I go for refuge in the Buddha.
I go for refuge in the Dhahamma
I go for refuge in the Sangha[177]

This chant and prayer called the *Three Jewels* or Refuges (Buddha, *dhamma*, *sangha*) is generally considered to be the center of Buddhist spirituality. This rendition is in the Pali language and comes from the Theravada Buddhist denomination. The practice of prayer, the intent of prayer, and the language of prayer differ from denomination to denomination and from culture to culture. The variety of expressions of Buddha's original experience and teaching at Deer Park are significantly diverse. Three of these are not only good examples but also solid branches from which others have sprouted. These are Theravada, Mahayana, and Vajrayana.

Everything is always changing.

Key Facts for Buddhist Spirituality

SPIRITUAL-ITY and RELIGION	PLACE OF ORIGIN	MEMBER-SHIP	KEY DATES	CENTRAL PERSON	BOOKS
BUDDHISM	INDIA	Fifth largest in the world. Among the smaller groups in North America	563-483, 220-552 BCE; 749, 1175 CE	SIDDARTHA GAUTAMA 563 (BCE) (BUDDHA)	The Dham-mapada
CORE ISSUE	**BELIEFS**	**RITUALS**	**MORALS**	**ORGANIZATION.**	**PROMISE**
Suffering because our conscious self is the result of craving and delusion.	Anatman: no eternal self; all is change Rebirth Nirvana	Yogas	Five precepts Eightfold path	Theravada Mahayana Vajrayana	Nirvana

The Spirituality of Theravada Buddhism

Theravada Buddhism claims to follow the original message and methods of Siddhartha. The signposts are a brief summary of its approach to the spiritual life.

Belief. Our spiritual life must recognize that all of life is suffering (duk-kha). Material progress, better products, better food and drink, sexual encounters, friendships, and pleasant music are only expressions of the suffering that surrounds us and is attached to all of these realities. Nothing but suffering exists because nothing is permanent. Everything is always changing. Only that which is permanent will satisfy us permanently—forever.

But everything is changing, including our very selves. There is no atman, no self. The only reason there seems to be such a reality is because we desire it and because of what we have done in the past and present (karma). There is no such thing as a god because there is nothing permanent: neither Brahman, god, natural laws, feelings, relationships—nothing. So what is left when we die, and when the entire universe ceases to exist? Energy? Bits of matter? Souls? Spirit? None of these, Theravada Buddhism replies. But, one might ask, what does last forever? The reply: We don't know.

Ethics and Ritual. The way we get to this I-don't-know state of life is by walking the eightfold path. It is open to everyone, but in actual practice, only monks and nuns can do so since they are able to concentrate on what is required. The lay person has other concerns to deal with: job, family, education, and everything else that goes into the daily living of most people's lives. The Five Precepts summarize the minimum of what is required: abstain from taking life, abstain from taking what is not given, abstain from sexual misconduct, abstain from false speech, and abstain from fermented drink that causes heedlessness.[178]

> You cause suffering when you ignore its causes.

Abstaining in these ways while trying to live the eightfold path should get you, in the next reincarnation, to the life of a monk or nun. You are helped in this upper movement of reincarnation by going to a *stupa*. These are important places dedicated to Buddha. Inside these dome or bell-shaped buildings are carvings of sacred spirits described in the stories of Buddha, probably a statue of Buddha, and places to walk and recite verses from the Pali Canon. In addition to visiting a stupa, an ordinary lay person should also give food and drink to the monks and nuns when they come begging. Young people, especially young men, should spend a few years in the monastery learning how to mediate and live an ascetic life. Mediation is an essential ritual in the Buddhist's spiritual life and is best learned from someone adept in its practice. In imitation of Buddha we can train ourselves to leave all, realize the fickleness of existence, and break into Nirvana.[179]

> Others can help you know suffering's causes.

Community (Sangha). In a spirituality that disdains relationships and emphasizes the fragility of togetherness, the *Sangha* is proclaimed as essential to its existence. Siddhartha's Middle Way, between the lonely wandering ascetic and the pleasure-filled lay life, is lived in community, especially the community of monks and nuns. Monks and nuns are an essential part of Buddhism. Here in Theravada Buddhism they are the ideal of Buddhist life. Living together they strive for the enlightenment obtained by Siddhartha.

The Spirituality of Mahayana Buddhism

Mahayana Buddhism, known as the Great Vehicle, is the largest of the denominations and is predominant in China, Korea, Japan, and Vietnam. This is the "greater vehicle" because it is a means for everyone to cross the river of samsara to what lies beyond. Three beliefs distinguish Mahayana from Theravada Buddhism: everything possesses the nature of Buddha; other heavenly Buddhas and compassionate beings (*bodhisattvas*) can help us become a Buddha; and *sunyata* (emptiness).

Buddhism says that everyone in one of his or her lifetimes can be enlightened. Theravada Buddhism recognizes that there is only one Buddha: one who became enlightened and continues to live so that everyone can imitate him and be enlightened. On the contrary, Mahayana Buddhism says not only that anyone can be enlightened, but also that anyone can return to this mode of existence to aid others. Each of us has this Buddha nature which is evident with our disgust with suffering, our wish for Nirvana, and our striving for enlightenment. That which made Siddhartha Buddha is in each of us and thus we are part of Buddha's cosmic body. One might say, that Buddha is manifested through Siddhartha and a cosmic Buddha is manifested in all living things. There is a third body or manifestation of Buddha in the heavenly realms. Consequently there are three Buddhas: cosmic, heavenly, and Siddhartha. What made Siddhartha Buddha was certainly enlightenment but even more it was compassion. It is compassion that makes one a Buddha. It is compassion that is part of each of us. The perfection of compassion takes many lifetimes, but it can occur. Those in which both enlightenment and compassion have occurred are called *bodhisattva*. These compassionate beings and those seeking to be compassionate help each other fulfill their Buddhahood. This is especially done through the six "perfections" (*paramitas*): giving, morality, patience, vigor, meditation, and wisdom. When practiced consistently, they lead to a compassionate style of life.[180]

Sunyata (emptiness) is a term found in Buddhism in general and is best understood by how it is applied in practice by the spiritual masters. Usually it is not understood as another way of saying zero, nothingness; instead, *sunyata* makes us conscious of the fact that nothing is what it seems because everything is always changing, and all of life is unsubstantial. Consequently nothing and no one is deserving of our total concentration and dedication. Our realization of sunyata is a step on our journey to enlightenment.

Varieties of Mahayana Buddhism: Pure Land, Zen (Japan) / Ch'an (China)

Namu Amida Butsu.
I place my faith in Amida Buddha.[181]

Mahayana Buddhism became more inclusive as it emigrated into China, Korea, and Japan with what became Pure Land Buddhism. The basis of Pure Land is the story of *Amitabha,* the heavenly Buddha, who lived in the heavenly region known as Pure Land or Western Paradise. This land was inhabited by gods and humans. Pure Land Buddhism says that you can get into Pure Land by calling on *Amitabha* with deep affection and trust at death to bring you there. In Pure Land one would be prepared for Buddhahood and enlightenment. The chanted repetition of the prayer *Namu Amida Butsu* (quoted above), especially at death, is the means to arrive in this heaven. *Jodo-Shinshu*, known in the United States as the Buddhist Churches of America, is part of Pure Land with one significant addition: *Namu Amida Butsu* is not a request to enter Pure Land but a thankful response to Buddha for his gift of the means to get there.

The devotional and to some extent survival spirituality of Pure Land coincides in many Asian cultures with a more abstract and disciplined type of Mahayana Buddhism known as *Ch'an* in China and *Zen* in Japan. We will review what happens to spiritualities when they blend with American culture in Part Three. Zen teachers of Buddhism emphasize two things: the necessary role of meditation with total concentration on the object of meditation, and the absurdity of using language and rational concepts to understand anything, let alone spirituality. Remember, there is only one major truth: you are Buddha. My suggestion of starting part two with a blank page would fit their approach. But they would also add that all the other words and ideas after that blank page are useless for understanding spiritual truth and realizing one's Buddhahood. Each Zen master has his or her unique way of coming to realize spiritual truth, which is hidden behind layers of desire and rationality (heart and mind). Two major Zen approaches to meditation are *Soto* and *Rinzai*. Both use sitting meditation as the major way to enlightenment. While Soto uses only sitting mediation, Rinzai also uses physical techniques such as a slap, a yell, or a push on the one meditating to shock the person into realizing the truth. *Koans* are also typically used as riddles to stop all rational thought. For example

Well versed in the Buddha way,
I go the non-Way
Without abandoning my
Ordinary person's affairs.
The conditioned and
Name-and-form,
All are flowers in the sky.
Nameless and formless,
I leave birth-and-death.[182]

Zen has influenced martial arts in China and Japan. It results in great concentration in the moment, such as pouring tea (Japanese Tea Ceremony), haiku poetry, and an approach to beauty that emphasizes the spontaneous and natural.

The Spirituality of Vajrayana Buddhism

Vajrayana (Tibetan/Tantric/The Diamond Vehicle/ Thunderbolt Vehicle) Buddhism is related to the Hindu Tantric tradition by way of Padma-Sambhava, an eighth-century holy man who brought it from India to Tibet and other places in Asia. As with all Tantric systems, *Vajrayana* sees the cosmos in pairs, male and female. Contrary to the Indian perspective, the pairs here are male and female Buddhas. One shares in these powers through the use of fasting, prayer, and repetition of magical formulas and action. One of the most powerful magical chants is *Om mani padme hum* (Om! The jewel is in the lotus, hum!). Many people chant this mantra, but only the initiates know its meaning. The prayer wheel, the *Mani* in Tibet, is a non-verbal way to continually invoke the mantra. It does so by being turned by hand, the wind, or some other mechanism. It is seen as a way to ward off evil and pray to the Buddhas for favors.

The most well-known form of Tibetan Buddhism is Yellow Hat Buddhism. Tibetan Buddhism shares with Buddhism in general its emphasis on the monastery and its monks. In the fourteenth century a reform movement among the monasteries was led by a group that became known as the Yellow Hat, or *gelug*, monks who wore yellow to display their intent to reform the monasteries. Celibacy, for example, was introduced. This reform movement dominated Buddhism in Tibet and spread to Mongolia, Russia, and Siberia. Early in the development of the Yellow Hat movement the idea of the Grand Lama, or with time, the Dalai Lama, developed. It began with the belief that the head Lama of each monastery was the incarnation of a Buddha. Towards the end of the sixteenth century, the title of Dalai Lama was reserved for only one person, the Grand Lama of the monastery at Lhasa, the principle city of Tibet. He is seen to be the incarnation of the Buddha *Avalokita*.

Comparing Buddhist Spiritualities

	Theravada	Mahayana	Vajrayana
Origins	483 CE	500 CE	700 CE
Also known as	School of the Elders	The Great Vehicle Chan, Tendai, Pure Land, Zen, Nichiren	Tibetan, Tantric, Diamond Vehicle, Tantrayana, Mantrayana, Shinogon
Inherent to (Minor influence in India after 250 BCE)	India, Siri Lanka, South East Asia	India, East Asia	India, Tibet, East Asia
Buddha is…	Siddhartha Gautama, the enlightened one	Cosmic Siddhartha Gautama	One of many male and female cosmic Buddhas
Texts	Pali Canon	The Lotus Sutra and Diamond Sutra are two of many	Most are transmitted orally. *Bardo Thodol* (The Tibetan Book of the Dead)
Pivotal concern	Enlightenment	Compassion	The power of enlightenment. (Vajrayana: The Diamond or Thunderbolt Vehicle)
Present model of human perfection	Arhat: One who has followed the Buddha in the Middle way of dedication to the dharma	Bodhisattva: the sharing in the compassionate empowering of self and others in their Buddha nature	Lama: one who possesses special magical powers revealing them as Buddha and bodhisattva

Seeking Harmony With All:
Taoism, Confucianism, and
the Origins of all Classical Spiritualities:
The Indigenous Experience

When the Great Way prevailed, the world community was equally shared by all. The worthy and able were chosen as office-holders. Mutual confidence was fostered and good neighborliness cultivated. Therefore, people did not regard as parents only their own parents, nor did they treat only their own children as children. Provision was made for the aged until their death, the adults were given employment, and the young enabled to grow up. Old widows and widowers, the orphaned, the old and childless, as well as the sick and the disabled were all well taken care of. Men had their proper roles and women their homes. While they hated to see wealth lying about on the ground, they did not necessarily keep it for their own use. While they hated not to exert their effort, they did not necessarily devote it to their own ends. Thus evil schemings were repressed, and robbers, thieves and other lawless elements failed to arise so that outer doors did not have to be shut. This was called the age of Great Harmony.[183]

Heaven is my father and Earth is my mother—all people are my brothers and sisters, and all things are my companions.[184]

***

The Tao that can be trodden is not the enduring and unchanging Tao. The name that can be named is not the enduring and unchanging name.

(Conceived of as) having no name, it is the Originator of heaven and earth; (conceived of as) having a name, it is the Mother of all things.

Always without desire we must be found,
If its deep mystery we would sound;
But if desire always within us be,
Its outer fringe is all that we shall see.

Under these two aspects, it is really the same; but as development takes place, it receives the different names. Together we call them the Mystery. Where the Mystery is the deepest is the gate of all that is subtle and wonderfull.[185]

Another name for *Tao* is "the way" or "path." Central to this great way, this Tao, is the existence of the harmony which is its foundation. Every spirituality seeks it. Near Eastern religions consciously acknowledge and search for it. The Tao cannot be named. It is imagined as a stream that is in constant motion. The only reality is the Tao, and only those who go with its flow are real. It is not a god nor is it the creator God. Words will never express Tao, but we must endeavor to do so to enter its flow.

> **Your spiritual path is our spiritual path.**

The religions of the Near East began, like those in India, before recorded history: in the deep mystery of the cycle of the seasons inherent to agricultural societies and the wonder of life and death that is so much a part of them. Where the Indian religions saw the dismal wheel of life-death-another life-another death, the Chinese saw the harmonious fruitfulness and interconnectedness of all life and death. The classical spiritualities of India sought to escape death's cycle by searching within; those of the Near East sought to embrace this fruitful interconnectedness with all its tensions. Both these spiritualities presupposed that the realities they experienced were ever present in a here and now with no beginning and no end. No mechanical clocks marked linear time, but rather, the ever-present repeated cycle of life and death defined all of existence, as well as the presence of the seen and the unseen, the presence of forces seemingly unable to be controlled with the technologies of the time, and the presence of personalities powerful enough to come out of nowhere to subjugate them and demand their obedience. This was a world of a hierarchy of spirits, of ritual magic, of earth, fire, wind, water, wood, and metal. This was a world of opposing forces of light and dark, of heat and cold, of male and female. When all these forces worked together harmoniously, there were good harvests, healthy bodies, comfortable families, long lives, and enlightened leaders. There was not chaos here but the *yang* and *yin* that accounted for the moon's phases as well as the sea's tides; the changes that could lead to life or death; the mystery of the way—the Tao (Dao).

Chinese Spirituality

Confucianism and Taoism best express this ancient religious culture. Confucianism originates with *K'ung fu-tzu* (551-479 BCE). The name, when transliterated into Western languages, is Confucius; if it was translated it would be "Great Master Kung." Taoism (Daoism) originates with *Lao Tzu* (604-520 BCE) and the famous spiritual masterpiece *Tao-te-ching*. Ancient stories link the man with the book. Modern analysts suggest that this is not so, but for our purposes, it makes no difference since both author and book share the same perspective.[186] Each of these perspectives finds its origins in the spiritual beginnings of the culture itself which has the following signposts.

Belief

> **A harmonious balance of self and society results in a happy life for all.**

The universe, if left to itself, is in harmony. In contemporary language we might say that the laws of the universe are unchanging. They are obvious expressions of a rationality we, as rational creatures, can discover. We are in trouble when we tinker with them as a result of what we discover as we create an irrational, chaotic, and disharmonious universe. Whether in the ancient Chinese perspective or the modern scientific perspective, humans are what cause things to come apart. We are presently in a world devoid of harmony and in need of the methods of bringing things together.

Essential to things being harmonious is the right proportion of those forces that keep it in harmony: *yin* and *yang*. Everything is composed of these two forces. A human male, for example, is predominantly *yang*; a human female is predominantly *yin*. But both are made up of *yin* and *yang*. To be fully human their *yang* and *yin* must be in balance. The *yang* force is usually described as one that is active, hard, warm, dry, bright, positive, expansive, procreative, and masculine. The *Yin* force is passive, soft, cold, wet, dark, negative, contracting, and feminine. As you can see, they are opposites. Everything is made up of these two opposing forces, which must come into balance to make things better. The more in balance our lives become, the more whole and spiritual we become. The more in balance everything in the universe is, the fuller and more harmonious we are. We achieve such harmony by doing the right things toward each other and the entire universe.

> **Reverence, loyalty, and respect sustain the harmony of life.**

Ethics and Ritual

There is an inherent power in all of us to do the right thing. This is called *te*, which many times is translated *virtue*. When people are virtuous, life is in harmony; when not, life is chaotic. Confucianism and Taoism have different emphases and interpretations of the role of virtue in life; common to both are the importance of it in one's life. They also share the importance of showing due reverence, loyalty, and respect to one's parents and all others in authority. They, in turn, are to show respect to you.

As with most ancient religions, the beginnings of Chinese religion also worshiped gods. These gods, if worshiped properly, determined the fertility of soil, the catch of fish, and a good harvest. Offering-rituals associated with temples, shrines, and home altars engaged the power of the gods to fulfill the wishes of those making the offerings.

Divining the future was also part of this ancient religion. The third century BCE *Book of Changes* (*I Ching*) is a classic in this regard; it has been used by people throughout the centuries to discover what will happen to them. It began as reading the cracks in dry bones or turtle shells to discern the *yang* (unbroken lines) and *yin* (broken lines) of the forces at work in our present that will soon be our future. The same basic approach is found in another example of ancient symbolic magic called *Feng-shui* (wind-water). This is based on another foundational conviction of the ancient Chinese: the role of *qi (ch'i)*. It has always been a challenge for translators to convey in English what this means. The closest, it seems, is that it means life-energy/force. Ancient healers built systems of acupuncture around these ideas of *yang, yin,* and *qi*. In *Feng-shui*, the forces present in nature are discerned for the betterment of the inquirer. When done, the house, furniture, windows, or anything can be arranged to provide a balanced harmonious location for the one seeking betterment.

Community

China, both yesterday and today, is an enormous land populated with millions of people. Today it possesses the third largest land mass in the world and the largest population. There is tremendous diversity. Until very recently the community was the village. The spirituality that developed focused on peasant life and the necessity of linking everyone together in a harmonious community. With so much diversity, so many people, and a large land mass, the challenge of any leader was how to bring it all together. The answer, for the most part, was by physical force. This resulted in constant war among the diverse local leaders and serial rule by emperors. Between the rule of two of these unifying imperial dynasties, the Zhou and the Quin (722-221 BCE), severe and constant war challenged people to look deep into their culture to bring about communal harmony. The challenge was taken up by two formative Chinese spiritualities: Confucianism and Taoism.

Community and Confucian Spirituality

The Great Master Kung (551-479 BCE), *K'ung fu-tzu,* was a teacher. His father died while Confucius was still young, but his mother nurtured him and underwent a great deal to see that he had a good education. He worked in the government bureaucracy until he was fifty. At that time he became one of the chief administrators for the local Duke of Lu. This did not work out and he left the position. For thirteen years he wandered from state to state teaching how to bring about political and social reform. He returned home to the district of Lu where he remained until he died at the age of seventy-two. The *Analects* (Lun Yu) are a compilation of his insightful sayings and works dealing with politics and society. Other works are attributed to him such as the *Book of Changes*, the *Book of Rites*, and the *Annals of Spring and Autumn*. It is probable that he used and edited these books rather than wrote them himself. His students were the ones who had the greatest impact on the culture. What they taught, what we call Confucianism, became the theoretical and organizational foundation for the Hun Dynasty (202 BCE-220 CE). During this time Confucianism became an essential part of Chinese culture.

Key Facts for Confucian Spirituality

SPIRITUALITY and RELIGION	PLACE OF ORIGIN	MEMBER-SHIP	KEY DATES	CENTRAL PERSON	BOOKS
CONFUCIANISM	East Asia (China)	Sixth largest in the world. One of the least represented in North America.	551-479 BCE	MASTER KUNG (CONFUCIUS)	The Analects of Confucius
CORE ISSUE	**BELIEFS**	**RITUALS**	**MORALS**	**ORGANIZATION.**	**PROMISE**
Disharmony – especially among classes of people	Each works for the whole Ideal person	Li (Good form, courtesy) all the correct rites and rituals proper to your role in society. Ancestor worship, spirit worship.	Inner and outer virtues. Jen (humaneness). Shu (reciprocity). Hsueh (self-correcting wisdom).	Shrines	Harmonious Society

What we have as a classical form of spirituality, then, is the result of centuries of development. Even with the distain of the present Chinese government, the spirituality continues to shape the world view of most Chinese. Confucianism looks back to the origins of the culture and proclaims it both good and necessary for life today. Just as we must honor our parents, so we should honor our ancestors who laid the foundations of this harmonious society. When we look back, we see that we are all part of a giant harmonic pattern of life in which each of us is to play our part. If we learn to perfect the pattern we are genetically and culturally destined to be individually and socially, we will, as individuals and communities, live in harmony with others, nature, and ourselves. Central to perfecting the community and ourselves is living a life of virtue. Virtue, after all, is pattern of living: a positive quality of a person that, after time and discipline, becomes part of her or his very being.

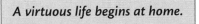

A virtuous life begins at home.

Our training in a virtuous life begins at home. It is here that we learn *jen* (humanity) and *li* (good form, proper ritual relationships). These are the two fundamental virtues of every whole person and every true social community. *Jen* is the disposition and mentality of putting others first in all one's actions. The "me first—I am the best" approach is abhorrent to this spirituality. It is never the "I;" it is always the "we." *Jen* instills in us the virtue of *shu* (reciprocity): never doing to someone what you would not have done to you. Jen also instills in us the virtue *hsueh* (self-correcting wisdom): a habit of always seeing if we have measured up to the ideal of *jen*: humanity. We know that we can never be perfect, but we also know that we can always improve to come closer to fitting the pattern of the ideal human being.

A virtuous life is achieved not only by desiring it and thinking of ways to achieve it, but also, and necessarily, by developing a set of virtues that support the desire and perfect the patterns necessary to sustain this life. *Li* is central for becoming virtuous. A person possessing *Li* is one who knows the right words, right dress, and right actions required in every social interaction, such as with one's parents, siblings, peers, teachers, and civil authorities. A person possessing *Li* knows how to command, to take commands, to love, and to show displeasure in the best way possible. A virtuous life is a harmonious life: a life of *li*. The signposts of this life are those of the ancients perfected through a life of virtue. The quote at the beginning of this section on Chinese spirituality provides a clear description of the harmonious, and thus peaceful, society that results from it.

> **A virtuous life never ends.**

Community and Taoist (Daoist) Spirituality

From out of the same cultural chaos as Confucianism came the foundation for what is called Taoism. As it exists today, there are two major foci within this spirituality with a common basis in ancient Chinese religion and an acceptance of disharmony as the major cause of our current chaos. Instead of the Confucian emphasis upon the balance between the inner and outer virtues as means to bring one in harmony with Tao, the first major focus begins by abandoning any hope of discovering the Tao through reason, conversation, and writing. Instead it demands a deep inward spiritual discipline to bring about personal and social harmony. Two ancient third century BCE texts reflect this focus: *Tao-te-ching* and *Chuang Tzu* (*Zhuangzi*). Together they reflect the core focus of the discipline necessary to achieve harmony: *wu-wei* which is usually translated as "active non-doing." The ancient tradition described in the Tao is an always present enlivening force. The Taoist tradition, represented by these two books, merely says let the Tao be Tao. Live simply. Act simply. Think simply.

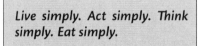

> **Live simply. Act simply. Think simply. Eat simply.**

Consider, for example, a block of wood.[187] As it is, without any carving, any paint, or anything being done to it, it has infinite potentiality. Let it be and the Tao will bring about harmony and further beauty. We do this first through natural simplicity. This is what we must strive for because it is closest to Tao and the harmony inherent to matching its patterns throughout the universe. We are all part of Tao and have great difficulty distinguishing ourselves from each other and the Tao. We are all equal as part of the Tao, thus social hierarchy and adornment should be rejected. Our daily adorned life is also one that is difficult to simplify because we are not sure of who we are.

The butterfly dream of Chuang Tzu highlights the difficulty. Chuang Tzu tells a story to one of his disciples in which he describes dreaming that he was a butterfly. He experiences life as a butterfly only to wake up and realize that he is not. He is, instead, Chuang Tzu. However, on reflection, he says he does not know if he is a butterfly dreaming that he is Chuang Tzu or Chuang Tzu dreaming he is a butterfly. The story highlights the difficulty not only of simplicity but also of discovering Tao. When one is caught in the mystical web of epistemological challenges, one may go the way of rational analysis or meditative concentration. Taoism, as with Buddhism and Hinduism, takes the way of meditation by offering various meditative techniques to discover one's identity, one's place in Tao, and the way to a simple life.

The other focus of Taoism is on explicit tangible methods of choosing the proper food and breathing and exercising correctly. There is also the ancient hope of mixing the proper chemicals together to provide an elixir for immortality. This approach is sometimes known as *Tao-chiao*, religious Taoism, or magical Taoism. It accepts many of the ideas we have just reviewed, especially the idea of

> **Exercising your body, mind, and spirit enables you to live the proper way.**

ch'i as is found in the I Ching and Feng-shui. When the ch'i enters into our sense world, it does so as yin and yang. Immediately, however, yin and yang become disharmonious as they enter into our world. Such disharmony is the cause of death. To bring ourselves into harmony with the Tao, we need to use what the Tao has given us to balance things. Tao-chaio provides the means of keeping balance in humans. It does so by searching to discover the correct mixture of food and drink that keeps one in balance and allows one to live forever. Proper breathing techniques, such as those expressed in tai-ch'i exercises, bring one into balance. A life of virtue is also seen as a means of accomplishing the yin-yang balance so we may have proper ch'i and become hsien, an immortal. Do not mistake this endeavor as an abstract joining of human spirit with ch'i. It is much more than that, for if one seeks to fully embrace this spirituality, one also has available temples, shrines, and priests to offer sacrifice to the universe of spirits and gods that influence our lives through the animate and inanimate objects that surround us.

Key Facts of Taoist Spirituality

SPIRITU-ALITY & RELIGION	PLACE OF ORIGIN	MEMBER-SHIP	KEY DATES	CENTRAL PERSON	BOOKS
TAOISM	East Asia (China)	Same as Confucian-ism	604 BCE	LAO TZU (604 BCE)	Tao Te Ching
CORE ISSUE	BELIEFS	RITUALS	MORALS	ORGANIZATION.	PROMISE
TAOISM Disharmony in self, nature, and among people	Yin (dark) and Yang (bright) forces or energies. Tao. Resist perma-nence.	Jiao (offer-ings) Zhai (purifi-cation rites)	Te (virtuous life) Wu wei (active non-doing) "In letting go all gets done." Being rooted in the Tao	Shrines	Harmony with Tao

Transcendence in Chinese Spirituality

The Chinese New Year, or as it is called today the "Spring Festival" in China, brings together in fifteen days of celebration the transcendent atmosphere present in the everyday life of Confucian and Taoist spirituality. Here we find the centrality of the virtues of Confucius, the magic of the Taoists, and the hierarchical world of the ancestral spirits. We also find, in the name change, the role of state support for the signposts of the religion.

The Chinese New Year is based on the lunar calendar. The Gregorian calendar that is used in Western culture became mandatory in 1929 and again in 1949. The Gregorian New Year is different from the lunar New Year that is celebrated throughout Chinese-speaking cultures. Since it is celebrated publicly and by many Chinese, we can see that just because something is official does not mean the people will follow the official version for important celebrations and rituals in their lives. All classical religions were, and sometimes still are, the established religion of a culture. As such, they helped establish the signposts of the culture. Chinese religions are no different.

Reflecting its rural origins, the Chinese people celebrate their New Year over fifteen days. The modern, quick-paced world pays little heed to the seasons of the year and the phases of the moon. The mechanical clock and the orderly, regimented life it introduced influence the New Year today. Few can take all the time necessary to prepare meals from scratch and bring all the family members together for the celebrations that are required by such rural feasts. Most people celebrate what is most important to them during the fifteen-day festival.

The central concern of much of the celebration is *Hsiao-Ching*, filial piety, which, by the way is also the name of one of the Chinese classics said to be authored by Confucius.[188] The home and its virtues are reflected in the gatherings throughout the fifteen days with diverse members of the family coming together from near and far. New Year's Eve begins the celebration with an elaborate dinner where places are also set for deceased ancestors.

The ninth day is marked by prayers to the Jade Emperor god. He is prominent among the Taoist gods. Among some Chinese, especially the Hun, he is seen as the god who saved them from extinction. Sacrifices of tea, fruit, and paper gold are offered in thanksgiving for the past and supplication for continued protection in the future. Many other Taoist gods, such as *Guan Yu*, the god of war and business, are also honored. The Lantern Festival marks the last day with lanterns lit to mark the way home for lost spirits. Firecrackers are set off to ward away evil spirits.

The five elements of wood, fire, earth, metal, and water, have corresponding colors: green, red, yellow, purple, and blue. Notice that red corresponds with fire. It is the color of warmth, joy, happiness, and luck. It is not by accident that the Chinese communist party uses red in its uniforms. During the New Year's celebration, red is found everywhere, especially in the red envelopes in which monetary gifts are placed and given to friends and loved ones.

The New Year's celebration is also an experience of transcendence: of moving beyond the "now" into the future. It combines the ancient means of transcendence found in Taoism and Confucianism with the various adaptations of the present. It is a perfect example of celebrating one's spirituality.

The Ancient Roots of All Spiritualities: A Harmonious Whole World Indigenous and Survival Spiritualities

Like trees, humans are rooted in the earth where they were born. Like trees, they stretch out to grasp what they need to live and grow. They seek to transcend their place. Unlike trees, they can walk and run. They can stretch in all directions. But they cannot escape the place where they were born. We are all indigenous peoples in some way. Usually this is reflected in the language we speak, the food we eat, and our body-sense of weather and environment. For example, those living in the dry Denver area find it particularly difficult in humid areas such as Florida. I was born in a small town outside of Pittsburgh. Most people in this area live on the sides of valleys and hills. This is how I grew up, and to this day, I feel at home walking on slanted surfaces.

The classical spiritualities we are reviewing in this chapter clearly indicate where they originated and the land that gave them birth. All classical spiritualities reflect their beginnings as they span the globe and the centuries. When we look at them at their current stage of evolution, we tend to forget where they came from. In doing so we may also forget the indigenous forces that are still part of them and us. As we have seen, many aspects of the spiritualities in Part Two have their roots in pre-history, the time when indigenous spiritualities dominated the globe. Although they do not dominate the globe today, their foundational themes are still found in all spiritualities.

Even though these spiritualities are part of us today, it is extremely difficult to clarify the processes that connect us with them. One of our principle means of communicating from generation to generation is through writing. There was no writing among ancient peoples. Spoken, not written, words, were their primary means of communication. That does not mean there was no source of information that tied one generation to another. Rituals, art, stories, and the very life of the people themselves tied generation to generation and, at the same time, help us understand their spirituality. Their burial grounds usually provide us with a great deal of information about their culture. Archeologists, anthropologists, and adventurers of all sorts are our principal sources of information for these spiritualities.

In Chapter Two we saw a significant difference of interpretation among these sources depending on the native culture of their interpreters. At times these commentators saw them as illiterates, primitive peoples, unlettered people, superstitious people, people untainted by the evils of our modern world, and people without culture of any sort. These negative views of other human beings have done little to help us understand them or ourselves in relation to them except, perhaps, to enable us to feel superior. I would like to suggest that the spiritual foundations provided by these oral cultures still resonate in contemporary spiritualities and certainly help us understand some of our deeper yearnings. This is true not only for those indigenous cultures of the past but also those that still exist in many parts of the world.[189] Here we concentrate on those ancient cultures that gave birth to the classical spiritualities. Some current, indigenous forms of spirituality will be described in Chapter Seven.

Let us begin by imagining an ancient world where we are all intimately connected and we seldom, if ever, experience anything or anyone outside the immediacy of this way of life. Let us imagine that this is a four-season world with spring, summer, fall, and winter. Let us imagine that we are fortunate to have a keeper of the fire: someone whose family somehow in the past obtained fire and has kept it burning. It is winter. We are fortunate to have fire. Yet we are constantly cold and hungry—very hungry. Many have not survived the cold. Some of us have died. My mate died giving birth last winter. Our child also died. We place the dead deep in the back of another cave. It is always dark there. We put their favorite tools with them and rub them with a red dye that looks like blood.

We remember, though, that as the hunger increases, the sun gets warmer and the nights get shorter. The snow will melt, plants will begin to grow, and more animals will be seen. If possible, we will kill these animals. We will dig roots as the earth warms and pick flowers as they spring up. Strawberries are the first fruit to satisfy our hunger. We celebrate their coming. We will eat these things. We will be hungry in the spring, but not as much as before. We know the places to go to find the roots and other edible plants as spring turns

> *No more hunger, no more pain, no more cold and wet.*

into summer and summer into fall. We know the places to go to find the animals to kill. We know how it feels on a warm fall day with the sun shining, the stomach full, and everyone feeling good, awake, energized. Most of those born in the spring are dead now, but some live on. We put the dead ones with those who died before them. Babies who have lived over many winters are men and women now. They, as us, have a few broken bones from the hunt, cuts and scratches from long journeys, broken and decaying teeth, but today we feel good. The day of celebration is near—the day to celebrate the goodness we feel at this moment of sun, of food, of drink, and of young people coming of age. We are whole. We live!

The air grows colder and the sun less warm. We return to the fire, to the cave with its drawings of our world and our life in it. There we will live amidst our stories, our fire, our drawings, our food, and our warm bodies. Winter is coming, but so is spring. Many of us will be there to greet it.

The drawings we made and the stories we tell remind us that this will all happen again. In the depth of winter, it is difficult to believe that this cycle is true. But it is; the stories tell us why and remind us of what is and what will be. They remind us that if we keep seeds and do not eat them, the seeds will change into something different when planted. They remind us that the wind that makes the trees and plants move is like the breath inside us, enabling us to move. When there is no wind, nothing moves. When there is no breath in us and in animals, there is no spirit and no movement. We only know the wind is there when it moves the trees and plants. We only know the spirit is there when it moves the person, the animal, the plant. The spirits, like the wind, are everywhere. The stories tell us how to treat the spirits of the wind, of the animals, of the plants, and everything. Our spirit is connected to their spirit—like the wind that moves the trees is connected to the wind that brings the rain; and the rain to the plants that grow; and the earth to the plants and animals we kill and eat. We are one. We are part of an eternal cycle.

Sometimes I see images in the clouds that look like my father, my mother, my brothers, and my sisters who have died. Up there are the sun that warms us and the rain that makes things grow. I feel close to my father when I use his club. I can hear his voice telling me how to use it; praising me when I am success-ful. Sometimes our special elder's spirit goes up to the clouds, the sun, and the rain and brings us the warmth of heal-ing for what makes us hurt inside or the hope for a good hunt tomorrow. This

> **Food, warmth, health, and love are in our future.**

elder's spirit is good and is able to hear and speak with the other spirits. The one who leads us has a strong spirit too because it enables him to know what to do, when to kill, and when to dig for roots and edible plants. Some spirits are good, just as sometimes the sun and the rain are good; some spirits are evil, just as sometimes the sun and rain can harm or even kill us. Many times, I meet these spirits after I go to sleep. I am in a different world from the world I live in when I'm awake. In the sleep-world, I meet those I have loved, those I have hated, and those I have feared. Many times, too, I can feel those I've met in the sleep-world close to me when awake. When I sit on a hill on a warm autumn day after feasting and being with my mate, I wish that all of life could be like this all the time; that the spirits and all the things of the earth would be as they are in that moment—in harmony. I know that time will come, but I know it is not now. The stories tell us why it has not come yet, and what we have to do to make every day as harmonious as possible.

* * *

Imagination can take us only so far. Descriptions of our ancestors can only provide so much insight. Analysis, however, can put both together to suggest the ancient foundations for contemporary signposts. Our signposts are the con-sequence of many centuries of experi-encing harmony and disharmony, hurt and pleasure, cold and hot, hunger and satisfaction, death and life. The basis to

> **My people and I have the power to make life better.**

it all is a cycle of these experiences in my lifetime and my people's lifetime.

These signposts are also a consequence of experiencing the exercise of power in the midst of an uncontrollable world. The power of my arm builds a shelter and plants a seed; the power of my legs carries me to fresh water and edible ber-ries. The power of our community's voices makes us feel and act as one: powerful voices, powerful people. Power brings a better life and power brings death. Sometimes this is a necessary death in the hunt or in defending our community. Sometimes, too, it is a destructive power done merely for the thrill of destruction and taking a life. It is always easier to destroy than to grow and build.

Actually, we can control very little: the weather, disease, fire, water, wind, productive earth, personal relationships, body, mind, and will. In the midst of power are always the unknowns, the uncontrollable, and the unpredictable. Only the cycle of seasons remains to divide our lives in the midst of the uncontrollable. We humans are equals amidst nature's diversity and cycle of life. The power to destroy, so easily used, does not produce the satisfaction our imagined person found on that warm fall day. Having everything in balance, however, does: sun, food, drink, people. Survival to the next warm fall day seems imbedded in our very being. What will direct us to living that day again? What are the signposts that guide us beyond the cave, and beyond the moment of exultation on the hill?

Out of all these experiences slowly evolved the signposts of transcendence that mark the way beyond the here and now of joy and sorrow. *Belief* provides a security for both today and tomorrow. It provides many stories, drawings, and artifacts about such things as the eternal cycle of life and death, spirits, the relationship between corporeal and incorporeal beings, the causes of suffering and death, and how to return to a time of harmony and fulfillment. A deep sense of affirmation and trust about the role of humans in bringing about this future is found in these stories.

Rituals embody this hoped-for security through a repeated pattern of action and word. Rituals bring the past to memory, enliven the present by making us aware of our connections, and offer us control over our future. Rituals bring the rain for our crops, the spirits for our healing, the animals for our table, young men and women to adulthood, and the dead to peace. A deep sense of holiness is always present in these rituals.

Ethics bind together a partnership of protection against evil and uncontrollable forces. Our ethical behavior guarantees harmony and means to purify us when we destroy this harmony. A deep sense of justice is felt when such harmony comes about.

Community provides a sense of fellowship with our peers, our leaders, all spirits (ancestors included), and everything we are connected to. Community provides a fellowship of support for happiness, supplication for help, and satisfaction of affective relationships. This land is not only earth but people, justice, and truth. It is all of me.

Transcendence and power are two sides of the same coin: to become more than I am here and now. This sense of power within me to kill; to make things

> *The elders' stories tell me so, the dances show me how, and our customs guarantee their promise will be fulfilled.*

for war, for food, for beauty; to bring forth life from the earth, from one's self, and from one's mind in stories, dreams, and imagination is a stretching out with one's whole being for becoming more and going beyond the here and now. This search for transcendence at its most fundamental level is a search for life, for daily survival against all odds, a search for food and drink, a search for security in knowing and doing what will bring life tomorrow, next season, and years ahead. This security is found in these signposts.

Signposts, Symbolic Immortality, and Spirituality[190]

In his many works, Jay Lifton reminds us that this search for total security is through symbols that connect us to our past, present, and future.[191] Thus we express and experience this seeking through our five senses (touch, smell, hearing, sight, taste). Such searching to make connections through what we have described above as signposts is, as Lifton also reminds us, a seeking for immortality; that is, we want to keep these connections forever and be secure forever. We find the evidence of this seeking through symbols of immortality. (Lifton calls this symbolic immortality.) These are present throughout human history beginning with our early ancestors who were the first indigenous people. What we find are symbols and patterns of symbols that realize transcendence through biological makeup, creative works and activities, religions, cycles of nature, and short-lived psychophysical experiences of transcendence. These symbols, resultant from the seeking of our first indigenous ancestors, are the foundation of the signposts of every form of spirituality.

The future is forever.

Biological Transcendence. Our genes connect us to the past and the future. Our progeny project our physical being into an unknown future. The experience of our parents forms the basis of how we trust, love, and hope. The gathering of family, clan, or tribe is a gathering of who we were, are, and will be. These are powerful symbols of immortality: I will continue on as *we* continue on.

Transcendence through Work and Art. The tools we make, the cake we bake, the stories we create, the broken things we fix, and so many other things we put our hands and minds to are expressions of creativity. Some of these may remain for centuries. Others, having been cast into the grave of an ancestor, may be unearthed millennia later. Many things we do now may have an effect later: A mother repeating a saying to her own daughter that her mother told her is a connection between the generations. The words, the cake, the stories, the help to improve someone's life, the new way of doing something are symbols that connect us and help us realize our immortal transcendence. I, we, continue through these symbols.

Religious Transcendence. Religions, as we have seen, offer patterns of symbols, evidenced in the signposts, constituting a way of life that not only connects generations but also provides a sacred canopy of symbolic patterns that say this world can be trusted, and part of this trust is that you and I, all of us, will live forever.[192] We will transcend the here and now of joy, happiness, sadness, and the ultimate barrier to transcendence: death. The stories tell us this is true, as do the rituals and ethical norms.

Transcendence in Nature. This same permanency is found in the cycles of nature and the surety of the laws that express such permanency. Upon death we are transformed into the nature that gave us birth and the nature that guarantees that some of what makes us who we are will continue forever as plant, animal, and the very earth itself. When we wake up in the morning and see the sky, we see a symbol of eternity and transcendence implicit in it.

Short-lived psychophysical experiences of transcendence are those obtained from drugs, alcohol, and other stimulants made by human beings. In many instances, they provide individuals with an otherworldly experience that satisfies, for a short time, their thirst for transcendence, but these experiences offer no permanent path toward transcendence.

Symbolic immortality is found in our living these symbols and patterns of symbols within our cultures, religions, and spiritualities. As we have seen so often, these three are bound together throughout most of history and much of our current world. When these symbols are vibrant, so are the people living them. When they are not, we experience stasis, separation, and disintegration.[193] Without the symbols of immortal life, we, individually and as a society, begin to experience

> **Where we live is where our future begins.**

death, not immortality. Aboriginal spirituality has seen and today does see the destruction of much of what offered them symbolic immortality. The destruction of their symbols of immortality reflects the decay of their ways of life. Everyone's spirituality is founded upon some aboriginal spirituality. The questions are whether our current liminal experience is seeing the decay of symbols of immortality without the growth of new or renewed ones and whether our culture will imitate that of the aboriginal ones and pass our signposts on to other ways of life.

Stable Signposts but Diverse Spiritualities

We must remember, however, that aboriginal/indigenous spirituality is multifaceted and extremely diverse. Certainly, over time, we humans have found the stable patterns of belief, ritual, ethical behavior, and community, but, while these signposts as such are found in every form of spirituality, the symbols manifested through these signposts are diverse and must be respected as authentic expressions of human spirituality. There are, for example, thousands of indigenous/aboriginal spiritualities. The only authentic way of understanding one of these spiritualities is to become a member of a tribe. Lacking that, we must exercise great care in bringing the signpost(s) of that tribe into our spirituality. It will not accommodate itself to our spirituality because of the vast differences between the two cultures (e.g. oral vs. written). Most attempts to bring these aboriginal spiritualities into a modern person's way of life usually deepens that person's sense of liminality and aloneness rather than providing stability to his spiritual life. For example, we might imitate Arctic shamanic practices in our Sedona, Arizona life, but the symbols and actions, now in a different context, have changed. The symbol-facts may be the same, but the symbols have changed radically.[194]

What these past indigenous spiritualities have given us is the gift of stable signposts in our spiritual lives. We open this gift as we live our spirituality that has evolved out of past indigenous spiritualities. These signposts provide us with a sense of immortality, as Lifton described. In this time of liminality, we must carefully translate the past into the future. This can be done with great care and seriousness. But it can be done.

The next chapter will review attempts to do just that: adapt ancient spiritualities to our contemporary liminal age. We will end this chapter with a short discussion of Shinto Spirituality as an example of how an aboriginal spirituality develops into a contemporary one.

Shinto (*kami-no-michi*) Spirituality

Shinto is indigenous to Japan. Japan is a chain of mountainous, volcanic, islands located along the eastern coast of Asia. Crops can grow on only 11 percent of the land, and most of them are cultivated on the sides of mountains. There are few natural resources—fish being the only exception. Earth tremors are common to the islands. There are eighty active volcanoes and the constant possibility of destructive earthquakes. Japan has four seasons with an abundant amount of rainfall.

Several excavations as well as the earliest writings give us an insight into the beginnings of Japanese culture and religion.[195] The origins of Japanese oral culture are between 4500 and 660 BCE. There were as many indigenous Japanese religions as there were gatherings of human beings who lived in what today we call Japan. They all envisioned their world as filled with spirits, some favoring one place, some favoring another. The word given to these spirits was *Kami*. While these spirits were found especially at these places, there were a few people who could contact them and act in their stead. These people, usually women, were called *miko*. They would travel in groups from village to village as ways for people to contact the dead, tell the future, and cure any illnesses. Storytellers described how the Kami originated as well as what they did. The storytellers also described the creation of the islands from the activities of the two first Kami. From these stories, the people came to know they were created as part of a world of spirits and humans who were to live in harmony with one another. Japan was the center of the universe. Harmony there was harmony everywhere. The leaders of the group, and later the Emperor, were specially chosen by the kami to fulfill their proper destiny. When the leader, the kami, nature, and the people were in harmony, things were good; when not, things were bad. When the people did something that broke this harmony with the kami, they had to be purified.

Because Japan was close to the Asiatic mainland, it came in contact with Taoism and Buddhism. As you may remember, the name Hinduism came about as a description of what was common to the diverse indigenous religions of India when first Islam and then European Christianity came to India. The same thing happened in Japan. As the contacts with Taoism and Buddhism increased, the name *Shinto* came to be accepted as describing what was held in common among these diverse indigenous religions. As these diverse indigenous groups were brought together to form the empire of Japan between 250 BCE and 250 CE, a common term such as Shinto would have been helpful to describe who they were. A symbol of this unity of people, culture, and religion is the shrine built in 4 BCE at Ise about two hundred miles from Tokyo. It is the shrine of the Sun Goddess *Amaterasu Omikami*, who is not only one of the most powerful Kami, but is also in the lineage of the emperor, who was also considered one of the Kami. The shrine became known in Japanese simply as "the" shrine, in comparison to all the thousands of others throughout Japan, because of who it was dedicated to and the emperor who is part of this same lineage. Even today, it is considered the national shrine.

Most commentators suggest that the word Shinto is actually two Japanese characters brought together to form one word in the Latin alphabet. These words, *kami-no-michi*, would be translated "the way of the Kami" when written separately. By 4 BCE, we have a strong cultural thrust toward one emperor, one shrine, one religion, one nation. History demonstrates, however, that

> **Our land. Our spirits. Our center of spirituality.**

such unity is always being threatened. Let us first look at this unity through the spiritual signposts of Shinto and then see how this indigenous religion of Japan is shaped by other religions and their spiritualities.

Spiritual Signposts of Shinto

Takaamahara Ni Kami Tsumari masu.
Kamurogi Kamuromi no Mikoto wo Mochite
Sumemioya Kamu Izanagi No Mikoto
Tsukushi No Himuka No Tachihana No Odo No
Ahagi Hara Ni Misogi Harai Tamau Toki Ni
Narimaseru Haraidono Ookami Tachi
Moromoro No Magagoto Tsumi Kegare Wo
Harai Tamae Kiyome Tamae To Mousu Koto No Yoshi Wo
Tamatsu Kami Kunitsu Kami Yaoyorozu No Kamitachi Tomomi
Ameno Huchikoma No Mimi Furitatete Kikoshimese To
Kashikomi Kashikomi Mo Maosu

Spirits of purification
created for order of and the mother
that they inhabit the Sky,
exactly as when
The God Izanagi no Mikoto
bathed in the narrow estuary
of a covered river with trees
permanently leafy, in the South region.

With all the respect from the depth of our hearts
We ask that they hear us, such as the spirit that hears our
intent, with sharpened ears, together with
Spirits of the Sky and the Land,
Take the badnesses, disasters, and sins and purify all.
Miroku Oomikami
You bless us and protect us

Meishu Sama
You bless us and protect us.
For expansion of our soul
And the fulfillment of your will.[196]

As we have seen, central to the Shinto belief are the Kami. Commentators have a difficult time translating the term and explaining who or what they are. Some translate the term as "gods," others as "spirits," and still others as "sacred."[197] The myths describe them with personalities similar to what we have seen in the gods in other religions, yet at the same time, other entities such as one's ancestors are called Kami. All in all, the kami may be seen as portals to transcendence. Where they are experienced as existing, especially at the shrines, they offer to the believer an opportunity to move beyond the here and now and transcend present time and space. They do this not only through the experience of the sacred so many times witnessed at these shrines, but also through the purification rites that are always offered there. The here and now, after all, is disharmonious, imperfect, and out of sync with the world of Kami. The way to bring everything into harmony and perfection is to purify whatever is causing the world to be disharmonious. This is done by rituals of purification.

The central religious rituals in Shinto are those associated with shrines and purification. A purification ritual is accompanied by prayers of various sorts, such as the one quoted above, as well as actions associated with water, salt, sand, fire, and sake. These are done at all shrines. Sometimes, especially at purifications of a new car or at the groundbreaking ceremony for a new building, a priest shakes a *haraigushi*, which is an instrument of purification made from a branch of a sacred *sakaki* tree with white linen or paper steamers attached. To some it may look like a pompon. A significant purification ritual is held at the Ise shrine every twenty years. As a part of that particular purification ritual, the entire shrine is torn down and rebuilt through a ceremony called *shikinen sengu*. *Shikinen* means "a set number of years" and *sengu* means "transferring the shrine." That has been happening every twenty years for the last two thousand.

The number of shrines in Japan varies between eighty thousand and one hundred thousand. Originally, the shrines were places in a forest, along a river or a stream, or at the ocean shore. They were special places to connect with the kami. Most homes had a shrine, though these would not be counted when enumerating the many shrines found in the countryside. Today they are more formalized, and other gods may be included with the kami in one's prayers and the intent of the shrine. This is not a place of worship but of petition. No images are found in the shrine proper but some other items may be there. In the shrine at Ise, for example, the eight-sided mirror of *Amaterasu Omikami*, the sun goddess, is always carried from the old to the new shrine. In Japan today there are also Buddhist and Taoist shrines. Each of these has been influenced by the other in architecture and decoration.

An item found in most shrines is the *ema*, a small wooden plaque on which people write their prayers and hang them at the designated place in the shrine. These are bought at the shrine and usually have some animal design stamped or painted on it that is associated with the shrine. One prays for whatever one wishes: passing an exam, falling in love, gaining a job, getting over the flu. One's prayers are limited only by one's desire for betterment in the here and now of daily living. The ideal would be that all one's prayers were answered and all the necessary purifications would occur. If done, the world would be in sync with the kami. Life would be harmonious.

Part of that harmony is the celebration of important days such as the New Year, which begins at midnight of December 31, the Girls' Festival on March 3, the Body's Festival on May 5, and the Chrysanthemum Festival on September 9. These ritual celebrations are examples of key times when Shinto spirituality seeks to bring together the necessary forces for harmony.

> *Our spirits protect us. Our rituals purify us. Our shrines transform us.*

Shinto *ethics*, while not as detailed as in some spiritualities, are naturally found in the totality of the Shinto lifestyle. Central to ethics and morality is what is central to all of Shinto: harmony. Consequently, central to one's ethical concern is to do the right thing and feel the right way. All such concern begins and ends with one's dedication to being in harmony with the wishes of those in authority such as parents, teachers, bosses, and the emperor. If we were to outline the foundation of Shinto ethics, it would be family, nature, cleanliness, reverence for kami, and harmony among all these.[198] This foundation is built upon as Shinto interacts with Taoism and Buddhism.

The *communal* nature of Shinto is found in the individual and communal acknowledgement that community, not the individual, is central to one's spirituality. The community, here, as it has been frequently described, is the entire seen and unseen universe. Shinto was built upon those first indigenous experiences in the struggle to keep alive in a land of mountains and water. It evolved into a national religion. What we see today are the resulting spiritualities whose core is the necessary harmony among nature, humans, and all living creatures, which, if broken, will destroy life as we know it.

Shinto today is best summarized by the Carmodys when they say:

> In defining itself, Shinto picked up something from Buddhist philosophy, Confucian ethics, and Taoist naturalism. The result was a nature-oriented worship with special emphasis on averting pollution. Furthermore, Shinto domesticated Buddhism as a religion of kami-bodhisattvas and it modified Confucian social thought to include the emperor's divine right.[199]

The development of Shinto from its indigenous origins to the present is contained in this paragraph. It is also an example of how an indigenous religion becomes a classical spirituality as it absorbs competitive ways of life into its core spiritual transcendental dynamic. Before we begin this brief description of Shinto's spiritual development we must remember that presently the Japanese culture is more religiously inclusive than exclusive. In other words, people have no difficulty claiming all three of these religions as their own at the same time. Such individual claims and social adaptation demonstrates a current openness to what has developed even though it has not been the case historically.

Historically, we can use the building of the national shrine at Ise as a marker of the national religion called Shinto. Confucianism came to the Japanese islands around 285 CE and Buddhism in 550 CE. With the introduction of Buddhism on the islands, centuries followed in which either Buddhism or Shintoism was the state religion. The embrace of the state naturally caused deep reactions in the culture as that religion began to take hold, only to have the other religion substituted for it centuries later. Substitution may be too strong a word here, however, because what we see is a gradual adaptation of one religion to the other. We have already briefly alluded to the fact that there are many Buddhist shrines as well as Shinto shrines throughout the nation. Shrines, as an important part of the Shinto religion, became a predominant expression for all religions in Japan. A brief description of two other well-known parts of Japanese culture may help us understand how such interplay between the religions resulted in significant changes in the Japanese version of all three of these religions: the Samurai and the tea ceremony.

Samurai originally meant those who were trusted servants of the nobility.[200] In America today, however, we see a great deal of sword fighting, blood, and guts depicted in movies about the Samurai but little of the deep spirituality that formed, by the twelfth century, an elite military force that fought for its chosen nobleman. This spirituality was highly influenced by Buddhism in general and Zen Buddhism in particular.

What seems to have happened is that when Buddhism came to Japan in 550 CE, Buddhist monasteries came along with it.[201] With time and their proclamation as the state religion in 594 CE, they became more and more wealthy. As these wealthy monasteries grew, so did the necessity to guard their treasures. Although there were strict rules against Buddhist monks taking up arms, some, along with the laity, did so in order to protect the monasteries. These same monasteries also became a place of respite for retired and wounded samurai warriors. Many of these monasteries were Zen Buddhist monasteries. Zen, as you may remember, emphasizes two things: the necessary role of meditation, understood as total focus and concentration on the object of mediation, and the absurdity of using language and rational concepts to understand anything. Meditation, when perfected, enabled one to be enlightened in this life. Death meant nothing. Japan was in constant war during these centuries. If anything was necessary for the samurai, it was to ease their minds between battles and focus their minds during battle. If the sword could become the object of concentration, a type of meditation might develop using that object and a new approach to fighting would follow. By the twelfth century, these historical circumstances and the ingenuity of the Japanese people produced what we know today as the samurai warrior.[202] Daisetz Suzuki summarizes this development best when he says:

> When the Japanese say that the sword is the soul of the samurai, we must remember all that goes with it: loyalty, self-sacrifice, reverence, benevolence, and the cultivation of higher feelings. Here is the true samurai.... He could never be separated from the weapon that was the supreme symbol of his dignity and honor. Training in its use was, besides it practical purpose, conducive to his moral and spiritual enhancement. It was here that the swordsman joined hands with Zen.[203]

This style of life is reflected in the typical list of virtues found in the twelfth century *Bushido* (Way of the Warrior) Code. The typical seven were justice, courage, benevolence or compassion, respect, honesty, honor, and loyalty. Three others are also revealed when reviewing the total code: filial piety, wisdom, and care for the elderly.[203] Recalling the discussion of ethics we had when dealing with Confucianism, Taoism, Buddhism, and Shinto, you can see the origins of the ethical signposts reflected here. The same can be said of the ritual meditation techniques used by the Samurai.

The sword is our very soul. The soul is loyal, reverent, benevolent and self-sacrificing.

War and combat are part of life. The Samurai developed a form of spirituality around it. The same can be said of eating and drinking—in this case drinking tea. The Japanese developed the ritual of drinking tea as an expression of an entire lifestyle. The development began in 815 CE with a cup of tea offered to the Emperor Saga by a Buddhist monk. From such humble beginnings, drinking a cup of tea developed into the intricate ritual that it is today: a ceremony that is both an expression of Japanese culture as well as the religions that are part of that culture.

If you have ever prepared a meal for dinner, set the table for the meal, shifted furniture around in the room in order for your guests to eat the meal more comfortably, and thought about how you would greet the guests when they came for the meal, then you have an idea of what goes into a Japanese tea ceremony. You may have also become aware of how all your preparations reflect the culture in which you live.

No culture does everything the same. Likewise, there is no one way of doing the tea ceremony as a formal ritual. There are diverse schools of thought on how to conduct the tea ceremony, most with traditions that go back centuries. One school does stand out since it influenced not only how to perform the ceremony but also Japanese art, landscaping, and architecture: that of Sen No Rikyu (1522-1591 CE). From his perspective, the specific steps of the ceremony symbolized four basic principles: harmony, respect, purity, and tranquility. Some would also add the attitude that each confluence of people, place, tea, and instruments for serving will never be repeated. All should be treated with the calm reverence that such uniqueness represents. These principles reflect both the Buddhism of the ceremony's founders and the Taoism of the land from which this Buddhism came.

The rooms are usually simple and reflect a certain pastoral atmosphere; the floors usually have *tatami* mats, which, as with everything else, are re-arranged according to whether it is the hot or cold season. Two types of tea may be served: thick or thin. Everyone will drink the thick tea from one common bowl; the thin tea is served in individual bowls. This is a very intricate ceremony with many different instruments handled in traditional ways. This description would end up as a checklist of items to be used if we detailed the entire ceremony. A list of rules and items for any religious ritual tells us little of what is happening. The only way to experience the spiritual depth of such a ritual is to participate in the ritual. Remember, though, that in doing so, you are never a full participant if you haven't lived a long life in that religious culture. At the same time, you might ask yourself if any seemingly ordinary rituals are part of your spirituality. In our contemporary culture, spirituality seems to be thought of only as an extraordinary state of living. The classical forms of spirituality in general challenge such a view. The Japanese tea ceremony, in particular, certainly offers us an example of how the ordinary can become a means of transcendence.

Experience of the Transcendent

The feeling of loyalty to our families and communities places us in harmonious continuity with all those who have gone before us and sustains the optimism of future remembrance by others of our families and communities. Jay Lifton suggests that such an experience is also one of symbolic immortality. The warrior in battle and the pouring of tea in one's home are two examples of stepping into this stream of immortality. A few minutes at a shrine, the purification of a new car, and the blessing of the priest at a wedding are all means of becoming part of a four-thousand-year tradition that has woven together a people into a nation and provides that nation with a sense of transcendence to overcome the challenges of the island upon which it survives. To become aware of such transcendence is the challenge to each person living this spirituality and the community within which she or he lives.

Seeking Eternity within and Harmony with All:
A Summary

Eternity: no place, no time, a limitless number of moments beyond our imagination. Do you wish this to be true? For thousands of years people have not only wished it so but have believed it and taken all necessary means to enter into this moment. The signposts of the East are there to mark the spiritual way.

The rhythm of the seasons is the rhythm of life that continues forever. We can never step out of it. We move with the flow of life; balanced, we continue human life to its outer limits. We petition the aid of all the life energies that surround us to reach that limit and ultimately become part of that which gave us life to enable it for others. The signposts of the East are there and offer the necessary balance to become part of life's flow.

If at the end of the last chapter the challenge was to discover God's name, the end of this chapter faces us with the possibility that there is no name, no time, nor reality at all since everything is illusion caused by ignorance or suffering.

PART THREE

LIMINAL SPIRITUALITIES: SPIRITUAL OFFERINGS IN A TIME OF RADICAL CHANGE

Oops
Wow.
Whoaaa!
This is narrow.
Can't stand long.
Sit neither.

Whoa.
That's a long way down.
Why are all the king's men yelling?

Whoa.
I might fall.
Then what?

Look!
There's others!
- over there, on the edge.
I wonder if I can move over
next to them?
Or to the Other?

Hey, over there.
Let's get together.

Hey.
Let's move closer.
Hey.
Can you hear me?

Whoa.
They want to what?

What?!
Measure the edge? Measure the fall?
Right now?
Are they crazy?

Whoa.
Feel that wind!
It'll blow us all off.
Look the king's horses are moving away.

Come on people. Let's get together.

Oops.

And all the kings' horses and all the
kings' men could not put all the
humpty dumpties together again.

* * *

Sin, Death, and Suffering are with us yet
As is mystery and paradox,
still encompassing,
While I continue striving to transcend all this.

Resurrection, Kingdom, and Heaven; Enlightenment,
Nirvana, Oneness with Tao and Nature—still not
here and now. Life's mystery remains.

Oops.
Now what?

* * *

Many people feel like Humpty Dumpty: buffeted by the winds of change , sitting alone—trying to make a living, trying to engage in a meaningful life with others, calling out in fear of personal and/or social disaster. Some might feel broken from running into the mystery of life too often, unable to be mended by the horses and men provided by the classical spiritualities. At least those who feel like Humpty are aware of what is happening. They scream out trying to make us aware of their deep crises. There are many more who don't feel anything. Psychically numb from the myriad choices offered by the winds of change, they repeat the routines of the past in the hope of surviving the present. But, feeling or not, both groups share the same ledge, buffeted by the same winds, waiting for something to happen. The transformations promised and promoted by the classical spiritualities have not yet benefited the vast majority of contemporary humans who sit on the ledge hoping not to fall.

The reason why people cry out or are psychically numb is because the foundations of our current culture are being challenged by deep changes in technology, warfare, economic inequality, the environment, and gender relationships. The quick expansion and application of sciences such as bioengineering, nanotechnology, electronic computers, and advertising have lead to the possibility of an entirely new world of telecommunication, medicine, education, and aging. Learning without a teacher and a classroom, medicines created for each individual, a majority of people over the age of sixty-five, and instant awareness of what is happening across the globe are new paradigms in society. Global warfare carried out by small groups organized on the Internet rather than in nation-states is new. Total nuclear annihilation, while not new, is ever present. A world without icecaps, increasingly warmer, fewer species, disappearing water resources, and ever increasing costs for foodstuffs is new. Uncertainty over gender interaction is new. Economic disparity, while not new at a global level, is new in the consciousness of most people in North America.[205] An example of this in the United States is that from 1980 to 2005, four-fifths of the total increase of American income went to the top one percent. Aside from increased debt for the ninety-nine percent with less actual income are the breakup of families, increased unemployment, home foreclosures, and psychological depression.[206] All these "new" situations result in the typical signposts of belief/truth, rituals, moral norms, and secure feelings of togetherness being uncertain. When signposts are moved, people have difficulty knowing where they are going as well as where they have come from. A culture without firm signposts is uncertain of itself. This is the context of contemporary living.

Contexts, as I have said repeatedly, are important for understanding our descriptions, analyses, and choices. Liminality, as we described in Chapter Two, is our context. Just as our language shapes our thoughts, expectations, and experiences, so the cultural context of liminality shapes us today as we stand poised on the here-and-now ledge of our lives. Our contemporary world is a liminal world—an in-between world of great ignorance, chaos, grief, alienation, and the perverse stability offered by leaders more interested in the continuance of an imagined past rather than healing in the present. In this world, classical spiritualities are lived by millions while modern spiritualities are evolving from our immediate past - spiritualities that were and still are marginal to both the classical and modern spiritualities. All forms of spirituality now exist in the context of liminality as they promise and promote a new personal and social future and the means to achieve it. We do not know precisely what a liminal spirituality looks like.

Those who develop spirituality in a liminal context are the models for future spiritualities. Their liminal spirituality will serve as an example of how to live in an age of uncertainty. The artifacts of past spiritualities surround us in names of places, buildings, literature, music, arts, modes of thought, and so much more. The new artifacts await those developing liminal spiritualities. Whether these will develop into the new classics is something only time will tell. The essential nature of a liminal spirituality is its "in-between-ness," its uncertainty of what has been given to us by the past and its solid hope that there is more to life now and in the future than the insubstantiality of what the current signposts of spirituality provide us. Shall we look at what we have here and now and create out of that the classics of the future? Will those spiritualities that have developed over the last two to three thousand years once again re-invigorate and lead us beyond liminality? Will the spiritualities that have existed throughout the centuries on the edges of cultures dominated by classical spiritualities now provide more certain signposts and become the dominant spiritualities? The following two chapters will enable you to answer these questions and respond to those answers within the framework of your own spirituality.

CHAPTER SIX

NEW SPIRITUALITIES: MODERN SPIRITUALITIES IN A LIMINAL AGE

Answer the following true or false:[207]
- *Few things are certain in life.*
- *No one can prove something is true.*
- *I enjoy texting, celebrating my teams' wins, and getting together with my friends.*
- *Things are good when I feel good.*
- *My community is made of those who look, think, act, and dress as I do.*
- *We can know and control our world without a god.*
- *Experiment and its mathematical interpretation provide us with certainty and truth.*
- *The fundamentals of leading a healthy, prosperous, and psychologically whole and happy life are found in the principles discovered by the social sciences.*
- *The basis of a strong community is the truth, discovered by science, and the agreement by the majority of that community on how to live together in peace and prosperity.*
(The significance of your answer may be found in endnote 207.)

***

E=MC2
~ Albert Einstein

I don't know Who—or What—put the question; I don't know when it was put. I don't even remember answering. But at some moment I did answer Yes to Someone—or Something—and from that hour I was certain that existence is meaningful and that, therefore, my life, in self surrender, had a goal.
~ Dag Hammarskjöld

***

180

The glory filled the old barn even as it filled the temple. Heavenly strains of music burst through yielded lips. Messages in many languages were given with interpretations – holy laughter and shouts of victory blended in one harmonious song or praise.

~ Alice Belle Garrigus (1858-1949)[208]

***

Something radical has happened to millions of humans within the past five hundred years. It has resulted in their becoming very powerful. It has impacted everyone else as they have spread their culture and overwhelmed others throughout the world with their armaments, sciences, technologies, ideas, medicines, and trade. That something has been the adoption of a modern (scientific) outlook.

As the modern advanced from its origins among a few scholars to others first in Europe and then in the United States, it challenged the classical and indigenous spiritualities by promising and promoting other means of transcending the here and now. As we saw in Chapter Two, what the modern approach promised and promoted has failed. Just as it gradually spread throughout the world and overwhelmed each culture it encountered, so too those forces that were to bring about its diminishment began to gather and threaten the modern world and its spiritualities. The result of this interaction between modernity and the forces causing its diminishment is our current age of liminality, or age of post-modernism as some call it. All those who are living a modern life have to deal with the consequences of this conflict just as those over the last five hundred years had to deal with the transition to the modern era. The twenty-first century is the Liminal Century.

Of course, everyone on earth is not yet modern. Nor are those living in a modern culture necessarily aware of the forces gathering to destroy it.[209] Some of those forces and the resulting changes are very subtle. Most everything in life is mixed. I can provide some clarity, however, as to what is going on; I can also offer some understanding about what is happening to your own spirituality and those of others. The descriptions of what I am calling "new spiritualities" will do that. These "new" spiritualities are derivatives of the modern outlook and those responding to the forces causing liminality. There is not enough space in this book to discuss all the new spiritualities, because there are too many. I will select representative samples of diverse responses to the modern and the

> *Spirituality must recognize the new: books for all; the mind capable of seeking and finding the truth; the world as predictable and manipulable; "I" as the center of it all.*

liminal. These samples will be selected based on the descriptions provided in Chapter Two. Although these spiritualities are from different decades of each century, they do highlight what happens when people encounter threats to their own spiritualities. That in itself is a lesson worth reflecting on.

The modern era brought to the fore many exciting and radical changes in people's lives. First, the written word became available in the form of books that everyone could read. There was a gradual understanding that the mind is capable of using science to discover a predictable world that can be manipulated through mathematics and technologies. The individual was viewed as the center and arbiter of everything. Scientists began using experimental methods to reduce things to their essential parts and determine which one of those parts the whole was dependent on.

The book as a source of knowledge was open to all who could read, not just the clerical elite; food, marriage, health, war, and wealth did not need prayer and ritual to succeed; if you developed modern skills and learned modern information, you could leave your place of origin to make a new, successful, life. What the modern promised was independence from the past to forge your future—a future filled with everything necessary for you to be happy. What it promoted was objectivity, learning, and being in control of your world—social, personal, and natural—through learning its laws and implementing them. None of this needed the classical religions and the spiritualities derived from them. None of this rejected the basic nature of a religion as a way of life promising and promoting total change or transformation. It did, however, deny the non-empirical world as the source of this empirical one and, with that denial, the foundation of the classical religions and spiritualities.

Classical religions and their spiritualities responded to the modern world and its denials in unique ways depending on the mindsets of certain groups. The *traditionalists* rejected all that threatened them and sought to return to what they described as the traditional ways; thus, some Christians demanded that Christian churches return to the fundamentals as reflected in the Bible. The *contemporalists* countered the threats of modernity by absorbing them whole, with little change, into their religious/spiritual lives while rejecting what no longer fit in the context of modern life. Christians with this mindset abandoned the cosmology of the Bible, accepted the sun as the center of the solar system, and accepted the existence of germs and microscopic life as the causes of disease and other ills. The *co-temporalists* sought to understand the basic nature of the modern era and its expression, so as to include them in a coherent way in their previous way of life, thus, using modern literary analysis, many Christian theologians accepted the Biblical stories about the beginning of the earth as stories about God as creator, not as scientific descriptions of what happened at the beginning of time.

These three divisions are clearly seen within Judaism as the Orthodox (traditionalists), Conservative (co-temporalists), and Reform (contemporalist) movements. The Orthodox retains all the ancient mitzvoth and celebrates the Sabbath and High Holidays in ancient Hebrew. The Conservative retain all mitzvoth still found viable in this modern world, and they use a mixture of ancient Hebrew and English in their services. The Reform has services on Sunday, in English, and sporadically keeps Kosher.

Traditionalist Spirituality

Now every little thing she did, from cooking to whispering to washing to holding hands with doctors, she did to try to keep the world from changing. It was an impossible task, she thought, but that is what we Chinese are good at. — Sam Meekings, Under Fishbone Clouds [210]

Fundamentalist Spirituality: A New Way of Looking at the Classics

The modern, as a way of dealing with reality, originated in the West and thus its first impact was upon Christianity. The United States, in particular, is seen as the example of a modern nation. As the modern way of life became more organized in the United States in the nineteenth century, some Christians took a defensive stance toward it by rejecting it. In making such a rejection, they developed what came to be known as Christian fundamentalism. The Scopes Trial (1925) was a prominent example of the fundamentalists' rejection of evolution. Behind this desire for the "old time religion" was an attitude and method of discovery that shared a great deal with the then developing modern culture. What they shared might be called "secular fundamentalism. It provided several signposts for Christian and other religious types of fundamentalism that are examples of a traditionalist spirituality.

Old is best and stick to the fundamentals.

Secular fundamentalism has not only shaped our modern world, but lies at the basis of Christian fundamentalism. Secular fundamentalism is a way of thinking and acting that millions of people subscribe to because they do not formally depend on God, nor do they need a god in order to function in modern society. Christian fundamentalism, while confessing a belief in God, supports this response. When we discuss any of the diverse fundamentalisms, and Christian fundamentalism in particular, in a pejorative or a complimentary manner, we are doing so based on what we encounter in those with a secular fundamentalist mindset every day of our lives.

183

Secular fundamentalism: What is it? [211]

Secular fundamentalism, referred to in the following as just fundamentalism, is a worldview in which all of life and its experiences are interpreted literally rather than symbolically; univocally rather than multivocally; uniformly rather than pluralistically. It is a way of seeing and interpreting our world that demands that the significant words that are expressive of meaning and belonging be identical from one context to another. It is also a movement of those seeking companionship among others of like mind and sensibilities so that the world is cast in an us-versus-them dichotomy. As both a worldview and a movement, its adherents accept certain conceptual signposts and normative attitudes as marks of the good and truthful person. This set of experiences, conceptual signposts, and normative attitudes make up the hermeneutical circle of fundamentalism. Each of these is connected to the other in such a way that one cannot exist without the other.

As a hermeneutic, it is a structuring of reality consequent upon a search for security and power.[212] It is carried out by drawing clear limits of meaning and belonging around the searchers, such that certain words are expressive of that meaning and belonging no matter what the context. This drawing of clear limits is dependent upon the fundamentalist experience, which indicates the end of the search and certain conceptual signposts that express that experience. Notice how modern such an approach is. It is attempting to do what the modern approach demands: to be objective. Objectivity means that, no matter what the context, we see the same thing. Something is real in the modern approach only when a successful experiment is performed anywhere and at any time resulting in the same results. Context of time and place are irrelevant. Fundamentalism demands the same objectivity.

The Fundamentalist Experience: Certainty within Uncertainty

The traditionalist, and in this instance fundamentalist, is a response to modernity as it enters into a person's life. Such an entrance may be the beginning of liminality and its uncertainties. Fundamentalism sees the present situation as filled with uncertainty. The experience of uncertainty can be invigorating and, therefore, a springboard for creativity or it can be frightening. Indeed, the glory of American life in the context of today's pluralism and freedom is frightening to many. Pluralism, for them, has

> *Truth is certain. Truthful people are good. We can tell the difference between the truthful good ones and the ignorant bad ones.*

become cheap relativism; freedom, promiscuity. They consider the traditions of the past a safety net because it set limits to pluralism and freedom. In many ways, that safety net has been destroyed by a cynical, scientific rationalism that fears and ridicules all tradition. Many people find themselves, in turn, afraid and without a clear sense of self or communal identity. The horizons of their lives, defined by their traditions, are distrusted and without communal support. No one can live long in constant fear and without some purpose in life. Those who have enjoyed the security of a particular faith will not allow themselves the agony of insecurity for a prolonged period of time. They will search for, and probably find, a worldview that offers what they seek. To find security, the fundamentalist seeks to experience life in a literal rather than a symbolic sense; to explain life and its experiences in a univocal rather than a multivocal sense; to live life and its experiences in a uniform rather than a pluralistic sense; to seek companionship among those of like mind and sensibilities such that the world is cast in an us-versus-them dichotomy.

Because of these life experiences, they accept certain conceptual signposts as marks of the good and truthful person. Let us look more closely at these experiences and conceptual signposts. The fundamentalist experience as described in this book is a conscious mentality. There are times when the fundamentalist feels the themes mentioned below so intensely that these feelings determine action(s) that express and reinforce the experience. These themes are listed here with no attempt at prioritization. They are experienced as a total mindset, with one theme perhaps dominating at one moment and another at another moment.

Several attitudes constitute the fundamentalist mentality. One is believing there is a strong, easily distinguished difference between those who are "good" and therefore speak the truth and those who do not speak the truth. There is uneasiness, sometimes bordering on anger, when some people describe themselves as sincere but really are not. These nominally sincere people may lack some of the conceptual signposts and/or the attitudes necessary to being a good person in the fundamentalist's definition. Whatever it is that these other people lack, the fundamentalist realizes that he or she does have these concepts and experiences while others do not. The reason the fundamentalist can claim such knowledge is because he or she has had the unique experiences that are the foundation of being good and truthful. The fundamentalist does not feel the need to investigate, to have oaths, or to engage in lengthy discussions. The fundamentalist senses quickly the presence of a truly sincere person because there are shared experiences between the two of you. One becomes accustomed to how it feels to be in the nominally good and truthful person's presence, and thus one learns to sense when a person is good and truthful and when he or she is not.

Fundamentalists have an optimistic outlook. This is not an abstract commitment but a deeply felt experience. Such an optimistic outlook can best be described as a feeling of confidence that if the world takes the direction envisioned by the truly good and truthful people, it will be the best possible world. The fundamentalist is optimistic that this world will come about if everyone has confidence and works hard to do what is necessary for this new world to come.

Because of this confidence, fundamentalists seem to have a special source of energy, vitality, and dynamism. Sometimes a fundamentalist is able to do things because of this confidence that he or she would never do on his or her own. Confident in her abilities and optimistic of the outcome, she is able to move to new heights of goodness and truth as a result of being at one with the true purpose of the universe.

To the fundamentalist, truth is experienced. It is felt, touched, and discovered. Such empirical truth is found in the written and spoken word. These words give security and provide a constant and clear authority in personal as well as communal life.

The fundamentalist expresses these feelings in his inner thoughts of gratitude for being good and for knowing the truth, and in hoping beyond hope that life will be good to him in return. In the midst of such inner thoughts she feels energized to such an extent that she believes she can do no wrong because she is associated with those who are good and who possess the truth.

These feelings result in easily identifiable words, phrases, and statements that establish a conceptual framework for one's experiences. Slogans, propaganda statements, advertising jingles, and repeated phrases and value statements are the ordinary ways in which these verbalizations are expressed. These verbalizations are a summary of the way the fundamentalist sees the world. They are also a ritual incantation that expresses the fact that one has had the experience and shares the common outlook to which these words bear witness. Agreeing upon such a common way of expressing oneself on the fundamentals issues in life, the fundamentalist is freed to do and think whatever he or she may wish.

Conceptual Signposts that Express and Reinforce the Experience

The fundamentalist slogans and statements may seem restrictive to a person who does not share the fundamentalist perspective, but these slogans and statements are freeing to the fundamentalist. They provide security by demonstrating what is true. These unquestioned presuppositions give rise to and reinforce certain conceptual signposts, such as the following:

- Truth is found in the use of words. By reducing the meaning of words to a precise and never changing significance, the truth of the matter at hand can be found. Each word points to, but does not participate in, another reality, which usually is founded on the basic experience.

- Thus, dualism is the best way to see the world, whether this is a dualism of object-subject, observer-observed, or person-thing.
- This dualism and reductionism allows analysis—the method of choice—to be used to full effect. All problems are to be analyzed by determining the causal link between the various objects (words) presented for analysis.
- In so doing, objectivity is claimed, since no emotion is found in the analysis and nothing is real beyond the empirical world that is analyzed.
- In the process, knowledge offers the fundamentalist a coercive power over causal processes. Truth is objective and beyond human feeling and subjectivity.

These conceptual attitudes are found, although recast in religious or spiritual terminology, among all spiritual fundamentalists.

Christian Fundamentalist Spirituality

Christian fundamentalism[213] is a distinct and important spirituality in our liminal times because it began as a Christian traditionalist response to the modern era while unknowingly accepting secular fundamentalism. It shares the history and signposts of classical Christianity, but it interprets that history and modifies those signposts in reaction to the modern mentality and its social consequences. It is very much a Bible-based form of Christianity. It begins with the challenging question of whether modern methods and the laws they discover are applicable to interpreting and living the Christian way of life. Will the natural laws revealed through mathematical analysis and scientific experiment enhance one's spiritual life? Will the modern methods for dating and reading ancient literature enhance one's reading of the Bible? Will the scientific discoveries and understandings associated with conception, birth, dying, and death deepen one's spiritual life? Can the social sciences such as psychology, sociology, and political science make a difference in our spiritual relationships? For the most part Christian fundamentalists reply to these questions with a strong "no," saying the Bible is their norm for living. They believe these sciences are valuable only once they have been judged by the Bible. From this standpoint of "no" to the modern present and "yes" to the ancient Bible, they form their signposts with the conviction that they represent an older and better way of life. As with many traditionalists, fundamentalists find a transcendent experience in the nostalgia of thinking about, talking about, and acting to embrace this vision of regaining the lost paradise.[214]

> **The words of the Bible have all the truth.**

This nostalgic experience begins with a profound life-changing event: conversion. American religious history is framed, in many ways, by the phenomenon of revival.[215] Revival is a powerful ritual in which, ultimately, the participants have the transcendent experience of Jesus's concern for them, their faults, their errors, and their sins. This concern is experienced in the intensity of Jesus's forgiveness and saving them from the fires of hell; bringing them into belief in His Word, the Bible, and joining them to the community of the saved. This experience, and its daily reinforcement by those who have undergone the same experience and share the same expectations about themselves and non-believers, are a powerful spiritual force in one's life. Although most books on Christian fundamentalism begin, and sometimes end, with the articles of belief, which are the fundamentals of fundamentalism, we can never forget that the basis of fundamentalism is the transcendent experience of salvation and the community within which it is shared.

Community: The Gathering of Believers

These are usually small communities. The mega churches are only considered "mega" in contrast to the fact that most Christian fundamentalist church communities are around one to two hundred people representing diverse family grouping well beyond a joining of nuclear families or individuals unknown to each other.[216] These were inward-looking communities more interested in the lives of fellow members and their mutual spiritual experiences than in politics. Gradually they have become more involved in the diverse political movements that

> *Life with bible-believers is transformative.*

have reached out to engage their energies against ways of life contrary to their own. As with other members of the evangelical movement, they are very adept at using contemporary media technologies and techniques. If you are interested in this spirituality, there are multiple means to get information and to contact others with similar interests. The seeming intimacy of such sites enables you to have a feeling of community without the physical necessity of being present at a church. A spirituality that has great difficulty with modern thought and its consequences has enormous expertise with the contemporary means of communication—whether it is the open air preaching and pamphlets of the nineteenth century, the radio of the twentieth century, or television, Facebook, Twitter, and online sermon podcasts of the twenty-first century. This expertise demonstrates that the fruits of the modern tree may be eaten without accepting what gave it birth.

Belief: The whole truth, so help me God

Fundamentalist belief begins and ends with the Bible. In 1878, the *Believers Meeting for Bible Study* summarized this fundamental belief by proclaiming in what came to be known as the Niagara Creed:

We believe 'that all Scripture is given by inspiration of God,' by which we understand the whole of the book called the Bible; nor do we take the statement in the sense in which it is sometimes foolishly said that works of human genius are inspired, but in the sense that the Holy Ghost gave the very words of the sacred writings to holy men of old; and that His Divine inspiration is not in different degrees, but extends equally and fully to all parts of these writings, historical, poetical, doctrinal, and prophetical and to the smallest word, and inflection of a word, provided such word is found in the original manuscripts: 2 Timothy 3:16, 17; 2 Peter 1:21; 1 Corinthians 2:13; Mark 12:26, 36; 13:11; Acts 1:16; 2:4.[217]

The Bible, in other words, is inspired by God the Holy Spirit and enjoys the inerrancy of God. There is no error in the Bible. But this is easier said than read. Notice that the statement admits that there are different writings in the Bible such as poetry, doctrine, and prophecy. With the modern approach to reading literature, one reads the text "objectively," according to the intent of the author and the actual type of literature being written. One reads the text as it was written a thousand years before Christ, not as if it was written in the twenty-first century. For example, how did people write and think about an historical event such as the creation of the world? Today if someone is writing an historical document and says that it took a day for something to happen, we think twenty-four hours. But is that the way they thought before clocks marked the day with seconds, minutes, and hours? Even more, how do pre-scientific cultures describe the beginning of the universe? Do they write history or poetry? They cannot write in a modern scientific manner since modern science did not exist. Or, is there another way not present in our culture for making such a description? This is God's word say the fundamentalists. If it is about an historical event it must be history. Unless the Bible says otherwise, a contemporary twenty-four hour day is a twenty-four hour day in the Bible. That is just common sense. History is history. It doesn't change. All the rest is just some university professor trying to give us his or her mixed up thinking about the Bible. The Bible is without error and should be read with this common sense, or literal, way of reading. Just the facts, not some interpretation of them gotten from outside the Bible or the imaginings of a non-believer's mind. These facts are found in each sentence and phrase in the Bible. Thus, God's words are *God's* words. We can read these words and be sure they are true and meant for you and me, each of us. There is no danger in taking these words and using them for preaching, teaching, inspiration, and daily living.

This method of reading the Bible is called "chain texting." In this type of literary analysis, linking together common ideas with their common sense understanding across diverse biblical books and diverse types of literature seeks to understand why God placed those words, and consequent ideas, in the Bible for our inspiration and life-giving direction. Studying the Bible is understanding it as a whole and linking the various ideas together for our spiritual lives. Each word, phrase, and sentence is God's, exactly as it stands, with no need for context or proof of what God thinks.

With such a way of reading the Bible in hand, Christian fundamentalists claim there are certain non-negotiable fundamental beliefs found in the Bible. The five listed below are generally agreed upon as the fundamentals. Most fundamentalists, however, have more than these five. There is disagreement as to what others may be added to the list of Christian fundamental beliefs.

- The virgin birth of Christ
- The inspiration of the Bible by the Holy Spirit and the inerrancy of Scripture as a result of this inspiration
- The belief that Christ's death was the atonement for sin
- The bodily resurrection of Christ
- The historical reality of Christ's miracles[218]

This listing of fundamentals was written in obvious denial of the modernist rejection of a supernatural world as causative of what happens in this one. Many classical spiritualities take the same stance with a different view of the other-spiritual or supernatural world and how

> **This evil world will end – soon!**

it affects this one. So, if your spirituality shares this view of the spiritual world as separate from yet causative of this one, it would either accept or reject the fundamentalist view for other reasons than those provided by modernity.

Another important belief for most fundamentalists is the expectation that the world is coming to an end. As the Niagara Creed puts it:

> *We believe that the world will not be converted during the present dispensation, but is fast ripening for judgment, while there will be a fearful apostasy in the professing Christian body; and hence that the Lord Jesus will come in person to introduce the millennial age, when Israel shall be restored to their own land, and the earth shall be full of the knowledge of the Lord; and that this personal and premillennial advent is the blessed hope set before us in the Gospel for which we should be constantly looking. (Luke 12:35-40; 17:26-30; 18:8; Acts 15:14-17; 2 Thessalonians 2:3-8; 2 Timothy 3:1-5; Titus 1:11-15)[219]*

Notice the chain texts at the end of this quote. This belief also highlights another important element in fundamentalist belief: prophecy is understood as foretelling the future. Fundamentalists are convinced the Bible is filled with all kinds of prophecy but especially those associated with the end of the world. Modernists speak of apocalyptic literature; fundamentalists speak of prophecies about the end of the world. Some fundamentalist churches have provided us with exact dates of the end; others, with strong proclamations that it is near. The establishment of the State of Israel in 1948 was seen as the fulfillment of biblical prophecies. Fundamentalist churches are strong supporters of Israel as a result of these prophecies and its linkage to the world's end.

Rituals: Phrases such as "Born Again," "Praise the Lord," and "Let Us Gather in His Name"

Although many Christian fundamentalists reject or modify central rituals of classical Christianity, such as the sacraments, they retain some as biblical commands (ordinances) and add others. We have already seen one of these in the brief discussion of revival and the concept of being saved. These are certainly highly individual experiences, yet they do happen in predictable steps with predictable phrases such as "praise the Lord" and "being born again." Especially

> **Spoken, personal, and sincere prayer stimulates the Spirit.**

if one was born into a fundamentalist family, one is socialized into what is expected of being born again: Sunday celebrations, modes of evangelism, ways of prayer, and the manner of interacting with those outside one's church. The words are Bible based; the actions are contemporary ways of performing biblical actions such as baptism outdoors and imbibing grape juice and not wine at the Lord's Supper. Most fundamentalist churches accept music and song as essential aspects of their worship services. "Spirituals" are central to many African-American fundamentalist congregations. To many they provide a deep sense of the spiritual life. Like Yoga in Hinduism, Spirituals have become part of mainstream culture sung by people with little knowledge of their words or heritage. Bible study groups are part and parcel of being a Christian fundamentalist. The ritual of studying the Bible has a long tradition that gives deep energy and spiritual life to those who continue it throughout their lives.

Morality: The Bible Tells Us What to Do

The sporadic court challenges demanding the public display of the Ten Commandments are many times the result of fundamentalist Christian beliefs. The other normative moral imperatives of classical Christianity usually do not get as much attention. Emphasis upon the Ten Commandments reflects an attraction to the Old Testament God of judgment, power, and the favoring of God's chosen people. This is not to say that the other imperatives of classical Christianity are not followed, but it is to say that other, more current, moral issues gain more attention. For example, contemporary market capitalism is recognized by modern historians as having its beginning at the end of feudalism. The Christian fundamentalist view, however, is that capitalism is based on the Bible—as are other strong markers of fundamentalist morality such as prohibitions against drinking alcohol in any form and dancing.[220]

With the Bible as its fertile ground, the fundamentalist expression of Christianity grows strong in both the context of the modern world and the liminal world that follows it. This is a spirituality of certainty and predictability. The signposts derived from the Bible provide the believer facts equal to any scientific experiment or mathematical demonstration. These facts are more easily found in the Bible through the common sense reading of it rather than in any scientific manual. As with scientific facts, these spiritual facts are equally applicable throughout the world and history. Context does not change them. The biblical certainty is affirmed with every reading of the Bible and every gathering of the saved. These are indeed God's people among whom we celebrate our mutual salvation—the actualized promise of total transcendence. Predictability is found in biblical prophecy that foretold Jesus's first coming and is foretelling his second at the end of this world and the coming of His kingdom.

Pentecostal and Charismatic Spirituality

Pentecostal and Charismatic Christianity is currently the fastest growing form of Christianity. It is truly a global spirituality adapting to every culture. It currently enlivens the lives of five hundred million people, one fourth of Christianity.[221] It is important not only because of its global strength but also because of its adaptability to every culture and, in the context of North America and the English speaking world, it provides the

> *The Ten Commandments carefully observed makes an observant Christian.*

culture with a great deal of its public images and language about spirituality. The quote at the beginning of this chapter is from the founder of Pentecostalism in Newfoundland.

Pentecostal and Charismatic spirituality are characterized by a deeply felt experience of the Holy Spirit's presence called "Spirit Baptism" and the signs that accompany this experience, particularly talking in tongues. The terms Pentecostal and charismatic are used to distinguish between those having this foundational experience and their institutional embodiments. Pentecostals are usually, though not always, those found in Bible-based, evangelical, and fundamentalist Protestant churches. Purely fundamentalist churches usually reject the Pentecostal assertion that the spiritual gifts present among early Christians are present today.[222] Charismatics are usually found in churches that are tradition based, such as Roman Catholic churches and mainline Protestant churches such as Lutheran and Episcopal/Anglican. They differ on whether to use modern tools in Bible reading, spiritual discernment, and how to include the Spirit's role throughout time (tradition) in contemporary ecclesial organizations and spiritual life. They share the deep experience of the Spirit and its fruits. It is what they share that is an exemplar of response to the modern and the liminal times. While the signposts of their respective institutions are of utmost importance to them, the deep experience of the Spirit's presence and the Spirit's direction throughout their life provides a privileged view of these signposts—placing the Charismatics in particular in possible tension with church authorities who have not undergone the same experience.

Pentecostal" is called "Pentecostal" because of its identification with the early Christian experience of the Holy Spirit at the time of the Jewish *Shavuoth* (Pentecost) (Acts 2:1-6) after Jesus's resurrection (Easter). "Charismatic"

> **The Spirit's language begins with baptized speech.**

is in reference to the gifts ("charisma" in Greek) delineated in several places in St. Paul's letters to the early Christians, especially in 1 Corinthians 12-14. These are called spiritual gifts both in the New Testament and in classical Christianity. Pentecostals and Charismatics believe that these spiritual gifts present among the early Christians are present today, indicating a profound renewal in Christianity. The gifts are many, but those continually emphasized within Protestant and Charismatic Christian churches are taken from the list provided in 1 Corinthians 12:4-12):[223] speaking in tongues as a witness to the indwelling of the Holy Spirit (after having been baptized in the Holy Spirit); wise speech (words of wisdom) understood as providing the proper way to give spiritual direction but necessarily tied in with discernment of spirits (understood as evil and good spirits); deep knowledge (words of knowledge) provides truths revealed by the Holy Spirit; faith; healing; and prophecy, understood as stating a message of God to those present rather than predicting the future.

Baptism in the Spirit, which includes speaking in tongues or glossolalia, is deeply moving to both the speaker and to those who listen. It is a central ritual of Pentecostal/Charismatic Christianity. Many times it occurs as the entire community gathers around the person to be baptized, laying their hands on that person, and praying for him or her. Many times, too, those praying are also praying in tongues. When the person breaks into a prayer that coincides with those praying around her, everyone is part of a profound spiritual experience. In the context of secular fundamentalism, it provides a marked certitude of one's spiritual way of life.

Identity Groups and Christian Militias

The various types of religious militias throughout the world remind us that religions and their diverse spiritualities are powerful motivators and an ever present temptation toward violent means to achieve spiritual ends. Christian Identity groups such as the Ku Klux Klan (National Knights of), The Arm of the Lord, The Covenant, Christian Conservative Churches of America, The Church of Jesus Christ Christian, Aryan Nation are examples of these. Members of these groups believe that when the Bible talks about chosen people, it is referring to white people of European descent who are the actual tribe that God chose. From this perspective, "white" is always right and the world should adapt itself to white European desires. Some even go so far as to see all non-whites as not having a soul. They nostalgically yearn for when England ruled the world and those colonized were to serve the whites who extended British rule. The spirituality of these groups is a mixture of Christian fundamentalist belief stitched together from strands of selected biblical texts. Their weekly, or sometimes more frequent gatherings provide a deep sense of fellowship around these texts and the rituals associated with military preparations and preaching about how they are being persecuted. Moral generalities centered on the family, the necessary sacrifices preparing for confrontation with the hated enemy, and treating each other with honor provide the substance of this signpost.[224]

Non-Christian Fundamentalism

A significant number of influential people in the modern world see religion as a hindrance to human development and human freedom. They seek to explain the world without dependence upon non-worldly causes. Modern methods have also sought to understand the world as if God does not exist. In fact, the term miracle came to be defined as an event caused by non-natural causes, meaning by God. Before the division of the world into natural and supernatural, it would have been inconceivable to think of miracles in such a way. But as the laws of nature were discovered, the use of these explanations was seen to be deleterious to a mature person's thinking and acting. All those outside the modern world, whether from an indigenous tribe or an ancient civilization, were seen to be slightly less human if they did not think and act in a modern way. As people within a society that was built with modern means rejected modern thought and methods, they too were viewed as not only immature but also dangerous to the essential progress demanded by modern sciences such as economics, medicine, psychology, and political science. Their way of life was dangerous to the modern way of life.

Commentators on the modern scene, such as journalists, began to use the term fundamentalist in a derogatory way, as a sum of all the immature ways of thinking and acting that would return the modern world to the "dark ages" of ignorance and superstition. One such journalist, Curtis Lee Laws, coined the term "fundamentalist" to indicate Christians who were willing "to do battle over the fundamentals."[225] These fundamentals had been spelled out in many places such as the Niagara Creed (1884) but in most detail in the series of pamphlets titled *The Fundamentals* published in 1909.[226] The "battle" that Lee suggested gained national prominence in *The Scopes Trial* (1925). The armies who waged the battle were described in the newspaper accounts of the Scopes Trial and in the plays, books, and movies that continued to bring it to national consciousness. The subsequent battles over evolution, curriculum, teenage dancing, prayer at school sports events, and teachers' freedoms to voice religious opinions while teaching in Public schools all served to keep these anti-modernist threats before the public's eyes. And don't forget the stereotypical radio and TV fundamentalist preacher who, to the non-fundamentalists, represented the worst example of ignorance of the natural world and its laws and threatened to return modern society to the restrictions and superstitions of the past.

When Middle Eastern cultures began to revolt against Western colonialism, it was seen by many in the West as a rejection of the modern way of life rather than a revolt against Western subjugation. Those in revolt also conflated the two. The concepts of religion and the separation of church and state were part of the Western culture by the time the revolts began. Religion as a separate entity from culture or state

> *Keep it simple. Say it with feeling. The truth of our holy book will win out.*

was unknown to the anti-colonial culture. Quite the contrary; some leaders believed that the way they were subjugated and the way their particular religion was practiced was the explanation for why they were powerless and poor. A return to the golden age of the religion was necessary for the people to climb out of powerlessness to powerfulness. This nostalgia for the past was formative of the dreams for the future. The term fundamentalist, in this context, has some validity. I use it here in the context of traditionalist spirituality within a secular fundamentalist mentality.[227] As with Christian fundamentalism, popular commentators on contemporary Islam join both fundamentalisms as attacks on the modern way of life and all the freedoms that issue from it. This may not be true. As with Christian fundamentalism, so with Muslim fundamentalism, it is necessary to study each purveyor of Fundamentalism since few agree among themselves on all the fundamentals. We should, however, spend some time asking what these fundamentalisms have to say to our own spirituality.

Muslim Fundamentalists

Muslim fundamentalists differ from Christian fundamentalists in three ways.[228] First, they use other sacred writings in addition to the Quran; Christians use only the Bible. Second, modern literary analysis did not directly attack the Quran as it did the Bible. Instead the modern sciences attacked both the supernatural worldview upon which all the sacred writings are based and the unified culture that grew out of these writings. Third, the law (sharia) that evolved from the interpretation of the sacred books, and is still evolving under the Muslim fundamentalist interpretations rejected almost all modern social development, such as many of the rights in the United Nations list of Human Rights. Christian fundamentalism, so far, has not publicly rejected human rights. Many exponents of both fundamentalisms do reject the United Nations, the most vocal exponent of Human Rights.[229]

The experience of colonialism has a deep and permanent influence on a culture. In the post-colonial period, the us-versus-them dichotomy of secular fundamentalism is present but without the clarity of purpose and intent. With the departure of the colonial power, the ever present "them" is gone. This leaves a search for identity that previously was found in opposition to the other. It is not so easy now. The scapegoat "them" is usually the former colonial powers and the United States.

Religion is always providing a way out of the here and now through its signposts of transcendence. It provided this when the oppressors were present. The formerly oppressed now look for it to do the same. Yet, once the oppressors are gone, the classic forms of religion that worked so well before to give hope and a vision of the future seem to lack the dynamism and future-telling ability as they had during the colonial period.[230] The nostalgia for that past time, awakened by charismatic leaders, focuses upon the beginning of the religion and the community that evolved out of it. There is always the presupposition that because the fundamentals of Islamic law and other signposts coincided with the beginning of Islam, it must be better than it is now. Devoid of contemporary historical methods and the historical consciousness that accompanies them, there is little to critique such a presupposition. These nostalgic longings for the early days of Islam seek to transcend present uncertainties by going to the distant past to determine the immediate future. The centrality of the Modern experience sets the scene for this return by offering a symbol of that past in a book honored throughout time as the actual and literal word of Allah. The commentaries on the book by Mohammed and others provide a sense of really knowing what the book means and how the community lived. The challenge for those we call fundamentalists, others call reformers, and some call Islamists, is to not only read these books for what is needed but to read them aloud in such a way that they give people the sense of hope they found in them while the colonial powers were present.

Within Islam, the official readers of the book are the *ulama* (scholars) among the Sunni and the *ayatollahs* among the Shia, also experts in the law. Within a fundamentalist context they provide us with two examples of Muslim fundamentalism: Iran and Saudi Arabia. The ayatollahs in Iran constitute the interpreters of the law that becomes *sharia* for all since it manifests Allah's will. In Saudi Arabia, sharia law is essential to the Saudi way of life, even though the government is an absolute monarchy. As such it must be interpreted by the *ulama* in Saudi Arabia. In describing classical Islam, we mentioned that this absolute monarchy is a dedicated advocate of Wahhabism, called *Salafism* by the Saudis, who believe *Salafism* is the foundation for worldwide Islam (*ummah*). They certainly provide their citizens with a clear identity and a spirituality that details the will of Allah in their lives.

These are only two examples of contemporary Muslim fundamentalism. Both retain the role of trained legal scholars in the reading and application of their way of life founded upon the Quran. Part of the return to the past has also been, among some Muslims, a return to looking to those beyond the community of scholars (ulama or ayatollah) for understanding that past. They look to the legal concept of *Ijtihad* to provide an interpretation closer to the Quran's original meaning as applied to contemporary times. Originally *Ijtihad* referred to a devout Muslim making a legal interpretation independent of the traditional sources when that interpretation dealt with personal matters. Some fundamentalists, however, see themselves as capable of making such judgment not only for themselves but for the *umma* at large, thus opening up the gates of interpretation through the use of *Ijtihad*.[231] With an ability to understand the Quran as it was intended using *Ijtihad,* these kinds of Muslim fundamentalists see themselves establishing an ummah of true fellowship and true submission to Allah. Certainly, in doing so, he provides a sharia for the present in a community of like-mindedness. The vagueness of identity lost by the withdrawal of colonialism is clarified based upon the newly found fundamentals of the faith.

There are numerous fundamentalist militant groups that use *Ijtihad* to forward their search for home, identity, and total control of their fate. Some might see both the Muslim Brotherhood and Hamas as such in their methods of understanding the Quran and Sunnah as the sole reference point for ordering the life of the Muslim family, individual, community, and state.[232]

Other Fundamentalisms[233]

There are many traditionalists who take the fundamentalist path. The communication tools that continue to reach out and bind the world together expose all those with proximity to television and the Internet to "the other" as a threat as well as entertainment; as offering a total way of life as well as an imaginary world of song and story. The modern way of life is very much a part of that threat. The Secular Fundamentalist mentality of our age instills a sense that a certainty of thought and fellowship are out there; one just has to discover it. Traditional fundamentalists seek in a nostalgic search in the past for the necessary fundamentals to provide this certainty of thought and fellowship. Part of that search is for the original and unifying elements of belief, ritual, morality, and community that will make a nation strong enough to stand alone, without compromise, against any threatening other. In this instance, nationalism and religion once again become constituent elements of a culture—no longer subject to the separations, isolations, and objectifications present in modernity.

A quick search on the Internet will bring you to groups representing the fundamentals of each of the classical forms of religion. From my perspective, they offer an ersatz nationalism built from contemporary desires more than past realities.[234] But my perspective does not matter here. Your spirituality may have this national element as part of it, or, in your search among the classical spiritualities, you may have found elements of a spirituality that demand you go to the homeland of the religion because it is only there that your desire for transcendence may occur. In Chapter Nine we will discuss some elements to consider if you feel you must make such a life-changing decision.

Recent historical developments may be of help in your search among the many spiritual fundamentalist groups around the world. If we take for granted that the Christian fundamentalists were on the front wave of reaction to the modern era, and acted out of a Secular Fundamentalist culture, then one evident development over the last hundred years has been the increase of such churches. There are thousands of such Christian communities and tens of thousands of people searching among them for a satiation to their thirst for the transcendent. The increase of churches is not so much from more people searching but from the same people searching in many churches at the same time.[235] Some churches are as small as two or three families. Certainly these places are available. Yet, with such continual multiplying of communities and seekers, we must also ask if this desire can be satisfied.

The classical spiritualities retain in their beliefs a completely new state of existence for everyone (heaven or Nirvana, for example) either after death or in the distant future. They do so, I would suggest, because their experience is that we cannot be completely satisfied in this life. The instant gratification demanded by many people in developed economies doesn't seem to be present over a prolonged period of time. The suggested drink, for example, that promises in a deluge of advertisements to slake our thirst, still leaves us thirsty for more drink beyond the moment when we finish the last drop.

The promotion and promise offered by secular fundamentalism for such instant certitude and fellowship has not been fulfilled either in the secular or the religious realm. Secular fundamentalism as well as religious fundamentalism share the premise of the modern mentality that truth and fellowship can be reduced to one foundational principle. This premise has been rejected by many, and we now live in a liminal age: the modern era has not kept its promise of providing a happy life that transcends the suffering and death around us. But there are many who have accepted *carte blanche* much of the modern world into their spiritualities. You may be among them. Let us look at some of these contemporalist spiritualities to help you discern if one fits you.

Contemporalist Spirituality

Many people wish to be current and up to date, fitting in with those they deem important. The term "contemporal" itself has been coined to formally acknowledge those who wish their spirituality to reflect this energy of life and to support those who are influential in keeping up with the times. But, as

> *Stay current. The news was yesterday.*

historians and older people know, times change. And, as sociologists and niche marketers also know, people's sense of trend setters are very much in the eye of the beholder. Witness how a president can be voted in with an overwhelming majority one year and the next be favored by only 32 percent of the population. Indeed, there are those who shift allegiances with the attractive phrase of a pundit, the enticing blast of a TV commercial, or an article in the style section of a magazine.

But many people do not. They hold on to what was current during a certain time in their lives and the spirituality that provided the dynamic energy of that time. Being contemporary once was enough for a lifetime. The contemporalist of yesterday is some people's old-time religion today. There are few religions that have not taken the route of contemporality sometime in their history. The times we are interested in are the modern and the liminal. We cannot describe, review, and analyze all of the attempts to keep up with the modern and liminal times. Therefore, we will look at the most influential.

Modern spiritualities are characterized by a Secular Fundamentalist outlook with one's certitude and fellowship derived from scientific facts and theories based on the hard and soft sciences. They reject any facts and theories based on a supernatural worldview. Liminal spiritualities are embedded with uncertainty, tentativeness, and suspicion of all ideologies and communities that demand one's total commitment over a prolonged period of time. They do so because of a deep hermeneutical suspicion[236] and historical consciousness that prevents them from saying "yes" to anyone and anything forever. These categories, formulated from a philosophical perspective, also represent dominant cultural perspectives in the West. We can see historically how religions, and the spiritualities they represent, have reacted to these perspectives. We have already examined this trend with the traditionalists. Now we will do so in the context of the contemporalists. Here we see how people have accepted almost *carte blanche* the dominant perspective of the surrounding culture. We will leave to the co-temporalists the difficult task of neither rejecting (traditionalist) nor accepting (contemporalist) the dominant culture. We will do so by providing brief descriptions of the religion and/or its spirituality. This should enable you, together with the references in the endnotes, to understand the spirituality and act accordingly.

One thing I would like to remind you is that most people know very little about religion and science. As a consequence, when they develop a spirituality which they may call scientific or which they will refer to as deeply imbued with certain religious perspectives, they are usually doing so with little reference to what professionals or clergy in those fields think or practice. When an individual or group of people adapt to the modern, therefore, there is a great deal of room for the imagination in the spiritual practices they build.

Becoming a Modern Spirituality

We've all seen children play "dress up." They dress imitating someone they may or may not know, but inevitably, they are limited by what is available in the form of clothes and shoes, and they exaggerate some aspect of who they are imitating. There is a lot of imagination buzzing around in those little heads.

Many times when individuals are striving to develop a modern spirituality, they seem very similar to children playing dress-up. They usually find their former spiritual means and signposts empty of transcendent energy. Yet they are driven by a need to create signposts for themselves that provide hope for transcendence among those they sense projecting such energizing hope. In contemporary life, there are many on the Inter-

> *"God" is so old. So get with the new.*

net and elsewhere who proclaim the availability of new scientific signposts to a spiritual life. These proclamations for a modern spirituality usually are found among three major movements: self-help, the "isms," and former classical religions appearing in contemporary dress. The following are some examples.

The Self-help Movements: Religious Science, the Twelve Steps, and Scientology

Particular self-help publications, communities, and websites promise and promote methods to satiate a person's desire to transcend her current life and exchange it for another one. Instead of the signposts of the classical religions, the self-help movement offers signposts that replace the supernatural with mental powers demonstrated, they say, by science. Émile Coué de Châtaigneraie (1857-1926) summarized it well with his phrase, "Every day, in every way, I'm getting better and better." He promises that this phrase, said at the beginning and end of every day, with full concentration and devoid of negative thoughts, with one being truly convinced that the former negativity in one's life will disappear, will make all negativity disappear. —Guaranteed! Experience proves it![237] Approaches such as these have abounded in Western culture since the nineteenth century. They are generally described as the New Thought Movement.

Deborah Whitehouse in her book *New Thought: A Practical American Spirituality* suggests that New Thought is still evolving and that "Many believe it might be the quintessential spirituality for the next millennium."[238] Whether it is "the" spirituality for the twenty-first century, it certainly was an important one in the nineteenth and twentieth. It linked the mind, science, mysticism, and positive thought in a way that has influenced the way many Americans think of spirituality.[239]

One example of New Thought in general and self-help in particular is Religious Science developed by Ernest Shurtleff Holmes (1887-1960). In his book *Science of the Mind* (1926),[240] Holmes creatively brings together many ideas associated with New Thought that were rumbling around in his culture. These ideas and the words that express them have a unique meaning to his spirituality. Yet it has attracted many followers over the years.

Holmes says that the only thing that exists is an infinite mind. We might call it God, Christ Consciousness, or Spirit. Since it is all that exists, it is always present. We are God, and the way we come in contact with ourselves, the Divine Intelligence, is through the spiritual mind treatment where we learn the necessary steps to achieve what we desire—our good. This "good" is always present in the infinite mind. We just have to know how to bring its presence into our presence. The infinite mind is non-judgmental, only wishing the good within itself to be shared with all. Within this sharing lies the necessary harmony for now and eternity. Our eternal life is the manner in which we share this harmony with the infinite mind and everything that surrounds us.[241]

Holmes influenced another famous preacher and author, Norman Vincent Peale (1898–1993), whose book, *The Power of Positive Thinking*,[242] and many other writings left a deep impression among many as to the function and role of a spirituality. He was able to combine his Christian Methodist background with his understanding of psychiatry to project a basis for spirituality that seemed both scientific and Christian. His quotes are repeated by many as an expression of their Christian understanding of belief and as a way to bolster their mental health: *Believe it is possible to solve your problem and it will be solved. Tremendous things happen to the believer. So believe the answer will come. It will. When life hands you a lemon, make lemonade.*

This self-help approach, which focuses on an individual's total control of the empirical world through the use of the non-empirical (mind, spirit, mystic), is found among many individuals and communities proclaiming spiritualities of hope that confidently promise and promote methods which, if practiced, will transform your life.

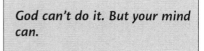

God can't do it. But your mind can.

A self-help movement that also promises you transformation, but sees such a transformation as occurring through the help of God and community in addition to a positive outlook, is Alcoholics Anonymous and its many derivatives. Twelve-step spiritualities imitate the twelve-step program of Alcoholics Anonymous with slight adjustments depending on the type of addiction that is their concern. Although AA began as part of the Moral Re-armament Movement in 1935,[243] a self-help initiative in its own way, its members today are as diverse as the human race. This same diversity is found among most twelve-step spiritualities. Their signposts demonstrate not only their embodiment of the self-help movement but also their beginnings in the United States. They were founded on the belief that humans can transform themselves by their own effort and/or conviction that a power greater than they will assist them. They form democratic communities of peers in which, through mutual help, they succeed. They meet regularly, and each meeting repeats the ritual of introduction, expression of addiction, and repletion of the successful use of the twelve steps. They are based on the conviction that a moral life builds character and results in life without addiction. American movies, songs, and publications repeat and reinforce the success of what happens through these twelve steps. Presently the twelve steps as provided by AA are as follows:[244]

1. *We admitted we were powerless over alcohol—that our lives had become unmanageable.*
2. *Came to believe that a Power greater than ourselves could restore us to sanity.*
3. *Made a decision to turn our will and our lives over to the care of God as we understood Him.*
4. *Made a searching and fearless moral inventory of ourselves.*

5. *Admitted to God, to ourselves, and to another human being the exact nature of our wrongs.*
6. *Were entirely ready to have God remove all these defects of character.*
7. *Humbly asked Him to remove our shortcomings.*
8. *Made a list of all persons we had harmed, and became willing to make amends to them all.*
9. *Made direct amends to such people wherever possible, except when to do so would injure them or others.*
10. *Continued to take personal inventory, and when we were wrong, promptly admitted it.*
11. *Sought through prayer and meditation to improve our conscious contact with God as we understood Him, praying only for knowledge of His will for us and the power to carry that out.*
12. *Having had a spiritual awakening as the result of these steps, we tried to carry this message to alcoholics, and to practice these principles in all our affairs.*[245]

"God" in these steps is not necessarily Yahweh, Theos, or Allah but may be seen as a "higher power"—a term which may be inclusive of the God of the Abrahamic religions. Yet a sense of the Christian God of the movement's origins permeates the twelve steps. Those uneasy with "God" language are also uneasy with this language no matter how much it is replaced with the term "higher power." In a culture still nominally Christian, however, most people are at ease with this language and the self-help attitude that is part of this spirituality. Both points are demonstrated by the many imitators of Alcoholics Anonymous. Here is a partial list of these groups: Celebrate Recovery, Gamblers Anonymous, Sexual Compulsives, Pills Anonymous, Marijuana Anonymous, Crystal Meth Anonymous, Debtors Anonymous, Overeaters Anonymous, Co-Dependents Anonymous, Cocaine Anonymous, Narcotics Anonymous, Adult Children of Alcoholics, S.O.S. (Secular Organizations for Sobriety), Cocaine Anonymous, Overeaters Anonymous, and Debtors Anonymous.

On the edge of these self-help movement spiritualities is a religion that pleads its modernity by claiming to be scientific. The Church of Scientology was founded in 1954 by L. Ron Hubbard (1911-1986). Its foundation was laid in Hubbard's early book *Dianetics: The Modern Science of Mental Health* (1950) and his science fiction writings.[246] Scientologists believe that we are eternal, spiritual beings. We are unhappy because the negative experiences that we have had in the past and present stay with us in our subconscious as metal aberrations called *engrams*. Only when these *engrams* are cleared will we be happy by returning to our eternal, spiritual selves.[247] The Church of Scientology claims that it can clear you of the engrams. It "…works 100 percent of the time when it is properly applied to a person who sincerely desires to improve his life."[248] It does this through a process called *auditing*, which includes the use of a mechanism called an E-meter. The number of sessions naturally depends on the individual involved—and the individual's ability to pay for each session. The total process does not stop with being clear because the person must discover who she or he really is. This discovery occurs by being led by an individual practitioner who has already made the discovery. This is a much longer and more involved process than becoming clear because each of us really is a *thetan*. Theatans created this material universe. But then they became so attached to what they created that they began to think they were the material body they created. As a scientologist becomes clear and/or becomes more knowledgeable about her *thetan* nature, she also becomes a deeply moral person. The more clear she becomes, she also realizes she is not her body. The nature of morality, mortality, and the precise nature of all the scientological rituals becomes evident as the practitioner advances in the church.

The 'isms: Nationalism, Scientism, and Humanism

Every form of spirituality, whether shaped from personal concerns and transcendent desires or accepted from surrounding choices, has a narrative. The science fiction stories of Ron Hubbard, re-told within the Church of Scientology, provide Scientologists with such a narrative about Thetans, their fall, and the necessary means to return to where they came from. A narrative is the pair of glasses through which we read the past, present, and choose a possible future. The narrative places the signposts on the road to transcendence and focuses our attention on how to walk that road, what may prevent us from taking that walk, and where the road leads.

Our socialization process includes bits and pieces of a narrative; this can be as subtle as discovering in childhood that school is closed on Presidents' Day. It can also be a central part of the story (Christmas celebrates Jesus's birth), or the entire narrative (the film *Little Buddha*). We hear many stories. Some of these stories become part of our spirituality. Joseph Campbell suggests that these narratives perform four functions: *cosmological*, because they explain how the whole universe works for and against us; *sociological*, because they affirm the necessity of keeping communal rules and customs in order for them to work in our favor; *pedagogical*, because they teach us how to act in order to live well; *mystical*, because in the telling of the story, there is the constant opportunity for a deeply spiritual, sacred experience. He, as many others, considers these profound and influential stories myths. To those outside the myth-telling community, these stories are false and misleading; to those within the community, they are sacred and never to be contradicted.[249]

Each of the 'isms we are about to describe is composed of many myths. Millions of people have died to protect the world they describe. These myths have invigorated many more people to live creatively in the present with a firm hope for the future. By now, commentators have reduced the entire story to a few descriptive sentences, which is helpful when doing a quick review. These short descriptions will provide you with the essential narrative upon which a certain form of spirituality is built.

One "ism" that has produced much death and exhilaration is *nationalism*. The nation and its expressions becomes the means through which one finds transcendence. Its founding documents, rituals, polity, and heroic citizens become, to its people, the object of their total obedience, loyalty, and dedication. The nation-narrative is usually composed of diverse themes brought together by an overarching need of the individual or group. In the case of the United States, this is usually seen as accepting the Constitution and the Gettysburg' Address as its sacred scriptures; holidays such as the Fourth of July, Thanksgiving, and Christmas as its rituals; hard work and equality as its moral necessities; democracy as its polity; capitalism, competition, freedom, and individualism as its core values. Its enemies are usually depicted as socialism, communism, and modern liberalism.[250] The nationalisms of Nazi Germany[251] and the former United Soviet Socialist Republic (USSR) are sometimes described in the same breath as the nationalisms of the United States, France, Japan, and China. Nationalism seems a natural tendency once a nation is formed and the people are seen to be an inherent constituent of the politics, policies, and culture of that nation.[252] Nationalism is a secular spirituality that has caused a significant amount of death in the modern centuries. Nonetheless, it has garnered just as much dedication, sacrifice, and martyrdom as any of the classical spiritualities.

> **Strongly held beliefs are the foundation of every nation.**

> **Our nation is better than your nation.**

Scientism makes the news occasionally when a scientist seeks fame and fortune by declaring God does not exist because there is no scientific proof that God is real. Most scientists believe in God, but scientism is most evident in the declarations of non-believers found in print and electronic media. The characters known as "Bones" in the television series *Bones* and "Spock" in the movies and television series *Star Trek* are examples of someone who lives by science and science alone.

The spirituality of scientism embraces only those signposts that express scientific facts. If you live according to scientism, your beliefs coincide with and are demonstrated by the scientific method and its results. Your rituals and moral imperatives encourage healthy human development and fit within the constructs of the social sciences. You associate with those who think as you do, and you find it exhilarating to hear new ideas and use new technologies. As with Spock and Bones, you have diffi-

> *Facts proven through experiment are the sole basis for the spiritual life.*

culty understanding and associating with those who are unorganized, illogical, and act primarily on feelings in their everyday lives.

Granted the overwhelming ignorance of both science and religion among most English speakers, many pundits, preachers, and politicians are free to use their imagination to create narratives describing scientific spirituality that may exist only in their own minds but attract people because of their "scientific" dressing. We have already seen some of this in our examples of the New Thought Movement. The fact of the matter is that most scientists do not make the scientific method the basis of their life. The scientific method cannot take into account God's existence to be effective. Most scientists' lifestyles do take into account God's existence.[253]

Usually we do not experience scientism like we see it portrayed by Bones and Spock, but it is there in so many other ways as people accept what they think the sciences, such as the social sciences of psychology and political science, tell us about our world. If we allow the sciences to determine what we do, say, think, and hope, we are living the spirituality of scientism. Secular humanism is sometimes seen as an expression of scientism rather than as an "ism" in its own right.

Humanism places the betterment of humanity and individual humans as the norm of everyday life. Its history is complex; its meaning is diverse. Many adjectives are adjoined to it such as secular, religious, Christian, Marxist, Chinese, Jewish, and Muslim. The methods for placing humanity at the center of all serious thinking divide most discussions of humanism.

Renaissance Humanism sought to understand the human by using what we today would call the humanities,[254] whereas secular humanism[255] seeks to understand the human by using science and the scientific method. Renaissance Humanism of the fourteenth, fifteenth, and sixteenth centuries brought the Greek and Latin classics back into the education system while emphasizing good writing and speaking (rhetoric) as the mark of the educated person. The critical thinking necessary for both good writing and speaking resulted in challenging the translations of some texts into Latin (e.g. the Vulgate Bible) and the authenticity of others (e.g. the Donation of Constantine). In the past most humanists were clergy.

Secular humanism takes the position of scientism by rejecting religion in general and Christianity in particular as providing the norms of what it means to be human. Instead of these ancient norms, it declares that human reason alone can determine what is best for humans. This physical, mental, or spiritual best should be determined by scientific reason, experiment, and the texts resulting from them. Both types of humanism provide a basis for understanding one's spirituality and that of others.

Renaissance Humanism, and its renewal in the Western Christianity of the 1970s, emphasized that the body and its emotions play a positive part in one's spirituality; the world around us is good and a healthy avenue to grow spiritually; all things in moderation are avenues to fulfilling one's spiritual life. Offered in addition to, but not necessarily contrary to those spiritualities of deprivation, deep asceticism, and fear of all things "natural," this type of humanistic spirituality offers a life in which the materiality of body, emotions, and engagement in nature deepen the energizing life of the spirit. Foundational to all of it, however, is learning: deep, expansive, and critically expressed through excellent speech and writing.

> **A human life perfectly led is a spiritual example for all.**

Led by the American Humanist Society,[256] *Atheistic humanism* has a strong and organized presence in contemporary life . The thrust of that presence is summarized in the 1996 statement of the International Humanist and Ethical Union:

> *Humanism is a democratic and ethical life stance, which affirms that human beings have the right and responsibility to give meaning and shape to their own lives. It stands for the building of a more humane society through an ethic based on human and other natural values in the spirit of reason and free inquiry through human capabilities. It is not theistic, and it does not accept supernatural views of reality.*[257]

It seems at times that most of its website and media attention is over its anti-religious positions rather than its positive outlook on the infinite possibilities open to all humans through reason, especially scientific reason.

It should also be mentioned that as niche marketing, educating, and politicking has increased in the twenty-first century, these 'isms have become imbedded in the isolated communities they produce. That means that there is little productive communication between niche communities. Sometimes they portray other communities as evil in their myths, thus enabling the myths to fulfill their primitive function in the modern era. Although there are hints of the existence of these 'isms in the past as the dominant narrative of large groups of people, they have come to fruition during the modern age.

Becoming a Liminal Spirituality / Former Classical Religions in Contemporary Dress

Contemporary liminal spiritualities abound. Many are discussed in the next chapter dealing with marginal spiritualities that have gained acceptance, though not adherence, among many in that culture. Wicca and witchcraft are examples of such spiritualities that have adapted to the spirit of liminality. Some of the modern spiritualities, in their attempt to remain relevant to the majority of people, gradually begin to accept the uncertainty, tentativeness, and suspicion present in contemporary liminality. There is, then, a tension between how they adapted to the modernity of the past and the challenge of adapting to the liminality of the present. If a spirituality is truly a contemporary one, then it will naturally seek to be liminal in liminal times and modern in modern times. A good example of this is the Unitarian Universalist Association, a current wave of spirituality with deep roots in past Christian cultures.

The diverse churches that united to form the Unitarian Universalists in 1961 provide a history of gradual adaptation to the surrounding culture where they, many times, took the lead in adapting to those liminal situations. It is only natural that over the centuries such continual adaptation would lead to a diversity of viewpoints as to what is essential to an appropriate spirituality. Such diversity has resulted, over time, in many different Unitarian organizations. We are looking at those that have contributed to the Unitarian Universalists. Their website provides the principles upon which this life must be based and the sources, or authorities, upon which these principles are derived.[258]

> *These principles and sources of faith are the backbone of our religious community.*
>
> *There are seven principles which Unitarian Universalist congregations affirm and promote:*
>
> - *The inherent worth and dignity of every person*
> - *Justice, equity, and compassion in human relations*
> - *Acceptance of one another and encouragement of spiritual growth in our congregations*
> - *A free and responsible search for truth and meaning*
> - *The right of conscience and the use of the democratic process within our congregations and in society at large*
> - *The goal of world community with peace, liberty, and justice for all*
> - *Respect for the interdependent web of all existence of which we are a part*
> - *Unitarian Universalism (UU) draws from many sources:*
> - *Direct experience of that transcending mystery and wonder, affirmed in all cultures, which moves us to a renewal of the spirit and an openness to the forces which create and uphold life;*
> - *Words and deeds of prophetic women and men which challenge us to confront powers and structures of evil with justice, compassion, and the transforming power of love*

- *Wisdom from the world's religions which inspires us in our ethical and spiritual life*
- *Jewish and Christian teachings which call us to respond to God's love by loving our neighbors as ourselves*
- *Humanist teachings which counsel us to heed the guidance of reason and the results of science, and warn us against idolatries of the mind and spirit*
- *Spiritual teachings of earth-centered traditions which celebrate the sacred circle of life and instruct us to live in harmony with the rhythms of nature*

These principles and sources provide the basis of this spirituality's belief system. The other signposts reflect their historical past. Worship services depend a great deal on the individual congregation. Naturally, there is great emphasis on reading, preaching, and learning while some rituals from all the classical religions may also be practiced. Their morality, while accepting the basic moral code found in most religions and reflected in the Ten Commandments, focuses on doing everything possible to help their neighbors. They have had an originating impact upon such things as prison reform, abolition of slavery, the women's movement, and civil rights. St. Lawrence, Tufts, and the California Institute of Technology are among some of the institutions of higher learning they founded. They see their origins in the Anabaptists movements of the sixteenth and seventeenth centuries, and in the Congregationalist churches in the U.S. in the late eighteenth and early nineteenth centuries. Their spirituality, then, looks to the religions, philosophies, and sciences of the world for their underlying beliefs; the basic thrust of humanitarianism for their devotion to human freedom; and their weekly gatherings for the communal support necessary to sustain these beliefs and the energy to continually seek that freedom.

A Spirituality without the Abrahamic God

> **Act as if God doesn't exist but keep the commandments.**

Science acts as if there is no God, and some people accept that methodology as ontology by declaring the same. Possibly without realizing it, they are usually referring to the God as presented to them by their Western culture and their socialization process: the God of Abraham.

We have already seen many of the classical spiritualities that do not recognize Abraham's God as their God. They may not even have a single all-powerful creator, just, and loving God in their culture, yet they have a spirituality that has promised and then provided means of transformation for millennia. What distinguishes these classical spiritualities from the more recent ones is historical development over the course of millennia versus a few generations. To sustain relevance and provide practical results for people over a prolonged period is a challenge for any public institution and ideology. Those institutions whose evolution is based on a contemporalist model are always adapting. Consequently, they lack a clear identity because they identify so closely with the surrounding milieu to which they are adapting. Yesterday, it was the Renaissance Humanism of the sixteenth century or the science of the nineteenth; today, it is the liminality of our modern world that determines the various contemporalist spiritualities to which people are drawn. The classical religions, somehow, have been able to change yet remain the same. They have done this by using, subconsciously, the co-temporalist model.

Co-temporalist Spirituality: Traditioning Spiritualities

Certainly the materials that encompass the classical spiritualities change: the paper upon which their holy scriptures is written, the buildings within which worship is celebrated, the words that Buddha, Jesus, or Abraham first spoke, the dress people wear, and the original language used to express the thoughts of the founders. Contemporary historical methods demonstrate that every religion and spirituality has changed significantly over the centuries in each of its signposts. So what is there about the classical spiritualities, or any spirituality for that matter, that is ageless? Shouldn't we all just change our spirituality depending on our feelings and culture and thereby be contemporalists? Is there really something about the classics that continues over the millennia enabling each of them to fulfill the promise of the life they promote today beyond new feelings and new cultures?

The *traditionalist* approach claims that the exact words expressed in the original literature as well as certain rituals, ways of acting, and organizational behavior never change. If you change the material expression of the way of life, you change it. To destroy those words, beliefs, rituals, moral demands, and ways to associate with those inside and outside the spirituality is to destroy something that has given a spiritual life to millions. The *contemporalists* say the opposite. When the previous manner of expressing the beliefs, rituals, morals, and communal life begin to age or change, so does the spirituality. After all, if you change everything about you—body, past, ideas, actions, and associates— what is there to identify you as "you?" The spirituality that people live today is nothing like it was at its origins. History demonstrates nothing is the same. Admit it. Abandon it. Develop something new that is more healthily lived in today's culture.

The *co-temporalists* admit the paradox of change and not change, and they accept the paradoxes we reviewed in chapter one, especially the one that said, "I am an immortal who dies." They understand that immortality as no change. They sense that out of the tension of the paradox comes the renewed vigor of a spirituality seeking its identity and meaning for contemporary life. They point to the history of how each spirituality is an example of what has happened over the ages and how there is deep and significant change yet something is the same about it. There is some pattern that continues that is not necessarily attached to the material realities of the tradition and that is independent of changing language and culture. It is not tradition that is central to a classical spirituality but traditioning—the enlivening pattern of the past in the present that is continually providing a deep spirituality for those who will live it in the future. It is this approach to spirituality that we will focus on in this chapter.

There are two ways of trying to understand how to go about developing healthy change: the mechanistic and the organic. The *mechanistic* seeks to discover the essential, abstract, core of the spirituality in as objective a manner as possible. This core is then used as the norm of all present and future development of a spirituality. In the process, the spirituality is reduced to its essential ideas, and from these one builds a healthy spiritual life. This can be likened to how one has an idea of a chair and then builds the chair. So, for example, Christianity is essentially doing good to one's neighbor, or it is essentially faith in Jesus as Savior, or, as in the third century Christian church, it is where bishops, the Bible, and the creed are found—all else is relative.

The *organic* approach recognizes the mystery of the spiritual life in its wholeness; realizes that life is not an abstraction; accepts the fact that organisms develop differently and sometimes better after birth; commits to a life of liminality; and continually looks at the present to see what is alive from the past to enliven the present and the future. One looks to the past not with a nostalgic sense of returning to the past as past, but with a transcendent hope in the present for the past's evolution to a healthy future. One does not know whether she is successful until after the fact. Only after living the spirituality over a prolonged period does one sense that he is in the tradition and has traditioned appropriately. We cannot be told what we experience is authentic to the religion or spirituality; we must experience it as such.

> **Grow your spiritual life.**

When we reviewed the classical spiritualities, we saw that there were different types of each of them. We could talk about Orthodox Christians, Catholic Christians, Protestant Christians; about Sunni and Shia Muslims; Theravada, Mahayana, and Vajrayana Buddhists; and so on for Judaism, Taoism, Confucianism, and Shinto. The co-temporalist thread throughout these religions reflects a number of characteristics. They retain many of their original expressions of the signposts; they contain remnants of the diverse ages within which they existed and co-temporalized in; they have an attitude of adaptation as a means of solving contemporary issues; they have a deep commitment to continuing their spiritual traditions by making them alive in the contemporary age; they find truth, beauty, and goodness both in their tradition and their culture. Thus, for example, the mainline Christian churches in the United States during the nineteenth and twentieth centuries accepted modern methods for interpreting ancient literature and applied those methods to the Bible; they rejected the ways capitalism denigrated workers and their families by preaching and applying the social gospel; they rethought Christian belief in light of the physical sciences by looking for other ways of describing miracles, the existence of heaven, the nature of the soul, and evolution; they accepted the core principles of psychology in its pastoral counseling and conclusive scientific evidence for daily living.

Every classical spirituality has had to deal with a new culture. Examples from the past abound. Pictures and statues of Jesus and Buddha reflect diverse cultures that each religion has adapted to and developed within over the centuries. The diverse types of architecture of the church, the mosque, and the Shinto temple all reflect the religion's entry into different cultures. Many times the actual place where the structure is built reflects the sacredness of the place. For instance, the church/mosque is built on the same site as the previous mosque or church which, in turn, was built on a previous holy site. Christmas is a typical example of such a development in terms of a holiday, as no one knows when Jesus was born, and the day itself was originally a day for celebrating Roman gods. Ideas such as "God" and the Christian creed are in constant development from the Jewish Yahweh through the Greek *Theos* to contemporary times when the theologian Paul Tillich, for example, called God "he Ground of Being."

As those living these diverse religions came into a culture, they had to act in a co-temporal manner. As those who came from that culture accepted the "new" religion, they did so in a co-temporal manner. They had no choice. Otherwise, they would have abandoned the new culture they were becoming part of. Those new to the culture learned the language, the central ideas, and the ways of acting and celebrating of the local people who in turn accepted the religion/spirituality as their own, and then chose words, ideas, and ways of acting and celebrating that they felt best expressed this new religion, now theirs. Both those old to the religion and those new to the religion took the risk of making the religion alive to their present culture. The risk is called hope, and the confidence that what they possessed could live in any culture is called faith. If indeed the spirituality is a classic and is meant for all cultures, then it must be co-temporal to be alive for these people in these times. Otherwise, it has an appeal only to a small group of people and must abandon its mission of being a way of life for all. The result today is a religion that has existed over the centuries. The challenge today for the classical spiritualities is to acknowledge that change happens to all of us; that spiritual change happens to all of us. All organisms must change or die.

Past co-temporal existence is easily forgotten by those who know it as the tradition. Such a spirituality is "just the way things are" to each generation.

New fruit from old roots

Thus, each generation lives the spirituality as if it never had a history and was timeless. An historical consciousness tells us otherwise.

Each spirituality today is faced with the quandary of what to do to sustain its identity. Some say, in a fundamentalist fashion, that everything must remain the same. Sameness is identity. Some say it's impossible to sustain a single identity in a liminal age. Sameness does not exist. And others say that only by traditioning the past into the present will the identity be sustained. For someone who accepts the co-temporal as necessary to developing a spirituality, these same co-temporal impulses are usually found at the local level, near where she lives. Especially in the cities and suburbs, there are sub communities of each of the religions and/or spiritualities. Certain ones in these sub-communities will risk the new while holding on to the old, seeing the sources of transcendence present within the signposts in a new way and embracing new sources never before recognized. This risk means uncertainty—something the other two options do not offer.

Every religion and spirituality tends to ossification and, consequently, restriction of where the transcendent may become manifest. They forget that their founders discovered a way of seeing life different from the religion they were brought up in. In their profound experience of transcendence and its associated feelings, they sometimes do not realize that other co-religionists in their own generation or the next generations have neither the experience nor the expectations they have in their ways of life. Co-temporalists would suggest that in what many authorities in the classical religions call secular or scientific is found the seeds of the future of religion and the spiritualities that enliven us.

Summary

As modernity became a cultural force in the nineteenth century, it changed the dominant way of thinking and speaking. Simple and clear ideas expressed in short, easily understood sentences were declared the ideal. Facts were declared the basis of all truth. The classical spiritualities responded to modernity in three ways: running away from it toward the past (traditionalism), adapting to its scientific and technological expressions (contemporalists) and a wary attempt to slowly investigate what was good in both the tradition and science (co-temporalists). The result was the three major spiritual movements that influence people today.

CHAPTER SEVEN

MARGINAL SPIRITUALITIES:
WHAT'S OLD IS NEW AGAIN

Arise, you sons of pleasure, and visit the Earth, for I am the Lord, your God, which is and liveth forever!

In the name of Satan, Move! and show yourselves as pleasant deliverers, that you may praise Him among the sons of men![259]

In this book, the reader will begin to understand that his physical life is a tiny segment of a vast circle wherein there is no beginning and no end; thus his spiritual life existed before the start of that segment and will continue after the end. Particularly in these troubled times—people find the idea that life ends only in oblivion extraordinarily distressing. — the reincarnationist views life not as a gateway to death but as an expedition into the next stage of the eternal journey of the spirit.[260]

Women…are moving to create a distinctly Americanized, feminized, democratized form of Buddhist spiritual practice…. The more basic appeal of Buddhist practice to women resides in the fact that Buddhism posits no god, crates no I-Thou relationship with an all-powerful father figure. A central tenet is that one must trust one's own experience above all else.[261]

The old people had runes which they sang to the spirits dwelling in the sea and in the mountain, in the wind and in the whirlwind, in the lightning and in the thunder, in the sea and in the moon and in the stars of heaven. I was naught but a toddling child at the time, but I remember well the ways of the old people.
~ Carmina Gadelica[262]

The more things you know or pretend to know, the more powerful you are. It doesn't matter if the things are true. What counts, remember, is to possess a secret.
~ Umberto Eco[263]

214

55. Q. *Why does ignorance cause suffering?*

A. *Because it makes us prize what is not worth prizing, grieve for that we should not grieve for, consider real what is not real but only illusory, and pass our lives in the pursuit of worthless objects, neglecting what is in reality most valuable.*

56. Q. *And what is that which is most valuable?*

A. *To know the whole secret of man's existence and destiny, so that we may estimate at no more than their actual value and this life and its relations; so that we may live in a way to insure the greatest happiness and the least suffering for our fellow-men and ourselves.*
 ~ Buddhist Catechism by Colonel Henry Steel Olcott.[264]

Man is also triune: he has his objective, physical body, his vitalizing astral body (or soul), the real man; and these two are brooded over and illuminated by the third—the sovereign, the immortal spirit. When the real man succeeds in merging himself with the latter, he becomes an immortal entity.
 ~ Madame Blavatsky[265]

Oh, East is East, and West is West, and never the two shall meet,
Till Earth and Sky stand presently at God's great Judgment Seat;
But there is neither East nor West, Border, nor Breed, nor Birth,
When two strong men stand face to face, tho' they come from the ends
 of the earth.
 ~ Rudyard Kipling, "The Ballad of East and West"

***

Are these the voices of those on the margin or in the mainstream of our current culture?

A marginal spirituality is one in which people live alongside of, in opposition to, or separate from the majority religious culture. Those of the majority religions often look at those on the margins with fear, curiosity, and abhorrence: fear because they do not understand the marginal; curiosity because the unknown always tempts one to promised pleasures and forbidden knowledge; abhorrence because their difference is so great that it is a deep threat to their way of life. Throughout history, and by some today, these marginal spiritualities are called sects, cults, the occult, the esoteric, the mystical, or the metaphysical. For the classical Western religions the marginal were seen as satanic, witches, pagans, idol worshipers, lost souls, or heathens. The Eastern classical religions usually described their marginal as ignorant, worshipers of powerless gods, uncivilized, or unenlightened. Of course the modern majority sees all religious ways of life as superstitious, unscientific, mere opinion, and uneducated. In liminal times, all spiritualities are equal among a populace that does not understand science, religion, spirituality, and is uncertain about most everything.

Marginal, obviously, is very much dependent on whether one is part of the majority or not. In pluralistic societies with diverse cultures, the marginal is both less threatening to the majority and, perhaps, less mysterious. In non-pluralistic societies, everything is more certain and clear. Yet in these same non-pluralistic societies, the marginal has always had a role in their continued health and development. It is on the margin that unconventional spiritual signposts are tested. Later they may be rejected or accepted by the majority. After all, every religion was a marginal religion sometime during its existence. In today's liminal, pluralistic societies the marginal spiritualities that were rejected in the past are publicized as equal to the classical since all are seen as equal from a pluralistic perspective. There are few threats to a marginal spiritual perspective as long as anyone can publish a book, create a website, and bring himself into public view. Many times what passes for news today is merely a commentary on the unusual. (Why tell everyone what they already know?) Thus, the news becomes a commentary on what is on the margins of society rather than among the majority of society. A story about what everyone already knows and does is considered boring, and thus not news.

If you were born into the dominant religious perspective or grew up aware of its existence, your entrance into a marginal religious life probably provides you with something positive and negative. Negatively, you probably have a weak or nonexistent spiritual compass when using the classical religious signposts. You may also harbor a sense of alienation from the majority religions even if you were not born into one. There may be things about the way the majority think and act that are not only distasteful to you but also oppressive. For example, you were born in a small southern town where most people belong to one fundamentalist Christian church that preaches the necessary subservience of women to men in all things. You are a woman. In this situation, you are a powerless individual. You find the belief and its consequent demands on you oppressive. The marginal spirituality of Wicca is not only freeing but also empowering to you through its beliefs, rituals, and gathering of like-minded women. Positively, you find something not available to you in the majority religion: like-minded co-religionists and signposts that provide meaning and direction. The marginal religion provides a sense of freeing transcendence not found previously in your life. For others who are perhaps living a boring, routine life, there may be the thrill of the unusual, dangerous, and unknown mystical Eastern spirituality. Ways of life that offer moderately dangerous unknown rituals and associates enable you to transcend your daily life for something more than the here and now.

Many marginal offerings are present in our liminal, secular fundamentalist culture. In such a culture all are equal, not only because they are opinions but also because of the basic religious ignorance present in the culture. This amalgam of cultural realities provides a current seeker with a multitude of choices outside the dominant religious atmosphere. The literal nature of secular fundamentalism enables the seeker to find common words, understood as common ideas, across both the classical and marginal religions. Words such as reincarnation, soul, God, religion, spirituality, and spirit, which are found within the classical religions, carry with them into the marginal offerings the power of antiquity and the experience of the classics even though they do not mean the same as in these classical contexts. The relativities of history mean nothing in a culture that believes that context, historical or otherwise, is useless in the face of the factual certainty of words and phrases repeated by those one trusts. Everything is new when you do not know what is old. Many of these liminal spiritualities are old marginal spiritualities dressed within secular fundamentalism to provide their adherents with certainty in a liminal culture.

Today's Trends and Themes in Marginal Spiritualities

Sometimes words and ideas have a way of growing to encompass more concepts into their original meaning. We have seen how the word "religion" grew from basically "my religion" in the late Middle Ages to include all Christian churches, then, in the late nineteenth century, to encompass all those who believe in God and, ultimately, all ways of life that promise and promote total transformation or change through sacred words, actions, and gatherings of likeminded people. "Spirituality," as it is used today, has and is experiencing the same universalizing trend as it moves beyond the early and medieval view of ways to engage in and live the life of the Holy Spirit to the deeper ways of living human existence. When this expansion is viewed from the perspective of Western culture, particularly U.S. culture, we see that the culture's former dominant religions have a decreasing influence on that culture. When these former dominant religions (Christianity in the U.S.) did have influence, the ways of life of such groups, such as witches, Satanists, and Gnostics, were considered esoteric, occult, and on the edge of daily life. Today, what was on the edge is part of a generally pluralistic and permissive culture that advocates acceptance of the odd, different, and counter-cultural. All spiritualities, no matter how destructive, are equal in this spiritual marketplace. Whatever turns you on spiritually is acceptable. In the process, the meaning of what is spiritual continues to expand so that it is almost unrecognizable from its origins. The current modes of communication reinforce the continued expansion of what spirituality is through the process they use to provide us with information about spirituality.

> As more things become spiritual those spiritualities on the margins become fewer.

All of these information delivery systems depend on someone's understanding of what categories of information will be listed under certain words or queries. A Google system, for example, has been set up to respond to the search term "spirituality" by an algorithm presupposing a certain meaning of "spirituality." The Library of Congress system, generally used in most libraries, will place certain books together depending on a certain idea of the version of spirituality presented in those books. Therefore, what is called the hermeneutical circle begins with our looking for spiritual books that are presented with a slightly different understanding than our own, and then, when we look next time, we look with this expanded view of spirituality.

Here are some titles garnered from diverse search engines during a search in February 2011. These were found on at least three lists.[266] Some of these books have been popular for several years and some authors have been publishing for decades.

- *Eat, Pray, Love: One Woman's Search for Everything Across Italy, India and Indonesia*, by Elizabeth Gilbert[267]
- *A Course in Weight Loss: 21 Spiritual Lessons for Surrendering Your Weight Forever*, by Marianne Williamson[268]
- *Jesus Calling: Enjoying Peace in His Presence*, by Sarah Young[269]
- *Heaven is for Real: A Little Boy's Astounding Story of His Trip to Heaven and Back*, by Todd Burpo, Sonja Burpo, Colton Burpo, Lynn Vincent[270]
- *The 5 Love Languages: The Secret to Love That Lasts*, by Gary Chapman[271]
- *The Power of Now: A Guide to Spiritual Enlightenment*, by Eckhart Tolle[272]
- *Be Love Now: The Path of the Heart*, by Ram Dass and Rameshwar Das[273]
- *The Heart of the Buddha's Teaching*, by Thich Nhat Hanh[274]

These books are representative of similar popular publications over the last hundred years. They, as do media blogs, social media, and other electronic means of communication, continue themes that first originated among marginal religions at their point of historical origins; then they became part of the normative culture and once again intensified in marginal spiritualities. Many of these current trends are actually themes begun with the first revivals and the enthusiastic religious expectations that evolved from them, such as the necessity of experiencing the transcendent in a life-changing event (Jesus saves!).

Some trends evolved from the millions of ethnic Roman Catholics with their saints, angels, monks, miracles, blessed relics, animals, holy waters, shrines, and talk of diverse types of spiritualities. As Catholics themselves became part of mainstream America, these items and other stories and expectations gradually seeped into the culture through movies, music, and talk shows. The same can be said of other immigrants as they came to America bringing their Voodoo, Candomble, and Santeria. The World Parliament of Religions in 1893 was a short but significant event that added to the mix by exposing the American public to articulate representatives of Hinduism and Buddhism. The Eastern classical religions were advocated by American intellectuals in the Transcendentalist movement, but it was the World Parliament of Religions that placed these religions, along with their colorful and exotically-dressed advocates, in the consciousness of the American public.

The continued growth of colonialism and such events as the Second World War continued to bring the ordinary person into contact with the people living these newly titled spiritualities. The growth of the self-help movements and mind awareness (science of the mind) provided a context within which the always-present needs of survival spirituality were able to be met in a new age. The result is a complex and expansive view of spirituality in contemporary America. The meanings of and means to spiritual experience are expected to embrace all these formerly marginal spiritualities, and all of them now retain an aura of sacrality inherited from their religious origins. After all, many would say, they are spiritualities: something good, beneficial, and not to be questioned because they provide an experience of transcendence that takes you away from the ordinary everyday life you live. The trend today is to consider something as spiritual when it provides you with a transcendent experience – takes you out of your ordinary way of life. The understanding that a spirituality consists of a set of signposts enabling you to create a better life for you and your community is diminishing. In the place of this connection is the immediate satiation of one's transcendent desire and a search for a lifestyle that will continually assuage this desire.

Marginal Spiritual Themes: Today and Yesterday

The easiest way is to review these important themes in the current populist idea of spirituality by summarizing each one with a single word or phrase and then providing a brief description of the theme along with a description of how it became part of the American way of life. The overall result will enable you to make distinctions in your current spirituality to make healthy choices in the future.

Contemporary spirituality demands that:
- *I experience it.*
- *I talk about it.*
- *It turns my life around in a short time.*
- *It is supported primarily by my heart not my mind.*
- *It makes my life complete and happy.*
- *It promises a new invigorated life promoted by those of deep spiritual wisdom.*

Witness. The Christians in New England whom we called Puritans required a person to rise in the assembly and witness to their personal experience of Jesus leading to conversion. Without this witness, a person was not considered a member of the church, which at that time was also the requirement for citizenship.[275] But the willingness to witness to their conversion experiences died out after the first generation. Only a few of the second and third generation Puritans were willing to stand witness to the same experience as their parents. The vast majority of those generations did not witness even though it meant the loss of voting privileges. They knew what was required. They had seen others do it, but they were not able to authentically witness to such an experience. Such authenticity was recognized by the speaker's sincerity and clearly recognized path to the experience.

A generation or so later, all at once, people from different Christian churches began to witness. The eighteenth century Great Awakening, or first great revival, rocked the colonies with people giving personal witness to Jesus's role in saving them. The stories usually followed a well-worn path of moral destitution, a life-changing event, and living in a new way (rebirth). This description of turning one's life over to Jesus has a long history in Christianity beginning with the well-documented "Confessions" of St. Augustine (354-430 CE). It is also a way of demonstrating the value of a marginal spirituality: removing one from a meaningless life, earth shattering experience, new way of seeing things, and my sharing that experience and new way of seeing things with you. Many times the purveyor of the marginal spirituality today, also adds world travel either in the spiritual search before the experience or afterwards.

Few classical religions require such personal witness to be a member of the religion. Only when one begins to restrict membership to adults does one face the "need" to ask for membership or to explain why it is important. None of the traditional Christian churches require a witness. This mode of religious witness is foreign to most cultures and many times is a source of friction between them and the Christian churches that require it.

Consciousness, Witness, Verbalization. Spirituality in the world of witness is restricted to those who are conscious of the roots of their spirituality and can talk about it to others or describe it in writing. Sometimes it seems that the distinction between religion and spirituality in contemporary literature is between those who are conscious of their transcendent desires and expressions and those who are not. Spiritual directors are necessary not only to discover life's direction but to talk about that direction and everything that accompanies it. Spiritual diaries perform the same function of bringing to consciousness one's experiences and capturing them in writing for a more thorough examination later on. A marginal spirituality must by its very nature be ready to speak up for itself in the face of the majority, thus highlighting the necessity of consciousness, witness, and verbalization.

Quick Life Change. The First Great Awakening and the ones that followed led to an expectation in American religion that one could turn his life around quickly once he had the proper experience of Jesus. Some authors would suggest that the American Revolution led to a cultural expectation that political and personal change could happen quickly. Certainly, the self-help movement has many books, articles, and websites that suggest such a possibility; for instance, some claim there are twenty-one spiritual steps to losing weight, finding eternal love, or stopping drug use. Just as the majority of religions do not see witness as a necessary requirement for their spiritualities, most do not seek a quick life change as a necessary warrant to the transformative power of the religion. Slow continual growth and depth in the religious way of life is usually seen as a marker of that transformative power.

Centrality of the Individual Person. Revival's designated purpose is to convert the individual to a new way of life. If individuals had the desired experience of salvation, its purpose was achieved. If it led to a worship service, so be it; but the worship was worthwhile only if the person had been saved. If it led to a moral life, so be it; but the moral way of life was only significant if it was an expression of the foundational faith experience. Most likely, those having the same experience would join together in a church: salvation first; church as a consequence. This was different from what was understood up to this time. The majority accepted as fact that the Church was always there. We join that eternal Church. The emphasis upon a voluntary gathering of believers was, at that time, marginal. Gradually, however, in the United States, it came to represent a majority view as churches were increasingly seen as voluntary organizations that depended on individual members for their financial support. Because of the First Great Awakening, the majority of churches were flooded with those demanding that their ministers experience the same salvific experience and camaraderie they had. The result was a division among many of the New England churches between those who demanded a faith witness and those who did not.

Distrust of Institutions. Obviously the institutional majority were not worthy of trust since they had neither the required experience that declared authenticity of life and belief nor were able to witness to either the experience or their own belief in a sincere and certain fashion. Institutional religion was seen as empty religion. Preaching that seemed prepared because it was read from a written script was lacking in sincerity. Preaching that was spontaneous, easily understood, and stimulative of one's emotions was true preaching. Formality, institutions, and complex theology were not what religion was all about.

Conscious Promotion of Spiritual Basics (Survival Spirituality). Spiritual basics are what I have called the Spirituality Of Survival in Chapter Five. There I described these basics as consisting of the signposts that provide the means of entering into, coping with, and coming out of the transformative events that challenge all of us: birth, suffering, marriage, death, job, personal relationships and, what we call today, self-image. Sometimes institutional religions and their accompanying spiritualities forget that people have to sense that their spirituality enables them to successfully deal with the central events in their life, including daily sustenance, justice, and living with dignity. The marginal spiritualities promise and promote this empowerment to those who have no power. Those who live the marginal spiritualities give evidence that they are "somebody" by supporting and living these spiritualities. Magic ritual, a signpost essential to those living a survival form of spirituality, provides that evidence. Magic rituals involve the same kind of repetition found in all rituals, but added to it is the conviction that the end of the ritual will be achieved if the ritual is done perfectly. This conviction seems simple, yet it contains the escape clause for failed magic. It demands perfect unity of mind and body. Thus, when the ritual does not achieve its end, the reason for the failure is evident. Either it was not performed properly or the practitioner and/or congregation did not have sufficient faith. Marginal spiritualities have a prominent role among the marginalized. The evidence they provide of their success gives the marginalized hope.

New Revelations. The old is never just old among marginal spiritualities. It is always "newly discovered." These newly discovered revelations, which many times are acknowledged in the spirituality as ancient, are usually described as being almost destroyed by the institutional religion of the time, or as ancient manuscripts or artifacts dug up in a field or found in an ancient monastery or library. But the old is new again because it offers a new spirituality to those bored by, offended by, or dismissive of the dominant contemporary spiritualities. Joseph Smith will find gold tablets that tell him of lost tribes (Church of Jesus Christ of the Latter-day Saints, also known as the Mormons). The Fox sisters will communicate in a new way by rapping with ancient spirits (Spiritism). Madam Helena Blavatsky and Colonel Henry Steel Olcott will travel to India at the request of a secret order of religious masters called Mahatmas to discover the ancient Indian religion that was destroyed by colonialism (Theosophy). As science becomes a major influence, the "new" is found in using scientific language (scientology) and technologies (the e-meter) to deal with bio-physical or bio-chemical changes (engrams). And certainly, just as scientists use their mind to rip the face off nature to discover what it really is and how to control it, so we can use our minds to power our interaction with people, things, and spirits (Science of the Mind).

Expert spiritual guides open the doors of spiritual mysteries. All are equal in the spiritual quest, but some are more equal than others. All of these marginal spiritualities trace their origins to a spiritual master: someone who has had a special revelation of transcendental reality. This particular master's revelation is to be transmitted to all. Belief in this revelation marks both the master and those who follow her or him as special in knowledge and unique in the spiritual quest. In an American context that also means that this view of the spiritual transcendental world opened up by the revelation goes into competition with all the other views present in this pluralistic culture. The exposure of this new revelation to the public beyond the first initiates is embodied in the spiritual master who manifests in life and dress the worth of this revelation. In a competitive atmosphere, the messenger and her or his theatrics in dress, word, and deed are sometimes what attract people to this way of life. The revelation itself, dressed in entrepreneurial garb, becomes part of the virtual realties that attract many to a new lifestyle, except now that lifestyle is a spiritual one.

Shopping for a spirituality that fits one's transcendent desires, hopes, and expectations is a natural expression of life in a consumer society. When people say they chose a particular religion, or when they prefer this one rather than that one, we have entered a new religious and spiritual era.[276] Religions must in some way become competitive with each other when they depend on individuals for their daily sustenance. Such competitiveness, built upon individual preference, has a profound effect on the diversity of marginal spiritualities that enter into the market. It becomes a market in which the god depends upon the people's choice rather than God choosing a people.

These are some of the themes that have repeated throughout the history of American spiritualities and religions. They will be found in the movements and institutions that we now describe. We can take two approaches to these descriptions: provide an alphabetical arrangement of spiritualities or suggest some historical connections between them. The cataloguing method is found among many New Age offerings. I have chosen the latter method by offering general categories that reflect what we have reviewed so far and that provide a means of understanding what the future will hold. We will begin with the culture we know best, the Western and dualistic, then review how some of the Eastern and monistic spiritualities are marginal in the Western world. These two broad categories have existed, in one form or another, for centuries. Consequently, it is necessary to suggest marginal spiritualities that have arisen in this modern and liminal age while retaining roots in the past. After all, what's new is old—again.

Western Marginal Spiritualities: Otherworldly Spirits, This-worldly Magic

Satanic Spirituality

To hear the words "Satan" or "devil" today usually brings together a multitude of feelings and ideas such as evil, tempter, rebel, endless pleasure, occult, chaos, evil's source, God's enemy, exorcisms, and hell. The history of Satan and the devil is long and fascinating.[277] Certain symbols and words associated with

Satan are sometimes used by some musicians to demonstrate their rebellious-ness. Sometimes these same symbols are burned into a tree or wall or marked into the ground as a hint of sacrifice and anti-establishment. In today's world, these symbols may be dualistic when people believe that Satan exists and is the sum of evil. But these symbols may also be completely this worldly with the celebrants of these satanic magical rites not believing in any sort of god or other world. Instead, they wish to demonstrate through these symbols that life is to be lived to its fullest without boundaries or rules. Both the otherworldly as well as the "this" worldly perspectives have been written down, sung, and institutionalized. When we look at these writings, songs, institutions, and other public displays, it does not take long before we realize that many of these are an exercise in imagination rather than reflecting any consistency in thought or action. Certainly in the past, many of the writings were from Christians who saw the presence of Satan in every word and action that expressed a distorted view of Christian thought and ritual. Today images of Satan are not only depen-dent upon Christians writing about Satan's working in this materialistic culture but upon those who wish to bathe in the satanic aurora to attract attention and/or to experience the thrill of danger and evil. Such virtual realties are well placed in a culture living and breathing other such virtual realities. Today, a satanic spirituality, unless totally dependent upon the author's imagination, views its essential beliefs from a supernatural dualistic or natural wholistic perspective.

Beliefs: Immortal Dualism or Mortal Wholism

References to Satan may be found in the holy scriptures of all the Abrahamic religions. There Satan may be seen as an otherworldly spirit or angel who, at the very least in these religions, tempts humans to forego God's will for their own; at the most, Satan is seen as the Lord of Hell, the leader of all

Satan is God's enemy.

evil forces fighting with God to rule humanity and the source of all illicit plea-sures leading humans from God.[278] Although not in the formal creeds, many people also envision Satan as the all-powerful, immortal force of evil over and against God, who is the all-powerful immortal force for good. Such a view is close to the Zoroastrian religion. Satan in all these instances is viewed in a dual-istic manner: otherworldly and opposed to God in an eternal contest.

The mortal, wholistic, perspective pays no attention to whether there is an eternal other world or even if there is a God or not. Instead, it encourages people to concentrate on the here and now of pleasure and power. Since this is a more recent approach to Satanism, it will be found in books published in the second half of the twentieth century such as Anton LaVey's *The Satanic Bible*[279] and the church he founded, The Church of Satan. The Temple of Set may also be seen in this tradi-tion if one identifies the Egyptian god Set with the satanic tradition of adversary.

The conflation of these two modes of belief occurs in many images and writings about Satan. For example, the Greek god Pan with his hooves and horns became identified with the devil as witchcraft began to be seen as heretical and evil. Portrayals in writing or painting, such as Francisco Goya, *le Sabbat des sorcières* (the Sabbath of witches) in 1797 conflated the idea of Satan with that of pan resulting in the image of Satan with horns and/ or hooves. At the same time, it conjoined the idea of the evil witches with the embodiment of evil, Satan. This resulted in an image of Satan that is found in a great deal of literature.

Another way we hear about satanic beliefs is the discussion about Left (Black) and Right (White) hand paths of magic where the left refers to dualistic satanic worship and the right to pagan, wholistic rituals. While the distinction originated in the West with Madame Blavatsky (1831-1891), the founder of Theosophy, there is so much dissention about this distinction that it seems that people pick their understanding of the terms depending on what they want to convey about their spirituality in general. [280]

> **Satan is a spiritual model of a satisfied life.**

Ritual among Satanists is considered magical and of two kinds: that which, when performed properly, brings to bear the infinite powers of the otherworldly Satan (dualistic) or that which concentrates the powers of nature to achieve the desired effects of the ritual (wholistic). Many times the same titled ritual such as the Black Mass is performed with the diverse presuppositions as to power. See, for example, LaVey's ritual[281] as compared to that described in Joris-Karl Huysmans (1848-1907) book *Là-Bas* (1891)[282] the latter, though fictional, became a template for later descriptions of the so-called Black Mass. I will deal with magic under a separate heading for esoteric / occult magic.

One ritual associated with dualistic Satanism that should be mentioned is exorcism. I always remember doing a weeklong workshop for the Roman Catholic diocese of New Orleans dealing with New Age religions. The Diocesan exorcist was present and active throughout the week. When we began a discussion of satanic cults and rituals to say he added another "dimension" to the discussion is putting it mildly. He

> **Satan can place his spirit in our bodies.**
> **Natural energies, properly controlled, can free us from our old taboos.**

strongly believed that Satan not only possessed people but was the cause of many societal ills. Keep in mind, this was New Orleans, which has a long history in the practice of voodoo! But it is also the view of many around the globe, and its claims are a constant attraction in the media.

Spirit possession and exorcism are a part of human history. Satanic possession and exorcism parallel the history and development of Satan in Christian history. Exorcists have always been part of that history. Throughout this book we have discussed the role of spirits as part of religious development in the West, as part of survival spirituality, and as prominent in religions that believed that its gods were spirits.

Spirits both good and evil have been part of the classical religions and spiritualities from their very beginnings. As these same religions entered into the modern world, the spirit-caused events such as possession, movement of articles across rooms, talking in tongues, reading minds, and being in more than one place at a time began to be called parapsychological events rather than miracles or spirit possession."[283] These were studied using the scientific method. The result was that when someone looked like she was being taken over by someone else, there were two ways of explaining the phenomenon and responding to it. One was to say the devil had taken over the person's spirit. The other was to say it was because of a psychosis, hysteria, mania, Tourette's syndrome, epilepsy, schizophrenia, or dissociative identity disorder.

Consequently, when people are possessed today, you will find those who want to help them very much reflecting the manner the classical religions responded to modernity: some will use religious ritual alone to deal with the possession; some will use scientific methods alone to deal with the possession; some will use both science and religion to deal with the possession. That exorcist I mentioned above, for example, consulted with psychologists, fasted

> *Greed is good. Lust is great. You are the center of your universe.*

and prayed, and used both his ancient rituals and contemporary chemical and behavioral means to care for the person. In a book on spirituality, I cannot emphasize enough that when we begin to deal with that which is beyond the ordinary humdrum of life, we walk upon a fragile path whether we describe that path using the social sciences or ancient mythical personalities. One thing all the classics remind us is that there are always good and evil spirits that surround us on the spiritual journey. We must always have a way of dealing with them. Ritual is certainly a powerful way of dealing with possession whether the ritual is religious or medical. [284]

When we look at the **moral signposts** of Satanism, we see that they consciously try to mirror the religious commands found in the Abrahamic religions by saying the opposite of what they say. It should be noted that a title of LaVey's *Satanic Bible* modifies an anything goes moral approach with the proclamation "Indulgence—not Compulsion."[285]

The diversity of institutions that are seen as Satanic becomes very complex because of the borrowing of ideas and interpretations surrounding the nature of Satanism. Every religion has to explain evil and suffering. Consequently, every religion will have as part of that explanation Satan in one of his or her manifestations both symbolically and ideologically. That leaves room in a Secular Fundamentalist culture for a free interchange of titles, rituals, and explanations by taking these out of their classical religious context and bringing them into a contemporary satanic one.

The Spirituality of Wicca and Witches

Witches and Wicca revive themes previously discussed such as immortal dualism, mortal wholism, left and right paths, magic, and the god Pan. Every Halloween we see many people dressed in costumes representing witches and Satan and hear news reports of some Wicca coven celebrating one of their festivals. We will focus on contemporary witches and Wicca. Sometimes it will be necessary to delve into history merely because the historical record may invalidate what contemporary practitioners may proclaim as historical fact.

Sorcerers, healers, cunning folk, and fortunetellers exist in every culture. The source of their power is many times said to be the manipulation of spirits and gods and/or harnessing of nature's power and energy. "Nature" here can also be understood as some internal quality of the person possessing these powers.[286] This manipulation or harnessing is done by words and deeds developed over the millennia. The purveyors of these rituals are said to do magic. Good, or right-handed, magic is beneficial to both the

> Witches follow Satan.
> Witches, sorcerers, healers, and fortune tellers control the forces of nature for their clients' good fortune.

conduit of power and the client. Bad, or left-handed magic, is a cause of misfortune to the intended person. The one who does all this is called a witch in English. In many lands and for a great deal of history these women, for they are almost always women, were seen as doing bad to people: making them sick, causing a tree to fall on them, destroying crops, bringing sickness into the community. Because they were seen to be the cause of suffering and evil, they were sought out and destroyed. People's experience was that once these witches were destroyed, life got better. Whether it actually did is not for us to say.

We can talk about four types of people we will call witches: good witches able to manipulate the spirits for good; good witches able to manipulate nature for good; bad witches able to manipulate the spirits for evil; bad witches able to manipulate nature for evil. Those who look to nature for this power are called Wiccans (wise ones), witches (but not the bad ones), the craft, or the followers of the old religion. Those ways of life that look to spirits rather than nature alone to produce this power are called Witchcraft, Voodoo, Santeria, Shamanism—to mention a few Western types.

Those who live the **Wiccan spirituality** *see themselves as following in the footsteps of ancient European women who worshiped their ancient gods before the advent of Christianity* and were, subsequently, persecuted by the Christian authorities while doing good for the people they lived among. Because of this persecution, much of their tradition was kept secret over the centuries, only to be revealed in the nineteenth and twentieth centuries by diverse masters and by these masters' experiences in performing the necessary magic handed down to them. Three authors in particular are seen as the founders of the Wiccan movement. Wicca has continued to gain adherents since these beginnings, and with new followers, modifications have been made to the insights of the original founders. Especially in the United States and Britain, these additions were influenced by the neo-pagan movement, which was gaining an increasing amount of attention in the middle of the twentieth century. These three authors were Margaret Murray (1863-1963), Gerald Gardner (1884-1964), and Robert Graves (1895-1985). Murray put forth the theory that there were women throughout Europe who bore the brunt of Christian persecution. These women gathered in groups of thirteen called covens wherein they worshiped a horned male god during a ritual sabbath. Gerald Gardner in his book *Witchcraft Today*[287] claimed that he was initiated into an ancient English coven that went back to Neolithic times. He is seen as the father of Wicca, a term he first heard at his initiation into the coven. Murray wrote the introduction to Gardner's book. Graves contributed several ideas to the Wicca movement: the idea of the Triple Goddess (maiden, mother, and crone) each representing both the female lifecycle and the phases of the moon; [288] the use of Celtic myths and poetry as descriptive of the power of ancient women; and, his Celtic Tree Calendar. All of these have become part of some Wicca covens. The historical and factual claims of Murray, Gardener, and Graves have been disputed by many throughout the years. But the dispute many times just adds to a member's sense of knowing what is right no matter what the elite intellectuals say about something—a consistent theme of Secular Fundamentalist culture.[289] Since its origins Wicca has developed to include many and diverse themes from different marginal spiritualities. If you are interested in this type of spirituality, the group(s) you contact may be quite diverse. Usually, however, if they are called Wicca, they will offer a natural spirituality of some sort, which we will examine later in this chapter. Wicca is also seen as a manifestation of feminist spirituality, which we will discuss later in this chapter. Whether Wicca, good witches, the craft, or followers of the old religion, their general spirituality would most likely include the following signposts.

> The magic of nature is given to us to survive and prosper whenever life is sorrowful and threatened.

Belief

Nature contains forces that, if not controlled, will destroy us. We control these forces through rituals (magic) that enable us to use them for our benefit. As we grow in the knowledge of how to use these powers and the trust in our ability to do so, we will become masters of our fate. "Energy," both positive and negative, is a common way of referring to these powers. The goddess of nature is the one to be worshiped through special rituals within which are contained magic formulas. The goddess manifests herself as a maiden (virgin), a mother, or a crone (old age), reflecting the powers of nature and the source of these powers. To worship the goddess is to worship the divinity within us and celebrate "female power, the female body, the female will, and women's bonds and heritage."[290] As a consequence, all living beings and the earth herself (Gaia) are holy.

Ethics

What one should do to fulfill these beliefs is, seemingly, obvious: live in reverent harmony with nature; keep the core values of personal freedom, self-determination, and autonomy; always maintain the two principles upon which life is based: as long as you harm no one, do what you want; whatever we do returns to us three times over, be it good or ill.[291]

Ritual[292]

There are four major *sabbats*,[293] or festivals, and four lesser ones. They depend on the relationship of the earth, sun and/or moon for the exact date of the seasonal ones. October 31, *Samhain*, celebrates the New Year. *Imbolic /Brigid*, February 1 celebrates the beginning of spring. May 1, *Beltane*, marks the great spring festival of fertility and renewal. Many times this is when the marriage of the god and goddess is renewed. August 1, *Lughnasadh*, marks the beginning of harvest as well and the end of the growing season. The four lesser *sabbats* mark the summer and winter solstice and the spring and fall equinoxes. Many covens usually meet at the beginning of the new moon and some meet once a week. These meetings are called e*sbats*.

> *The gods of old joined with the new visions of today result in a life without end.*

Many covens have rituals unique to them. One common ritual is the circle seen as both a sacred space concentrating the positive energies to those gathered in the circle and dissipating the negative energies that hinder magic. The basic goals of this spirituality are seen as physical and mental health, wealth, relationships, and the common good.

Community

Although there are solitary Wiccans, many enjoy the company of each other as they gather in covens. The Wiccan/craft/witch/old religion/neo pagan gatherings are usually independent of each other. There are some who attempt to place the curious in contact with each other as well as link diverse covens together. Dianic Wicca, Covenant of the Goddess, Church and School of Wicca, and Church of the Old Religion are some of these. Of course the Internet, as well as the yellow pages, will put one in contact with a coven. This is a noticeable difference from the, not too recent, times when there would be a noticeable outcry at their existence.

When Witches Look To The Spirits For Power

Witches, Vodoun (Voodoo), Santeria, and Shamans look to spirits, gods, or saints to cause good or evil. The Wiccan movement is still seen by many within the context of this kind of witch. Perhaps this is because it is easier for people to think of life in terms of spirits rather than natural energies. Nonetheless, these spirit-beliefs are the way many people conceptualize and experience life. We look at these four manifestations of spirit-belief as examples rather than as an exhaustive list of those spiritualities that attempt to manipulate this world for their own purposes. It is this manipulation of the spirit world that Christian authorities in the late Middle Ages feared. They saw it as the devil's manipulation of people rather than people's manipulation of evil forces. The Christian church believed that God alone knew the future; God alone was responsible for true miracles; God alone permitted contact with the spirits of the dead; God alone gave us healing shrines, sacraments, and prayers. Anything that did not carry the warrant of the Church, Protestant or Catholic, was of the devil. Those who tried to do things similar to what the Church did without her permission was a tool of the devil and, in some way, possessed by him. At least that is what the authorities and most of the people of the time believed. Consequently, those who healed the sick, contacted the dead, foretold the future, controlled people, animals, or objects through magic[294] were seen as threats to society and treated as criminals

Belief in another world possessed of powerful spirits is central to this spirituality. The exact nature of that "other" world differs among the diverse spiritualities that see both worlds as populated by spirits. Spirits may be disembodied human beings or other beings without a body. The other world may be one of the Abrahamic God with good spirits (angels), bad spirits (demons and devil),

> *Good and bad spirits surround us and seek to contact us.*

human souls in heaven (good) or in hell (bad), saints who are special human souls with intercessory powers with God to effect certain goods—for example, St. Jude if you lost something. The other world may be one of many gods (polytheism) each with a special power, and probably a consort of spirits. All these spirits are understood to have a will and intellect similar to humans and thus may be influenced to do things in much the same way that humans are swayed: such as pleading, offerings/gifts of various goods (food, liquor, sweet smells), and threats (not paying attention to them, destroying their earthly habitat). Contemporary otherworldly witchcraft, without historical or tribal connections, usually describes this other world based on imagination and a conflation of anthropological findings.

Voodoo and Santeria, however, have their origins in tribal past that has been reinforced by generation upon generation of lived experience. These religions are an amalgam of African slave religion and the religion of those who brought them to work their lands – the Catholic colonizers.

The **Vodoun** worship the goddess *Gran Met*, portrayed as a black mother, and the snake god, Damballah, represented by a python or boa. However, it is the other gods, or *loa*, that are contacted for any kind of favor be it violent, sexual, vindictive or generous. The gatekeeper to the spirit world of the *loa* is *Legba*, called "papa," and usually portrayed as an old man walking with a stick or crutch. Only *Legba* can allow a *loa* into our world.

> *Papa brings the snake god to make life better and defeat our enemies.*

Santeria (Regla de Ocha / La Regla Lucumi) beliefs are easily traced to the West African religion of Yoruba. The combination of the slave's Yoruba religion and Roman Catholicism formed the roots from which this spirituality sprang. The supreme god is *Olorun* (Olodumare) and the *orisha*, lesser spirits or saints, are sought after for their specific specialty of malevolent or benevolent goods. The *orishas* are enticed into helping their petitioners through various means especially animal sacrifices such as chickens. [295] It is believed that the *orishas* possess people, using them as their instruments in this world. Aside from the aid of the *orishas* in daily living, one's ancestors, the *Ara Orun*, are always available for guidance and help. As mentioned previously, these spiritualities are not always open to the public. Their beliefs, rituals, and moral imperatives are handed down orally. In all these communities, the priests are the principal conveyors of these traditions.

The rituals of these spiritualities include the use of magic in its many forms.[296] In practice, anything can be used to create their magical spells. In Santeria, for example, a *santero* (male priest) will use any part of the *bombas ceiba* tree: the roots and leaves help cure venereal disease, the bark cures infertility, the tree trunk and the ground surrounding it become a place to conjure evil spells. Coconuts, too, are used much like the *bombas ciba* tree to summon that special *orisha* to perform special magic for the petitioner. Many *vodoun* ceremonies use a long ritual rattle made of calabash and containing eight sacred stones of different colors. The rattle is a means of hearing the *loa* speak in response to their requests. A *botanicas*, which is a store specializing in things used in Santeria, will have the necessary items for performing these rituals.

Shaman is a term that has come to include many of the things witches do: healing, divinization, casting spells, controlling the weather, identifying lost or stolen property, communicating with and traveling among spirits. Shamans have performed their craft since the beginning of humankind. What is unique to them is their ability to travel into the spirit world at will, to self-initiate the ecstatic experience that places them in that world, and the processes of initiation into this role within their society. What began as a term, *saman*, used in Siberia and Central Asia, quickly became a way of describing diverse individuals doing more or less the same thing throughout the world.[297] As we find the re-conceptualization of witches in today's liminal age, so too we find the existence of neo-shamqns.

Shamans in indigenous cultures are different from the neo-shamans. They live on the edge of society, yet in most tribes, they are essential to its planning and communal living. One becomes a shaman because one's father or mother was one or because in some way, many times an illness, the person is chosen by the spirits as their conduit to this world. Central to shaman spirituality is a *belief* in the immediacy of the spirit world and one's ability to enter into it and engage the spirits' power for either one's own benefit or that of one's clients. The *rituals* are similar to those already mentioned above. Remember, however, that they are unique to the culture in which they exist as the dance, music, potions, and bodily disciplines bring the spirits world into ours for the threat or benefit of like-minded followers. The initiation rites are always difficult and a challenge to the initiate while being unique to each tribe. Being a shaman is not easy. It is a difficult way of life, lived on the edge of society, and always in danger of losing one's way in the spirit world and/or being attacked by evil spirits. There are many offerings on the internet for initiation into and details of how to live a shamanistic spirituality. As with anything on the internet, one must be careful of what one buys.

> *Secret knowledge is a powerful force for good.*

Gnosticism, as with everything we have reviewed so far, comes through the sieve of the liminal age in which we live. Gnostics left few historical documents describing the details of their spiritual life. Most of the information we had until 1945 came through the writings of those who saw them as threats to their faith. In 1945 at Nag Hammadi in Egypt, fifty-two fourth century manuscripts were found in an earthen jar. Many of these were Gnostic manuscripts.

Since then others have been found. Manuscripts entitled *the Gospel of Thomas, Gospel of Peter, Gospel of Philip, Gospel of Judas, Testimony of Truth,* and *Apocalypse of Peter* provided insight into a movement known as Gnosticism. Scholars recognized that these manuscripts provided a more complete view of what third, fourth, and fifth-century Christians called Gnosticism. When these texts were translated, some academics claimed them equal to Christianity. These writings were considered a severe threat to Christianity. Controversy followed, as did expansive media coverage. Others, including these academics, offered them as an answer to those on a spiritual quest. Consequently, that left those in search of an authentic Gnostic spirituality in the difficult position of trying to sort through the portrayals of Gnosticism by the early Christians, the Gnosticism of the new scholars and media commentators, and a spiritual life called Gnostic by Gardner and others. Some people tried to live a life based on ideas and practices derived from these sources. Their lived experiences seemed to affirm the value of this way of life. And, today, one hears a great deal about Gnostic spirituality.

What seems certain is that Gnostics hold that there is a secret knowledge founded upon an experience of otherness of one's body from one's conscious spirit. This spirit is a remnant of the divine: like a spark of spiritual light in the darkness of our material body. The real is the spiritual; the unreal is the material world that we ordinarily experience through our senses. This experience and the knowledge handed down over the ages provide a Gnostic with the conviction that the material world, which includes our body, is evil, created by an evil god. This evil god, called Yahweh by Jews, takes us away from what the true god revealed to us in Jesus, who was the true spirit of God living among us. Jesus revealed to us that there is a cosmic struggle between the good God and the evil god. We must choose sides. We demonstrate such a choice by disciplining our bodies. They are of no import, and if we allow our bodily desires to be fulfilled, our bodies can distract us from the war that exists between evil and good both within and outside the body.[298] The Jewish holy book, the Tanakh, therefore, was considered a worthless document and should be eliminated from one's spiritual life.

> *To know our inner divinity enables us to become divine.*

As mentioned, we know little about Gnostics, this especially pertains to their rituals and codes. We do know that the hatred and fear of the material world was a constant theme within Gnosticism, which led in many instances to condemnations and sometimes crusades by church authorities against its adherents such as Albigensianism (Cathars) and Manichaeism. Gnostic spirituality today comes in many forms such as the Church of Gnosis, Apostolic Gnostic Church, and The Thelemic Gnostic Church of Alexandria. They have in common a dislike of

Western Religions, especially classical Christianity; a belief in the absolute reality of the spiritual world and the falsity of the sensual one; rituals, many times called sacraments of initiation which lead one more deeply into the mysteries of the belief; and, websites as portals to their information and connections with the community. Most people find the websites as the easiest place to begin their search for the gnostic spirituality.

Not so with our next source of transcendence claimed by those in the neopagan and Wicca movement. *The Kabbalah* has a long history and documentation to prove its worth. You may have noticed a strong trend among both classical and marginal spiritualities away from wholism toward a dualistic view of nature. They seek to transcend this world of suffering and death to an immaterial one of immortal spirits and happiness. The Gnostic, unlike the shaman, does not seek otherworldliness to influence this "real" world but to transcend it permanently. A similar desire is found among the ancient, but not necessarily contemporary, devotees of the Kabbalah (Cabala, Qabalah, Kabala). We will review both the ancient and the contemporary. Both ancient and modern have their roots in a Jewish marginal spirituality that developed over the millennia. Its cosmology is reminiscent of Gnosticism, and it shares with most marginal spiritualities secrets not easily discovered. Many websites and books that purport to have made this discovery offer the spiritual seeker the means to take advantage of the esoteric lore they offer.

Once one becomes convinced that an immaterial transcendent world exists and one desires to enter into it, the immediate question is how to achieve entry. The response to both the desire and the method is both personal and mechanical. In the ancient *Kabbalah*, personal development involved a sustained desire for perfection, intense discipline, dedicated discipleship and a dedication to learning the necessary skills to enter into the divine world of immateriality.

> *The world of the senses is not real. The wisdom of the ancients reveals all that we need to know for a deep spirituality.*

Transcendent desire is most easily sustained when you perfect your skill in interpreting the Kabbalah and in learning its techniques for transcendence. Realistically, you need a good teacher to learn both technique and interpretation. Becoming a devoted follower of the teacher places you not only in the presence of the teacher, but also in the teacher's community of followers and their shared experience.

The Kabbalah is essentially an oral tradition of interpretation of the Tanakh; a tradition claiming to originate with the creation of the earth. There are many methods of exegesis of these sacred writings. Three in particular developed: the obvious meaning of the words themselves; the allegorical interpretation of words, laws and stories; and, the uncovering of secret meanings hidden by God in the letters, numbers, and images in these sacred writings. This last is associated with the Kabbalah. Gifted rabbis developed means of interpreting the inner meaning of the sacred writings by discovering the meanings hidden there. The methods of using such numerical and alphabetical methods were called *gematria* (the most popular), *notarikon*, and *temurah*. These were essentially ways of breaking the divine code within the holy writings.[299]

Though the methods of interpretation most publicized today were developed in the twentieth century, historians usually acknowledge two major schools of Kabbalah: Jewish and Western Occult/Esoteric. The Jewish school of interpretation is rooted in the entire Tanakh and in the intense mental and physical disciplines necessary for discovering God's mysteries. The Western Occult tradition looks to fifteenth- and sixteenth-century Jewish sources such as *Zohar for* the appropriate methods for discovering and controlling the principles of existence.

The way of understanding the cosmos, according to the ancients, begins with God's creation of it through a divine light emanating from God to arrive at what we sense around us, the created world. This process is illustrated in the Tree of Life or *Sephiroth*. According to the *Sepher Yetzirah*, or *Book of Creation*, God used thirty-two secret paths of knowledge in creating the world. Each path, or emanation, is called a *sephirot/sefroit*. These paths are how God comes into our world and we can enter into God's world. The ancient *Sephiroth* is found in most articles dealing with the Kabbalah both for its description of the cosmology and for, along with the numbers associated with the Hebrew alphabet, an object of meditation to bring one into the presence of God. The base of the Tree of Life (*Sephiroth*), *Malkut*, represents the world and the top of the diagram, *Keter*, represents God. The other avenues are descriptions of our necessary development from this base world to a divine one following the path of the emanations. Many moderns will understand the *Sephiroth* from a more modernistic perspective that replaces God with diverse natural energies. They believe that through the use of the magic and numerology contained in such books as the *Zohar*, one is able to control these energies for one's own purposes.

The Jewish tradition was influenced by several books in addition to the oral tradition. The earliest book is the *Merkabah* (+/- 500 CE). Aside from demanding intense fasting and the chant of divine names, it provided magical talismans, seals, and incantations to move through seven heavenly mansions to enter God's throne room and obtain direct contact with God. The *Sefer Yetzirah* (Book of Creation) was written somewhere between 500 and 800 CE. It gives us the first written descriptions of the Tree of Life. The *Sefer ha-Zohar* (Book of Splendor) was written in 13th century Spain and laid the groundwork for the majority of kabbalistic interpretations from that time onward. It suggests that we are all connected and, consequently, when someone advances up the Tree of Life that person brings the rest of creation along with her or him. Only one who has purified his body, mind, and spirit may advance up the tree. As the *Zohar* spread into Europe in the fourteenth and fifteenth centuries, Isaac Luria Askenazi (1534-1572) provided new terminology, symbolism and interpretations for the *Zohar* which still influence its devotees. Hasidism, which we already discussed in dealing with Judaism, still uses some kabbalistic ideas.[300]

Today much of the Western Kabbalah tradition comes by way of California (The Kabbalah Center). Two individuals brought a great deal of popular awareness to this tradition: Eliphas Levi and Aleister Crowley. Crowley's *Hermetic Order of the Golden Dawn* brought Kabbalah, Tarot, astrology, and Freemasonry together to create a comprehensive spirituality. The Kabbalah Center has simplified the entire Kabbalah by providing a visual ten-step process to enlightenment. This simplification of belief and ritual along with the magic of a red string tied around the left wrist in a prescribed manner gives one a connection to the protective energies surrounding the tomb of Rachel described in the Hebrew Scriptures. Many famous people such as Mick Jagger, David Beckham, Madonna, and Paris Hilton have found their rituals and ideas helpful as they live in the public eye.[301]

The Kabbalah along with the *Hermetica* may be seen as central to much of what Western marginal spiritualities promote. A brief review of the *Hermetica* will provide you with both its contents and also a sense of other ideas and magical performances found in discussions about the occult, esoteric, New Age and marginal spiritualities.

The *Hermetica* are remnants of a collection of books said to contain ancient Greek and Egyptian knowledge and techniques (magic) for controlling one's environment (alchemy), for dealing with one's destiny (astrology), and for directing any unseen powers in one's environment and destiny (theurgy). They are found written in many languages such as Coptic, Arabic, Syriac, Armenian, and Greek. There are purported to be forty-two books written by Hermes Trismegistus, the greatest of all

> **To know and control what is above makes us who we are below**

philosophers, kings, and priests. We do not have all these books, and there are always claims to new discoveries and additions to the total corpus. For example in the Nag Hammadi finds (1945), the Gnostic discoveries included among them descriptions of hermetic initiation rites. Ever since their discovery during the fourteenth and fifteenth centuries, they have been controversial as to authorship, content, and dating.[302]

A short work, the *Emerald Tablet* or *Table of Hermes Trismegistus* contains a saying we hear among many Satanists and Wicca devotees: "As above, so below." Although there are many meanings given by commentators, the most prominent is that what happens in the heavens will affect us here on earth. Astrology interprets this saying as the movements above (the stars, moon, sun, and planets) affect us below (human destiny). Another interpretation understands the "above" and "below" in supernatural terms, where what happens in the supernatural world (heaven) effects our natural (earth) world. The gods, spirits, and saints work their power through the magic we exercise in their name and the name of their followers. Finally, it is also understood as a microcosm (below) macrocosm (above) relationship where there is more of an equal relationship between the two. Thus, if I can control myself, microcosm, I can control the macrocosm such as weather, physical objects, and national destinies. The means to achieve this control is found in magic as well as our relationships with the spirits and/or nature.

It seems quite clear that the idea of *metempsychosis* may be found in the *Hermetica*. This is not the belief found in many Eastern spiritualities that believe the self-conscious desirous ego seeking continual change will ultimately disappear; rather, this is a continual reincarnation of a conscious ego able to carry a clear knowledge of previous selves from body to body until one escapes from the body to enjoy a consciousness of continuing fulfilled desires and relationships.

Hermetic beliefs and magic become part of such groups as the *Hermetic Order of the Golden Dawn* and *the Rosicrucian Order*. There they join with the developing ideas of the Kabbalah Center to provide many people with a sense of transcendence amidst the ordinariness of life.[303]

Between East and West: Marginal Spiritualities

When a spirituality has been marginal and secret for most of its existence, our understanding of it, as outsiders, is dependent upon brief glimpses of its actual effect upon other human beings. The effects of the classical religions and spiritualities are public. We can easily see how Christians, Jews, Muslims, Buddhists, Hindus, and followers of Shinto lead their lives. For our glimpse of marginal spiritualities to make sense, we need some context—some means of interpreting what we see, hear, and, perhaps, smell. Since they have been on the margins of culture until recently, we have not seen them as we do the classical religions.

We have just discussed some of those marginal religions using the Western context. In this section, we will discuss some of these from an Eastern context. There are some marginal spiritualities, however, that seem to defy all context. They embrace both Eastern and Western contexts in a seemingly contradictory manner. Their thought processes and the words and actions used to express them share in this same ambiguity and contradictoriness. Especially today on the Internet, we find a great many of these seeming to invent the religion out of some mescaline-filled air, drawing pictures from the smoke and their imagination; using the sounds of those around them as a meditative chant to deepen their spiritual discoveries. They are not always as nonsensical as I am suggesting, obviously, because they have gained followers over the generations.

In this section, we will examine a spirituality that has gained a significant amount of attention; we do this to provide you with one example of a spirituality that exists on the extreme margins of contemporary culture. Once again, we review this approach to spirituality from the perspective of English-speaking Western culture.

Theosophy

Madame Blavatsky and Colonel Olcott, the founders of Theosophy, crossed a variety of boundaries the most important of which are the cultural ones. Madame Helena Petrovna Blavatsky (1831-1891) was born in Russia. Her father, Peter von Hahn, was an officer in the army; her mother, Helena Andreyevna, a novelist. From an early age, she was said to hear the voices of both animate and inanimate objects as well as to have conversations with the spirits that surrounded her. At seventeen, she chose to marry Nikifor V. Blavatsky but left him after a few months to travel the world for the next ten years, two of which were in Tibet studying with the masters. She returned to Russia only to leave shortly after her arrival with an opera singer, Agardi Metrovich. He died on the boat while they were going to Cairo. She then founded the *Societe Spirite* for occult phenomena.

When she was accused of fraud in 1873, she left Cairo for New York City. She began to make a name there for her psychic abilities. While visiting two famous mediums, William and Horatio Eddy, in Chittenden, Vermont, she met Henry Still Olcott (1832-1907). A match made in heaven (or some astral plain) because these two became good friends and collaborators. They left their mark on the religion they created, theosophy; the anti- colonialism of India, Sri Lanka, and South East Asia; and, the image of Hinduism and Buddhism within and outside those places. Colonel Olcott was highly educated, served with distinction in the Civil War, became a lawyer, and wrote for the *New York Daily Graphic*. They formed the *Theosophical Society* in 1875. They left New York and went to Bombay, India where they relocated the Theosophical Society in Adyar, Chennai in 1879. Eventually Blavatsky went to England where she died. Olcott remained in India and died there. Both had traveled the world and encountered many spiritual ways of life, and this had changed them. Olcott, in particular, had changed significantly from the husband of a Presbyterian's daughter in New Rochelle, New York to welcoming seekers to the psychic adventures of Madame Blavasky in the New York City, to officially converting to Buddhism and being considered by some Buddhists in South East Asia as a Bodhisattva.[304]

They brought many issues to contemporary discussions of spirituality: the need to pay attention to psychic reality across cultures, the importance of spiritual masters in conveying this reality, an emphasis upon the ancients of Greece and Egypt as more knowledgeable about spiritual realities than moderns, a familiarity with reincarnation and karma as essential ingredients to any spiritual discussion.[305] All of these ideas were systematized in the Theosophical Society and its publications both past and present.

Part of this systematization envisioned the world we live in as an evolving consciousness. Everything, including humans, evolves from an individual monad.[306] Human evolution, and consequently each human being, becomes manifest through seven reincarnating bodies. The soul is one of these manifestations and is, essentially, a human's complete and authentic existence. The material body, as all material things, is ephemeral to our ability to live an authentic human life. These souls (humans) evolved through seven stages. At this time in human history, almost everyone is stuck at the fifth stage that developed on Atlantis. With time and effort, we will develop through to the seventh, and final, stage in which we will have a certain permeability of conscious realized in the unification of material, soul, and the physical.[307] No one religion or ideology has the necessary means to bring such an evolution to its completion. At the same time, each religion is helpful in providing us with some of the necessary means to achieve our own perfection.

> *We are still in the early stages of human development. Our way of life speaks that development.*

Theosophical resources, to aid us in this quest are found on the internet and in its suggested publications. One particular individual should be mentioned because he was groomed to become the world leader by the directors of the Theosophical Society: Jiddu Krishnamurti (1895-1986). He left the society to become a famous teacher in his own right. He taught that each of us must search for the truth on our own, and he emphasized that this search can only be done by abandoning all talk and ideas of the search itself. As he stated in writing:

> *Order is necessary, complete, absolute, inward order and that is not possible if there is no virtue, and virtue is the natural outcome of freedom. But freedom is not doing what you want to do nor is it revolting against the established order, adopting a laissez faire attitude to life or becoming a hippy. Freedom comes into being only when we understand, not intellectually but actually, our everyday*

239

life, our activity, our way of thought, the fact of our brutality, our callousness and indifference; it is to be actually in contact with our colossal selfishness.[308]

Eastern Marginal Spiritualities: Looking West to See East

The farther west you go in North America, the closer you come to the homes of the Eastern Religions. Going as far west as you can in the United States to the islands of Hawaii, this is even more so. Where we stand determines who we see. It also conditions, as we have said so often, how we see. In this section we will review how Eastern spiritualities are viewed in North America and how, in turn, they view themselves. In this perception of themselves, they become less marginal to North Americans and more marginal to practitioners in their Eastern culture. Sometimes the ideas and practices of the marginal spirituality are plucked from that classical spirituality and formulated anew by a North American spiritual entrepreneur.

Let's begin with one typical misinterpretation of marginality: Most Asians in North America are Christian. Hinduism, Buddhism, and other Asian religions represent 1.1 percent of the U.S. population [309] and 2.9 percent of the Canadian population.[310] Few people in North America convert to Hinduism. A significant number have converted to Buddhism. A large number of these live in the western states and provinces. As you might remember from the chapter on Eastern spiritualities, Hinduism is very diverse within India and has few adherents outside India. Buddhism expanded throughout Asia and changed as it did so. When either of these spiritualities comes into North America, it comes as having been lived by people from a certain area of Asia — much like an old Sicilian neighbor, who whispered to me one day that he never knew he was an Italian until he came to America. Until then he was a Sicilian. When people from Asia come to the United States or Canada, they often take for granted that the religion they grew up with is the religion of their home nation, not realizing, many times, that it is actually a variation of one of the classical religions lived within the context and tradition of the region and/or tribe they grew up in. Thus, we find that the understanding of the classical religions by most Americans comes from those individuals or communities of individual Buddhists and Hindus that established themselves in America. The signposts we have provided are not necessarily the same signposts in emphasis and substance that those immigrating into North America have. The same modification of signposts occurs as religious professionals from these spiritualities begin to offer their services in North America.

All the classical spiritualities change in a North American milieu. Marginal ones are no different. Several forces from American culture affect these spiritualities and shape them to adapt a more American perspective. As a result, they stand between the ancient classical forms and the American way of life itself, bringing something unique to both. While these statements are a simple bullet-list itemization, each is a significant challenge to some classical Buddhist spiritual schools.

- Women are in leadership positions and they emphasize working together through positive relationships, open communication, and togetherness.
- The community (*sangha*) becomes essential to Buddhism, not only for monks and nuns, but for everyone.
- There is equality among all. Monks and nuns are not of a higher status than the householder.
- Meditation is not the sole means to enlightenment.
- Mediation must not result in one's evasion of community and improving the common good.[311]

Changes such as these easily lead those who encounter these classical spiritualities in North America to think that what they encounter is authentic Buddhism or Hinduism. They are not. They are one small example of the classical religion as it has taken root in North America. Many times people mistake the part for the whole; for example, accepting an Indian guru's writings, lectures, and programs as an exposition of Hinduism when it is only his perspective on parts of the whole. The same can be said of the types of yoga that are found in most cities in North America. Like pizza, they are an American creation.

The following three types of Hinduism have somehow become "Hinduism" to many North Americans. First, there is *The Vedanta Center*, a branch of Ramakrishna founded by Vivekananda in India. It operates the Vedanta Press and has become a significant print source of Hindu literature, i.e. Ramakrishna literature, in North America. Second, there is *The International Society for Krishna Consciousness* (ISKCON / Hare Krishna Movement). It was founded in the United States by Divine Grace A.C. Bhaktivedanta Swami Prabhupada (1896-1977). As the title indicates, it focuses on attaining unity with Krishna. In the past, the followers of Krishna were seen in public areas such a bus stations and airports singing their mantra "Hare Krishna" (Praise to Krishna). Its publishing house is Bhaktivedanta Book Trust and its magazine is *Back to the Godhead*. Third, the *Self-Realization Fellowship* was founded in 1925 by Paramahansa Yogananda. The classical form of yoga meditation is central to helping one redirect one's energies from engaging with phenomena outside the self to focusing on the goal of self-realization. Those interested in Hindu spirituality usually come in contact with one of these versions of Hinduism.

Buddhism, like Hinduism, has not brought a large and diverse representation of its various spiritualities to North America. It does, however, provide clear options among the classical Buddhist schools of spirituality as well as adaptations of entrepreneurial spiritual masters. Vietnamese Buddhists are the majority of Buddhists in the United States. The *International Buddhist Meditation Center* in Los Angeles is the largest of their organizations. The *Buddhist Churches of America* are spread throughout the United States representing the Mahayana approach to Buddhism. Chinese Buddhism may be found in the *Dharma Realm Buddhist Association*. The Dharma Realm Buddhist University is part of this organization. One finds here most of the diverse Chinese schools of Buddhism. Tibetan Buddhism, *Vajrayana*,[312] is the educational wing, and the Shambhala press provides much of its written material. All of these are, in their own way, faced with how to communicate their spirituality to others. *The Order of Buddhist Contemplatives* at Shasta Abby is a good example of a group explicitly dedicated to such communication.

Yet these institutions, though significant, are not the major means of communicating the Eastern Spiritualities to most people in North America. Meditation, Yoga, Zen, reincarnation, karma, Karate, Shamari, Chaka, and I Ching are not only words to many Americans, but they evoke images as well. One would be hard pressed to see these as marginal to American culture. They have become as ubiquitous as pizza and tacos, and as with pizza and tacos, they indicate that certain ideas and techniques have entered into the mainstream of the culture. They may be representative of an ancient way of life, but when taken out of that context, they are something altogether different.

When these spiritualities are introduced into Western culture, it is not ancient wisdom and techniques that are offered as a spiritual method, insight, or way of life. The entire classical way of life seldom accompanies the offering. Transcendental Meditation (TM) is a case in point.

> Ten spiritual masters gave birth to the final spiritual master: the sacred Sikh Guru Adi Granth.

The movement, and the mantra meditation technique known as *Transcendental Meditation*, gained Indians' attention in the mid-1950s. Maharishi Mahesh Yogi (1914-2008) then brought it to the West. It became part of public discourse in the 1960s when the Beatles and other public figures told us they had learned how to meditate transcendentally. When others said that they had learned to levitate by using advanced Transcendental Techniques (Yogic flying), the media provided intense coverage of both Maharishi Mahesh Yogi and the controversies surrounding his meditative techniques and spiritual doctrine. People now knew what "meditation" was and what it could achieve. Why did people meditate? TM said that it would help you relax and, consequently, benefit your health. The Maharishi also said that TM could help you concentrate and touch your inner self. The belief was that you could meditate to improve your health, be better at your job, and be more creative and focused. Does any of this sound like the goals of the Hindu bhakti yoga? What began in the 1950s as Hindu bhakti yoga had transformed by the 1970s in Western culture into an emphasis on the scientific basis for its meditative technique (Yogic Flying excepted), and today it emphasizes its spiritual and scientific nature as it adapts to the culture that surrounds it.[313] Such complete abdication to the culture seldom occurs at the Hindu and Buddhist centers mentioned above, but it does exist many times as the individual entrepreneur attempts to and gains followers.

An example of a spirituality that is both marginal to North America as well as its native land is *Sikhism*. The two major religions of India and Pakistan are Hinduism and Islam. Sikhism offers a synthesis of both by bringing together Sufi Islam and Hindu *bhakti* devotion. In North America Sikhs are easily recognized as the men wearing turban, beard, and ceremonial sword (*kirpan*). Their reputation as fierce fighters has a long history and adds, at times, to the fear that surrounds them as a marginal spirituality. Contrary to stereotypes, however, theirs is a spirituality of compassion, devotion to the one God, and service to others.

Sikhism is founded upon the experiences and insight of ten gurus and the final Guru Adi Granth, which is the sacred Sikh scriptures.[314] The ten gurus lived from 1469 to 1708. When the final Guru died, he said the future Guru would not be a human one but instead the living word. Each morning a copy of the *Granth* is enthroned at the central temple of the Sikhs in *Amrithsar*

> **Listen to the final guru's word: worship only Ik Onkar and speak his word for eternal life.**

and put to rest at night. During that time, it is read continually. This practice is followed in most Sikh temples throughout the world.

What one finds in such reading, reverence, and honor to Guru Adi Granth, and throughout Sikh teaching, is the conviction that humans are good but ignorant of who/what they really are. This ignorance is caused by attachment to our selfish desires and is expressed in anger, lust, greed, pride, and the worship of everything but *Ik Onkar*. All of these are considered idols that we worship when instead we should adore *Ik Onkar*. We must get beyond our ignorance by experiencing *Ik Onkar*, the reality that embraces and wishes us to become one with that which is beyond our words and images. If we cannot do that, the law of karma demands we be reincarnated until we do. We break out of this wheel of reincarnation through devotion to *Ik Onkar* (God/Reality/Being) by thoughtful repetition of Ik Onkar's name, especially in the morning.

While bathing, we sing the *japji: Ik Onkar: the true name, the creator, without fear, without hatred, timeless, self-existent, known by the Guru's grace*.[315] Such thoughtful repetition throughout the day connects us to the ever-present *Ik Onkar*. And we look forward to total absorption, and cessation of reincarnation, *in Ik Onkar* as our final destination. We are aided in this goal by finding our own guru to aid us in the necessary steps to discovering the necessary discipline and acts of compassion necessary to walk toward our final transcendence.

This short description provides us with a glimpse into a spirituality that has existed for five hundred years on the margin of Islamic and Hindu cultures, and for one hundred and fifty years on the margins of Christian Western culture. This is a long time. Sikhism has not existed in secret, as many of the marginal offerings we have reviewed in this chapter, but out in the open for all to see. Sikhs may be rejected by those who see them, but they are there.

Like the classical forms of religion, they are divided into fundamentalists and moderates. The issue for most Sikh fundamentalists is their desire to a return of the ancient joining of the Sikh religion with the land and culture of the Punjab. In pluralistic cultures such as North America, the Sikh fundamentalists are faced with the same challenges the classical forms of religion have faced: to return to an older form of the religion (traditionalist), to accept the modern world and practice their religion in it as they understand it (contemporalist), or to adapt their religious way of life to the current liminal existence (co-temporalist). The Sikhs, as all marginal religions, are faced with the same choices. The same three challenges that face both classical and marginal spiritualities also face spiritual movements that arise in our current liminal era.

As examples of current spiritual movements, we will examine three: nature spirituality, feminist spirituality, and spiritualities of the powerless. They have their contemporary origins in movements responding to denigrations in the physical environment, intense inequality among the earth's human inhabitants, and seemingly inbred convictions about male-female relationships.

Marginal Movements in a Liminal Age: Advocates for the Earth, the Sea, the Air, and the Human Spirit

A movement is like throwing a snowball down a hill: it gathers more snow or it stops dead, right where we throw it. What might be packed together are ideas, negative feelings like hunger, positive ones like nationalism, or a sense of alienation from major segments of our culture. They become packed together by happenstance or human design and then are thrown onto the momentum of changing culture. They do or do not influence that change depending upon myriad circumstances. In liminal times, the culture is changing more quickly than at other times. When the movement is thrown into the culture, it is not necessarily the number of people that join it but how long it lasts and how many are influenced by it that makes a difference. An example of this would be if the snowball we threw stopped dead but shook up enough snow to start an avalanche or, if the snowball melted and was no longer a snowball.

In a liminal age, there are many expressions of uncertainty and need. Many movements are initiated to respond to the changes threatening people's signposts. As these movements affect the culture, they become testing grounds for what will gain traction and provide permanency within that culture sometime in the future. In other words, they are transitional subcultures acting as agents of translation between what is old and what is new. Those whose spirituality is found within one of these movements will experience, on the one hand, a sense of fulfilling their desire for transcendence and of fellowship with those who are part of the movement. On the other hand, however, they may be viewed by society as odd, and so they may feel alienated from society and its primary religions and spiritualities. To some this feeling of alienation coincides with a picture of themselves as rebels with a cause fighting against all odds. This type of alienation, of course, has a long history in American myths of the lonely outsider coming to save the oppressed town, nation, or business. To others in a movement it may be a cause of depression and deep apocalyptic feelings. No matter what the individual feelings are as the movement continues, it births its songs, sacred places and celebrations, heroic myths of founders and enemies, ways of dressing and eating, and a set of normative values. The civil rights movement of the last century is exemplified by Martin Luther King, the slogan "We Shall Overcome," the shootings in Birmingham, non-violent resistance, peace, and equality for all.

Three challenges to our way of life have led to three movements and their coincident spiritualities: the possible destruction of our physical world, the unjust treatment and brutalization of our fellow human beings, and, in particular, burdening more than half the human race with the task of serving those of a different gender. We will

> **Can we be free, secure, and have a voice in government – even when marginal?**

describe the spiritualities surrounding each of these issues by first describing why it is important, what the current scientific thought is regarding the issue, what the religious perspectives are, and the consequent response by some of the spiritualities.

In order to describe the responses of the major religions and clarify the spiritualities evolving out of these responses, I have to take a brief side road that will enable us to clearly mark the signposts found in these spiritualities. That side road is the current linkage between religion and politics in the United States. This side trip will enable us to clarify the primary religious perspective and the major marginal movements it has spawned. It may be you are part of a movement and do not know it. After all, when everyone around you thinks the same, it's hard to think there are many who do not!

When your ideas have never been challenged, you seldom think about them. You just live them. So the status quo regarding the environment, economic injustice, and the rights of women were never thought about for centuries because people were not conscious of them. Slowly, however, some people became aware of certain issues; for example, the dangers of high population density and the consequent famines, the cultural changes caused by the growing cities, and, finally, the chemical imbalances in the atmosphere that would destroy life as we know it. Gradually some people recognized that people's freedom and a society's creativity were being severely restricted by demanding each person follow a strict social script according to her or his gender characteristics. The inequality inherent in past societies increasingly challenged some people's consciences first in religious and social movements that rejected slavery, and then in demanding children be offered an education to cope with the changing economic environment while prohibiting their labor for meager wages. These are some examples of how people slowly became aware of what was happening around them. Today, in the global awareness of the twenty-first century, everyone must deal with issues that previously were unthinkable because they were unrecognized. Recognition does not bring agreement about how to respond to what people see, however. Many still advocate slavery even when it is recognized. People still strive for and support inequality based on birth through diverse caste systems, even when they're consciously aware that people are starving to death because of this inequality. Some people, however, do strive to eliminate the evil they see.

People began to recognize the systemic nature of certain challenges: population growth, child labor, environmental degradation, and injustice among people based on age, sex, and the color of their skin. Political parties became identified with what was to be done about these issues. Another factor, one

> **Are women, the poor, and nature itself marginal?**

that is very significant for our purposes, is that religious people have become identified with one political party that seeks to maintain the status quo in these matters as much as possible. In other words, the spiritualities of people are reflected, for the most part, in the political party they belong to. That is not to say that every member of a certain political party supports the status quo for all of these issues, but the majority do. Furthermore, the majority of the members of that party belong to a certain spirituality within their religion that supports the status quo.

During the last forty years, a number of factors unique to American culture have come into play. These factors have resulted in a clear delineation of positions regarding these issues based on whether one is traditionalist, contemporalist, or co-temporalist. A quick survey of recent cultural trends described by sociologists of religion will mark the logic of the development. We will use for our guide an excellent summary of those trends: the book by Robert D. Putnam and David E. Campbell titled *American Grace: How Religion Divides and Unites Us*[316] as well as the research provided by the Pew Foundation.[317]

Americans always have been and still are an extremely religious people.[318] But today the alignment of which religion they belong to is becoming more fluid as an increasing number of people see that they have a choice of which religion they will join (if they join one at all). Religion has become something they choose rather than something that is part of them as it was for their parents, grandparents, and great grandparents. This fluidity and choosing means "that people gradually sorted themselves into likeminded clusters—their commonality defined not only by religion, but also by the social and political beliefs that go along with their religion."[319] These likeminded clusters resulted in an extreme polarization among people, which had consequences on their spirituality and the diverse religious institutions that gave birth to these spiritualities. Many times people had more in common with those in other religious institutions than with some in their own. That means that before this change, you could be fairly certain that if you were talking to a Presbyterian, Catholic, Muslim, Jew, or a Baptist, the perspective of the one you were talking with would be more or less coherent with their co-religionists; there would be a coherent pattern among co-religionists in each religion.

> The power of the majority is economic, religious, and political.

This no longer exists except in a few situations where the clergy and the institution itself clearly, loudly, and actively promote one coherent view that damns the changes taking place, seeing them as the disintegration of American civilization and offering little hope for America's future. The result is that in the first two decades of the twenty-first century, Americans' religions and politics are significantly coherent.[320] There are the two extremes: the liberal secular pole (contemporalists) and the conservative, evangelical pole (traditionalists). Joined to the evangelicals are other deeply religious individuals from other religious institutions who share their worldview, such as conservative Roman Catholics.

There is now unity, for the first time in American history, among diverse religions based on a common spirituality[321] where its adherents have a strong belief in God, frequently attend religious services, pray outside of these services (especially before meals), and affirm their religion as central to their lives and identities. If these markers reflect your spirituality, more than likely you also feel that your values are deeply threatened by the current American culture and you must do everything you can to protect these values. Between this grouping of liberals and conservatives there is a very weak coalition of mainline churches (co-temporalists) advocating dialogue and a search for common ground.[322]

Mainline churches are those that have been the backbone of American religion since its founding: Episcopalians, Presbyterians, Methodists, American Baptists (not Southern), Disciples of Christ, Congregationalists, United Church of Christ, and Lutherans (not Missouri Synod). They are no longer in the religious majority. The liberal secular pole is growing but does not match, religiously, the conservative one. The mainline churches are slowly losing members as are Roman Catholics, who lost one-third of their non-Latin members during the last twenty years. That leaves the question of marginality and marginal spiritualities a difficult one to answer until one looks at the majority in terms of wealth and institutional power, not just membership numbers. In doing that, it is quite clear that those who oppose the traditionalists are the minority whenever they advocate protecting the environment, reducing armaments, protecting and advocating for the rights of the powerless, and demanding equality among the sexes.

Chicken Littles or Prophets? New Marginal Religions Confront the Old

The position of the majority of scientists and the experiential and experimental basis of their positions are recognized by everyone. For example, there is an iceberg four times the size of Manhattan floating in the North Atlantic that has broken off from Greenland, an obvious example of decades of glacial melting; China holds over a trillion dollars of U.S. debt; China and Saudi Arabia are buying land in African countries to raise food for their people; most workers receive less than subsistence wages for their work; huge numbers of people are migrating from have-not countries to wealthy ones; pre-teen wives are stoned to death for leaving their aged husband in many countries, and females receive less education than males in most countries. Finally, we can never forget that nations possess enough nuclear weapons to destroy the world and all living things. The facts are there. Interpreting them and what to do about them varies. Since we are discussing current issues, the probabilities are that you not only know the issues but know your position on the issues. In stark terms they may be stated as follows: 1) The world is going to end if we don't get back to traditional religious values, and we solve these problems as individuals, not as a government or business (traditionalist); 2) The world is going to end if we do not act quickly, use contemporary technologies to deal with these problems, and make systemic changes in society to deal with them (Contemporalist); 3) The world is going to end if we do not combine both the necessary technologies, systemic change, and the spiritual lifestyle to bring about a new world that protects us from the roots of these problems (co-temporalist).

Religion and spirituality are essential to the discussion because many in camps two and three see the religious world view of the first group as causing these problems and because groups one and three see religion and spirituality as essential to dealing with them.

During the 1960s, a certain view of Christianity began to be seen as the cause of the diverse crises. For our purposes, we will call it the traditionalist one. It saw Christianity as an extreme, dualistic, man-centered religion that viewed the non-human world as necessarily subservient to humans. The role of; humanity was to gain control over nature and, in the process, gain an eternal, spiritual reward. The Bible clearly demonstrates this by ordering man to subdue the earth (Genesis 1:27-31), women to be subservient to man (Genesis 3:16), and to acknowledge God alone as holy (Leviticus 11:44-45; Deuteronomy 5:7-9). God's laws reflected the natural and spiritual ordering of all creation: God, spiritual beings, man, woman, animals, and all other living and non-living things (nature). The result of this set of values is that the Abrahamic religions and Christianity in particular have broken the natural harmony present in nature and radicalized the opposition between the sacred (God) and the secular (nature).[323] This harmony was recognized by the aboriginal religions and many Eastern religions especially Tao, Shinto, and Jainism. Christianity does not recognize the sacredness of nature, the necessary connection between all living and non-living things, and the right to life of each of these living things. If this Christian perspective is not abandoned, the critics holding the second and third position say, we will commit ecological suicide.

Contemporalists accept the necessity of rejecting the religious perspective offered as giving birth to our ecological degradation. Some reject all religion and join movements that try to get governments and businesses to change their dangerous ways.[324] Others reject all the classical forms of religion and return to the spiritualities that existed

> **Is classical Christianity the cause of contemporary marginalization?**

before Christianity arrived into Europe and the Americas such as Wicca, Celtic, and Native American spiritualities. These are known as nature spiritualities or nature mysticism. In many ways, these continue Western culture's deep love of nature expressed in the works of the Transcendentalist thinkers, Romantic poets, national parks, suburban housing, and backyard gardens. But they are also done with a conscious rejection of the traditionalists' image of God. Many Wicca, for example, will follow Eileen Holland's proclamation that we need to worship the Great Goddess in order to truly follow the ancient Wicca craft.[325] Contemporary followers of American Indian (aboriginal) religions speak of attending to the wishes of the Great Spirit.[326] Followers of these spiritualities will usually be strong supporters of secular movements advocating for the rights of women, prevention of further harm to the planet, and equality among peoples.

Co-temporalists, present in most of the classical religions, look at the evidence and see it as probative; look at their tradition and see it as life giving; and, seek to discover the ideas, values, and actions necessary to achieve the same goals as the Contemporalists. Mainline Christian thinkers will point out that the Bible also says that all of nature is "very good" (Genesis 1:30-31), that the New Testament proclaims that the kingdom to come is one of harmony,[327] and that creation groans for this harmony to be restored (Romans 8:18-23). The Christian tradition witnesses to the resurrection of the body to eternal life and sees God as acting through nature in many ways. The sacramental system is one in which water, oil, spit, bread, wine, and beeswax play central parts in how God becomes manifest and operative in this world by transforming as instruments in bringing about a new one, the Kingdom of God. St. Francis was one of many saints declaring the necessity of respect for all living things. These thinkers readily admit that an emphasis on stewardship, a totally transcendent God, and dominion of the earth conditioned many in the West to look on nature as an inanimate tool in human hands. At the same time they also ask people to consider that it was not these Christian ideas alone that led to where we are right now. The ancient Greek view of the dominance of reason over material things, the modern view of reality as only that which is empirical, the economic theories that see financial growth as central to happiness, and living a life patterned after the seven deadly sins also played a part in bringing us to where we are right now.

Instead of a radical division of God and nature, and a hierarchy of powerful and powerless, co-temporalists offer the inclusiveness of Process Theology, where everything is connected to everything and God is part of the futuring of existence, and communities of consciousness-raising are birthed by Liberation and Feminist Theologians. Their biblical foundation is laid with such quotes as "There is no such thing as Jew and Greek, slave and freeman, male or female: for you are all one person in Jesus Christ" (Galatians 3:28; also Colossians 3:11). Many co-temporal Christian theologians also believe strongly in what is called the Communion of Saints, which holds that everyone, the living and the dead, are interdependent and part of Jesus's resurrected body (mystical body). And, with the declaration of St. Paul (Romans 8:18-23), they are groaning together to become perfected. co-temporalists will also support most of the actions advocated by ecological, feminist, and rights movements.

Traditionalists are not standing idle in their response to the ecological crisis. Some in the biblical Green movement accept the scientific data and the scientific interpretations. They do differ on how to react to both. Their reaction is within the context of stewardship and individual responsibility.[328] Within that context they support many of the calls to action by such groups as the Earth Policy Institute of Lester R. Brown.

The other classical spiritualities reflect many of the diverse Christian responses to these issues. They have not been the target for blame regarding environmental degradation because the sciences and technologies that caused it began in the West with roots in both Christianity and a tradition of blaming Christianity for multiple psychological and social evils. Within the context of the United States, we can easily identify those of the traditionalist perspective

> **Where do the classical spiritu- alities stand vis a vis women, the poor, and environmental degradation?**

since they are, as mentioned above, deeply religious and usually members of the Republican Party. Those who take a Contemporalist position do not have to be considered because they accept the scientific findings describing the crisis. Therefore, in summarizing the position of the classical spiritualities, we will look at the co-temporal positions in the classical religions.[329]

This natural world, for all the Abrahamic religions, is real, created by God, but is not God, and has a beginning, end, and purpose known only to God. But we must care for it. Judaism looks to its oral and written traditions and finds four principles to be used in dealing with the natural world: to acknowl- edge that this is God's world and respect, maintain, and treat it with rever- ence.[330] To haphazardly destroy the natural world is immoral. According to Isma'l Al Faruqi, a Muslim theologian, Muslim political and religious leaders have a moral obligation to guarantee that all new development cares for the environment.[331]

The Eastern classical religions, as we have seen, take a very different approach to our natural world. In the beliefs of Hinduism and Buddhism, nature is not real; it is an illusion caused by our own ignorance and/or desires. Yet Mahayana Buddhism also sees nature as a means of bringing compassion to all living beings. In Taoism, nature is essential to life because it is part of the ever-changing process in which the harmony and unity of the Tao is present. Shinto sees nature as the means through which the kami come into our lives. In Confucianism, nature is considered real and necessary for human living, and it brings this living to fruition as we all become more ordered and in har- mony with each other.

When co-temporalist thinkers look at the Eastern religions, they begin with these basic beliefs regarding nature. They also begin with the very evident reality of extreme environmental pollution. Some may blame this on Christi- anity as argued in the 1960s, but the fact is that things are bad. For example, going to an Indian website designed to highlight how bad it is, *GIT4u*,[332] provides the overwhelming facts. The most symbolic fact is that the sacred Ganges itself is highly polluted. A *small* part of this pollution is 1.3 billion liters[333] of sewage per day from towns along its shores. In 2016 CE, there will be 1.26 billion people trying to survive on this land. China is also highly polluted. What do their religions have to say about this?

Hindu thinkers emphasize the interconnectedness of all beings as expressions of Brahman. Thus, there is a kinship among all living beings who are reincarnations of other living creatures, perhaps a human. A respect for cows, a general teaching of non-violence, and vegetarianism reflect the norms emphasizing this belief, thus leading to a better environment. Buddha's teaching of loving kindness for all beings (*metta*) should lead to care of the environment. The concept of karma also says that what we do has an effect on us no matter how private or public the action. Our "doing" destruction to nature will affect our karma. Jainism, of course, with its deep-rooted belief in non-violence toward all living things, summarizes the desire of most ecologists in the necessity to respect nature.

Taoism has always respected nature because nature is essential to our being as the Tao undergoes the eternal process of birthing the future. The model of this eternal process is the changing seasons where we see birth (spring), life (summer), fall (fruition), and winter (death). What goes around comes around. To cause and/or increase disharmony of this eternal process is only to increase the depth of change as the next season arrives. For example, if we cause a great deal of snow (winter), then we cause a great deal of water and flooding, then we cause a shorter spring, and, perhaps, then a more intense, heated summer. Wu-wei, the practice of active non-doing, is the best way to deal with creating electricity, food, and pure water. We will certainly know by 2030 CE whether Taoism, as with all the Co-temporalist approaches to the ecological crisis, makes an impact on our mutual future.

The book *Exploring Religious Meaning* offers a distinction that may be helpful in thinking about your approach to these diverse responses to the ecological crisis.[334] It is also a quick review of what I have just said. The authors suggest that there are three basic approaches to a spirituality of nature, and they coin three terms to describe these approaches: *symbiosis, apobiosis,* and *diabiosis. Symbiosis* is when you want to live in harmony with all natural things. You want to feel at one, and perhaps have, with the trees, grass, animals, microorganisms, stars, the universe—all organic and inorganic reality. You do not want what you perceive as the natural order of things to be disturbed. You would rather adjust to nature than try to change it to fit your needs. The environmental crisis is a call to return to this oneness with nature and will only be solved if we learn to live in harmony with all living and nonliving things.

Apobiosis is the opposite of symbiosis. In symbiosis who you are is essentially who you, organic and inorganic reality, are. We are one. In *apobiosis* all that surrounds us is different from us. It is "other" to "me." The only way to deal with nature properly is by treating it objectively: like a machine with diverse parts which, if discovered and manipulated properly, will improve my spiritual life. Nature is not a reflection of God, but our learned ability to master nature reflects the deep spiritual and God-like power we possess to create a world in our image. To honor nature as if it is God and as if it is the origin and fulfillment of our lives is to kneel to an idol; it is to place the source of spirituality in a reality that does not provide true life. The environmental crisis is a call to use our imagination, reason, and technological abilities to remake nature in such a way as to make us better human beings, provide the context in which we can truly live a full spiritual life.

Unlike both symbiosis and apobiosis, *diabiosis* views all organic and inorganic reality as almost something evil, something holding you back from a full spiritual life. The spiritual life is beyond material things, which are so far from what is truly real and transformative that we must avoid thinking that they matter. Because nature does not matter! It only tempts us to forget who we really are and what we really might become. Our true home is beyond this natural world. Our true home is a spiritual, supernatural one. The environmental crisis is a distraction from what really matters. Is the solution to the environmental crisis one of these approaches? Perhaps none of these? But reflecting on how you perceive nature might help in dealing with the crises surrounding it.

Before moving on, one last fact regarding the environmental crisis must be recognized: it is intensifying. In his book *World on the Edge* Lester R. Brown repeats a question we must all answer before closing this section because its answer determines how quickly we must find solutions to the crisis. *"A lily pond has one leaf in it the first day, two the second day, four, the third, and the number of leaves continues to double each day. If the pond fills on the thirtieth day, when is it half full?"*[335] Our environment is filling with leaves. Which day do you think we are on? And remember, when we are at day thirty, it is too late. Do your spiritual signposts include this calendar?

Is It Natural for Women to Be Subservient to Men, for the Rich to Get Richer, and for the Poor to Get Poorer?

For some, all these questions are social questions and do not deserve a place here because we are discussing spirituality, not sociology. Yet, many advocates for peoples' rights experience this advocacy as a transcending experience and view their goals as deeply transcendent ones. For many Christians, for example, such advocacy is answering the call of the Sermon on the Mount or the norms presented by Jesus judging the sheep and the goats. For many Buddhists, it is the height of compassion to advocate for the betterment of people's lives. For all social questions are spiritual questions: reject them, embrace them, and/or to live their responses.

The lines drawn in our discussion of the ecological crisis are repeated in responding to the questions that head this section. The majority of people throughout the world will answer "yes" to these questions. They were taught that this is what is natural. What they were taught enlivens their lives, offers promises of transcendence, and, at times, provides glimpses of what the world offered by the tradition will give them. For a minority of people throughout the world, the answer will be "no" to these questions. The nature of things is not, necessarily, how we were brought up, and there is evidence that it can be quite different. Let us follow that evidence and reject how we were brought up. Develop a spirituality of nature, of womanhood, of liberation for all. As these people embrace a meager vision of what will be and forge the necessary road and lay the signposts to travel to its completeness, they experience the transcending change that gives the vision and signposts a sense of sacrality: a sacrality that must be protected at all costs and made ready for the next generation. Finally, there are still others who look at the evidence and, instead of believing it, they are fearful of scientific predictions about the environment, economic change, and gender differentiation. They look at what they have been given and what will probably come. They realize that what was cannot be. They seek, somehow, to sustain the vitality of the past in the present and into the future. They seek not to build something new from the saplings growing among today's marginal spiritualities but to remake from the ancient timbers a new spiritual home that will withstand the coming storms. Which of the three will prevail? The window to the future needs to be open to see. But it is only our present spirituality that enables us to open it.

Two things are evident: there is much we can predict, and there is still more we cannot. More than thirty years ago I began teaching an introductory course on Gerontology. In the economics of societal aging, every text said we would be faced with funding pensions, especially public pensions, in the near future. No one listened to what was obvious. As I write this people are protesting about public pensions. Instead of planning yesterday, they complain today. It seems we did not pay attention to those leaves gathering in the lily pond. At the same time the protests have gained less media attention. The largest tsunami and earthquake in Japanese history has devastated large sections of the nation. Japan was the best prepared for such events of any nation in the world. Obviously, the preparations were not enough. Sometimes the wind fills the lily pond after the first leaf.

Ah, the mystery of life, of death, of human reason, of human survival—of the necessity of energizing, supporting, and deepening the human spirit. Those who are the Chicken Littles and the Prophets are only known long after they have shouted their messages. But we cannot wait to know who is who before making a decision. Not making a decision today creates the future.

Summary

Today's trends have enlarged the meaning of spirituality and brought former marginal spiritualities into the mainstream. The abandonment of the Abrahamic God by commentators has resulted in a re-interpretation of some of the classical western spiritualities by replacing God with Mother Earth (Gaia) or natural energies. The world of spirits has replaced the one created by God for the followers of these marginal spiritualities. They are more comfortable with belief in nature's gods than the God who created nature; with magic rituals than biblical sermons; an ethic that expands life's pleasures than restricts individual freedom. Marginal spiritualities have stepped from the edge of cultural existence to very public roles in music, film, literature, and the arts. But while the marginalized of the past gained recognition as visible spiritualities, the marginalized of the present shout to be recognized as a necessary part of every religion and spirituality. In stark terms, many of them declare that every form of spirituality must provide security, freedom, and a political voice for all women, all people rich and poor, and all of nature. If certain spiritualities do *not* do so, they predict, the majority of people will abandon the core of the Western spiritualities they profess.

PART FOUR

TESTING THE SPIRITS:
CULTURAL AND PERSONAL

Life is like a box of chocolates. You never know what you are going to get. (Forrest Gump)

What's life? Birth, death. Everything in between is a drag.
(Lou Grant on the Mary Tyler Moore Show)

Vis, Veritas, Vita.[336]

Satyagraha[337]

Life is not a true and false test. It's an essay written by you and ending at your last breath.

***

Louie was having a what day, which was better than a how day, and infinitely preferable to any day that demanded she concentrate on why? All the same, she could have done without it.

So much of life was an imitation of itself that deciding whether a thing was real gave her problems. Sometimes really obvious things weren't real at all, they were merely pretending....

In an odd way, Louie could see something of herself in the black-clad teenager she followed through the door of Borders Books. The girl's obvious irritation with idiots who had no idea where they were going, plus her reluctance to pay much attention to traffic lights on the way were qualities with which Louie could identify.[338]

***

Oh, where have you been, my blue-eyed son?
And where have you been my darling young one?
I've stumbled on the side of twelve misty mountains
I've walked and I've crawled on six crooked highways
I've stepped in the middle of seven sad forests
I've been out in front of a dozen dead oceans
I've been ten thousand miles in the mouth of a graveyard
And it's a hard, it's a hard, it's a hard, and it's a hard
It's a hard rain's a-gonna fall.
~ Bob Dylan

***

When the hard rain falls we are tested. As the complete song says, we are tested through what we see, what we hear, and who we meet. Although verbal conversation is usually the primary test, the radical tests are faced in the conversational dialectic of action. How we interact with those most radical of all human activities of death and suffering are the ultimate test of our spirituality. The spirituality that springs forth from these testings either energizes or stunts our foundational uniqueness.

The last two concluding chapters of this book are about those tests. Chapter Eight brings all the spiritualities of this book into conversation with each other over how you should think and act in the face of death, after-life, suffering, and evil. Chapter Nine asks you to re-affirm your choice among the spiritualities and to make that choice consciously and with intentional purpose. It also provides you with the means to act upon what you have thought about during the reading of this book. Chapter Nine reminds you that you are responsible for your spiritual life, which is the ultimate test.

Chapter Eight

Spiritualities in Conversation: Death, Afterlife, Judgment, Suffering, and Evil

Beginning the Conversation

Thin as a telephone pole. Tall. Maybe six feet and still growing.
Narrow face and eyes like sparkling blue water. Dark long hair falling over her shoulders.
There she sat in the back row.
That way, the teacher said, others could see.

Back there she sat. Looking into another imaginary world. Mind wandering,
Wandering outside the classroom lights, hard back seats, boring books, and broken clocks.

"Tammy, did you do your homework?" the teacher asked.
At least that is what she thought she asked.

Back there in the back seat, she sat.
Beyond the world of boys stepping on her shoes and girls giggling about her breasts, she sat.
Feeling deep within the urge of foreverness;
the thrilling flight of spirit-freedom;
the beat of a heart that wants to go beyond all this;
that can go beyond all this; that will….

"Tammy, stand up and read your homework!"

* * *

The room smells of fresh urine. Naked and unshaven, an old, spindly sweating man is lying on the bed in a passionate embrace. His arms form a gentle circle of comfort around the emaciated woman lying next to him. Gasping for breath, spittle oozing from her mouth, she struggles to complete her circle of love with arms weakened from suffering.

"Go," he whispers. "Go…there's nothing more to do…go…. I love you. We love you. It's time…go…."

Near the door of the room three middle-aged children stare with sleep-starved eyes and unspoken pain.

Outside the pop, pop of a drug deal gone bad. People screaming. Police sirens rocking the walls of the apartment buildings….

Suddenly the man disentangles himself from the woman's arms, leaving them askew on the bed, and stumbles toward the door.

The woman stares as her breath squeezes into the humid air….

In a near perfect chorus the children cry, "She's dead!"

The father turns, looks, and stretches his arms out toward her…to be clasped by his children as they form a circle of grief, crying, crying, crying….

***

A Conversation about Death

A Conversation about Death as Spiritual or Secular

Is this last scene spiritual? If this were the European Middle Ages, there would be no doubt. It is. The town would have been called to the woman's bedside by the ringing of the bells and the chant of the priest as he came to perform the Last Rites. The woman would have had an opportunity to speak her last will for those gathered around her before she died. She and her community's spirituality would have been evident in ritual and shared grief.

Not so today. People often die in our economically powerful society: old, out of the public eye, alone—and oftentimes an agonizingly slow death. The woman in our scene was fortunate her husband and children were there. Someone who spent seventy-three years of her life struggling, happy, sad, throwing parties, directing large groups of people, winning and losing all kinds of games and opportunities, and becoming a famous musician. She is gone. Here was someone who suffered and died. Finis! Nothing! Useless!

Some may consider her as just another item to be picked up and thrown into the cemetery—our landfill for the dead. It's nothing to be concerned about; nothing terrifying, chaotic, or tragic; nothing that captivates us and repels us; nothing that constructs and deconstructs identities while redrawing borders and shifting margins in life and society; nothing that challenges our sense of transcendence. Everyone dies.. It's rather ordinary, and certainly, it's not spiritual.

But is that really the case?

What about Tammy sitting in class, wanting nothing more than to escape to follow her dreams? What about her imagination, her sense of freedom and foreverness, and her desire for transcendence? Are these also banal and secular? After all, everyone imagines. Everyone has a sense that he will be forever...live forever. She's just another spindly pubescent waiting to fly free of the cocoon. It's ordinary.

Does your perspective change when you come to know that the old woman in the second scene is Tammy?

It is spiritual, but...

When death happens, life ends. When the children cry, "She's dead!" they recognize that this woman, their mother, is no more! The "who" is now an "it." That "it" may now be buried, burned, or otherwise disposed of. It does not move. It makes no sound except the unheard sounds of decay. It is cold. It becomes rigid. It stinks. It begins to fall apart. It is dead.

When death happens, life with that person ends. In the above scenario, the woman is not part of the circle of grief. Ultimately, she is frozen both in body and memory. She becomes the possession of each one of the four in the room. She is no longer free because she lives in their memory, their words, and their genes. She is finished. Tammy is gone!

The spirituality of what was happening becomes especially evident when we are aware of both scenes: Tammy alive and forever and Tammy dead and gone. The spiritual experience is a paradoxical one: one of continuity and embracing the dying; and one of discontinuity, wrestling with the fact that she is no more. You and I will be no more. Both continuity and discontinuity, wrestling and embracing are part of this foundational experience of life called death. This realization is palpable in the early moments of this family's grief when they stand holding each other in the midst of death's chaos. They recognize that with their mother's death, they face the challenge of holding on to the past enlivened by her presence while forging a future without her—but with a deeper realization that they too will die. Spiritual transcendence is wrapped up in human decay, tears, and hope for a better tomorrow.

Every time dying and death occur, it is a spiritual experience. Whether it is a baby three months old, an entire village destroyed by a bomb, the guts of a suicide bomber splattered over a building, or a famous politician cut down by a murderer's bullet. All death is spiritual because it is the final act of each human and all humans—an act in which the hero is destroyed and turned to dirt. It is the final moment when each of us realizes that we are not the center of the universe, we cannot control everything, and we will be no more. And those of us in that circle outside of the dead are faced with the realization that although we too will die, we must, somehow, realize that the dead must remain in their bed and we must connect with the living and move on from this death and, for a while, thoughts of death itself. It is spiritual because it is at the root of all spiritual experiences: it is a foundational fear constitutive of every act we perform. It has produced and destroyed civilizations. It necessitates religion and spirituality. It is inherent to every individual and social identity. It is the foundational cause of transcendence, and it challenges us to be free and creative. It is the final paradox of an angel who defecates.[339] It is a spiritual event that is capable of bringing down the final curtain on all of humanity while attracting each of us to stand ready for something we do not wish to happen.

Some Hear It, Some Don't: A Context for a Dialogue between Spiritual and Secular Death

It is not unusual that some people hear things one way; others, another. We listen to such diversity daily in politics, sports, movies, art, and music. Why is this not the case when it comes to talking about death? Its multiple meanings and experiences are there because we need others to live. We need others just as we need our limbs and senses. And just as continued use of our limbs and senses results in patterned expectations and interpretations enabling us to live, so too these same expectations and interpretations are disabled when we lose a limb, sense, or another person. The resultant emotion from such disabling is grief, the emotional response to the loss of a significant other.[340] As survivors, we need connections and patterns to continue living. Grief is the process through which we recognize what has been disabled or lost, and we begin enabling new relationships. Grief is essential to death for both the one dying and those having to let go of her or him. Not all grieving is the same. Grieving depends on what is lost. When one is lost through death, it is part of death's spiritual nature, sketching out through various emotions the uniqueness of the one who died as well as his or her commonality). Death-grieving tells us something about ourselves as well as the world we live in while building a new one. We transcend the death of a significant other through grieving. We experience the spiritual throughout grief as we let go of who was for what is. In that experience, we face the fear of our own demise while seeking to transcend it in word, action, and belief. We die when they die. Grief breathes new life, thus enabling us to make new connections that can occur only because of the other's death.

At the same time, the word death contains within it several references which we should clarify before talking about what people see and do not see. Death may refer to the suffering that occurs during the entire dying process; to the moment the person is no longer considered a human being but instead is viewed as an object; to the time after that moment, usually referred to as being dead. Grieving, in contemporary society, occurs during all these times. I am suggesting that death is spiritual in all three meanings.

Why Some Do Not Perceive Death as Spiritual and Cannot Enter into the Conversation

Death, especially the moment of death, provides us with many symbols and emotions besides spiritual ones. Grief, revenge, winning, relief, threat, excitement, and revulsion are a few of the others. Television newscasts enable us to experience death with a feeling of luck, gratitude, and, perhaps sympathy in relation to the one pictured on the screen. Politicians' claims of military victories provide many with a sense of revenge and competitive

> **Dead is dead: No more!**

exhilaration. Hospices and hospitals keep death private. Death is never a simple fact with only one meaning. Instead, it is a symbol mirroring as many meanings and emotions as we humans are capable of experiencing.

Yet, the attraction-repulsion transcendence of death as a symbol of the spiritual is often missing in our pluralistic society. These mirrored symbols of death may also shade the self from encountering the threat offered by death's spiritual dimension. Just as we can destroy our ears by listening to loud noise for any length of time, so we can destroy ourselves by listening to death's complex spiritual nature for too long. Remember that what we are asking you to encounter in the depth of this spiritual experience is the realization that no matter what you do or who you are, you will cease to exist. Just as you need to eat, breathe, drink, and defecate, you need to die. This is not easy to reflect upon mentally or emotionally. Consequently, we try to avoid it.

Freud said that our subconscious mind cannot imagine our own death.[341] Perhaps that is one reason we refuse to acknowledge death as a spiritual experience. Geoffrey Gorer suggested that we imagine other things than death itself when we encounter death.[342] Perhaps, he says, just as in pornography, we replace human lust with animal lust; we lose the sense of human death when we see contemporary portrayals of death in the media, literature, and the arts. Certainly, the world at the beginning of the twenty-first century is different from Gorer's in the middle of the twentieth. We are surrounded by portrayals of death as people grieve daily on our TV screens, our military uses it as an instrument of national power, and the first wave of Baby Boomers enter their time of dying, late old age. Death surrounds us. Our diverse responses to death in a pluralistic society challenge us to enter into a very serious conversation about death's place in our lives.

One of the greatest contemporary myths is that death should occur only in old age. Our modern sanitation, nutrition, and life-extending technologies have led to the expectation that death is natural and that it naturally occurs in old age. All other deaths, such as a childhood accident, are unnatural.[343]

> *"Death" as No more? Is this an opinion or a fact?*

Such an image of death is a direct obfuscation of death's spirituality because part of death's spiritual nature is that it should not be happening to me. To deny that dual nature of death ("I'm finished" versus "I must live") is to be blind to the spiritual nature of death (attraction-repulsion transcendence) as a symbol of the spiritual. For a healthy life and society, we must encounter death as a whole and continue that age-old quest to overcome it. We must simultaneously wrestle with death and embrace the living. This is what defines us as human. It does not happen only when we are old, and we should not feel it is the only thing left to do as we enter old age.

Analyzing the Dual Meaning of "I'm Finished" and "I must live"

The spiritual image of death is woven by our experience of grief. Grief takes the strands, now broken, of those relationships built over the years with the now dead person, and weaves them into a new identity of both the dead person and the living. Beyond the scenes favored by the media of people crying is the multitude of other grief expressions. These expressions always do two things: they look to the dead past, thus recognizing the fragile nature of each human, and they look to the hoped for future, thus recognizing the heroic, questing nature of each human. Grief, in its own way, is also very spiritual. Here we have the spiritual nature of death: an end and transc**end**ence. When we grieve, we recognize that the person is no more in all their myriad relationships to us. When we respond to that recognition with certitude, and when we begin to weave the past and the present into a new future, then we have recognized the deep spirituality of death. For we have embraced the dying and wrestled with death and are transcending the death of the significant other. We have acknowledged the finality of "I am finished" and the continual challenge of "I must live."

We humans have been doing this forever. We've looked at death by starvation one day and planted a new field of crops the next. We've looked at death by freezing and begun to build fires. We've looked at death by ignorance and begun to educate ourselves. Humans have looked death in the face and said *we are more than that* through our technologies, our art, our language, and our civilization. The spiritual nature of death has brought us to where we are today. It has also challenged our ingenuity for explaining it. Religions and philosophies have functioned as the meaning-giving vehicles for cultures to not only do what it takes to transcend death but also to think, believe, and imagine beyond the moment of death. Every one of us has deep within the urge to be more than death and the conviction that we *are* more than death. But, as in all things human, we need others to affirm this urge and support this conviction. These others are found within our culture. In the past, our culture, our religion, and our philosophy of life were one. A pluralistic culture, by its very nature, means there are many religions, many philosophies, and many cultures immediately impinging upon our grieving in competition for how to weave our future.

Competing for Meaning: Agreeing on Transcendence in the Conversation about Death

Transcendence is the sense that there is more to life than the way it is right here and now. Some look to get away from the "here" and some from the "now." In one way or another, humans seek to transcend both. Death is spiritual because, on first reflection, it says no to transcendence. The person no longer moves and no longer communicates as before. Everything who was that person slowly disappears. Yet we humans have consistently said no to the possibility of impending death. There is more of that person than meets the senses, and there is more for that person to do even though everything is slowly disappearing. With a confidence sometimes boarding on naiveté, we have expressed our disagreement with this evident reality through our songs, our literature, and our religions. From a Western perspective, we have formulated several questions with expected answers: Do I have a future? Do we have a future? Will that future be good or bad? Is there anything I can do to make it good? Will my death or the end of the world affect that future?

Using a language evolving over the millennia, we in the United States use two words that help us describe a human person and thus answer those questions: body and soul. American culture emphasizes the individual and his or her ability to control his or her own destiny. Most are interested in what happens to "me," and death is seen as what destroys the body. Most opinion polls,[344] therefore, describe transcendence as "life after death," where the soul lives a pleasurable existence with friends and loved ones in a place called heaven.

Although many believe in a place of punishment called hell, they do not believe they will live there. They believe that they will live in heaven because the power of their imagination, or some use the word "belief," will get them to heaven. This way of seeing things, believing, or imagining strongly creates the afterlife. In a seemingly contradictory finding, many are of the opinion that they cannot prove anything about an afterlife while also believing that people may experience the afterlife in what is called near-death or afterlife experiences. The belief in an afterlife experience is that someone dies, the soul or spirit goes out of the body and experiences what is beyond death, then returns into the body and thus rejoins this present, earthly life. The typical American culture and language is reflected in this belief: the body dies and the soul goes to some soul or spirit world, thus, the soul creates its own future. This body-soul distinction, as well as the ability to create one's own future, gets in the way of someone from the United States culture understanding the afterlife views of those who do not have such a distinction in their language. Those without such a distinction may also believe that you may live an afterlife of suffering and/or that your individual afterlife is of no consequence. The future life of the tribe is more important than your individual life now or later.

Although cultures differ, it seems we humans share a common desire to think and prepare for that future, which effectively transcends the present and that barrier of time called the moment of death. This continual link to some future life is a necessary part of human identity. The psychologist Jay Lifton called this a deep human need for "symbolic immortality"—a need to continue and express the connections to body, mind, and community into an endless future.

> No more? But we continue to live in many ways.

These symbols of immortality surround us. Many aspects of ourselves are passed on in our genes while our thoughts, values, hopes, desires, fears, and hates continue through our words and actions as received by others. Somehow who we are continues. This is especially clear in the continued existence of famous people through street names, building names, memorials, songs, and films.

In religious symbols, we find how humans have answered these questions throughout time. We will look at some of these symbols from our individualistic perspective in the next section.

There have been two root responses to transcending the moment of death: some do so by redefining the human person existing here and now, and some do so by defining the significance of the individual person in the here and now—and both are done in the face of contemporary scientific evidence.

Contemporary culture is paradoxical in claiming that what is real is the natural world; what is opinion is everything else, including afterlife. Thus, only what we can see, feel, touch, smell, hear, and measure is real. Instead of viewing death as spiritual, we consider it the natural consequence of living. It's what happens. When we die, what we see, feel, touch, and communicate with also

> **Spiritualities claim we are much "more" than this dead body.**

dies. Each of us is as important as any other human, animal, vegetable, or mineral. Death is not spiritual. It is natural. Only the natural is real. Challenging this interpretation of human death is the spiritual view of death that claims that the human person is more than what is disintegrating before our eyes.

What "more" are we?

One central response to this approach is the affirmation of the spiritual. We are more than we sense and measure. We love. We hate. We imagine. We are free. We are more than the transience of what some call the body. What that "more" is varies depending on the culture. There is the *non-sense more*, the *quasi-sensible more*, the *"I don't exist" more*, and the *new improved more*. Of course, these are given more traditional titles, such as, soul, ghost, reincarnation, and resurrection, but sometimes other titles are used to clarify what the traditional ones originally meant. All say that when we die, that unique aspect of us that makes us who we are continues. Let us look at each of these in more detail.

We continue as an entity beyond all sense and measurement; in this book, we refer to that as the **non-sense "more."** Some call this the soul. The soul is what is unique about each of us—a uniqueness that is more easily intuited than reasoned to, yet it very much reflects the insubstantiality of ideas rather than the substantiality of material things. I existed before I was born, and I will continue to exist after the moment of death. Death is spiritual because it keeps in tension the disintegration of the body and the final integration of the soul.

We continue as an entity that, while truly unique, also continues to share some type of permanency that is sensible; in this book, we refer to that as **the quasi-sensible "more."** Some individuals can see it. Some can feel it. I am a quasi-sensible person who exists within my body. Like the soul, I am not affected by hot, cold, broken relationships, and earthly disintegration. Death is spiritual because it allows some, but not all, to sense my continuation after the moment of death. This permeable entity is like the breath that changes shape yet moves where it wills. Although many people refer to this entity as a ghost, do not mistake it for what we are discussing. Movies generally portray afterlife ghosts as replicas of people living a different existence who have all the characteristics of this existence. Aside from being contradictory (the perception that afterlife will be exactly like this life), none of the spiritualities we have discussed have such a view.

We always have the ability to move beyond not only the now but the here; in this book, we refer to that as the *"I don't really exist" aspect of more.* We exercise this ability when we realize our ignorance and misinterpretation of our present state. Sometimes this happens in deep meditation. All our desires and thoughts take us away from this one realization: that we are the universal, unchanging one. The uniqueness, heroism, and permanency that we sense within us is actually who we really are: the entire sensible and non-sensible universe. If we realize this, death has no meaning. The moment of death enables us to relax into the ocean of Being that we are. If we do not realize this, the moment of death is the beginning of a new life in this sensible universe perhaps as a human, but we may also begin another life as an animal, plant, or other sentient being. Death is spiritual because in its disintegration, it usually highlights our failure to move beyond our ignorance and desires while intuiting deep down that we can move beyond them. Reincarnation is the result.

We are who we are; in this book, we refer to that as the ***new improved "more."*** When we die, we're dead, but God will bring us back again better than we are right now. Our relationships to things, people, thought, and the universe will be clarified and heightened. This world has within it the capability of being a new and better world than it is right now. Our death is spiritual because it is a marker that the time has not yet come for this new world to begin. All the work, play, love, and thought we have put into this world, while beneficial, have not yet brought about the promise of a resurrected one. When that promise is kept, the entire universe resurrects together.

These four ways of perceiving our survival and reinterpreting who we are focus on the individual as being more than what he and others sense, which is his present body and its limitations. There are other ways humans perceive as transcending the moment of death. Notice that all of the above, except resurrection, discount the importance of the body.

One other way sustains the notion of the spiritual by seeing one's uniqueness as becoming part of the tribe or society. It begins with the idea that the individual is not as important as the tribe or the community, and we are who we are because of our relationships. It admits and affirms the uniqueness and significance of each person. It does not accept the various notions that place the personality within an immaterial entity. Instead, in affirming the importance of each person, it places that importance in those to whom the living person was kept in existence by his/her relationship to the people of her community. The moment of death is spiritual because it tries to balance the aliveness of the person's relationships with the fact that the source of that unique set of relationships no longer exists.

These varying spiritual views of death need to become part of an ongoing conversation. For too long they have existed without serious dialogue taking place among us. Perhaps such a conversation will begin with the testing that occurs in a truly pluralistic society.

The Terror of Death in a Pluralistic Society

Pluralism and individualism within an epoch of great change, such as we are experiencing in the twenty-first century, results in great freedom for the individual but little support for the individual's identity. We need others to validate who we were, are, and hope to become. To fulfill that need we have evolved into various niches (subcultures, gangs, or tribes) reflecting our taste in music, clothes, mechanical devices, and religions. Although the niches exist because of pluralism, pluralism exists because of a global economy. To live we must move between niches. In making such moves, we come to realize that our niche and all its symbols of life are transient. Moving from niche to niche, we sometimes find ourselves dizzy with the change. All our permanent symbols are broken as we move from niche to niche to make decisions that affect our lives. Our "body social" is destroyed. We live with the inherent fear of destruction. We must wrestle with death every day.

Our classical religions mostly evolved during a time when they were the only dominant religion, an essential part of the culture in which it gave birth to texts, songs, doctrines, moral imperatives, and rituals that were also part of that culture. These religions' answers to our questions about the future were also ingrained in that culture. Classical religions are faced with the globalization of life now just as individuals are. They fear for their future identity because we are all caught in the cacophony of niches banging against each other. We are all faced with the challenge of embracing the disappearing past, wrestling with the future, and encountering in all its sensuality the reality of the spiritual. Only in doing so are we able to go beyond our fears. What we have learned from death will enable us to live only if we have heard death's spiritual lesson and enter into a conversation with others about it.

Death and Afterlife: A Conversation among the Classical Spiritualities [345]

Many of the spiritual lessons about death are taught through the signposts of the classical religions. These lessons have sustained billions over the centuries as they faced death in all its multifaceted forms. Whether the symbols embedded in these signposts are adequate for our liminal times is a question being answered by those living these spiritualities today. Those adhering to a traditionalist or co-temporalist approach for answering these questions are very involved in struggling to speak a thoughtful answer to the questions associated with afterlife in our liminal age. What follows is the starting point for their responses.

Western Culture: Christianity, Judaism, Islam

Christianity

Many descriptions of afterlife surround us even when we state we are describing those put forth by one religion. The symbols of Christian architecture, song, art, and literature express not only their original intent but also the meaning given them over the centuries. The same holds true for the center of Christian life, the Bible, which was composed and compiled over two thousand years ago, with parts of the Tanakh (Old Testament) being over four thousand years old. We have already reviewed its development over the centuries. Its portrayal of death reflects that development.

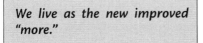

We live as the new improved "more."

Jesus and the first generation of those who followed him were Jews born and raised in what is now Israel and Palestine at the beginning of the Common Era. As Jews, they inherited the symbols and understanding of the afterlife present among their people. By Jesus's time, there were two dominant views of afterlife: at death one enters more deeply into the history and life of the Jewish people; at death one ceases to exist but will resurrect when the world as we know it ends and the new one begins. It is important to understand the beliefs that are inherent to these views of afterlife. One is the belief in God as creator. The only reason anything exists is because God keeps it in existence. Humans are kept alive because God keeps them alive. If we live after death, it is because God continues to create us after we die. If God chooses to do that immediately after death, at some later time (e.g. the end of the world), or in some other manner than God does it right now, that's God's choice, not ours. Another belief is that God's covenant is with Israel. Our life after death is as part of Israel. Israel does not need our individual existence for its continued existence. The tribes of Israel, not the individuals of the tribe, are dependent on God's power to increase and multiply forever.

The first generation of Jesus's followers believed that he was the first human to be resurrected—not resuscitated. In other words, after his death Jesus was living as a human in a new way from the way he had previously lived; thus he was resurrected. He was not merely made alive in the same body (resuscitated).

They also believed that they would be resurrected when they died and that this resurrection would happen to them at the end of time if they followed Jesus's way of life. They rested in peace until the end of the world when they would resurrect.

The followers of Jesus's way of life increased. Many of these followers were from the Greco-Roman culture, which surrounded the Jewish culture. This culture, and its language, contained the body-soul division inherent in many of the cultures of the Western world today. It was not long before the followers, now called Christians, began talking about a person's body and soul. In doing so, they had to confront another idea inherent in the Greco-Roman culture: immortality. To the Greeks and Romans, immortality meant that you were a soul. Your body was something you lived in while you did what was necessary to return to the heavens from which you came. This soul was eternal. It was not born and thus it did not die. For the Jews and the early Christians, God was eternal and only God could live forever. In order to keep their faith in God as creator and the resurrection of humans, they conceived of humans as both body and soul, as the Greeks did, but that God created both the body and soul when a person was born. Death separated the body from the soul. The body decomposed; the soul rested until resurrection.

With time, and a gradual acceptance of the "heavens," as the place of light and perfect materials, and as a place for the soul, which was also light and perfect, Christians of the West began to believe that when people died their souls went to heaven to be with God while their bodies decomposed in the earth. At least the souls of the Christians who followed Jesus's way went to heaven. Those souls who did not follow Jesus went to a place devoid of God—hell. At the end of the world, the church authorities stated, everyone would be resurrected and go to heaven or hell. Some theologians thought that at the end of the world only the good people would live forever. The others would not.

Over time, and the interaction of cultures with the Christian way of life, the afterlife also gained a population of angels and devils. The place of both heaven and hell also changed as people's views of the cosmos changed. At the beginning, heaven was above the clouds with mountain peaks marking some of heaven's boundaries, then it shifted to the edge of the solar system, then to the edge of the known cosmos, and finally to a dimension beyond the senses. Some stopped talking about heaven as a place and saw it as a relationship with God which intensified as we lived our lives here on earth and then later in other dimensions. Hell, as a place, was usually seen as the opposite of the heavens, at the center of the earth—a place one could also enter through caves and volcanoes. Ultimately, it too, as a place, was posited in another dimension beyond the natural senses. It too was seen as a relationship where those who rejected anything of God lived their life without God—forever.

For some Christians, especially Roman Catholics, a place, or later a relationship, called Purgatory developed. Purgatory was where those who died needing purging or purifying went to live temporarily. They spent their time in this place called Purgatory becoming a better person until they were prepared to live with God forever. Since Christianity was seen as a community (communion of saints) who helped each other in this life, it was understood that they could help each other in the next. So people prayed, fasted, and gave money to the poor in order to help those in Purgatory become purified of their sins just as they were supposed to help them in this life. Of course, this communion of saints worked the other way around: those in heaven could help those on earth. Thus, for example, the dead saints were prayed to for a good harvest, a healthy child, or a lost job.

Another afterlife place developed as Christian thinkers tried to understand two seemingly contradictory parts of their belief. Some believed that people could only enter heaven if they are baptized and believed in Jesus and followed his way of life, but there were many good and innocent people who had never been baptized. How could these people go to hell? The tentative response to this seeming contradiction was answered by the concept of Limbo. Limbo was where these good, innocent, people lived their lives apart from both God and the devil in the best possible life after death.

Christians, then, have a variety of answers to the question of their individual futures after death. Today most of them would say that their souls have an afterlife in heaven with friends and God. This afterlife is one in which a person has a memory of her life on earth as well as her life in heaven. Some of these Christians also believe they will live again as some kind of body-soul after this world ends (i.e., resurrection). Evil people go to hell where they suffer now and after the resurrection. People go to heaven or hell depending on whether they believe in Jesus and follow his way of life.

Judaism

Ancient Judaism's view of the afterlife might be seen to begin with God's creation of humans (Genesis 2:7) when God breathes into the dust the spirit of humanity, thus creating the first human. Death, to the first Jews, was when this breath of life returned to God and the dust of the ground returned to being dust. Each human was a unity of earth and spirit animated by God. In Genesis 12:1-3, God promises that the Jewish nation will live forever, but there is not an explicit promise that each individual will.[346]

Gradually this vision of ancestral life after death develops into personal life after death through resurrection. Initially resurrection is portrayed as the Jewish dead rising from their graves to provide an army for Israel (Ezekiel 37:7-10). Then this prophetic vision is applied to all humans and their judgment at the

271

end of time (Daniel 7). By the time of Jesus, resurrection is the dominant Jewish view of afterlife, and it becomes embedded in the culture with the destruction of Jerusalem (70 CE). This literal view of our bodies returning to life is a seed for further development over the next two millennia.

These ancient views of afterlife are retained among contemporary Jews within a culture that sees the human person as a composite of body-soul. Some Jews will say our afterlife is found in how our children and our children's children remember us. Others will say we will resurrect at the end of the world. Still others will claim our soul lives forever with God and there is no such thing as bodily resurrection.

Islam and the Concept of Death

Islam begins and ends with the oft-repeated proclamation, "There is no god but *Allah*, and Muhammad is his prophet." Allah causes life, death, and afterlife (Surah 22:66). Islam shares with both Judaism and Christianity the dominant view of afterlife in its original, seventh century, culture: bodily resurrection. It also shares the common challenge to the belief in bodily resurrection: what happens to the person while she/he waits for resurrection to happen. Judaism and Christianity answered the challenge in two ways. One was to say we rested until the resurrection. Another, which accepts the body-soul view of the person, believes the soul go to heaven upon death while waiting for the resurrection.

The dominant view within Islam understands the rest of sleep to be a time when we return to God. It is also a time for eternal rest. Thus, when we go to sleep every night, we enter into God's world. Our death is a permanent entry into what we experience every night. We are able to communicate with those who are in eternal rest through our dreams. Upon awakening from eternal rest through the resurrection, the good will enjoy the pleasures and wonders of the afterlife; the evil will suffer the pain and torment of eternal punishment. The majority of Muslims retain these original views of afterlife contained in their holy scriptures, the Quran. Foundational to the Islamic view of judgment is the conviction that God is all merciful: ready to gently bring us into a beneficial afterlife if we have done some good in our lives.

How Western Religions View God's Final Judgment of an Individual's Life

Contemporary Western culture many times escapes responsibility for action through a scientific explanation for action. Ancient cultures, and the religions that originated within these cultures, affirmed that we are responsible for all our actions and these actions are part of

> *Judgment determines if we will ever be any "more."*

who we are. Depending on what we have done, we are a good person or a bad person. Contemporary Jews, Christians, and Muslims include in the understanding of a good person the intent and wish of that person to do something good. Most legal systems are based on a combination of intention, willfulness, and what the accused person has actually done. One religious symbol of our continuing into the afterlife as a good person or a bad person is the act of judgment by God or one of God's delegates, such as an angel.

All three religions have some version of a judgment scene—either upon the moment of the individual's death or at the end of the world before or after resurrection. Since the concept of the soul did not exist in ancient Judaism, judgment was first seen in reference to the nation of Judaism being judged as it carried out its covenant duties with God. As the idea of resurrection developed, so did the concept of a judgment at the end time that resulted in either resurrection to life or damnation to destruction (Ezekiel 37:11-14; Daniel 12:1-2). Christianity inherits and elaborates upon these images of judgment from its understanding of Jesus' role as Messiah. The last book of the Christian Bible, Revelation, provides an especially vivid judgment scene and description of the place where God dwells, the heavenly Jerusalem (Revelation. 21: 22). One is judged in Christianity as well as in Judaism according to how he has kept the covenant obligations. Of these obligations, one obligation in particular is highlighted in both religions' visions of judgment: how the nation and/or the individual care for the poor. The judgment scene in the book of Mathew in the Christian Bible perhaps summarizes this emphasis best when it describes Jesus coming at the end of time with all the people gathered around his judgment throne. He begins to divide people according to whether they gave drink to the thirsty, food to the hungry, and clothes to the naked. Those who are rejected ask, "When did we see you like this?" and the judge, Jesus, says, "When you didn't do it for the least of those near you, you didn't do it to me" (Matthew 25).

As both Judaism and Christianity entered more deeply into a culture and language that emphasized the individual and accepted the concept of the soul, the vision of judgment at the end of the world began to be applied to the individual immediately after death. In Christianity, for example, the Ten Commandments were not central to norming the moral life for the first fifteen hundred years of the Christian tradition. Until the Protestant Reformation, the Seven Deadly Sins were central in envisioning how people would be judged. From the sixteenth century onward, the Ten Commandments held center stage. And, interestingly enough, when we look at what the priest confessors concentrated on when judging the penitent, we find they spent more time on issues of social justice than sexual practice. This is demonstrated by the fact that the moral manuals between 1598 and 1716 that formed the basis of training these priest-confessors had twelve pages dedicated to matters of sexuality and one hundred twenty-nine dedicated to matters of stealing and justice. God's judgment at death and resurrection, therefore, would reflect these norms.

Islam also has the symbols associated with judgment. As we've seen, Islam also reflects more of the Greco-Roman world that surrounded it. Both the judgment of the soul as well as the resurrection of the body is present within the Quran. The souls of the wicked are torn out of their bodies and questioned immediately upon death. Not recognizing God or his prophet, they are condemned to the fires of *Jahannam*. The good person's soul is not interrogated by the angels of death but gently released and led into the sleep of the faithful until the resurrection. According to some accounts, the good soul is led by the angels into the garden of life to await the resurrection (Surah 16:28-32). The original judgment is affirmed at the resurrection and the consequent afterlives described as living in the garden of sensual delights for the good and the horrible tortures of *Jahannam* for the evil ones.

Eastern Culture: Hinduism, Buddhism, Taoism, Confucianism, Shinto

We have seen how Judaism and Christianity adapted to the Greco-Roman culture's view of the soul. There were many other ideas and ways of life that were modified as Christianity became part of the Greco-Roman culture and, later, the cultures of Europe. Similar changes happen as the non-Western cultures enter the Western world through such avenues as the English language. Four adaptations, or translations, have special consequences for discussions of afterlife in the English language: the nature of the "I" that lives in the afterlife; the relationship of the afterlife to this life; the nature of ultimate reality; the manner through which the afterlife becomes better than this life.

> The "I" does not exist.

When those in the West ask the question, "Do I exist?" They usually identify "I" with an awareness of the world around them, an ability to think, to desire, to will to do things, to remember, and to wish for a future that is beneficial to the one who is thinking, desiring, willing, and remembering. If they are members of one of the Western religions, they believe that God is somewhat like them and possesses some of these same characteristics while still being completely different. Humans are not God. As members of these religions, they believe that what they do and believe in this life affects their lives in the next; they have only the one chance of this life to prepare for the next life. Time is linear. God is totally different from humans. There is an actual afterlife with this God.

Eastern religions do not look at life or afterlife in any of the ways we described above. The "I" as such does not exist since we are really all one. The universe, both seen and unseen, is one. Time is cyclical. The western word "God" is not applicable to ultimate reality. There is no afterlife as such; only this life lived in the right or wrong way which we live repeatedly until we get it right. Lived correctly, one realizes and becomes one with the universe which we are: a universe which itself is nothing (Buddhism).

In *Hinduism*, the real "I" is eternal, is divine, and is actually the universe. Everything we sense is false and leads us away from the true reality of this universe. Death, too, is a moment marking the false world we have and are creating. Everything we do creates our futures. Until we act and think correctly, we are destined to live forever, incarnate in the false world we create. Life after life, reincarnation after reincarnation, follows our inability to rid ourselves of our karma, our creation of false lives. Only through liberating knowledge will we discover the true nature of the world we are and break the endless cycle of birth, life, death, and rebirth. In experiencing knowledge that we are the divine, we, as conscious, sensing, thinking, willing, remembering, entities cease to exist. Various types of meditation enable us to have this experiencing knowledge. Another way to stop this false existence is through the way of devotion. In this instance, one focuses one's attention on one of the many gods in the Hindu religion. In the *Bhagavad-Gita,* for example, Krishna promises freedom from this illusory world if we fix our attention on Krishna alone and follow his way of life.

Buddhism, with its origins in Hinduism, looks at the individual's future in much the same way: affirming the ideas of continual rebirth or reincarnation; the falsity of this world as we sense it and become attached to it; and the need to escape from this false existence. While Hinduism emphasizes that ignorance binds us to this falsity, Buddhism emphasizes the fact that our desires create and bind us to a false mode of existence. We must extinguish all desire to be conscious, thinking, willing, remembering, and feeling. When we are nothing, we are in Nirvana, saved from all craving.

> The "I" keeps coming back until it doesn't exist.

Between death and reincarnation, many other worlds exist in Hinduism and Buddhism. Some of these occur while we are dying, others immediately after death, and sometimes for long times after death—before we are reborn into this world. These worlds are populated with beings who try to pull us into their false worlds, thus preventing us from being reincarnated or entering Nirvana.

Taoism understands ultimate reality as harmony resulting from the two complementary and interdependent forces of *yin* and *yang*: the positive and negative; being and non-being; light and darkness. Humans are one aspect of the *Tao* whether alive or dead. Death is part of the everlasting harmony of the universe. Our wills, desires, memories, feelings, freedoms, and bodies do not continue beyond death. One's present life may be extended by such actions as living a moral life, regulating our eating, esoteric sexual activities, and interaction with others. Confucianism is much like Taoism in its emphasis on harmony, the extension of this life by natural means, and the denial of an individual's soul existence after death.

Shinto understands ultimate reality as kami, a spiritual force that transcends and yet is expressed in all things. Life is a mirror of this kami energy; death is its mirror opposite. It is important for one to live a life worthy of being remembered as famous ancestor. Those who were famous enough as an ancestor would be remembered by all as worthy of becoming part of the eight hundred kinds of kami in the spirit world.

Hopefully this quick survey of death in the classical spiritualities has given you an opportunity to not only listen to the diverse understandings of death but also to reflect upon how you understand death as spiritual symbol. Such a survey can easily leave out the reality of Tammy and her family 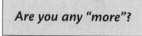 in the introduction of this chapter. It can also tend to not listen to the deep suffering that accompanies dying and death. We cannot leave the foundational spiritual event of death and afterlife without returning to dying and suffering as participating in such a spiritual occasion. Ultimately, our afterlife begins in this life with its mixture of suffering, evil, and the wonderful exhilaration offered by the life around and within us.

Spiritual Conversations about Suffering with the Suffering

The death of another person is a painful reminder than we are interdependent. Grief many times brings back the joyful memories of interdependence: loving touches, harmonious laughter, and quiet presence in shared danger or prideful success. The symbols of the person's presence surround us. In their grief-filled and haunting presence, we remember that all we have are the symbols—he or she will never again freely touch, laugh, or spontaneously share our lives. Our joys as well as our sorrows are multiplied by a number equal to those with whom we are interdependent.

Our interdependence, however, did not grow up serendipitously—without consciousness, without pain, without joy. There is a style of interdependence that characterizes the way those who share life deeply differ, one community from the other—a style that gives *this* community of people a certain direction that is different from *that* community of people. In the context of this book, perhaps the word spirit is better than style. One group of people is distinguished from another group of people by their spirit, their style. A spiri-tuality" is the conscious recognition and acceptance of a certain spirit or style of life as normative for present and future living. A religious spirituality is the conscious recognition and acceptance of a spirit of living that manifests and causes an ultimately, whole, healthy, responsible, belonging, and meaningful life. We have both witnessed these various group-spirits as well as shared them: Our team has a different spirit than your team. Our school has a different spirit than your school. Every group's spirit and spirituality is linked together by symbols of memory and a certain spirit that enlivens both these symbols and the memories associated with them.

Grief finds us remembering. Grief finds us at times dispirited. Grief finds us at times dispirited and alone in our memories of those who are important to us. The spirit, the memories, and the symbols of interdependence pour forth when we are asked, "What happened?" The response to a simple question such as this begins the story of the death and the life of the person for whom we grieve. This story also reflects his or her spirituality and the spirituality of those who remember.

Stories, Plots, and Values

Every life's story has a plot. As we apply for a job, make small talk, recall our early adventures to our children, we tie our lives together in some sort of plot that shows that our lives do make sense. The way we tell our stories speaks volumes about our style of life: why we do the things we do, what we think is important and unimportant, and how we prioritize our values and valuables. But telling a story is more than an expression of what has happened; it is also an indicator of our future direction. To be able to enter into the story of the storyteller—to affirm by a nod of the head; to question by the raise of an eye-brow—is important for the storyteller as well as the listener.

Questions in Life and about Life

Every life story has its exclamation points, periods, and question marks. Here we are interested in the question marks. We ask questions about life as it hap-pens as well as when it is over. Noticing a cut on my daughter's arm, I ask, "How did it happen?" Facing a dentist's drill I inquire, "Will it hurt?" Being told that I'm getting laid off, I demand, "Why me? What did I do to cause this?"

Questions have a way of probing the world around us. They stretch to the past and probe the present in order to allow us to live better in the future. To know that my daughter's cut was caused by a piece of metal on her bike, that the dentist will give me something for the pain, and that everyone fifty-nine and older was let go makes a difference for future living by allowing me to plan for that future.

Some questions and answers are larger than themselves. They point to larger questions and answers than are presently available. Why do we suffer? Why do we die? Do we have a future? These types of questions are never fully answered. Our attempts to answer them make a difference in the way we live our lives. These are what might be described as *making-sense questions*: questions, when asked and when answered, bring our stories together differently than if they were not asked or answered. They express the plot of a person's life story. To even ask these questions about suffering, death, and the future is to proclaim that we know these experiences and to suggest that the world should have some purpose; otherwise, why ask? To receive an answer to these questions, no matter how tentative, suggests a plot for one's own life story and that of everyone she knows. To live one's life with an awareness of that plot is to test both question and answer. It is not unusual that in living the answer, we discover a new question. Making-sense questions are like that—once we think we know whether they make sense, we are anxious to know if they are really non-sense.

> **Questions seeking answers: Why do we suffer? Why do we die? Do we have a future?**

Questions and answers are never individual questions and answers. Because we are interdependent, because our stories are part of a mutual history, questions and answers are shared. Questions and answers about suffering, death, and future are also shared. The questions you have are all part of larger communities of shared questions and answers. These may be national, religious, philosophical, or cultural groups that have developed ways of asking and answering these making-sense questions over time.

When we suggest large categories of thought and action, we always risk leaving someone out and/or not allowing room for mixtures of categories. Such a risk is worthwhile, however, when we are able to present paradigms that are easily understandable and useful for dealing with those who grieve and suffer. There are four famous answers to our three most common questions: Why do we suffer? Why do we die? Do we have a future?

Four Answers to Life's Questions

"It's absurd." Life is absurd. Death is absurd. It's absurd to even ask the question about the future since all we know and experience is the here and now. After all, life is just one damn thing after another, so what is the use of even thinking about it?

278

It is no use thinking about it, but there is a benefit to doing something about it. You prove you can beat life's absurdity. Get up in the morning and face the boredom of life knowing that in facing it you prove you will not let its absurdity do you in. To be human and alive is to thumb your nose at the boredom, absurdity, and stupidity of life itself.

The ancient myth of Sisyphus is a good example of this response to our questions. The story is told that Sisyphus was condemned to push a large boulder up an enormous mountain. Through rain, snow, sleet, cold and hot he strained to get the boulder to the top of the mountain. Day after day, night after night his only goal was to push the boulder to the top. Strained muscles, scraped knees and arms, bruised shoulders and face did not stop him. Every day he pushed. Every day he inched his way to the top. Then one day he reached the top. In exultation, he paused in triumph. While he paused, the boulder rolled down the mountain. His eternity was to push the boulder to the top. His humanity was to look from the top of the mountain at the boulder below and with shoulders square, turn to begin again. Death? Suffering? Future? "Absurd! But damn it, I'll keep pushing!"

> **It's absurd but keep living.**

"That's life," is another response. Some see life as a set of immutable laws, patterns, relationships, or recognized expectations, which, if broken, result in suffering or death. The immutable laws may be titled natural, physical, social; they may be seen as the deep and expected relationships between all beings. Whereas the "It's absurd" perspective looks at life in a negative way, this perspective may have a positive or negative outlook on life. But it is accepting of what causes the suffering or the death because it views all of life from a give-and-take perspective where everything must be balanced. It is enough to say that the person died of cancer or that the war was caused by people's dislike of their dictator. The future, from this perspective, is determined by the present. There are no surprises. If one does everything that is proper physically, socially, and emotionally then one will live forever. Life is an interlocking network of impersonal relationships which, when broken, cause suffering and death.

> **Just accept it and don't expect answers.**

"Down deep, we don't suffer," is a third perspective. Some believe that all that is tangible and passing is not real. Suffering is derived from being too attached to what is passing. All that is real is what is intangible and thus permanent. This permanent reality may be called the soul by some; self, by others; god, by still others. There are many names used to describe this permanency, but behind the names there is either a claim that there is some personal individu-

> **I don't suffer or die. The real me isn't effected by life.**

ality which never changes or there is a common, shared oneness that we all are. In either case, when we get caught up in this changing world, suffering occurs. When we get caught up in our changing individual desires, suffering occurs. Death is the deliverance from this suffering. But awareness that all of this is not real is also a way to move beyond the suffering. To realize that down deep, where the real me is, there is no suffering; to go beyond death is to attain a reality that stands still; there is no difference between past, present, and future.

"It all fits together somehow," is a perspective many of us have since it is dependent on our Western culture. It sees time and reality not as some permanent circle, but as a vector, a line going somewhere because it has reasons to go somewhere. Our personal history takes a personal direction that results from

> *It hurts but somehow it will all work out for the better.*

the interplay of our freedom, loving, and working with the world we are part of. We are very much our body, our changing emotions, and our relationships. We would be nothing without these dynamic realities.

The "why" question is very important to those who approach life from this last perspective because its answer indicates the direction of their future and the reasonableness of their death. Suffering and death must fit into something more than one's self. This something may be titled history, God, God's will, the Kingdom of God. Again, there are many images for the plan, but behind the plan is always a suggestion that it is a personal plan. The universe and all of life is the consequence of a relationship between the individual, all living and non-living beings, and that which supports the life and direction of this universe and life. When one asks why we suffer, from this perspective, the expected answer is along the lines of, "Why did your parent or friend hang up the phone?" The expected answer is a personal one involving love, responsibility, value or something similar. The "why" question in the other three perspectives is an impersonal question and looks for an impersonal answer. The question "Why did he die?" when asked from an "It's absurd" mentality expects a response of, "There is no reason; it just doesn't makes sense." The question "Why did he die?" when asked from a "That's life" mentality will understand an answer framed in impersonal logic such as "It's a terrible disease. Almost everyone dies because of it." The question "Why did he die" is seldom asked by those with a "Down deep, we don't suffer" mentality. If asked, the expected reply would indicate that the person has not been changed by death, that we really never knew him, that suffering is part of the life we live until we dig deeper into life and get to where it is really lived. The "why" question may be asked of the "it all fits together somehow" mentality without expecting an answer.

The way one phrases the unknowns of the cause is significant. We just don't know what it's all about. We think that what happened is bad, but we know that even from bad good may come. Or, in a sort of ultimate personal relationship, we describe how God suffered and died and that this seems stupid yet it is believed. Notice that the generalized mentality of "it all fits together somehow" is accepted, but how it all fits becomes lost in the mystery of the stories that are part of this approach.

Questions and Answers within Classical Spiritualities

These four answers are really spiritualities: a spirituality of the absurd, of consequence, of illusion, and of providence. We live as well as speak questions and answers. When recognized and affirmed as the plot of life, they are recognized as a spirituality that directs our lives. These four answers are also institutionalized in specific historical religious traditions. Humans have faced suffering and death since the beginning of time. The manner in which they have responded to these two basic realities has become enfleshed in a number of traditions. Traditions, after all, are our patterned response to the foundational realities of life. We have traditions of eating, of sleeping, of speaking, and suffering. This patterned response to suffering and death may be found expressed in each of the foundational human realities. Thus, we have traditions of bodily care, social ritual, emotional linking, and seeking for meaning associated with death and suffering. Because suffering and death are so all encompassing, so involved with the foundational realities of life, the traditions that are deeply involved with these questions are those we generally describe as religions. Religious communities have always responded to the whole person in their dealing with death and suffering. Some commentators in the last century, because of their philosophical orientation, suggested that religions always were concerned with the future, especially the future after this life. But if one looks at the major classical religions and their embedded spiritualities, one sees a wholistic commitment to the alleviation of suffering and care for the dead. There is care from the perspective of physical well-being. Care and concern for the sick and infirm have been so much a part of religion. Especially in the West, we have the tradition of hospitals and the vocation of the doctor as evidence of a long tradition of the care and cure of a person's ills. Every form of spirituality will have a way of dealing with those who suffer. The one suffering should be aware of this; those who aid the sufferer should be aware of where religious help may be obtained. Online search engines are easy sources of information for housing, food, grief, and/or other physical needs.

Every religion demands right living or right morals from its members. Right living looks toward the diminution of suffering by erasing its immediate cause. It

> **Care for the suffering. Bury the dead. Share with the grieving.**

sets the stage for a world free of the suffering caused by humans. Judaism, for instance, has given us many principles of justice and concern. The statement of God in Hosea 6:6, "…what I want is love, not sacrifice," sets the prophetic theme of justice and love for all. Nathan's statement to David, "You are the man" (2 Samuel 12:7), meaning, you are responsible and accountable to God for the suffering you cause, places the burden upon the individual to relieve suffering. The Christian's obligation vis-a-vis suffering is found both in Jesus's words on the Sermon on the Mount (Matthew 5:1-12 and Luke 6:20-26) and in his example in healing the blind, the lame, and the deaf. Islam's Five Pillars include a direct attack on poverty and demands the giving of alms. As the Quran says, "Did he not find you wandering and give you guidance? As for the orphan, then, do him no harm; as for the beggar, turn him not away" (Smriti xciii). For the Hindu, right living consists in specifying duties for each state of life. If lived, they decrease the suffering in the world. In essence, one should cause harm to no one. Buddhism and Hinduism find a common bond in a compassion that seeks unity with the suffering of others in order to destroy all suffering. These are some of the ways the classical forms of religion deal with the suffering that surrounds them.

Religions also offer many means of engaging the emotions surrounding suffering and death. This engagement of the emotions is found especially in the tradition of devotion and the tradition of mystical union. Not everyone within the various religions engages in these two traditions, but they are present in most religions.

Devotion is embodied by prayer and a lifestyle committed to a significant religious figure, such as Krishna or Jesus. Prayer is a communication with this most significant religious figure. Our suffering takes on a meaning because of our relationship to this figure. At the same time, our consecration to him or her opens up patterns of endurance,

> **Love others as God loves you. Love diminishes suffering and death.**

compassion, and forgiveness because we want to base our lives upon the object of our devotion who has also suffered.

Mystical union is consecration brought to completion by accomplishing oneness with the ultimate in our lives. We see this in the Eastern religions, where the ultimate identity of each of us is found in the permanent (Brahman); or in the Far East, in Tao, where we can reach an inner perception of and unity with Tao. The union is with that which is beyond the here and now. In the union, there is no suffering.

The social dimensions of the religion are many—most of which have become enshrined in ritual. The rituals surrounding the preparation of the disposal of the body, the rituals associated with the days and/or weeks following the death, and the prayer rituals within the gathering of the community petitioning for health or comfort. Ritual action copes with suffering in many ways: for example, by enlisting the support of the religious community as in Jewish mourning practices of Shiva, or the Catholic Mass, or by placing sufferings in a positive frame of mind by putting them in contact with their ultimate concern and consequently relativizing the suffering. Some ritual actions, such as faith healing, are believed to reduce suffering itself.

> *Gather with your community and share your grief.*

Every wholistic approach must also include the human drive to understand the surrounding world. The religious traditions in response to the "why" question have developed signposts of belief over the centuries to help respond to this question. Especially in those religious traditions that acknowledge a personal God (Judaism, Christianity, and Islam) there have been various attempts to understand why we suffer, why we die, and what influences our future. There are three basic responses: the instrumental, the punitive, and the redemptive.

The instrumental model of suffering is found, for instance, in the Islamic belief that suffering is an instrument of God's purposes; in Christianity, that God made Jesus perfect through suffering (Hebrews 12:3-10). In any discussion of suffering, this way of understanding the "why" of suffering comes to the fore as we tell one another that few good things are produced without pain or as we ask how we can develop into mature persons without suffering. The belief is that suffering is an instrument, sometimes sharp, sometimes blunt, of individual and communal development. A personal God uses it to bring about his goal for humanity.

Suffering considered as punishment changes the emphasis slightly yet significantly. Punishment highlights the judgmental character of a personal God. We suffer because we or others have sinned. Suffering is a way of righting the imbalance of evil over good. As Rabbi Ruba (1500 CE) said, "If a man sees that painful suffering visits him, let him examine his conduct." This approach is found in many prayer books of classical religions.

But classical religion is not alone in such an approach: The blood of many people flows in reparation for the sins of their colonial forefathers; a woman in public office is hounded from it for an offense committed in her teens; those who commit crimes against society are punished for past deeds. The model of suffering as a punishment for wrongdoing is evident to anyone who makes a child suffer because of some misdeed. It is a short step to complete the circle and ask of the sufferer what he or she has done wrong because suffering is supposedly always linked to wrongdoing. As a Sufi saying puts it, "When you suffer pain, your conscience is awakened, you are stricken with remorse, and you pray God to forgive your trespasses."

The belief in *suffering as redemptive* is found in many stories and songs: Someone takes upon himself or herself the sins and burdens of others so that all will be free of the consequences of sin. In this view, whenever anyone suffers so that others may live, redemption occurs. The prophets of Israel make

> **Help sufferers by sharing in their questions and answers.**

this clear in describing the role of the Babylonian captivity in the nation's life. Isaiah summarized it when he said, "By his suffering shall my servant justify many, taking their faults on himself." John's Gospel applies this same principle to Christianity when John the Baptist claims that Jesus is the one who takes away the sins of the world (John 1:29).

Listening to the Spirituality of the Sufferer

Most spiritualities find their home in one of the classical religions. These religions originated long before our modern world. They presuppose a closeness of community and a continuity of religious membership which their contemporary adherents may not recognize. Nor are they minutely aware of all the details of their religious signposts. Yet they may vaguely expect their professed religion or spirituality to provide them comfort when facing dying and death. How many times do they hear people being interviewed on television news say they have found their faith a powerful tool in the face of adversity. Hearing this in the midst of a cultural expectation that religion's role is to bring personal and communal peace, they seek some of this peace in the religion they know. They seek religion's power to reduce the pain from this prolonged, painful encounter with death. Yet many times they are ignorant of the rituals, devotions, literature, and stories that provide such relief. All the habits that usually result from regular practice are lacking: there is no habit with which to deal with the numbness of the suffering that is part of the death event. In typical secular fundamentalist fashion, they seek to pick off the shelf of religion some item of belief or practice that will help them survive this ordeal. Yet they do not have the context provided by the signposts that provides that belief and practice its power to embrace the painful suffering.

A funeral ritual, for instance, may be found in most of the classical religions. Let us use the Episcopal Church as an example. Someone may have been born, baptized, and confirmed in this faith. She may also not have gone to church for twenty years and neither have her close relatives gone to church. The person's spouse dies at seventy-two years of age. She expects the church to provide a funeral ritual for her deceased, the priest to preach a homily, and the parish to support her in her husband's death. The probability is, however, that she will not understand the ritual because these symbols and stories are foreign to her; the homily will not be personal because no one knows her or her husband; and, the service will be attended by few because of her and his age. This person's professed religious membership did not reflect her true spirituality, which easily may have been a style or spirit quite foreign to her religion. She may actually have a spirituality more akin to Wicca or a Contemporalist approach.

When we listen to the suffering present in this person, who may be ourselves, we may gradually become aware of the lived spirituality of the person, not the presupposed or easily articulated one from childhood as found in our example. The questions we asked above are helpful for hearing what the person is actually saying. When we ask, "What happened?" the response engages us in the other person's spirituality. The dos and don'ts of spiritual listening, plus recognition of the categories we mentioned in reviewing death and suffering, help us to discern that spirituality. Their present encounter with death or deep suffering may be an overwhelming challenge to that spirituality or it may not be. Our ability to understand the story and its underlying spirituality will determine the level of our involvement with that person's spirituality. The following are practical markers for enhancing their spirituality.

Respecting the Questions and Answers of the Sufferer

Get to know the values within their stories. The only way to know something about a person is to enter into conversation with him or her. We enter any encounter with our own categories. A professional counselor, for example, comes to the interaction with certain categories of diagnosis, prognosis, and remedy. The client comes to the professional to take advantage of this skill and knowledge. The skill, the knowledge, and the expectations are generalized. In dying and death situations, whether we are a professional or not, we face the universal realities of death as they occur in this human being. No one is exactly like everyone else. We should be able to discern the communality and uniqueness of the one we listen to. The principal way to exercise this discernment is to listen to the person's story. "What happened?" is always a more important first question than "How do you feel about it?" As you listen to the story, asking questions in sincere conversation for elaboration or repetition helps you know more of the story and what the person values. How does he make sense of the world? Not in the abstract "why" question that we began with, but in the specific questions of "Did you love her?" "What are you going to do now?" "Can I help?" These are just a few questions that can bring out someone's spirituality of the absurd, of consequence, of illusion, or of providence. But each person also has answers to life's questions of suffering, death, and future. We must be careful not to give our answers to the questions of those who suffer.

Respect the importance of their values and their stories. We meet most people for a short time each day, each week, each month. No matter how much time we spend with a person, it is a relationship that does not span her entire life. These making-sense answers are foundational to a person's life. One does not change the foundation of life easily. Anyone who has attempted to change a habit of eating, smoking, or speaking knows a fraction of what is involved when one tries to change a foundational habit of life that is expressed by these answers. It is better to enter into the person's story and, within her setting, urge her to be authentic to her spirituality. That means that you must avoid intolerance and proselytizing: respect her view; be humble about yours.

Provide opportunities for seeing and establishing connections. A story makes sense as the connections become evident. An enjoyable mystery story is one that leads us down one path only to realize that it is a dead end or going outside the story's plot. To know how the story is connected is an amazing experience. The story of life is no different. When we can see and live the connections, life itself becomes whole and more enjoyable. Making-sense questions and answers enable people to put it all together and realize how together their lives really are. Thus, it is important that we help those we listen to see and live the connections inherent in their spirituality. We do this by encouraging them to make connections with the community most akin to their spirituality. If this is a religious community, this is best done by attending to following:

- *Encourage them to make connections with their public and private religious rituals.* If they have an active religious spirituality, the first hearing of their story should be sufficient to give you an idea of which rituals are of significance to them. Rituals encourage any of the items mentioned under classical spiritualities. We do not have to know the rituals. It is enough to ask the person we are talking with. If she is actively involved with her religion, she will know her own inclinations. What she needs is encouragement to initiate the ritual action and support as she engages in it. Take night prayer, for instance. A Christian with an established spirituality will have a place for regular prayer in his or her life. This easily may surround preparations for sleep. The intense suffering surrounding dying and death many times throws the person off his religious rituals—the rituals of suffering challenge the rituals of spirituality. If the client is not actively involved, but claims adherence to, a classical religious tradition, you will need another hearing of his story. What was important to him in his childhood? Are his patterns of later life suggestive of another spiritual pattern? It would certainly be appropriate to encourage a devotional approach to someone who easily establishes personal relationships with others.

- While encouraging the development of his spirituality, *be willing to become involved with his story* when it becomes highly emotional—emotions are constitutive of every spirituality.
- *Provide opportunities for the sufferer to see the connections between her experience and her belief system.* Every spirituality has beliefs that are helpful for encouraging a person to stretch beyond her current hurt to another way of life. Each classical religion gives reasons, founded within its belief system, for dealing with suffering, death, and the future. These systems have proven quite effective for thousands of years. The person whose spirituality is founded in one of these systems should be encouraged to talk about what her co-religionists believe about suffering, death, and the future. More than likely, the person, in speaking about the others, will suggest the lines of thought that he or she is more comfortable with.

When Questions and Answers Do Not Match

Our spirituality of suffering is a story written by our answers to the foundational questions of life: do I have a future? What can I hope for? What should I do to bring about my future and establish a hope in it? Sometimes the answers suggested by a person's religion are dysfunctional to her spiritual life. Instead of the religion affirming the person's responses to his or her suffering, it intensifies that suffering. Certainly various religions have grown out of the blood of martyrs. Certainly too, all religious stories include ways of living through suffering. There are times, however, when we may be faced with clear evidence that a person is being destroyed physically and psychologically by her religion. The religion as lived by our conversant is destructive of that person.

If we understand personality as a human pattern of response to the internal world of consciousness and the subconscious and the external world of interdependence, we realize that a dysfunctional religion is one that destroys or inhibits the growth of this patterning. The manifestation of certain psychoses together with prolonged aimlessness suggests destruction of the personality. If we also find that the religion and/or spirituality causes the person to destroy his relationship with others and with his physical environment, there is no doubt something must be done.

Many of us would be hesitant to withdraw our support for a person's religion. After seeing its importance for one's spirituality, we might hesitate to acknowledge its destructive capacities. But we must. If we answer "no" to the following questions, we must suppose that this person's religion is destructive of his or her spirituality.

1. Does the person's religion deepen his or her relationship to others? Suffering can disrupt or at least fail to build community when it isolates persons from one another, destroys individuality, and neglects the demand of sufferers for recognition. If the person's religion intensifies this disruption, it may be destructive of her spirituality.

2. Does the person's religion contribute to his or her personality development? If so, it is a source of life. Self-actualization is a process of becoming more and more of who we are and everything that we are capable of becoming. It implies progression through a sequential series of stages toward increasingly higher levels of motivation and self-organization. We grow in confidence and personality development by making good choices and being responsible for them. If we find, therefore, that our religious way of life narrows our view of the world, that we are becoming self-centered, sarcastic in our humor, and rigid in action, then it is obvious that our religion is destroying us and reducing our ability to cope with life.

3. Does the religion lead to the person's engagement with the foundational questions and the hope associated with them? Religion must provide a person with hope. A hopeful attitude may not be easily articulated in the midst of deep suffering, but it certainly is expressive in the person's conviction of transcending this immediate suffering. A hopeful attitude enables a person to hold on when life's purposes seem to be at an end.

If all these questions are answered "no," it becomes evident that the person's religion may be destroying his or her spirituality rather than enlivening it.

Deepening Our Spirituality in the Midst of Suffering

We cannot become embittered toward all religions because of the way this person's religion is affecting him or her. Religion is a powerful force for good and for evil. The way each of us lives it varies, and thus its personal embodiment will differ. Our spirituality depends on the spirituality of others. When we encounter certain masochistic forms of religion, it is easy to be overwhelmed by the evil present in what we presupposed was consummate goodness. Sometimes we may forget the mysterious nature of both religion and suffering. To forget such mystery is to unnecessarily test the limits of our own spirituality. If we remember that we are not alone, that we cannot do everything, and that

288

sharing suffering is shaping it, we will enhance rather than weaken our spirituality.

You Are Not Alone

You friends, your family, and the person's family are all in some way facing the suffering with you. Friends are present with their knowledge and skills to assist you both in encountering the suffering of others as well as in dealing with your own reaction to that suffering. Your family members and those who are closely tied to your life are there to sustain your spirituality in difficult times. The person's family, too, is an essential component of this network. They are a way of connecting to those who suffer client and a means of becoming aware of their spirituality.

You Cannot Do Everything

When you engage in enhancing the spiritualities of others, there is always the danger of losing yourself in their story. If you listen to enough significantly different stories, you may sometimes forget your own. What are your significant values, stories, and the celebrations of these stories? You must attend to your spirituality in the midst of engaging the spirituality of others. Sometimes the most prudent thing to do is to refer the person to someone else when you sense that your own spirituality is disappearing.

Sharing Is Shaping

Ultimately, we all face the fact that suffering is an encounter with life's mysteries. An engagement with mysteries of this sort is an engagement not with a simple question and answer but with a question and an answer that affects us and is part of the complexity of being human.

Spirit always goes beyond simple answers and simple solutions. Spirit always hovers within chaos bringing it together in some mysterious way. Your spirituality brings together the personal unknowns of past, present, and future and enables you to live. Dealing with the chaos of your conversant's suffering, you many times must imitate the spirit that silently hovers over all chaos. You must reach out in non-verbal ways to share the suffering of those you listen to. A held hand, a silent waiting, a back rub, a phone call of concern—these are all significant answers to questions brought about by suffering. And sometimes, just sometimes, your answers enhance the spirituality of those you deal with: your spirit speaks to theirs at this moment in life. At this moment, you share their suffering, their deaths, their grieving, and their future because you have helped life make sense at its most profound level. In these truly spiritual moments—when you or others have been broken by suffering—life opens to a deeper sense to all concerned. In your sharing, you shape the spiritualities of others and yourself as you seek that never-ending conversation that is your spiritual life.

Evil: Where the Conversation Ends and Hope Endures

Evil is present in everyone's life. Evil destroys life, threatens hope, harasses desire, and obliterates both past and future. We experience it, expect it, fight against it, and yet are unclear as to what it is. But we know we want to escape its clutches. Every culture and thus every religion and spirituality has stories, art, and music describing its origin, its destructive nature, its faces, and how to deal with it—including its ultimate disappearance. The advancement of human culture is the story of human attempts to overcome the evils of war, poverty, hunger, ignorance, suffering, and death. We have seen what classical, modern, and liminal spiritualities view as destructive of a full life. All our descriptions and reviews of the spiritualities in Parts Two and Three as well as suffering and death in this chapter have dealt with the causes of evil and the means of eliminating it. What we present here is a broad-stroke comparison between Western and Eastern perspectives on evil so that we can more clearly test our spiritualities.

Religion: Seeing a World without Evil

In its broadest sense, a religion is a way of life that promises and promotes total change. Religions describe the reasons for the evil in our lives, how to rid ourselves of that evil, and what our world would be like without evil in it. When looked at from a global perspective, there are currently two major religious perspectives on evil: Eastern (Hinduism, Buddhism, Taoism, Confucianism, Shinto) and Western (Judaism, Christianity, and Islam). As we have seen, there are many other perspectives, but, for the most part, these two dominate the lives of most of the people on earth and a review of them brings more people into the conversation.

The West: God Created the World and Continues to Create it So that Evil Will Disappear

Judaism, Christianity, and Islam believe in the same God—a God who created the world and everything in it. Combined with the stories about the creation of the world in the Bible is the story about evil, which is present with humans at the beginning and continues with us to this day. And, with the story of evil's origin and continuance is the intellectual challenge inherent in the religious belief in a good, all powerful, just, creating God. To help understand fully the intellectual challenge of good and evil, many thoughtful people in the

West have found the distinction between moral and natural evil helpful. Moral evil is evil caused by humans. War is an example of moral evil. Natural evil is caused by nature. Earthquakes, hurricanes, and tsunamis are examples. Of course, nothing is as simple as this distinction, especially today when humans continue to pollute the natural environment and thus are a cause of many natural evils. When the creating good God is also thought to be all-powerful and therefore responsible for the continuing existence of everything, including good and evil, the distinction becomes even less clear.

Added to this view of a creating God is a sense among many people that this God is like the Greek god Fate who is an impersonal determinant of everything that happens on earth. In this latter instance, the previous distinction made by theologians and philosophers is useless in the face of God's all-encompassing direction of the world and the demand for a type of faith advocating that God knows best, that God knows all, and that God is good and, therefore, everything that happens is for the best. Evil becomes good in the face of this vision of God.

Each of these three religions emphasizes God's relationship to evil differently, but they begin at the same place. Each also offers different rituals and prayers to deal with evil, but they do offer such rituals and prayers. They do not just allow evil to happen. All affirm that it is God's will that we alleviate evil. All realize that we must go much further than the simple command to love each other. They go beyond this command to show how evil will be diminished only if we follow God's commands dealing with the environment, each other, marriage, eating, and property. Some of the names such as heaven or kingdom of God will be similar, some different when it comes to describing the end of all evil, but it will always include a description of the end of evil when God will be tangibly present to earth's peoples while they live in peace with each other.

A Matter of Perspective: West and East

Evil has many faces. One of the more famous is that of the devil who is seen by many in these religions as the totality of evil and the cause of much of it. Evil has many famous places. One of the most famous is hell, the dwelling place of the devil and all who accept the devil's beliefs and way of life. We humans face evil during our lives. We either add to the evil in the world by doing bad things or conquer it by doing good things. Ultimately, it is God who conquers evil in its totality because evil surrounds us, limits us, and many times overwhelms us. Such overwhelming evil can only be overcome by an all-powerful God. Those who believe in ajust, good, all-powerful, creator God believe that God will always conquer all evil. Humans cannot deal with evil alone. They need God.

A world without evil is called Heaven, the Kingdom of God, and Paradise. A world without evil, in the Western religions is very wholistic. In the final world created by God, humans are always described as having body, mind, and spirit while enjoying a world without pain, suffering, ignorance, alienation, and purposelessness.

Those who do not believe in such one God who is creator, all-powerful, and just naturally understand the battle between good and evil differently. Actually, those who come at the experience of individual and communal evil from the perspective of the Eastern religions do not believe evil is as real as those in the Western religions. Neither do they believe that the destruction of evil resides outside the human being in some type of personal, all-powerful, all-knowing, just God. Actually, they do not believe in such a God. From their perspective, the evil human's experience, while hurtful and destructive, will disappear when humans realize its cause. When we realize its cause the means to alleviate it is obvious, and the world as we know it will disappear along with the evils inherent in it.

The religions of Southeast Asia (Hinduism, Buddhism, Jainism, and Sikhism) see this evil world as caused by karma, which will continue death after death, birth after birth, increasing both individual and communal evil. We are not so much a body and a soul but rather the consequence of what we do. If we do evil, we become, and contribute to, evil. We must escape this continual rebirth and be liberated (Moksha in Hinduism; loka in Jainism; Nirvana in Buddhism). We and the world we experience disintegrate when we are liberated. Such liberation will occur if we adhere to dharma, which is the proper individual and communal path to liberation. The religions of East Asia (Taoism, Confucianism, Shinto, and Mahayana Buddhism) experience the chaos of evil but see it as caused by disharmony. As we have seen, each has its own means of bringing back the original harmony of the universe.

The Modern, Religion, and Evil

This review of the major religious influences in our world only scratches the surface of why evil exists, ways to reduce or destroy it, and stories that foster hope for a world without evil.. The religions and their embedded spiritualities offer a complete way of dealing with evil: thoughts, actions, and gatherings with other people. Each religion has its stories describing how evil began, how it continues, and what the universe will be like when it no longer exits. Each religion has its rituals and prayers for dealing with evil. Each religion commands its people to deal both with the roots of evil and with the evident evil that surrounds us. The classical spiritualities and some of the marginal ones have existed for thousands of years. Obviously, people have found them valuable tools for facing the evils of life.

People also have always had ways that were not explicitly religious to deal with evil. We have seen one particular way that has developed over the last five hundred years. Modern science and technology have arisen to deal with many evils that have destroyed humans such as hunger, disease, ignorance, and inhospitable weather. During the last one hundred years in particular, the sciences have provided ways for people to live comfortably and longer than ever before. Before the turn of the nineteenth century, science seemed to offer unending progress and the destruction of all evil. The twentieth and twenty-first centuries are a clear witness that humans need something besides science and its handmaid technology to overcome life-destroying evil. Science during this time may be enabling many people to live comfortably and longer, but it also is providing some people with the power to destroy the entire earth. The twin evils of universal destruction and treating humans as commodities of commerce challenge contemporary religions, spiritualities, and sciences to look more deeply into why evil exists, how to rid ourselves of it, and how a world without evil will come about.

Along with the detailed ways of life offered by the religions is the equally persistent rejection of living these ways by those who profess adherence to them. At the minimum, religion and spirituality instill in us the hope that evil can and will be destroyed; at the maximum, it offers us the means to do so. Yet, there still seems something within us individually and communally that refuses to embrace the means for transcendence and wrestle with the consequences of such an embrace.

Spiritualities will proclaim sin, the devil, ignorance, lack of positive thought, or human egocentricity as the culprit. Whatever the title or the cause, the effect is clear to all of us: we choose evil sometimes even when we proclaim loudly that we do not. We war. We kill. We lie. We steal. We do all kinds of things our spirituality affirms as destructive of self and others. Every form of spirituality offers means of redemption, purification, forgiveness, and ways to start again. We need to discover these ways to begin again—and to begin!

Summary

Our death and suffering, and that of others, always questions our spiritual life because it challenges the fact that we are a whole person who transcends our here and now. It challenges and demands an answer to the questions, "Do I have a future?" "Will I transcend my death and suffering?" All classical spiritualities answer "yes" to those questions. As you enter into this conversation, what is your answer to those questions? Do you or do you not transcend the here and now of suffering and death?

Chapter Nine

Hard Choices: Conversing with Self and Others to Discover Your Spirit

We had just moved. Our five-year-old son was preparing for kindergarten. After all the visits, talks, and preparations the first day arrived. All clean, dressed, fed and watered, my wife was walking him to the school bus when I shouted, "Good luck, Rudy!" He turned, looked me in the eye, and said, "Don't call me Rudy. I'm going to school. My name is Nathan." Ah, growing up—the loss of self; the gaining of self, all wrapped up in a name change.

***

Throughout history, the traveler has been forced to recognize the fact that leaving home means a loss of innocence, encountering uncertainty: the wider world has typically been regarded as haunted, a place of darkness: "There Be Dragons," Or as Othello reported, "Cannibals that each other eat, The Anthropophagi and men, whose heads Do grow beneath their shoulders." "As the traveler's map is redrawn, parts in unsettling and tragic ways, voices might whisper, 'Stay home.' Don't. There are opportunities to be had."[347]

***

Who am I? And do I have time to find 'me' before I answer the question?

***

When you talk to yourself, who are you talking to?

***

Mirror, Mirror on the wall. Who is the most spiritual of us all?

***

W e've been on a spiritual journey, haven't we, peeking into the spiritual lives of others both past and present; testing their signposts through evil, suffering, and death to discover and understand their paths to transformation of self and the world. Now is the time to look over what we have described, reviewed, and thought about; to make choices about what we have done; to close the book, and, hopefully, to take some of its lessons into our own spirituality. To fulfill the twofold purpose of ending and beginning, we will first look at the spiritual self as we described it until now. We will see how that spiritual self relates to others and how that relationship enables us to transform to a better life. Finally, we will outline the steps that must be taken to make the necessary choices that will create the habits of a healthy spiritual life.

Which Self Is Making the Choices and Having the Conversation?

My five-year-old had life all figured out as he stepped into the bus. Little did he know what the rest of his life would bring; nor do any of us, no matter what our age. Gradually, experience teaches us that we are always growing up— always getting into another bus. Never finished, we never can be as sure (as he was) as to who we are, because there is always something more we wish to be; there is always more that we have become. Each spirituality has a way of describing that someone who is seeking to transcend the here and now. Many in our culture call it the self. In much of our discussion of spirituality until now we have reflected upon the relationship between the body, the soul, and the self. Let's try to bring all those ideas together in one image.

This "world" that we live in was described in Chapter One as life's mystery. Let's imagine we are fish in an aquarium. Life's mystery would be everything that is part of our current existence: the here and now of all our senses, of our minds, of our souls, and of our spirits. As with the fish, what makes up our here and now (the aquarium and everything in it) is both part of who we are and the limit of who we are. An important experience in growing up is recognizing what is not me (the aquarium and everything in it). In its own way, this is "other" than me: the water, the aquarium walls, the flora and fauna, the other fishes in the aquarium with me. Each spirituality deals with this relationship of the self and others; how we live out this relationship marks our growth in the spiritual life. Part of contemporary spiritual language in the West contains terms such as body, soul, mind, and spirit. If we are to understand who we are, these terms have to be part of that explanation. Their meaning differs from spirituality to spirituality. Again, the index will help you review those meanings if you need to.

> *Who are you? Put an "x" next to your favorite way of describing the "self."*

There are four ways of understanding the self in contemporary spirituality: the self as here and now but not yet (Western), the self as neither here nor now (Eastern, Indian), the self as here and now, there and then (Eastern Chinese and Japanese), the self as here and now (Survival). In other words, these are in the aquarium but are destined to be outside of it (West); not part of the fish or the aquarium (Eastern, Indian); part of the aquarium and whatever it becomes (Eastern: Chinese and Japanese) ; a fish in the aquarium (Survival).

I Am Here and Now, but Not Yet

Judaism, Christianity, and Islam differ radically in many ways, but they are one in their core beliefs: there is one eternal creator God; all of creation has a purpose given it by God its creator; that purpose will be fulfilled by listening to what God tells them to be and do; and that all of creation, especially humans, has a role to play in fulfilling that purpose. When God said, "It is good," the "good" included humans. Yet humans do bad things that are a result of not listening to God, thus preventing them, and all of creation, from becoming better. Consequently, who they are right now is neither who they should be nor who God wishes them to be. They have further to go in their personal and interpersonal relationships. Who they are here and now will be perfected in the future. That future is described by such words as new world, resurrection, heaven, and paradise. No matter what this future is called, God is always essential to its creation. We humans cannot do it all by ourselves. Who am I? I am one of those co-creators of my individual and communal future. The signposts that guide me to that future are unique to each of these spiritualities but common to them all is a book: a book with many of the same pivotal characters such as Adam, Eve, Abraham, and David; a book of warriors, prophets, mystics, and poets. The book will be re-interpreted by those who followed Jesus and read it through the eyes of the good news they heard (New Testament). And both the New Testament and the Tanakh will be re-interpreted through what the Prophet Mohammad heard, recited, had written down, and submitted himself and others to. The Quran, Bible, and Tanakh are central to understanding who we were, are, and will be. Say "yes" to who you are and who you will become. In doing so, you say "yes" to God.

I Am Neither Here nor Now

The varieties of Hinduism and Buddhism all calmly plead for us to stop, to be, to cease; to end this foolishness of desire that reveals our ignorance and intensifies our suffering; to remove ourselves from our past actions that have placed us in this foolish situation. To follow the sound of "om" beyond its inner origins to its true source and discover that the seeker and the one being sought are the same as are the speaker and the listener. There is no here and now and no there and then. There is no time and no place. Say "no" to your seeking and "yes" to your true being. The wisdom of the tradition, sometimes reflected in the ancient writings, energizes and directs you to do this. Follow the path that fits your needs whether it is devotion to one of the gods, experiencing true wisdom, or acting in the proper manner. Certainly, your past bad acts have to be dealt with as well as your present ones. Walking the proper path, directed by those who walked it before you, will enable you to realize you have always been at both its beginning and its end—an end described as heaven, Nirvana, or Brahman—an end of who you are. You can do it. Others have.

I Am Here and Now; There and Then

All is in balance. All is harmonious. But today, all, including you, is unbalanced and disharmonious. One act, one chance happening, one thought is enough to unbalance our lives. Balance and harmony come about when we begin and continue to build a perfect character that recognizes our part in the whole. We build this character by perfecting the necessary ways of acting and speaking that embody the harmonizing rituals that make us part of the whole. Foods, words, actions, interactions, breathing, and drinking: all must be in harmony. Peace, harmony, and a long life as part of an embracing community are the destiny we deserve and can achieve together with others. Our present is one with our future when all are in harmony with each other. You can be this fully mature and healthy person. Let it be.

I Am Here and Now

Survival is about food and drink; pleasure and pain; warm and cold. When life is short, distances long, and pains a constant reminder of present realities, there is not much time for reflecting on the future. The story is told of a tribe of pigmies who were brought out of their forest to a large savanna. They could not recognize distances because distances were never part of their experiences. To us a boat in a lake far away is a boat in a lake; to them it is a stick on a pond. When one's spatial and temporal horizons change, one's spirituality shifts along with them. That deep yearning to be more than I am at this moment and place is still present: matched in its own way by the stories and rituals handed down by my ancestors and the power provided by my mind, muscles, and instruments of death and life. I know I can be more than I am. But such knowledge is more hope than reality, and all the signposts direct me to perfect the here and now. In such perfecting life is good, life is longer, and pain is diminished. I live!

Body, Mind, Soul, and Spirit(s)

The principle thrust of the Western tradition identifies the person with all he or she affirms as "me." This "me" carries over into the perfected future with some consciousness of the past. One must remember that present consciousness of the past is never perfect. It is often formulated in terms of present concerns and future expectations. Yet the Western tradition always affirms and honors

> *"Mind, body, soul, spirit," which of these best expresses where you are? (When it is gone so are you.)*

the value of the present individual in the final transformation. To affirm the reality of mind, soul, and spirit is to provide hints to this final transformation because each of these realities provides experiences beyond the here and now. They enable "the fish" to swim beyond the confines of the aquarium and provide it with the hope of life outside of it. The Eastern tradition affirms and honors the reality of the impersonal dynamism of the universe whether it is Tao, Brahman, or Sunyata (nothingness). Neither mind, body, soul, nor spirit is real in the sense that this dynamism, who you are, is. To speak of mind, soul, and spirit is to remind us that we are more than our senses. But as long as "you" are being reminded and "you" are experiencing, you distract yourself from who you really are. The final transformation is becoming one with this dynamism. "The fish" and the aquarium must disappear along with your soul, mind, spirit, and body. The Survival tradition sees body, mind, soul, and spirits as part of this present life. Brother Fox and Mother Earth, while highly metaphorical to present technological humans, are made very real in daily intimate relationships that result in one's survival. Everything and everyone is part of an infinite aquarium where we swim together for the benefit of all.

Others

Others, here, are everything and everyone "other" than me (the self). We need others to exist: food to eat, air to breathe, earth to walk, people to love, to be loved by, argue and play with. Without them we die. Without them we are not born.[348]

Do others include "my" body, "my" mind, "my" soul, "my" spirit? If so then I probably say I "have" a body, soul, mind, spirit; if not then I am body, soul, spirit, mind, or all in a unique combination that makes me, me. Those questions and their answers may seem like abstract musings until we ask what we hold sacred in our lives. How can we talk about spirituality without talking about holiness, specialness, sacrality, and spiritual or religious experiences? We can't. So what is there about "you" that you hold sacred? What is there about you that you spend the most time cultivating? What is there about you that you would never give up—that you value the most? And, finally, do any of the answers to those questions include body, mind, soul, and/or spirit?

Certainly, "others" include human beings and nature. How should we characterize our relationship to these others? What part do they and this relationship play in our spiritual lives? When we described each spirituality, we saw how they dealt with these relationships. Each of them described others in community, as part of our ritual, as inherent to our moral life, and as necessary conveyors and supporters of our beliefs. Each spirituality provides its adherents with a way of life that enables them to think and act about real life situations such as how to help the poor, the suffering, others in our community, money, those of a different gender, and nature itself. Before moving on to look at making choices about our spiritual life, I would like to take a few pages to talk about our relationship to others, especially human others, in terms of mutual responsibility.

Mutual Responsibility for Each Other: Growth in Maturity

Recognizing a relationship with someone or something is affirming a connection of some kind with them. Recognizing we *need* something or someone is acknowledging a needed connection of some kind with that other. When the link is made between our need and that someone or something, responsibility comes into play. We are connected. In some way, we are part of each other and responsible for keeping the needed connection intact. A sense of fellowship

> Who are five people you are most responsible for?

affirms the connection; a sense of grief follows the disconnection. Knowing or providing a name for the other usually marks the type of needed relationship; for example, Mother Earth, Brother Fox, band of brothers, Dick, Sally, Bishop, Dad, president, master, and officer. Responsibility happens with the interconnectedness marked by assigning names. I am accountable for treating them as brothers, my bishop, or a police officer. In turn, they are responsible for acting as Sally, Dad, and a teacher. Responsibility marks our becoming whole since we take on the task of recognizing and fulfilling the needs that indicate what to do for mutual growth. That is why we are accountable. Our accountability to another is really accountability to ourselves because that is how our basic needs are satisfied and our "self" develops.

As every classical form of spirituality reminds us, our actions may be good or bad: they add to our karma, they help determine entry to heaven, or they build the kingdom of God (or not). A little reflection also reminds us that persons and things are not the same. Therefore, our responsibility differs in relationship to them. When I plant a vegetable garden in the spring, I become responsible for the life and death of those plants. Their lives do not depend on me entirely, but a great deal does. When I take my wife out for a romantic meal, I take responsibility for trying to set the atmosphere, but so does the restaurant and my wife. They are more free to do what they wish than the plants. The freedom and spontaneity of a human always makes mutual responsibility a challenge. Obviously my responsibility varies a great deal depending upon who or what the other is (how they are named) and myriad other circumstances.

A way of clarifying this may be to say that my responsibility will vary depending on whether I am connecting to an "it," a personal enemy, a passing acquaintance, an acquaintance, someone I do something with such as work, play a sport, or a friend, a lifetime friend, or a lover and friend. Philosophers such as Martin Buber will say it matters a great deal whether I relate to someone as an *it* (plant) or a *thou* (my wife). All that I offered in the above list was a few possibilities between the extremes of "it" and "thou." As we accept responsibility for our relationships, we are recognized in our society as growing up, maturing. The law recognizes this when certain ages are designed for drinking, driving, voting, and marriage. As we pass certain chronological markers, we are seen to be able to accept more responsibility for our actions. Spiritual life is no different from the rest of life in this regard.

Our modern world is filled with many humans who are turned into things; they have been made "its". In the current recession, we hear of escalating unemployment and more families living in poverty. Millions of human beings are without a job, but their plight is reduced to numbers and statistics. In political discussions about balancing the federal budget, we hear of the necessity to cut food stamps, unemployment insurance, and to deport illegal immigrants. Again, millions of feeling, crying, and hungry human beings are turned into numbers.[349] They have been reduced to *its* that can be manipulated with ease when those in power do not have to look them in the eye and say, "Sorry, no food for you!" When the mafia boss in the movie says, "Sorry, it's not personal; it's just business" and kills someone, he may be saying a great deal about our culture.

In modern business, we must treat people like things to achieve monetary ends. We cannot succeed in business or modern life without turning people into things. It is especially easy to see individuals as things when they are large groups such as unions, big business, a government, and a nation. Perhaps that is why many people want government to be run like a business: by the numbers. For some reason, the excuse that "it's just business" seems to absolve large groups of people from any moral imperatives and, thus, responsibility. Turning an individual and/or a large group into a thing seems to take away responsibility. We need habits of thing-making to survive in the modern world. Surrounded by these humans transformed into "things," it is no wonder human laws and morals decrease even as the coercive power of war, guns, and the police increase to take the place of human interaction.

It may also be that we are accustomed to seeing people as things when hearing that they favor an opposing political party, sports team, or brand of music. When we turn them into things, we are absolved from talking with them and listening. A thing does not have a free will. Rational argument, shared stories, needs, and desires do not move things to connect with us or us with them. No. We turn others into things to be absolved from the responsibility of connecting with them. Who are your enemies? Who do you fear? Will your friends only be those with whom you share a great deal in common? How much difference can you put up with and still call someone a good friend? Are there certain patterns of spirituality you consider completely irrational and inhuman among those we have surveyed? Are we responsible for those most unlike us?

These are important questions for spirituality in general and yours in particular. If the practice of spirituality inherently deals with transformation and transcendence from our present reality, then we are going toward a reality that is different from the one we are in right now. For example, in Christianity and Judaism, some religious thinkers call God the totally Other. How can you say you want to become like God when you cannot relate to a person who is different, other, than you?

Those who are different from what is considered "normal" by society represent the mystery of life itself. Infinite difference has many names in our human history. You have heard them repeated frequently in these chapters: God, Buddha, Brahman, Kami, and Tao. Those different religions, politics, sports fans, and cultures are openings to the totally other, the realm that is completely different. To remain in the security of our niche is to stunt our spirituality. To grow and mature in our spiritual lives we must get on the bus, then start and continue our journeys into the infinite.

Our transcendent desire is matched by the symbols of the infinite that surround us. The "it" of sunsets, warm breezes, delicious food, and people are means through which the infinite is present. The presence increases as we encounter animals of various sorts, pets, acquaintances, co-workers, friends, deep friends, and a friend-lover. All these offer tastes of transcendence and opportunities to grow. Our spiritual signposts indicate the means to respond to this presence.

In the last chapter, we examined events that none of us want to have happen to us or to those we love: evil, suffering, and death. Our response to these is indicative of our maturing spirituality. Even more, our response to these in those we fear, hate, and disdain because of their differences is indicative of our maturing spirituality.

The words used in the diverse spiritualities for experiencing that response are love, compassion, empathy, and mutual responsibility. In a book I once read, the main character was one who felt the pain of others. In situations where her enemy would actively try to kill her, she had to defend herself. In doing so, she hurt as much as they did when she hit them. Love, compassion, empathy, and mutual responsibility may hurt a great deal. C. S. Lewis once said that grief is the price we pay for love. Loving those who are different may easily lead to hurt. It may also lead to joy. We all know that growing up is not only experiencing the joy of the race but the pain of a fall. We also know that it's all worth it as we grow beyond it.

Hopefully, others will acknowledge that worth when they have love, compassion, and empathy for us, their "other," their "very different person," their "it." We are all an "other" to each other. That is why we are mutually responsible for sustaining the authentic relationships that breed the creation of the ideal world that such relationships will bring about in which sameness and difference lead, in an infinite dialectic, through dialogue, toward a better spiritual life. But none of this happens unless we value our lives, our conversations, and the necessary choices to growing this spiritual life.

A Question of Value:
Choosing to Grow; Choosing to Mature

We were interviewing realtors to help us in selling our home. One man who was tall, had broad shoulders, piercing blue eyes, and a deep voice sat down for the interview. He, rather than us, began the interview by asking us, "Do you want to sell this house?" We thought it was obvious that we did. But this foundational question made sense. If this was our number one priority, then everything else would fall into place. So the question we should have started with in the introduction to this book should have been, "Do you want to deepen your spirituality?" Because if you do not, then everything we say from this point on makes no sense. I take for granted that you wish to grow and to deepen your spiritual life.

The realtor's question also was a demand to know what we considered important. It was a question of values and pivotal value. "Value" many times refers to money in our consumer society. Sometimes it will refer to the quantitative value of an item when someone asks, "How valuable is it?" Value, in this book, is used in its older sense of importance or significance to the individual or community. So, to rephrase the question, "Do you value a spiritual life?" If you do, here's how to discern the values you have associated with it and to bring what you do value into your life.

Values: Answers to Questions beyond the Technical Zone[350]

Imagine you are a security guard. It's your first night on the job. Light in hand, you move slowly from door to door checking whether each is locked. You come to one door. Test the knob. It turns. Opening the door, you slowly shine the light around the room. An ax with something red on it lies on the floor; a torn dress has been discarded in a rumpled heap; there's an overturned chair. You hear the voice of two people arguing. You carefully walk through the room stepping over a coat, hat, and boots, enter a narrow corridor, and see the shadows of two people through the thick curtain before you. They are yelling and hitting each other. Suddenly you hear a loud noise from a dark corner to your right. You swing your light toward the sound. Too late. A gun flashes its horrible message. You fall to the floor and reach for your gun as the house lights go on to reveal that you have walked through the dressing room of the local theater to the back stage where some actors are rehearsing. Your flashlight had enabled you to walk comfortably, but its light hadn't been far-reaching enough to help you make a connection between the objects you saw.

Many questions are like a flashlight in a dark room. We focus the light (questions) where we wish, but we see only what is lit (our answer). Consequently, we see little of the entire situation—our beam is too tight. We lose the connections and context between where the light shines. Because it is so evident, we mistake what we see for what is. We need something more than sight to see beyond what is so evident. We need values and patterns of values—not only subconscious values, but especially those that are consciously chosen, spiritual values. These values provide the insight to see beyond the immediacy of the tangible and isolated spots of light. They connect our beams of light. If we do not know, understand, and provide for these values from beyond the technical zone, our technology is useless.

Arnold Pacey expands on this last point by describing why hand pumps failed in India. During a period of severe drought in the 1960s, drilling rigs went from village to village drilling for water. Hand pumps were devised to draw up the water from the bottom of the boreholes. By 1975, there were 150,000 pumps throughout the country. Two-thirds were broken. The broken pumps were replaced, but within two to three weeks, they too were broken. After a lengthy investigation and many wrong answers, it was discovered that the pumps failed because no one was taking care of them. It was obvious that the technology of the pumps had to include the administration and maintenance of the pump. Otherwise, the pump would not function. The machine might be technically perfect, but it did not work as intended. The technical design had to include the values of the people who were to use it.

The solution to the problem of the breaking pumps was held up because everyone failed to realize that a piece of technology that worked well in one culture did not always work well in another culture. The relationship of this piece of technology to people and their history had to be understood in order for it to work for its intended purpose: providing needed water. If technology is not seen within its entire human context, it is like those surgeons who claim an operation was a success because of its technical perfection, but they never mention that the patient died. Pacey calls the reason for such failure "tunnel-vision." As he says:

> *Any professional in such a situation is likely to experience his (sic) own form of tunnel vision. If a management consultant had been asked about the hand-pumps, he would have seen the administrative failings of the maintenance system very quickly, but might not have recognized that mechanical improvements to the pumps were required. Specialist training inevitably restricts people's approach to problems. But tunnel vision in attitudes to technology extends far beyond these who have specialized training; it also affects policy-making, and influences popular expectations. People in many walks of life tend to focus on the tangible, technical aspect of any practical problem, and then to think that the extraordinary capability of modern technology ought to lead to an appropriate `fix'. This attitude seems to apply to almost everything from inner city decay to military security, and from pollution to a cure for cancer. But all these issues have a social component. To hope for a technical fix for any of them that do not also involve social and cultural measures is to pursue an illusion.*[351]

Our spiritual lives are many times shaped by the same pragmatic forces that produce tunnel vision. We face our daily challenges with the hope of a technological fix—a better iPhone to communicate, a soaking tub to relax, a supermarket with nourishing foods, thirteen-step meditation programs to discover our true selves. Questions from beyond the technical zone many times shock, anger, and puzzle us because we practical people see them as too vague. The now, the concrete, the-practical matters at hand dominate our vision and our expectations. We are most comfortable in the technical zone of bottom lines, getting the job done, numbers, immediate results, and clear and precise answers to clearly articulated questions. We like our beam of light tight and clearly demarcated. We like having definite answers so that we can fix things. Creating an atmosphere for growth is too vague. Organic talk of growing out of a situation just doesn't "work" when what is required is to fix things. In other words, life-questions are best left for vacation time, not daily practical living.

Yet questions from beyond the technical zone, beyond the pump, are not only necessary but essential. We must go beyond the "how" to the "why" and "what ifs." We must go to questions of value to know who we are, where we are headed, and how we will get there.

Questions of value connect the spots our light has missed. They connect the ax, dress, people arguing, the gun—and the theater stage. They connect the pump, the Indians, their idea of foreign technology, their sense of importance, and those who are significant in their village culture.

"Value" is a word we use for indicating something is extremely important. I realize "value" has many meanings in our society. Foundational for many of these meanings, I would suggest, is "that which is most important." Values shape a culture and a personality and give them coherence. Values find expression in the symbols that make up our lives and that of the culture we live. To know people and their culture is to know their system of symbols. To know their system of symbols is to know their values.[352] However, the discovery of someone's symbols and their values is easier said than done. Let us begin with the easy part: what happens when values are not operative. Afterwards we will offer a process for discerning values and their presence.

Are Significant Values Present

Ennui, boredom, alienation, and discomfort are all emotional indicators that our present values are absent or not functioning. From his experience in the Nazi concentration camps, Viktor Frankl argued that anyone who has a "why"—a meaning in life—will find the "how" of living that life. Without a "why," we are bored. We have a sense that nothing is important. Nothing matters. Life is just one damn thing after another. To not be bored, Frankl argued, one must have values, for values pull us beyond ourselves. In going beyond ourselves, we grow, and in growing, we deepen our identity and our joy of living.[353] We shape our spirituality.

> *Are you experiencing any of these feelings: ennui, boredom, or alienation?*

Abraham Maslow suggests that a sense of ennui characterizes a person without values. Someone who looks back at his or her life and can never point to a significant moment of wholeness, experience, or peak experience usually lacks a sense of value. Values encourage peak experiences.[354]

Extended use of the *Purpose in Life Test*,[355] a test developed from the ideas of Frankl and Maslow, indicates that a failure to sustain a valuing life is associated with psychological alienation and discomfort. Certainly, boredom, alienation, and discomfort will destroy any individual or group. How do we enliven ourselves and our communities? We will do so not only with new technologies and sense-stimulating items, but also by supporting the enhancement and development of values.

> **Name seven of your termi-nal values. Name six of your important instrumental values.**

Many people have values. The question is not whether they value but what they value.[356] Here are two lists of values that provide an opportunity to see that what your values are and whether they are a means to an end (instrumental) or an end in themselves (terminal).

TERMINAL VALUES	INSTRUMENTAL VALUES
Comfortable life	Ambition
Exciting life	Open-mindedness
Sense of accomplishment	Capability
World at peace	Cheerfulness
World of beauty	Cleanliness
Equality	Courage
Family security	Forgiveness
Freedom	Helpfulness
Happiness	Honesty
Inner harmony	Imagination
Mature love	Independence
National security	Intellect (rational, consistent)
Pleasure	Self-control
Salvation	Logic (consistent)
Self-respect	Love (affectionate)
Social recognition	Obedience
True friendship	Politeness
Wisdom	Responsibility

Is Our Value an End (Terminal) or a Means (Instrumental)?

We may argue over which values are ends or means, but what is important is that we do not confuse end-values with means-values. A clean desk is easily achieved if it is our end-value; just dump everything into the wastebasket. But as a means-value, it is much more difficult to achieve, since our empty desk suggests something else is occurring. A country may say it values up-to-date military hardware. As an end-value, it sacrifices the education and health of its citizens to obtain such hardware. If getting up-to-date hardware is a means-value, not an end-value, then maybe it has to be adjusted when the actual end is its citizens' safety. If most of its people die from a disease that could have been researched and destroyed, what use was it that their government had the latest military technology on hand?

Is It Imaginary or Real?

Many times when people talk about values, they talk about their hopes—their imagination of idealized principles of action. In stating their values, they realize that they seldom act on them. Such imaginary, or idealized, values may prompt us to act, but they are products of the mind. If someone has many values and never acts on them or always falls short of his stated values, we must ask what he really considers important. What does he really value? Our spiritual life is determined by our values. Values are what drive our lives forward and what actually judge our everyday actions. Sometimes what we say are our values are actually our imaginary hopes.

How Do We Discern a Real Value?

Values are not "out there" waiting to be picked up like isolated pieces of gold or lovely flowers. Values are lived. We are valuing people only if we associate with people who speak and act values. When we experience others living a healthy life, we sense what is important to them and try to imitate them. The sharing of values results in building good communities. Healthy communities share basic values and celebrate this sharing in symbolic acts, words, and deeds. We search for values individually, sometimes communally. We recognize our values by what we do. Values are the ideals, words, and actions that we choose, prize, and act upon. We will look at these steps in more detail later in this chapter.

Our choosing may be in imitation of others, as I have already suggested, but many times, it is a conscious affirmation of the values lived by our parents and significant others as we grew to maturity. Those values are part of us, but we never consciously chose them. Conscious choice is essential to valuing. Many in our country, for instance, have been brought up to treat others fairly. Justice, or fairness, may even be seen as part of our American way of life. We may never have reflected upon this value. Yet because of circumstances, we have to reflect on what is fair. We become a parent of five children, become a member of an Affirmative Action committee, or lose in an administrative competition to someone of a different race or gender. Actually, we will define "fairness" in the way we respond to these situations, as we become conscious of the necessity for being fair and act accordingly.[357] Conscious of fairness, we then decide whether it is for us or not. We choose to act fairly. We prize fairness when we publicly state its importance and act fairly. When we do this repeatedly, we can presume that it is a value. In acting fairly over a prolonged period, we establish the habit or virtue of fairness.

Does acting fair make us happy and result in enormous rewards? Of course not. But we're not bored in the process! Moreover, down deep, we do have a sense of wholeness that sustains us in the midst of the controversies that surround our decision to act fairly.

Real Values Are in a Set or Pattern

None of us has only one value. We have a set, or pattern, of values. This set of values is usually consistent from late teens until death. What varies is which value provides primary direction to our entire set of values. The same can be said for a culture such as the United States. For example, if Americans value private property, liberty, independence, usefulness, clear cut moral imperatives, and choice, there may be times when one of these rather than the other provides order to the set. Thus, property may be more important than liberty; clarity of moral positions more important than choice. A spiritual life is bound together by a set of values that one can see embodied in spiritual signposts as people go about their daily lives. When we consider spiritualities other than our own, we tend to misunderstand their pivotal values because our own pivotal value prevents us from seeing theirs. With our compass needle pointing to our own true north, it is difficult for us to see the alternative north(s) offered by these other spiritualities unless we are disciplined in the art of spiritual discernment. Much like the flashlight of our security guard at the beginning of this section, our pivotal value and value set tends to keep our focus on ourselves rather than on others.

Sets Operate According to Priorities that Vary According to Circumstances

Why do our priorities shift at various times in our lives? They do so because we are living creatures adapting to an ever-changing world in which we search for some still point that centers our change. This adaptation, which is a response to the external changing environment, is also an adaptation to the internal necessities that govern the life cycle. We are constantly choosing, prizing, and acting. A new choice of priorities results in a new direction of our life vector. In other words, the same set of values is present now that has provided direction to our lives in the past, but because of external and/or internal circumstances, our lives take a new direction depending on our primary or pivotal value. Psychological maturity is one of the best determinants of what is leading one's value choices. It is also one of the better determinants of what might be characterized as life cycle spirituality.

Eric Erikson has provided us with an excellent way of describing such life cycle spirituality. [358] We begin life, Erikson suggests, with the alternating tensions and challenges of trust and mistrust. If we experience consistent and continuous love in our early years, we will probably become hopeful and mature. We also experience tensions and challenges between autonomy and doubt. If we have opportunities to try out new skills, we will probably develop a mature will because we will not be afraid of acting on our own. The ability to deal with these tensions and challenges at this stage of development enables us to enter into the next stage well prepared to meet its challenges. According to Erikson, this is the same with all subsequent stages.

Later in our childhood, tensions and challenges between initiative and guilt offer us an opportunity to accept life as purposeful. Solving the tensions and challenges between industry and inferiority during our school years allows us to have a sense of competence. If we have been praised for our appropriate actions, we will have this sense of accomplishment. The resolution of these tensions and challenges gives us a good start in facing the adolescent tensions and challenges between identity and role confusion. An ability to recognize continuity and sameness in our personalities in different situations and with different individuals enables us to know who we are without depending consistently on others for our identity and for their approval of our actions. We can have a sense of fidelity to self and others as we have a sense of who we are.

Knowing who we are, of course, isn't everything. How we interact with others is also a sign of maturity. A resolution of the tensions and challenges between intimacy and isolation in early adulthood leads to a mature ability to love. Gradually, we are able to fuse our identity with another in such a way that we are able to be intimate with that person.

Yet love is not everything. How do we compete with others? An overly competitive and combative relation with others only leads to isolation. How do we face the tensions and challenges between being absorbed in ourselves and our own goals and being concerned with others? Solving these challenges results in our being a caring person—one who can reach out and help others for their good and for the good of the world, or being a narcissistic individual—one who is only concerned with her own good.

Finally, all of us are faced with the tensions and challenges of giving up hope in the face of suffering, injustice, and incomprehensible death. These tensions and challenges always surround us, but they begin to dominate much of our lives in the later years. To be able to face disintegration is to be one who is wise. A mature old person is one who has the ability to look at disintegration in self and the world and choose wholeness and life. This is wisdom.

Maturity is never made in a moment nor celebrated by a birthday. Spiritual maturity, which has a value set composed of the values indicated by Erikson, is also not easily attained. Maturity is a constant challenge of life—a challenge that is never complete. We are always growing older. How we meet the above crises determines our way of life. Each of us may be spiritually mature or immature depending on how we deal with these tensions and challenges.

This chart summarizes what we have said so far.[359]

Pivotal Value (What's important)	Value Conflict	Vision of Self (How I feel.)
Hope	trust vs. mistrust	Forming *There is more to life than I experience right now, and I can obtain it.*
Will	autonomy vs. reliance	Beginning recognition in things and others *I want to do it myself.*
Purpose	initiative vs. guilt	Inside/outside (fantasy) *I will do it myself.*
Competence	industry vs. inferiority	Action and friends *I can do it.*
Fidelity	identity vs. role confusion	Ideals *Doing it is part of who I am.*
Love	intimacy vs. isolation	Goals *Here I am. Treat me with care. We can and will do it.*
Care	generativity vs. self absorption	Relationships *Look at what I/we did. Let's keep it going.*
Wisdom	integrity vs. despair	Memories *Everything is disintegrating. I'll keep it all together as long as I can.*

If we begin life in a situation where we are not loved—where our pleas for warmth, for food, and for cleanliness are not heard regularly—we will probably grow up not trusting our environment. The first stage of Erikson's theory suggests that if we do not experience trust in those first months of life, we will not be able to develop as a maturing person.

> **How old are you? Does your chronological age match your pivotal value?**

From a Christian spiritual perspective, for example, we will have a difficult time accepting a trusting God or living a balanced church life. If we never experience trust and love, we will never know the meaning of the symbols of love and trust. To describe a "loving" God is to describe a reality beyond our experience if we never knew human love. Our spiritual development is wholistic and thus always influenced by the way we are human.

Developmental theory, however, does suggest that we can catch up on our development at a later stage. It is possible that during adolescence, for instance, we can struggle through trusting again. All the challenges of past stages of life can be relived and won at another stage of life.

The consequences of understanding developmental theory are many, but certainly one is an ability to understand the all too common experience of being bored with our everyday spiritual lives. Some people notice that, at times, their church is boring. It is not responding to their concerns, or it even rejects what they hold dear. In some of these situations, our present developmental needs are in tension with those of the religious community we were socialized into during childhood. A young family going to a church where everyone is over sixty cannot expect to share many of the same interests as their fellow congregants. Many times our spiritual ennui is the result of those we associate with on a regular basis. If everyone in our niche has the same value set we do but a different pivotal value, it can easily be that we have a sense of deep alienation without recognizing it. It is not us or the classical spiritual way of life that is causing this feeling, but rather the fact that there is no community support for where we are in the spiritual life cycle. We must set about choosing either a more supportive community, new values for our set of values, or a pivotal value more in accord with our stage of life.

> *How does your value set match your present spiritual compass (Chapter Three)?*

Choosing Our Values[360]

When we congratulate individuals for a job well done or punish them for harming another, we do so because they own their action. They chose to act one way instead of another, and as a consequence of that choice, they accept the responsibility of that action. It is their act. They own it. Our legal, ethical, and everyday culture is founded on the concept of free choice. At the same time, we are surrounded by those who wish to control our choices to achieve their goals. Contemporary free choice must always be considered within the context of personal responsibility and communal control. As a result, whenever we discuss choice in its spiritual context, we must consider the nature of choice itself, its freedom, and the various theoretical and practical attempts to destroy or control this freedom of choice.

The Nature of Choosing

Every living thing moves: birds fly, dogs bark, wasps build nests, and bees sting. Within a certain range of activity, living things move in a purposeful manner: there is a pattern to their movement and a selection from among possible movements. Living things seem to do *this* action rather than *that* action because of some inner purpose. The human observer easily projects onto all living things both human feelings and thought. When we see the dog bark, the bee sting, and the bird fly, we many times presuppose that the dog, bee, and bird are doing something like we do—they *choose* to bark, sting, fly. Such a projection upon our surrounding world is part of those magical years of childhood when the child talks to the stuffed animal and listens to its answer. It is part of primitive tribal life when the whole world is animistic and filled with lives like ours.

Some contemporary scientific methods reverse this common experience by suggesting that human actions are like animal actions. Behaviorism, a type of determinism, suggests that all living things act as a consequence of the causes that surround them. There is no such thing as free choice because everything is already determined by forces outside of our control. Religious determinists claim that God, Tao, or inner karma determines what we do; psychological determinists claim that our mental and emotional makeup determines what we do; sociological determinists claim that society determines what we do. For determinists, human free choice is purposeful activity performed as a result of the inanimate forces that surround us. *They* own the act, not we humans.[361]

Although these deterministic theories are favored by many in the social sciences, our contemporary culture is based on an entirely different principle. Our prison, education, legal and political systems are based on the principle of responsible free choice. Our culture demands an answer to the question, Whose fault is it? Who performed such a wonderful job? The answers determine reward and/or punishment. Our system of rewards and punishment is based on the presupposition that people, not circumstances, are responsible for their actions. Spiritual life has the same presupposition. One's spiritual life grows out of responsible free choice. People act based on freely chosen goals and purposes. Our culture, as well as our spiritual lives, recognizes that humans can surprise us, do something unexpected and different—something beyond scientific systems and attempts to explain. There is something about the human being that enables him or her to say "no" when everyone expects a "yes" and "yes" when everyone expects a "no." There is something unique about us human beings that enables us to create something new. We have not made our homes the same way throughout time because we have freely chosen to do otherwise. Activity by animals and humans is not the same: we choose to act. Somehow, we can take what is outside us, bring it inside us, and, because of certain ideas, choose to change what is outside us.

Choice Is an Action

Choice is not only an internal decision; it is also an outward action. Our choices are revealed in what we do. Choosing and doing are irrefutably linked. Certainly, we think about things, we reflect upon things, we imagine things. But choosing is an intimate link between our personal, internal goals, principles, and habits and how we affect the world around us by operationalizing those internal thoughts, thereby creating our own world through choosing what will comprise it.

Choice Is an Action We Intend

What we select, whether as part of our world or to intervene in another's world, is purposeful—we want to do it. It is not necessary that we have the intention of doing something every time we do it. Many of our choices are not intentional as to *this* choice here and now. Most of our choices are part of a more extensive intentionality of wanting, for instance, to be a spiritual person, to be a generous person, or to be an industrious person. In light of these general intentions, we build habits of goodness or virtue, and these good intentions constitute the intention for our specific actions.

Because a spiritual individual makes choices based on such general intentions, his or her life has such consistency that others can say, "She or he is a spiritual person" and expect a consistent set of actions that constitute that spirituality.

Spiritual Choice Is a Free Action We Freely Intend

Freedom is the possibility and the ability to make choices. Such a definition of freedom is easy to read but difficult to apply. We are not freer simply because we have more choices. We cannot quantify freedom. A blind person does not have to wait for sight to live freely. Those of us who are surrounded by the constant attempt to control our political, economic, educational, food, drink, and dress choices through advertising should not say we were forced to vote for a certain U.S. Senator or drink a soft drink because advertising dominates the airwaves and limits our choices.

At the same time, we should realize that there is a great deal of subtle manipulation of our choices. Advertising is sold on the claim that our choices can be manipulated by the advertiser. In our modern, technological, consumer culture, choice is never had without someone trying to influence it. Most of the social sciences began as disinterested attempts to understand human behavior, and now they are frequently used to attempt to control that behavior for economic or ideological purposes. One must develop a strong character to choose freely and wisely in the modern world.

When we concede the necessity and the possibility of free choice in contemporary society, we also concede the responsibility that accompanies it. A spiritual life does not consist of freedom alone or in choice alone, but in free choices that result in our acceptance of the responsibility for our actions. A free choice may be a bad choice or a good choice. Both make us who we are and shape our spiritual lives.

Choosing the Necessary Values for a Spiritual Life

The values that must be present in a spiritual life are those that make up our spiritual signposts (belief, ritual, moral imperatives, community, and transcendent desire) and our spiritual compass (beauty, truth, self-discipline, order/harmony, loving, doing, and togetherness). In one way or another, they make up our value set. Their presence in our set, or pattern, of values is the result of our socialization process or of our conscious choices throughout our lives. We are always responsible for those we consciously choose and usually responsible for the choices we make by omission or by lack of awareness.

Socialization Process and Lazy Values

"Nature or nurture?" is the question that is always asked when talking about development, but to choose one or the other is too modern, too reductionist, too Secular Fundamentalist. This is because nature, nurture, and free choice work in concert to make us who we are.

Certainly, both nature and nurture contribute to our choices. We make our value choices because of our genetic makeup and the people who influence us throughout our lives. These value choices are embedded in thoughts, ideas, ideals, words, and actions. Socialization is how this society of people influences us to think and act in certain ways. It embeds language distinctions such as body, soul, spirit, and mind, as well as concepts that make no distinctions: moral understandings such as karma or divine judgment; life goals such as the Kingdom of God or Nirvana; and even time sensitivity, such as the impression that one's life is going somewhere, or that one's life is an illusion and nothing can be done about it.

Using stage theory, the socialization process may be described in the following way. First we learn how to act (kneel in church). Then we recognize the feeling associated with such an action (reverence). Then we learn the norms associated with such actions and feelings (only in church, in a certain direction), and the ideas associated with such actions, feelings, and norms develop (Jesus is present in the bread up in the front of the Church so we must kneel and feel reverent). Finally, we question the behavior, feelings, norms, and ideas in order to modify them into a better way than what we're doing at present (In Asia we bow to show reverence; it's better than the medieval habit of kneeling; rice bread is better than wheat bread for the Lord's Supper). This socialization process usually goes unnoticed as we grow up. Most people never arrive at the last stage.[362] This growing up is a process of both the individual's entering more deeply into the life of the community and the community's increased recognition of this person as an authentic member of that community. The entire process is happening in a complex and systemic manner. It usually does not call attention to individual values or to any reason to make conscious choices in relation to them.

Awakening to New Ways of Life and Lazy Values

The only time conscious choice of values comes to the fore is when an aspect of the expected behavior, feelings, norms, or ideas is clearly challenged. Before we are challenged, these lazy values are who we are. The challenges to individual values or patterns of values are most evident in crises and most profound in slow contextual change where one does not remember how the set of lazy values of one stage of our lives shifts to another set during another stage. Both value changes may lead to either an entirely new set of values (a Christian becomes a Buddhist) or a shift of a pivotal value and its expression (a right-to-life Christian only concerned with abortion becomes someone who is concerned about everyone's right to life, not only the fetus's/baby's).

Some authors use the term "conversion" for a sudden awakening to the dysfunctionality of one's former way of life and the necessary means and ends values of another way of life. Usually such sudden conversions are accompanied by a long, detailed story or confession describing how that former way of life led one astray. What is certainly evident in both the story and the conversion experience is that they are the result of a conscious choice of thought, word, or action that was not present before the awakening moment of conversion. What is also present are sets of lazy values both rejected and accepted that one only becomes aware of with the passage of time after the initial experience. It takes a while to know the newly accepted modes of behavior, feelings, norms, and ideas relative to the signposts of belief, ritual, moral imperatives, and community life. Sometimes this is done somewhat easily as one becomes aware of these new signposts; sometimes it is not.

In either case, new habits must be learned to accompany this new spiritual life. This may include new dietary norms as one moves from a meat eating spirituality to one that disdains eating meat, for example. It may include new challenges to one's practice of sex as one moves from one set that easily accepts the use of contraceptive methods to one in which they are utterly prohibited. It may include worship services held whenever one wishes to visit a shrine rather than on one day a week with the same community.

Changing habits is hard—especially as months and years pass after the initial experience and subsequent choices. It is hard because it brings to the fore not only our conscious choice of a certain way of life, but of the many ways the specific values of that way of life have become habituated—which causes us to face the many ways the new habits have to be formed.

Changing Values and Hard Choices: Conversations with Your Self and Others

Habits express our values. The feelings we have associated with our habits help to build them and destroy them and our values. As our surroundings change, so do our feelings, values, and habits. We must pay attention to all of these to understand and change our spiritual values.

The feelings that move us toward change are associated with the root fears we described as part of the spirituality compass: boredom, grief, loneliness, chaos (confusion), pain (losing self-control), ignorance, and the unattractiveness of everything around us. As one or some of these feelings intensify, there is a perceived need to deal with them. In a pluralistic society, there are many claimants that offer ways to deal with this hurt that digs deep into our very existence and identity. Ideologies, drugs, alcohol, self-help programs, counselors, therapists, and volunteer opportunities are some of the avenues one may take to care for these hurts. But it is not only negative feelings that may impel us toward changing our spiritual values; positive ones, again paralleling the compass, may do so as well. Examples of these are a great idea; an opportunity to be part of a vital community; being able to use our skills and knowledge to enmesh ourselves in actions beneficial to others and ourselves; developing our bodies to their upmost capacities; comprehending ideas that provide an understanding of important matters in our lives; and the deep feeling of love we have for another—all these may lead to change. The most recognized reason for making a change in spiritualities is marriage.[363] Strong feelings of love for another human being can lead us to make individual patterns of change in our spiritual values.

External factors also come into play, sometimes in ways we do not recognize at first, such as moving to a new part of the country or world where core values we once took for granted no longer apply, such as democracy or equality of the sexes or arriving for meetings on time. New technologies, war, changing economic fortunes, environmental change, shifting political majorities—all have significant influences on individual values and shifts in pivotal values.

For example, one could not have as a pivotal Christian value the reading of the Bible until Bibles became available (printing) and people could read (education for all). The same question of value holds when people in oral cultures have no written language. We cannot value what we do not have. We can hope, but values are what we actually hold as important: what we select, prize, and act upon. Until the technology was developed, one could hope to read a Bible, but it was not actually a value. It is never a question of having values or no values. It is always a question of which values one has within the dominant value pattern of society and one's unique spirituality.

Hard Choices: The Conditions

The following conditions have been found significant in helping you change and/or deepen your spiritual life:

- *Motivation.* The difficult question of why you want to do this must be answered. In answering it, you may discover other reasons, but you will also discover the core motivating factor for what you are doing. It may be as simple as "I love him" to a more complex "To better the lives of others" to "I want to discover my destiny."
- *Communal support.* Certainly isolated holy people walk the streets of our cities whether in New York or New Delhi. But they are unique in living a spiritual life without the support of others. If you look more closely, even they depend on others for sustenance or recognition as being a holy person. Self and others are essential for living in general and spiritual living in particular.
- *Repetition.* Habits become habits by doing the behavior, feeling, thinking, and normative living over and over. With a set of habits, a spirituality develops.
- *Positive and negative reinforcement.* When you do the right thing, you should, with time, have a sense of purpose and a positive attitude about you. The instances of failing to behave, think, and feel based on the new value(s) should result in negative feelings of guilt, uneasiness, and failure. These positive and negative repercussions to your newly chosen life or value set are indicators (but not goals in themselves) of a developing spirituality. The goal is to build your life around these chosen values.
- *Distance* from the previous environment (physically, mentally, or socially) provides the space to be your new self. How to do it and the consequences of distancing yourself from previous habits usually means distancing yourself from those who shared these habits with you. New values lead to developing a new self, and with your new self you gain

new relationships. It is a challenge to keep both old and new together, but it can be done. In doing so, it also may be your opportunity to love others as they are (along with your former relationships) while developing into someone different. In the beginning, when trying to develop a new set of values and grow a new spiritual life, it is best to put some distance between you and your former life.

- *Time.* Things take time. Americans are always demanding instant solutions to organic problems. The only instant solution to something or someone that is growing is to kill it/them. Clearly that is not the best solution, so it's wise to remember that it takes time to grow, to mature, and to interact with all the necessary realities that will make us who we are.

Hard Choices: The Process

Just as the conditions discussed previously enable you to implement the choices you make, there is a paradigm for making those choices. It is simply to select, to prize, and to act. In more detail, this paradigm may be described in the following steps. Remember that when we are talking about values here we are not talking about abstractions but embodied values in thought, word, and deed. Here is the way this may look in daily life.

- *Dream, hope, imagine, experience, and remember.* From these you build a treasure chest of values from which you may choose at the opportune time.
- If you live in partnership with another, make a point of *selecting values you both want to bring into your life and you can reasonably expect to act on* at this time. If you are just beginning to change your spirituality, it is important to experience some initial success in making such a change. Such success is best had by making the easy changes first.
- *Think through the consequences* of such choices. This may be a practice in imagination since much of what you expect may not happen, but it does cloak the choice in an atmosphere of reality.
- *Take steps to change* your life in clear accord with the newly adopted values. In this instance, you are acting on your values and beginning the repetition necessary to move from the hope of making something or someone important to actually making it so.
- *Publicly act and speak in accordance with these values.*

The process of helping someone else make and sustain spiritual values is somewhat the same as when doing it yourself. Both processes follow the basic model of all value choices: select, prize, and act. If you are helping someone else, here is a brief recipe for doing so.

- Encourage the person to make choices and to make them freely.
- Help the person to discover and examine available alternatives when faced with choices.
- Help the person weigh alternatives thoughtfully and reflect upon the consequences of each.
- Encourage the person to consider what it is he or she prizes and cherishes.
- Give the person opportunities to make public affirmations of the choices made.
- Encourage the person to act, behave, and live in accordance with the choices made.
- Help the person to examine repeated behaviors and life patterns (virtues) in relation to the choices he or she has made.
- Console in failure; encourage in success; remain a friend.

Hard Choices: The Substance

Judging between illusion and reality is difficult yet necessary. Snow White learned the hard way that just because something looks like a red, nutritious apple does not mean it is edible. People investing with Bernie Madoff learned that because their friends told them this was a great investment and because they trusted Mr. Madoff did not mean that it was a good investment. Actual, real change is many times in the eye of the beholder. Spiritual change is no different. Spiritual life is real life—not opinionated, irresponsible, and living by feelings or logic alone. It is whole. It is real. When the values and the ideas, words, and actions that constitute one's spiritual life change, that change has real consequences for the individual and society.

Consequently, when change is occurring in the signposts of your spiritual life and you are not consciously aware of that change, you may be feeling bad and not know why. When that change is occurring to many people, an entire society may be doing things and feeling certain ways and not know why.[364] You may see examples of this change in many ways. For example, one can proclaim, and deeply believe, that she believes in God, the Father Almighty. The words may be the same; the feeling of belief may be the same. But are the substance of the belief and the words the same in 2013 CE as they were in 100 CE? In 100 CE, the science of the time said the total potentiality of the human was in the male sperm and the woman was passive; that heaven was above the clouds; that the power of the warrior's arm and sword was the best means to change history; and that the language of the scriptures was Aramaic or Greek. In the twenty-first century, biological science provides evidence that both male and female are essential to the beginning of human development; that telescopes and travel to the moon have not found evidence of any physically divine-inhabited space; that people can plead for change by peaceful means rather than coercive force; and that hundreds of translations from the Aramaic and Greek have been made. The same can be said of marriage. In 100 CE, it was usually an exchange of property and involved marriage rights and duties among diverse families; in 2013CE, marriage is primarily seen as two people deeply in love promising to continue that love forever in a tight bond of friendship, care, and concern. Some things may seem like they have not changed, such as the word "God" and marital life, but substantively they have. They may look the same in both eras (the word G-o-d; two human beings), but what they mean and how they function is very different between the two time periods.

Many times people experience the feelings associated with change, such as boredom, ignorance, and loneliness, without realizing that substantive change has occurred. They do not know why they feel the way they do. They, and many others, deal with these feelings associated with substantive change by high substance abuse, mutual alienation, scapegoating, increased following of charismatic leaders, and a shrinking vision of what is acceptable to self and society. Deep change has occurred but because they see, hear, and act as they have in the past, they think nothing has happened, when in fact, a lot has.

Hard Choices: The More Things Change, the More They Are the Same

We have described, reviewed, and analyzed many spiritualities with long histories. They exist today with claims of continuity and authenticity to origins thousands of years ago. Some have reflected deeply upon their present connection with their past origins and development; some have not. Those that have not are satisfied with the communal sense that they are an ancient spirituality, providing the promises and means of transcendence that have enlivened millions throughout time. Millions today may have the feelings associated with value loss, but the leaders and thinkers in these traditions focus their attention on what is highlighted by the enthusiasms, good or bad, stimulated by their present social, ideological, technological, and cultural environment. Scapegoating the present, they look to their sense of a common tradition to provide them with a discernment of identity and a promise of a better future devoid of the present environment. Other thinkers within these spiritualities will go to great pains to demonstrate that their spirituality is the same now as it has always been. For example, sacraments are signs instituted by Christ, so in doing them, you do what Jesus did. Chants are found in the Vedas, so chanting them is doing what has been done by Hindus for millennia. The shrine at Ise has been there for millennia, so when I go there, I am doing the same today as what was done two thousand years ago. Literal imitation demonstrates that this is what people really believe. Still others will carefully detail how things said and done at one time were "really" the same as they are doing today. So "God" was "always" understood as all-powerful, all-knowing, and just. The incidentals of cultural interpretations—of how a baby is made, how the universe is inhabited, or the best way of motivating people to do good—are incidental to the reality behind these descriptions, which is that God is who God is: creator, all-powerful, the all-knowing director of history. These thinkers have provided a spirited defense that things are the same because the words and/or actions are the same; or that the essence of what is done, no matter what the change, is somehow the same even though one is not doing exactly what was done before.[365]

But in terms of making individual choices, these claims by religious experts, sometimes, are not enough. How do I know that this is the right one for me if I cannot rely on identity as a means of authenticity? How do I know whether I am being misguided by the loud shouts of approval and disapproval that mark thought and action in contemporary life? How do I know my present or hoped for spirituality has substance, and is true?

Your answers to these questions may follow the stages offered by Kohlberg and found in Chapter Four.[366] I feel this is the right thing to do or believe because such action and/or belief gives me pleasure; it is what all my friends or everyone does or believes; it is authenticated as true by authorities independent of pleasure-pain or majority opinion. In the light of Kohlberg, we realize that the use of each one of these questions as the definitive norm will coincide with one's maturation process. At the same time, the answers to these questions may be seen as true when normed against the answers to the following questions.

If you answer yes to three of these questions, you can be reasonably sure that your spirituality is developing in the proper direction.

- Is it reasonable? Does it fulfill the conditions of deductive and inductive reasoning?
- Does it agree with the tradition of your spiritual community?
- Is it supported by an authority in what you are deciding? (His or her learning and experience affirm your decision as the right one, or the expert is an authority because his or her religious role affirms this decision is correct.)
- Does it feel correct? Is it pleasurable? Will I get hurt?

But "truth" does not exist separate from those who speak it, hear it, and live it. Questions about living the spiritual truth we choose to live must also be asked. Again, as with the questions above, if you can answer "yes" and affirm a positive answer to the following questions, you are on the road to deepening your spiritual life. A "no" and negative answer should make you stop and reevaluate what in particular causes such a response within you. Talking to someone knowledgeable about the spiritual life should help you see the choices you need to make to continue your spiritual development.

- Does it destroy or deepen your relationship with others?
- Does it form or deform the life you live with others?
- Does it contribute to your personality development?
- Does it improve your ability to live creatively with ambiguity, uncertainty, and chaos?
- Does it lead you to engage with some of the foundational questions of life? (These are questions of justice, peace, health, responsibility, belonging, and meaning.)
- Does it help you love and live better?
- Does it intensify those values that are appropriate to where you are in your lifecycle?

Simple questions and simple answers do not complete the embracing wholeness of a spiritual life. Transcending life's boundaries always leaves behind the memory of the transcending experience and the inherent boundaries of life's deep mystery. The sharp distinctions inherent in well-reasoned analysis always leave behind what reason cannot embrace; the exhilarating emotions touching the edges of each sense stop because they cannot touch, smell, hear, taste, and see beyond the material world they enliven. Spirituality seeks satiation

> **Simple questions and simple answers do not complete the embracing wholeness of a spiritual life.**

to transcendent desire and final answers to abiding questions. We dive deep into mystery for satisfaction and answers. Well-worn signposts offer a path. Within us, a yearning for truth, justice, beauty, togetherness, health, meaningful activity, and direction provide the breath of life in mystery's depths as we seek a true path to discover completeness. Completeness "now" is still "not yet": now is the promise embedded in the thought, the ritual, the authentic and just action, the bond with another, the experience that touches us and pulls us forward; the "not yet" is the promise's fulfillment. We live in now-not-yet. Our developing spirituality is at one time like a strong, rushing river that embraces all in its path; at another, a calm pond reserved for just us to slowly, very slowly enter until encompassed by its warm, wetness. But it is ours. It is yours. Live it. Never abandon its promise for it will be fulfilled.

Summary

After choosing the best description of self, you were asked to use words in the English language for where the "self" resides. Doing that, you went on to examine your relationship to and responsibility for others. Once done, the process of clarifying your most important relationships and responsibilities was begun.

Values never stay in our heads and heart alone. What is valuable is what is important. We know our values by looking at our actions, not our desires and imaginings. Values stimulate our transcendent desire. They bring this desire to fulfillment. Values are central to any spirituality. In this chapter, you entered into a never-ending conversation to discover self, others, and your spiritual life.

Appendix

Dos and Don'ts of Spiritual Listening

Dos

- Prepare by learning about spirituality, particularly the signposts and how they affect a person's spiritual perspective.
- Learn to recognize religious emotions such as the sacred, the supernatural, the mystical, loyalty, devotion, obedience, and justice.
- Protect the environment of the encounter with the other.
- Listen and be sensitive first to the emotions, then the words, and finally the meaning of what is said.
- Nurture the moment within a memory of the past and a hope for the future.
- Listen to what is valuable to, of, and for the other.
- Establish an atmosphere of mutual concern.
- Stick to the basics.
- Keep in mind that while concentrating on listening to one person, someone else is not being attended to.
- Life is more important than listening; remove yourself from dangerous situations.
- Reflect on the event as soon as possible afterwards and record your reactions to what you have heard and what you have not heard.
- Change takes time.
- Act on what you hear.

Don'ts

- Interrupt, give advice, jump to conclusions, or argue.
- Demean or turn away from the other mentally or physically.
- Embody negative attitudes toward the other.
- Be too active (instead, just be present; don't spoil the atmosphere; let it become).
- Be troubled by silence.
- Be upset by embarrassment.
- Be frightened by overwrought religious emotions.
- Be afraid of the unknown.
- React quickly unless in danger.
- Expect too much.

GLOSSARY

Agnosticism: a belief that you cannot prove that God exists

Ahimsa: a Sanskrit-derived word meaning to avoid all harm. Usually translated "to do no harm" to any living thing (do not kill). This is part of the belief system of Hindus, Buddhists, and Jainists.

Ali: the husband of Fatima, Mohammad's daughter, was fourth Caliph. His death is seen as the beginning of Shite Islam since he was seen as the true successor to Mohammad.

Allah: the Arabic word for God

Amaterasu: Shinto goddess of the sun worshiped at the Ise shrine since the seventh century. The Japanese emperor is believed to be a direct descendent of Amaterasu.

Amitabha: the celestial Buddha of Mahayana Buddhism

Analects, the (ca. 475- 221 BCE): a collection of Confucius' sayings by his close disciples

Anatman (no atman): the Buddhist belief that no permanent, substantial, self exists

Anicca: the Buddhist belief that everything is always changing

Animism: the belief that everything is a living, willful, intelligent entity

Apocalypse: a description of total destruction, usually of the earth. In the Roman Catholic Bible, it is another word for the Book of Revelation or a type of storytelling within the Bible.

Arhant (Arhat): a Buddhist title for one who has attained Nirvana

Asceticism: a principled way of life designed to control one's mental and bodily desires

Ashkenazim: Jews who lived or came from Europe and Russia

Atheism: a belief that God does not exist

Atman: the Hindu word for the breath, soul, spirit, and the true self that you are

Auditing: the process in scientology of asking a series of questions put to the ones being audited in order to clear them of all barriers so that they may realize their true identity

Avalokitesvara: the one who embodies the compassion of Buddha

Avatar: In Hindism, this refers to the incarnation of one of the deities, usually Vishnu, Shiva, or Ganesha.

Avidya: In Hindu belief, this is the means by which a human being naturally mistakes that which is unified as being diversified.

Bar Mitzvah: the coming of age ceremony of a young Jewish male

Bat Mitzvah: the coming of age ceremony of a young Jewish female (not held in the Orthodox community)

Bhagavad Gita (Gita): The "song of god" is a Sanskrit text providing the revelations of the god Krishnathat he exists within each of us, and the means to realize this presence in its entirety.

Bhakti yoga: a way of devotion for gaining freedom from samsara

Bible-Believing Christians: those Christians who accept the literal reading of the Christian Bible as the sole norm of faith, science, and daily living. The current reading of the Bible and the preaching of charismatic individuals provide the normative expression of Jesus's way of life.

Bodhisattva : the process and/or consequence of enlightenment in Mahayana Buddhism; someone who has attained Buddhahood

Brahma: the Hindu god of creation

Brahman (Brahmin): ultimate reality; the mystery of life

Buddha (the enlightened one): anyone who has attained perfect enlightenment; usually in reference to Siddhartha Gautama, the supreme Buddha

Bushido: the title given to the way of life of the Japanese samurai

Cabala (Kabbalah): a marginal perspective on the relationship between humans and the universe. Originating and still in existence within Judaism, the written materials foundational to cabalistic teaching have been used by many marginal spiritualities as instruments of instruction and ritual within their own unique spirituality. These interpretations are significantly different from those within the Jewish tradition.

Caliph: the leader of the Muslim Ummah (community) and successor to Mohammed

Canon: the normative writings of a religion and/or spirituality

Caste (Varnas): the four ancient divisions of Hindu society that determine one's dharma. These were the teacher and priest caste (*Brahmana),* the warrior caste (*Kshatriya*), the farmer and trader caste (*Vasya*), and the caste of manual laborers (*Sudra*).

Catholic: usually refers to Roman Catholics, those Christians who accept the pope as their final authority in all matters and the successor of Peter the apostle. Some Christian churches also call themselves Catholic based on the original meaning of the term "universal."

Ch'an Buddhism (China): a variety of Mahayana Buddhism

Charism: Within Christianity, this term refers to a gift of God. One list is found in 1 Corinthians 12:8-8: wisdom, knowledge, faith, healing, miracles, prophecy, discerning spirits, tongues, and the interpretation of tongues.

Charismatic: As a general term, it refers to a person's ability to inspire others to thought and/or action. Within Christianity, it refers to one who has a charism (see above).

Christian Fundamentalism: In imitation of secular fundamentalism and founded upon the perspective of the traditionalists, this way of life seeks the uniformity of literally derived beliefs, laws, and rituals from the Bible to build a society prepared for the Second Coming of Jesus Christ.

Christians: followers of Jesus, the Christ. Usually divided into Roman Catholic, Pentecostal, Protestant, Lutheran, Anglican, Presbyterian, Methodist, Evangelical, and Greek Orthodox. There are thousands of titles for communities who follow Jesus.

Chuang Tzu (Fourth Century BCE): a Chinese intellectual and thinker responsible for a foundational book of Chinese culture of the same name, Chuang Tzu

Classical Spiritualities: See *Glossary of terms for discussing spiritualities.*

Clear: a term in Scientology referring to the attainment of a state of mind devoid of emotions and thoughts that prevent one from making decisions helpful to her or his true Thetan nature.

Cleric: a member of the clergy

Confucius (551-479 BCE)**/Great Master Kung/K'ung fu-tzu:** a teacher and author who had a profound impact on Chinese culture. He detailed methods (virtues) for building a harmonious society.

Conservative Judaism: Jews who reject both Orthodox and Reform Judaism; Thus they observe some of the laws and have both English and Hebrew in their religious ceremonies.

Contemporalists: those who seek to harmonize the selected core values of the past with the central values of the modern and its technologies in order to change the present into a better future.

Conversion: moving from one spirituality to another with the understanding that the new spirituality provides you with the promise of final transcendence and the signposts to achieve it.

Co-temporalists: those who look to a literal imitation of the modern, manifested in the diverse sciences, as a way to transform the present world into a better one.

Coven: a community of witches

Covenant: the mutually binding promises made between God and the Jews in which God promises to watch over them forever and they promise to worship only God and follow his laws.

Cult: a marginal religious or spiritual group. Sometimes this is also used to refer to a mode of worship.

Dali Lama: the leader of the lamas in Yellow Hat Tibetan Buddhism. Tibetan Buddhists see him as the incarnation of compassion.

Demons: evil spirits who fight against the good spirits, especially God

Dharma (dhamma): first used in Hinduism to describe the proper order of both universe and society. Sometimes seen as the laws one must follow to obtain enlightenment.

Diaspora: the dispersal of people from their homeland. Many times this is used, in the West, in reference to the manner of Jewish migration from Israel, especially after 70 CE.

Doctrine: the teaching of a spirituality that is accepted as absolute truth

Dogma: a set of normative beliefs. In Roman Catholicism, dogma is the highest in a hierarchy of official beliefs.

Dualism: a vision of the world as radically divided in two, such as creator and created; good and evil.

Ecumenism: the movement within Christianity for greater unity in doctrine, ritual, moral norms, and polity; not to be confused with "interfaith," which refers to interchanges among diverse religions

Eightfold Path of Buddhism: This is a method of stopping desire through having the right views, right intention, right speech, right action, right livelihood, right effort, right mindfulness, and right concentration.

Enlightenment: an eighteenth century European movement emphasizing reason and the scientific method as the means for discovering truth

Enlightenment: the process and achievement of total transcendence within Buddhism usually resulting in Nirvana

Eschatology: the study of events surrounding the end of the world and the entire universe

Ethics: the study of what is right and wrong; good and bad; systems of morality

Evangelical: a protestant movement emphasizing personal salvation by Jesus, the centrality of the Bible, and the necessity of telling everyone about the good news that is Jesus.

Exodus: a central story in Jewish spirituality. It is the story of their leaving a life of slavery in Egypt to a life of freedom in the Promised Land.

Fakir: a Sufi Muslim beggar and mystic; also, a mendicant wonder worker in Hinduism

Feng-shui: Chinese practice of orienting buildings and plantings according to the energy lines present in the Tao.

Five Pillars of Islam: the foundational acts required to follow Allah's will—to believe that there is one Allah and Mohammad is God's prophet; daily prayers, almsgiving, fasting during Ramadan, and a pilgrimage to Mecca

Foundational Attitudes: meaning, belonging, purpose, and well-being. These are present in every form of spirituality.

Four Noble Truths of Buddhism: All life is suffering; the cause of suffering is desire (attachment); stopping desire will stop suffering; you stop desire by following the eightfold path.

Fundamentalism: See the definitions elsewhere in this list for secular fundamentalism and/or Christian or Muslim fundamentalism.

Gemara: rabbinic commentary on the Mishnah which, when combined with the Mishnah, are the Talmud.

Gita (Bhagavad Gita): The "song of god" is a Sanskrit text providing the revelations of the god Krishna, that he exists within each of us, and the means to realize this presence in its entirety.

Gnostics: In general, Gnostics claim a secret knowledge founded upon the experience of otherness of their body from their conscious spirit. The spirit is a remnant of the divine, now living in materiality. Gnosticism provides the methods for this divine spirit to return to its original spirit world.

Gospels (Good News): Accounts of Jesus's preaching, miracles, and life, usually in reference to the four gospels in the Christian New Testament: Matthew, Mark, Luke, and John.

Grace (gift): In Christianity, this designates God's gift of God's presence, mercy, and love to humankind. Christians have developed an intricate system of commentary around these gifts.

Guru (master, director): This term is typically used in reference to one who directs one's spiritual life in Hinduism.

Hadith: Mohammad's word and actions used to provide an understanding of God's revelation in the Quran.

Haggadah: the detailed description of the Jewish Passover ritual. Some Jews use this term for the actual Passover ritual.

Haij: the sacred and mandatory Muslim pilgrimage to Mecca in Saudi Arabia

Halakah: all Jewish law

Hassidic Judaism: a Jewish eighteenth century ultra-orthodox movement begun in Eastern Europe. It is characterized by ecstatic prayer and consciousness of God's continual presence. Their way of dressing, which reflects the style of dress worn at the time of their origin, makes them easily recognizable.

Hejira (hejira): the first year of the Muslim calendar, which began when Mohammed left Mecca for Medina in 622 CE

Horned god: one of the important gods in Wicca and other neo-pagan spiritualities; usually associated with sexuality and animality

I Ching (The Book of Changes): an ancient foundational text of Chinese spirituality that contains ways of understanding self and the future

Iblis: the devil in Islam

Idolatry: giving illicit primacy to things, people, and ideas; the worship of anything but God

Imam: an Islamic scholar of the Sharia; many times in the United States he is seen as the leader of a mosque

Immortality: living forever; usually before and after human bodily existence

Incarnation: in Christianity, the belief that Jesus is both God and human

Indigenous Spirituality: See "Key Terms for Discussing Spiritualities"

Instrumental values: those people and/or things that are a means to an end

Ise: the major shrine of Shinto spirituality

Jainism: followers of Nataputta Vardhamana (579-527 BCE) who advocate total non-violence

Jen: the virtue of "concern for others" in the spiritualities based on Confucius

Jihad (struggle): the command that a Muslim must do everything possible to live out his/her spirituality. Sometimes Jihad is understood as doing everything possible to defend the Muslim community from evil.

Jina (conqueror): the Jain description of enlightenment

Jinn: the Muslim designation of both good and evil spirits

Jiva: the self; in Jainism, the jiva is one's eternal soul; in Hinduism, one's temporal self.

Jnana yoga: the way of knowledge for gaining freedom from samsara

Kaaba (cube): The most sacred shrine of Muslims located in Mecca, which is composed of a large black rock cube and other items.

Kabbala: Originally an ancient Jewish method for understanding the Tanakh, it has become a method used by many marginal spiritualities to help understand the individual's relationship to the universe.

Kali : the "dark mother;" the goddess of death, destruction and renewal

Kami: the diverse beings and forces that inhabit Shinto spirituality

Karaism: a Jewish movement that rejects all subsequent legal authorities after the Tanakh

Karma yoga: the way of action for gaining freedom from samsara

Karma: the effect of our past actions upon our present role in the cycle of life and death (samsara)

Khalsa (pure): members of the Sikh military fraternity who wear the five Ks: *kesh*, uncut hair; *kangha*, comb; *kachh*, short pants; *kara*, steel bracelet; and *kirpan*, sword.

Kosher: Jewish dietary laws

Krishna: a Hindu god, considered by many to be an avatar of the god Vishnu, who plays a central role in the Bhagavad-Gita

Kuan-yin: a bodhisattva to East Asian Buddhists and an immortal to Taoists. To Buddhists, she is the goddess of mercy.

Lao Tzu (Old Master): the founder of Taoism and author of *Tao-te-ching*

Lent: a Christian time of fasting, prayer, and almsgiving lasting forty days—from Ash Wednesday to Easter Sunday

Li: The central virtue in Confucius's system because it is the sum of all virtues and thus demonstrates how one is to act in achieving a harmonious life. It is made up of all routine human interactions, from getting up in the morning to going to sleep at night; from eating breakfast to talking to one's parents.

Life's Mystery: the recognition that we are limited in every way yet yearn to go beyond those limits. It is the desire for more than the here-and-now and the conviction that there is a there-and-then.

Liminality: existing in between two modes of existence or, in this book, cultures. *Individual* liminality is living in between different identities and senses of self; communal or *cultural* liminality is existing in a time of uncertainty and distrust of politics, economics, language, and spiritualities. See *liminal spirituality* in *Glossary of Key Terms for Discussing Spiritualities*.

Lotus Sutra: Many times translated into English as the "Sūtra on the White Lotus of the Sublime Dharma," this ancient text is one of the most important for Mahāyāna Buddhism and several schools derivative from it.

Magic: may be understood in both a this-worldly and otherworldly sense. In essence, however, it consists of a ritual of words and actions to bring about a desired end. The conviction of the magician will interpret the nature and working of the ritual.

Mahayana Buddhism: most Buddhists adhere to this way of spirituality. It is called the "greater vehicle" because it is open to everyone, not just monks. Through the proper practice of compassion, anyone can become a Buddha.

Mantra: a word or group of words in Hinduism considered having power to shape one's spirituality

Marginal Spirituality: See the *Glossary of Key Terms for Discussing Spiritualities*.

Mecca: the holiest Muslim city and part of the obligatory pilgrimage, the *hajj*. It is the original home of Mohammed as well as where the Quran was written. It is in Saudi Arabia.

Medina: the place to which Mohammed fled and established the first Muslim community in 622 CE

Meditation: a term with unique meanings in diverse spiritualities. Common to all is the necessity for deliberate and concentrated focus upon achieving a preset goal as designated by one's spirituality.

Messiah (the anointed one): a Jewish and Christian term indicating one designated by God to fulfill God's will at the end time. "Christ" is the Greek word for Messiah.

Mahdi: This word is Arabic for "the guided one"—a descendant of Muhammad who will restore justice on earth. In Shi'ite Islam, a Mahdi is a messianic imam who will appear to end corruption.

Minyan: the ten adults required in Judaism to perform ritual activities such as public prayer

Mishnah: in Judaism usually used to indicate that aspect of the law that was transmitted by word of mouth.

Mitzvah / Mitzvoth: the commandments of Jewish law (613)

Moksha: Hinduism's term for liberation from the cycle of life-death-life (samsara)

Monism: the belief that everything we see and experience is actually one (the opposite of dualism). See *Monistic Spirituality* in *Glossary of Key Terms for Discussing Spiritualities.*

Monks: those who have separated themselves from everyday life and dedicated themselves to a religious ideal. Most monks live in a community of monks.

Monotheism: the belief in one eternal, creating, all-powerful God. See *Monotheistic Spirituality* below in the *Glossary of Key Terms for Discussing Spiritualities.*

Moksha: freedom from samsara –the cycle of life-death-life; the final act of breaking through to enlightenment.

Mosque: a place of public prayer for Muslims

Muslim fundamentalism: In imitation of secular fundamentalism and founded upon the perspective of the traditionalists, they seek to provide new interpretations of the Quran based on additional written materials and the unique insights of charismatic individuals. Their main thrust is to provide a uniform way of life devoid of non-Islamic cultural influences.

Mysticism: In current spiritual parlance, this is a nebulous term indicating some intuitive connection with the root causes of the universe. Before the twentieth century, it usually indicated a method for uniting with God and/or bringing about personal enlightenment.

New Thought: This is the core presupposition of many self-help movements, which is that the human mind has the inherent power to change its physical and moral environment.

Nirvana (Buddhism): the destruction of lust, hatred, and delusion and with it any sense of a permanent ego. Total freedom from all conditioning, including death, leaves us with an admission of a new existence without the images to think or desire it.

Om (Aum): a primitive chant derived from ancient Hindu rituals that, when sounded by the righteous in the proper manner, is believed to align both earth and heaven

Orthodox Christians: This term is usually used in reference to Eastern Orthodox Christians who originally looked to Constantinople, now Istanbul, for their center. The date most commonly given for the split between Eastern (Orthodox) and Western (Catholic Christianity) is 1054 CE.

Orthodox Judaism: Jews who meticulously follow all the Jewish laws and their interpretations

Pali canon: the normative list of writings for the Theravada Buddhists

Pantheism: the belief that everything and everyone is God

Paradox: anything that on the one hand is filled with contradiction and, on the other, provides us with a sense of truth and wholeness. See: *Seven Spiritual Paradoxes* below.

Pentecostal Christianity: a Christian movement that emphasizes the charismatic gifts, particularly talking in tongues and baptism in the Holy Spirit. It is the fastest growing form of Christianity.

Pharisees: an ancient Jewish movement that was the basis for rabbinic Judaism that formed in opposition to the Sadducees. They believed in resurrection and deemphasizing ritual and emphasizing the mitzvoth and prophecy.

Polytheism: the belief that many gods exist and interact with our universe

Prajna: the virtue of wisdom and insight as indicated in Buddhism's eightfold path

Predestination: God's determination of a person's or society's life

Prophet: one who speaks for God

Protestant Christianity: a Christian movement first begun as a rejection of Medieval Roman Catholicism and an advocacy of the Bible as the sole norm of faith and faith as the sole means of recognizing God's love for us

Puja: ways of expressing one's devotion to any of the Hindu gods, such as prayerfully touching it before leaving the house

Pure Land Buddhism: a variety of Mahayana Buddhism

Quran (Quran): Muslim holy book. Muslims consider it the actual word of God as heard by Mohammad and written down by those to whom he dictated it.

Rabbi: a religious functionary in Judaism whose main concern is teaching Torah. In the United States, rabbis have become acculturated and are also seen as preachers and leaders of prayer.

Ramadan: a mandatory month of fasting in Islamic life. It is the ninth month of the Islamic calendar. The fast is from food and drink during the day. Prayer during this time is also encouraged.

Reform Judaism: Jews who accept the Torah as the inspiration for living one's life and adapting the mitzvoth to contemporary living

Reincarnation: the belief that after death a person's essence may again be born on this earth, if the person has not lived his/her pre-death life properly

Resurrection: the belief that at the end of this world all humans who have lived will once again live in some new bodily form

Revelation: God's disclosure of God's will for humanity. The written accounts of this disclosure (Christian Bible, Tanakh, and Quran) are the most common forms of acceptable revelation by the respective religions and/or spiritualities.

Rites of passage: rituals associated with the major events of one's life that result in movement from one status to another such as birth, puberty, marriage, and death.

Ritual: the repetition of word and act by an individual or community

Roman Catholic: a Christian who belongs to the Church of Rome on the global level. Usually this occurs through a local Roman Catholic Church or other religious institution.

Sabbath: In Judaism, it begins at sundown on Friday and ends at sundown on Saturday. By analogy, some Christians use the term for Sunday. In both religions, it is the weekly day of rest and religious reflection.

Sacred: separate and apart from the ordinary and deserving of respect and honor

Salvation: the attaining of perfect transcendence

Samadhi: the highest level of meditation. To some this is when the meditator becomes one with her or his object of concentration; to others, it is when a person attains a state of perfect distance from all change.

Samsara: the never-ending cycle of life and death. For humans this is a cycle of continual re-incarnation.

Samurai: Japanese warriors originating in Zen Buddhism and living a life of self-sacrifice, reverence, benevolence, filial piety and care for the elderly.

Sangha: term for Buddhist monastery or community

Satanic spirituality: This belief is twofold: this worldly or otherworldly. These are two distinct groups of writings and claims. This worldly interprets "Satan" as a natural force and everything about him is so interpreted. It concentrates on the here and now of a life of total pleasure. The otherworldly interpretation sees Satan as opposite to God and everything about this spirituality is a way of life contradictory to Christianity. Its focus is upon Satan as the father of all evil and how to cooperate with him to bring evil into our world.

Secular fundamentalism: This is a modern mentality that rejects the values inherent in the scientific method and seeks power to change the present into a future based on uniform ideas, customs, and essential experiences.

Secularism / Secularization: Three meanings dominate contemporary life: first, the Christian church has little influence on the direction of the culture (society is secularized); second, church members no longer hold to some or all of the beliefs of the church (norms of the secular world such as divorce are present in the church); third, the experience of the sacred is now also found outside the churches. The sources of this sacred experience are not always found inside the churches.

Sephardim: the descendants of those Jews who lived in Spain and Portugal before the Spanish Inquisition

Seven Spiritual Paradoxes: I am an immortal who dies. I need a "we" to be a "me." To be alive I must change and remain the same. I am one and many. My spiritual life is both free and earned; gift and purchased. I must fight to be in harmony with all. I am the same and different.

Shakti (power; might): a goddess whose power enables her worshipers to gain their inmost desires

Shaman: This term refers to a person who, much like a witch, is able to heal, cast spells, control the weather, communicate with and travel among spirits.

Sharia: the laws that govern the Muslim community

Shia (Shi'te/Shite) Islam: Shia is short for Shi'atu 'Ali – followers of Ali, the husband of Fatima, Mohammad's daughter. They accept Ali and his successors and the leaders and interpreters of Islam. They accept some Hadith that Sunni do not and thus differ in what laws should govern Islam. They are a minority within Islam.

Shinto Spirituality: the diverse spiritualities inherent to the Japanese culture

Shiva: the Hindu supreme god who is destroyer, creator, preserver, and revealer

Shruti: Hindu sacred books that are considered of divine origin

Siddhartha Gautama (563-483 BCE): the founder of Buddhism and a Buddha in his own right

Smriti: This word means "that which is remembered": foundational, but secondary to Sruti, sacred texts in Hinduism.

Soul: The essence of a person that some see as immortal and incorporeal; others, as inherently linked to the body; others, as the source of thought and will.

Spirit: This term has many and sometimes contradictory meanings, among which are similarity to soul, God, ghost, and the inner meaning of the person, event, or community.

Spiritual: There are many meanings of this term, all of which are dependent on the term "spirit." In this text, it refers to the experience and/or the actuation of transcendence.

Spiritual feelings (experiences): See the *Glossary of Key Terms for Discussing Spiritualities*—the basis of all spirituality.

Spiritual edol: See the *Glossary of Key Terms for Discussing Spiritualities.*

Spiritual signposts: See the *Glossary of Key Terms for Discussing Spiritualities*

Spiritual sources: See the *Glossary of Key Terms for Discussing Spiritualities.*

Spiritual: See the *Glossary of Key Terms for Discussing Spiritualities.*

Stupa: something built, usually mound-like and circular, that has close association with Buddha, such as his relics, his memory, or a statue.

Sufi Islam/Sufism: a mystical movement within Islam that developed methods for experiencing God's presence

Sunni Islam: This group represents the majority of Muslims who follow the law as established by the Quran, the Hadith, and the consensus of the Muslim community.

Sunyata (emptiness): total change in ourselves and in our environment

Sura (sutra): a way of dividing the Quran into paragraphs or chapter. There are 114 suras in the Quran.

Survival Spirituality: See *Glossary of Key Terms for Discussing Spiritualities*

Symbol: anything and/or person that places us in contact with a reality beyond our self. It has many meanings and provides diverse experiences. For instance, an image of the American flag places us in contact with the nation it represents. To an American, this is usually a positive experience; to the Taliban, it is usually a negative experience.

Symbol experience: the feelings associated with our coming in contact with a symbol. These may be very intense (crying, fainting, inability to talk) or slightly intense.

Symbol fact: anything and/or person without meaning and the ability to place us in contact with a reality beyond our self; for example, the actual color, cloth, and design of what we label an "American flag."

Symbolic immortality: Jay Lifton's term for the symbols that give us a sense of continuing beyond our own death.

Synagogue: the Jewish place of prayer, study, and community gatherings. The term "Shul" is used by Orthodox Jews; "temple" by Reformed Jews; "synagogue" by Conservative Jews.

Talmud: the commentary on the Torah by rabbis as contained in the Mishnah and the Gemara

Tanakh: Jewish Holy Books: Torah (law), Prophets (Nevi'im), and writings (Ketuvim)

Tantra: spiritual methods that accept the reality of the here and now while providing ways to transcend it. In the United States, this term has become associated with sexual practices that bring a deep sense of spiritual union to the partners.

Tao/Dao (China): The harmonious path which, when submitted to, fulfills us individually and socially.

Tao-te-ching (Laozi) an ancient Chinese text by Lao-Tzu written sometime before the fourth century BCE

Terminal values: those people and/or things that are ends in themselves

The Middle Way: Buddhism

Theology: the systematic and academic study of one's religion and/or spirituality

Theosophy: This movement sees the present world as an evolving consciousness that manifests itself through diverse reincarnating bodies of which the soul is one of these incarnations. The diverse religions help us evolve through these manifestations.

Thervavada Buddhism: the oldest of the forms of Buddhism. It promises total enlightenment and offers the Middle Way of Buddha as the means to achieve it.

Torah: the first five books of the Tanakh and of the Christian Old Testament. The word Torah is frequently translated as "law," but it is more a reference to God's revelation to the Jews both written and non-written.

Traditional Christians: those Christians who accept that the Christian church is the presence of Jesus in this world and accept the signposts developed over the centuries as valid and normative expressions of Jesus's way of life.

Traditionalists: those who look to a literal imitation of a former time and place to defend themselves from the perceived threat of the modern, thus transforming this present world into a better one

Traditioning: an essential process in the co-temporalist movement, it enables the beliefs, rituals, morals, and polity of the past to change in order to provide the same empowerment to the present and the future

Transcendence: a state of total change permitted to an entity (heaven; Nirvana)

Transcendent: that which exists beyond the here and the now of everyday living. "The" transcendent is usually referred to as God in the West.

Transcending: the process of movement and change to bring about the promise of one's spirituality (baptism; meditation).

Ummah: the community that is Islam

Upanishads (1000 BCE): a collection of texts within the Vedas that are accepted literally by Hinduism, re-interpreted by the Bhakti movement, and rejected by Jainism and Buddhism.

Vajrayana Buddhism: the Buddhism of Tibet and Tantric methods, to name a few, that promises to provide its followers with the power of enlightenment capable of being used now and in the hereafter.

Values: that which (and who) is important. They are the ideals, words, and actions we choose, prize, and act upon.

Vedanata: a synonym for one part of the Vedic texts, the Upanishads. For some it refers to those texts that enable one to come to a realization of the nature of reality itself.

Vedas (2000-800 BCE): the basic texts of Indian culture and spirituality

Vinaya: Buddhist discipline

Vishnu: the supreme Hindu god with the main task of keeping everything in existence

Wahhabi (Salafi) Islam: a reform movement within Islam advocating a strict Sharia; puritanical in nature. Saudi Arabia is a model of Wahhabism.

Wicca: a this-worldly spirituality that uses the forces of nature to bring about the desires of its adherents. Followers of Wicca usually claim to follow in the footsteps of ancient European women who worshiped ancient gods before the advent of Christianity.

Witches are viewed as two distinct lifestyles: this-worldly or otherworldly. This worldly are individuals who claim to control the forces of nature in order to bring about their wishes. Otherworldly are those who are either in the control of Satan or use Satan's power to satisfy their desires.

Wu-wei (active non-doing): The belief that if you live simply, act simply, and think simply, harmony will come.

Yahweh (YHWH): the name of God as first worshiped by the Jews and later by Christians and Muslims. Many Jews do not say this word because of its sacrality, instead replacing it with "Lord."

Yang: a force inherent to the Tao that is active, expansive, and procreative.

Yin and Yang: two essential forces that constitute the Tao

Yin: a force inherent to the Tao that is passive, contracting, and negative

Yoga: In current language, yoga is both a disciplined practice of mind and body and a general designation for diverse spiritual paths to enlightenment in Hinduism.

Zakat: In Islam, this is the duty to share some of one's wealth with the poor.

Zen Buddhism (Japan): a variety of Mahayana Buddhism

Zionism: a movement within Judaism beginning in the late nineteenth century that advocated an independent homeland for all Jews. This became the state of Israel.

Zohar: a group of books that form the core of the Jewish Kabbalah

GLOSSARY OF KEY
TERMS FOR DISCUSSING SPIRITUALITIES

The basis of all spirituality is the experience of transcendence (going beyond our present existence). It offers the hope of continuance and provides the foundation for future transformations that will produce a world radically different from the present one. Other experiences sometimes constitutive to and/or flowing from the transcendent are experiences of the sacred, the mysterious, the holy, the supernatural, duty, obedience to a cause, fellow feeling, belief, discipline, dedication, and/or a power or energy beyond the individual and all humans that determines and directs where and how we live our lives.

A religious spirituality is the conscious recognition and acceptance of an institutionalized spirit of living that manifests and causes an ultimately whole, healthy, responsible, belonging, and meaningful life.

A spiritual life promises and promotes the vision and means to change the present into another, better world in the near or distant future. Both vision and means are culturally dependent. The shift in pivotal means is expressed in the spiritual true north indicated by one's spiritual compass.

Spirituality is a way of life seeking a beneficial transformation and transcendence of self and community.

Collegial spiritual listening is an ability to attend to the whole person: body, mind, and spirit. It demands we be silent and listen to silence; we hear the words the other utters as valuable; we see the actions that person make as conveyers of meaning; we honor the thoughts he expresses as sacred to him. It demands we honor her ideas as well as her feelings.

Spiritual listening is attending to individual and communal yearning to change the self and the world for the better as evidenced in their words and actions.

Spirituality many times is bound to the lifecycle values described by Erik Erikson that occur from childhood to old age: hope, willfulness, purposefulness, competence, fidelity, love, care, and wisdom.

- It consists in patterns of symbols expressive of a whole.
- It is the conscious recognition and acceptance of a certain spirit or style of life as normative for present and future living.

- It promises and promotes a unique way of dealing with both mystery and paradox.
- It provides its adherents with a way of life that enables them to think and act about such real life situations as helping the poor, the suffering, others in our community, money, those of a different gender, and nature itself.
- It provides us with steady signposts for the road of life.

Spiritualities Based on Our View of God (as distinguished from god)

Agnostic spirituality promises and promotes an ability to live wholistically in the midst of acknowledged continual uncertainty as to human betterment and positive change. Many times such agnosticism is seen as essential for living in liminal times.

Atheistic spirituality is usually defined by what it rejects—an all-powerful and knowing creator, God, of all that exists. In contemporary culture, it is many times understood by atheists to be the total adherence to the promise promoted by scientism and the means of perfection offered by the sciences.

Monistic spirituality envisions present, past, and future as one. All reality is unified in such a way that the promised use of the means provided enables the practitioners to remove the barriers that prevent them from realizing their oneness. This does not rule out the presence of gods and spirits in our present deformed state of existence. Many of these spiritualities recognize such entities as necessary beings in the human evolution to oneness. Eastern spiritualities are usually referred to as monistic.

Monotheistic spirituality envisions time as linear and history as causal of present existence. The one God who is creating this world is seen as the force that will bring it to perfection in the future. The means provided to humans sets the scene for this perfecting action. There is only one, unique, God; any other gods, spirits, and animate or inanimate realities are dependent upon God for their existence. Western spiritualities are understood to be monotheistic and may be described as dualistic.

Polytheist spirituality may exist within a cyclical, linear, or unified view of time. This world, and any possible evolutions of it, results from the interaction of gods and spirits, usually present in a non-empirical world, with this one. The power of a god or spirit is unique to each god or spirit yet it is usually envisioned within a hierarchy of gods. Eastern spiritualities are seen to be polytheistic. Western spiritualities may be also be seen as polytheistic when spirits of all sorts, such as angels and devils, are part of that spirituality, and when God is seen as a spirit like the others but with supreme power over them.

341

Spiritualities Based on the History of Western Culture

Survival/indigenous spirituality. The promise of a perfected present in the future is promoted by the myths and rituals engaged in by individuals and community. Any imperfections of the present are overcome by using the rituals provided by tradition. In doing so the necessary food, marriage arrangements, secure personal interactions, and healthy life are enabled.

Medieval spirituality. This form of spirituality was founded on the vision and hierarchical nature of Roman Catholicism between 900 CE and 1500 CE. A life with God is promised and promoted by the proper use of sacraments and through the encouragement of habits to avoid the seven deadly sins (lust, gluttony greed, sloth, envy, anger, and pride), and to attain the virtues opposite to them (chastity, temperance, charity/generosity, diligence/hard work, patience, kindness/compassion, and humility).

Modern spirituality promises a future world made perfect through the sciences and their derivatives. Many modern spiritualities are characterized by a Secular Fundamentalist outlook with one's certitude and fellowship derived from scientific facts and theories based on the hard and soft sciences.

Liminal spiritualities are embedded with uncertainty, tentativeness, and suspicion of all ideologies and communities that demand one's total commitment over a prolonged period of time. The signposts of the past that embedded the ancient religious visions, promises, and promotions are experienced as unproductive in resolving present challenges. Yet hope is the energizing force shaping, or reshaping, these signposts. Such hope too easily attaches itself to charismatic personalities who offer a salve to present pain by energizing hope for a tomorrow obtained with little personal effort.

Spiritualities Based on Longevity and Adaptability

Classical spiritualities share the longevity and signposts of the classical religions. While the past is no predictor of the future, their ability in the past to change while remaining the same suggests they will evolve to live beyond these liminal times. Their greatest challenge, however, will be in their ability to somehow transform those aspects of their promises and promotions tied to one culture and still be recognized as the same. The current seeming necessities of environmentalism, pluralism, and gender equality are special challenges to such identity of culture and spirituality.

Classical spiritualities have existed for centuries, usually over a thousand years, and have the capacity to awaken individuals to the transcendent experiences available to them. They are composed of classic texts, music, art, ideologies, and architecture. Each spirituality has been and many times still is constitutive to the major world cultures. They share a common transcendent desire and the necessity of all five signposts. They differ significantly regarding their sense of time, deity, and humanity.

- **Eastern classical spiritualities** find their origins in the religions of India (Hinduism, Buddhism, Jainism, and Sikhism) and of East Asia (Taoism, Shinto, and Confucianism).
- **Western classical spiritualities** find their origin in religions of Judaism, Christianity, and Islam.

Marginal spirituality expresses the vision of those who have rejected the classical spiritualities throughout history. Their language and imagery sometimes reflect that of ancient oral cultures, and at other times the experiences and rhetoric of contemporary charismatic personalities. Most contemporary marginal spiritualities are composites of visions and signposts picked from ancient writings and imbued with contemporary language that titillates one's transcendent desires. Today the most common synonyms for marginal spiritualities are sect, cult, occult, esoteric, mystical, and metaphysical.

Spiritualities Based on an Authoritative Source of Promises and Promotions

A worldly spirituality is one that promises and promotes individual and social transformation to a clearly articulated way of life through a clearly designed process for getting there based on a current means of empirical verification, which is its authority for claims of truth.

An otherworldly spirituality promises and promotes individual and social transformation to a metaphorically described way of life through processes warranted by spiritual authorities based on this-worldly reason and experience found in a book, person, ritual, religious community, or personal experience.

Spiritualities Based on Geography

American spirituality is shaped by the conviction that every spirituality should focus on the individual rather than the community, have easily understood beliefs, separate church and state, have a special book such as the Bible, an experienced spiritual leader, prayer, a personal God, a special day of worship, and a simple, clear set of laws to guide one's moral life.

Niche spirituality's vision, promises, and promotions are dependent upon one's current community and its language, culture, values, and symbols. The experience of home that is part of every spirituality is especially important here because the niche is one's physical and/or virtual home.

Spiritualities Based on a Response to Modern Culture

Traditional spirituality, different and many times at odds with its classical religious history, rejects the modern world as devoid of God's signposts and advocates a world described as "traditional." This idealized traditional world is developed within a Secular Fundamentalist milieu and enveloped with a nostalgic feeling productive of a sacral experience.

Contemporalist spirituality accepts the modern world as described by science and usually transforms this description into a prescription for spiritual life. The social sciences in particular become normative for the determination of a mature spiritual life. Although the sciences are offered as the norm, their practical application is ordinarily derived from extremely popularized versions of the results of these sciences and their relevant technologies.

Co-temporal spirituality accepts the validity of the sciences and the particular classical spirituality under consideration. Sometimes this acceptance takes the form of declaring that each sphere, the religious and the scientific, has separate norms for truth and action. One's spirituality, then, may be lived without fear of contradiction because science has nothing to do with or say to spirituality and vice versa: Science may be developed without fear of religious contradiction because it is concerned with a reality and way of life separate from it. Most of the time Co-temporal spirituality accepts truth and this world as one; it also accepts the challenge of discerning the commonality of scientific and religious truth and engages in both the scientific and religious ways of life with the conviction that both will energize and transform the world we live in.

Spiritualities Inherited from Medieval Europe (*spiritualitas*)

As a mode of being: opposite of corporality
- The *spiritual* realm (e.g. clergy)
- The *temporal* realm (e.g. laity)

As a way of acting
- *Active life* such as that involving work, family, sensuality, and the ordinary
- *Contemplative life* such as those activities comprising the mind, the ethereal, and the sacred

Five Spiritual Signposts

The five spiritual signposts are words and actions—tangible expressions of a person and/or culture that enable us to promote our spirituality and experience the promises of transcending this current life

- **Belief** many times is found in stories, songs, poetry, creeds, and formal communal declarations. It is expressive of a desire for truth and trust.
- **Ritual** is discovered in the sacred times of the day, week, month, year, and season and in the repeated prayers, expressions of joy, sorrow, and conviction of salvation. Whether as repeated expressions of belief combined with action or action alone rituals express a desire for harmony and predictability of formative actions that remind us of the past and provide hope for the future.
- **Moral or ethical norms** (doing the right thing) are the agreed-upon communal ways of acting and speaking that reflect the community's view of truthful relations to the world as they know it and expect it to become—a world of fair, loving relationships that will birth the spirituality's vision of total transformation.
- **Community** is all of us supporting one another's beliefs through ritual actions and knowing that we can depend on each other to act in a just and life giving way toward one another. The formation of a community is a reflection of a desire for togetherness, belonging, and fellow feeling.
- **Desire for transcendence** is the continually energizing force that urges us to move beyond the present to a changed future. This force, when being satisfied in a spiritual experience, is described as the sacred, the mysterious, the holy, the supernatural, duty, obedience to a cause, fellow feeling, belief, discipline, dedication, and/or a power or energy beyond the individual and all humans determining and directing where and how we live our lives. The desire for, and satisfaction of transcendence, is what gives value to all the other signposts.

Spiritual Sources: Anything and everything has been found a source of spiritual life, touchstones of the sacred and transcendent. These times, places, persons, words, actions, things, and communities are believed to be a means through which one is in the presence of that power, energy, principle, or persona that sustains all existence. Spiritual Sources are the tangible constituents of each signpost.

Spiritual Idol: An idol is anything or anyone we affirm as our ultimate means of transformation and source of total transcendence who/what is incapable of being so.

Resources

If you are looking for sources for a specific topic covered in the text, they are best found in the footnotes. The easiest way to find them is to use the index to find what you are looking for and then to search the endnotes of that particular chapter.

The resources provided here are meant to aid you in your search for pertinent materials dealing with your spiritual discoveries. The books were chosen for their ability to expand on what was provided in the text. The websites were chosen to update you on materials that were in the text and to provide gateways to further discoveries.

Classical Spiritualities and Religions

- Classical Texts: Six volumes of the sacred texts of the major world religions and their embedded spiritualities: *The Tanakh* (Judaism), *The New Testament and Apocrypha* (Christianity), The *Qu'ran* (Islam), *The Analects* of Confucius (Confucianism), *The Rig Veda* (Hinduism) and *The Dhammapada* (Buddhism). *On Searching the Scriptures: Your Own or Someone Else's: A Reader's Guide to Sacred Writings and Methods of Studying* is the introductory volume by the editor, Jaroslav Pelikan: New York, Quality Paperback Book Club, 1992.
- Robert E. Van Voorst, *Anthology of World Scriptures* (Belmont, CA: Wadsworth/Cengage Learning, 2011), 11th ed. This book provides a helpful introduction to the writings of the classical religions and their associated spiritualities.

The following are two excellent series that include texts, commentaries, and reflections upon diverse spiritualities:
- Orbis press's *Traditions of Christian Spirituality Series* and *Modern Spiritual Masters Series*. For the books within each series see http://www.orbisbooks.com/msm.htm
- Paulist Press's *Classics of Western Spirituality*. The list of available books may be found at http://www.paulistpress.com/bookSearch.cgi?page=series_westernspirit

The Internet is also an invaluable tool for reading and reflecting on the classical texts. Simply type into a search engine the titles of the texts mentioned above or as found in the body of this book. The result will be a site for whatever text you are seeking. Select the translation that you are most comfortable reading. At an introductory level, the differences in translation are not that significant.

The same can be said for all the spiritualities reviewed in this text: type in their proper name and the official website will provide all the information you need for further review of their signposts. Some terms are unique to this book and will not be found on the Internet.

Marginal Spiritualities and Religions

Texts

- Cowan, Douglas E., and David G. Bromley. *Cults and New Religions: A Brief History* in Blackwell Brief Histories of Religion Series. New York: Wiley-Blackwell, 2007.
- Flowers, Stephen. *Lords of the Left Hand Path: A History of Spiritual Dissent.* Runa Raven Press, 1997.
- Harvey, G., and C. Hardman, eds. *Paganism Today: Wiccans, Druids, the Goddess and Ancient Earth Traditions for the Twenty-First Century.* New York: HarperCollins, 1996.
- Hutton, Ronald. *The Triumph of the Moon: A History of Modern Pagan Witchcraft.* New York: Oxford University Press, 1999.
- Ziolkowski, Theodore. *Modes of Faith: Secular Surrogates for Lost Religious Belief.* Chicago: University of Chicago Press, 2009.

Two websites may be helpful in your investigations: For a translation of some of the books of the marginal spiritualities, see the Alchemy website: http://www.levity.com/alchemy/corpherm.html.

For a collection of other commentators on the texts and developers of the tradition, see *The Hermetic Library* at http://hermetic.com/.

Classical and Marginal Spiritualities and Religions

Some comprehensive texts that provide further depth to what we have offered in this book.

- Bellah, Robert N. *Religion in Human Evolution: From the Paleolithic to the Axial Age.* Cambridge, Mass: Harvard U. Press, 2011.

- Chidester, David. *Patterns of Transcendence*. Belmont, CA: Wadsworth, 2002.
- Hemeyer, Julia Corbett. *Religion in America*. Upper Saddle River, NJ: Prentice Hall, 2006.
- Corrigan, J., Denny, F., Eire, C., and M. Jafee. *Jews, Christians, Muslims: A Comparative Introduction to Monotheistic Religions*. Upper Saddle River, NJ: Prentice Hall, 1998.
- Lindner, Eileen W. *Yearbook of American and Canadian Churches 2008*. Nashville, TN: Abington Press, 2008. This book provides essential information about religious organizations. Online access provides constantly updated information.
- Mead, Frank, and Samuel Hill. *Handbook of Denominations in the United States*, 12th ed. Nashville, TN: Abingdon, 2005. This book provides descriptions of the beliefs, worship practices, ethical imperatives, and organizational forms of the various religions in the United States.
- Laboa, Juan Maria, ed., *The Historical Atlas of Eastern and Western Christian Monasticism*. Collegeville, MN: Liturgical Press, 2003. This book provides a good overview of the development of monasticism.
- Young, William A. *The World's Religions: Worldviews and Contemporary Issues*. Englewood Cliffs, NJ: Prentice Hall, 2005.

The following web addresses provide quick access to up-to-date information concerning all the spiritualities we have reviewed in the text.

- *http:// www.religious tolerance.org/ Ontario Consultants on Religious Tolerance.*
- *http://csrs.nd.edu/* A site for the social studies study of religion.
- http://pewforum.org/about/ and http://relegions.pewforum.org/ reports. This site provides basic information about specific religions, recent surveys, and opinion polls.
- http://web.archive.org/web/20060907005952/http://etext.lib.virginia. edu/relmove/ This site provides detailed profiles of more than two hundred marginal religious groups and movements.
- *http://www.about.com/religion/*
- *http://www.adherents.com/* The religions of the world are enumerated here, and descriptions of various religions are provided. Some referral sites are not as objective as first indicated.
- *http://www.beliefnet.com/* This site is devotional in orientation yet provides quick comparisons on subject matter across diverse religions, such as discussions about the end of the world.
- *http://www.thearda.com/index.asp*

- *The Association of Religion Data Archives* (ARDA) supports this site. Data included in the ARDA are submitted by the foremost religion scholars and research centers in the world. Religious membership by zip code is found here. Research ability may be limited by one's professional competence.

NOTES

1   Such consciousness is extremely difficult to achieve. The felt-answers to these simple questions are, in turn, difficult to sustain over a prolonged period of time. To even understand the nature of consciousness is a struggle. See Eric Schwitzgebel, *Perplexities of Consciousness* (Cambridge, MA: MIT Press, 2011).

2   I am not equating consciousness with perception. Our consciousness is a multilayered reality. See Eric Schwitagebel, *Perplexities of Consciousness* (New York: MIT Press, 2011). A major limit to our current consciousness is our niche. See Eli Pariser, *The Filter Bubble: What the Internet is Hiding From You* (New York: The Penguin Press, 2011).

3   There may, of course, be more dimensions than four as argued in mathematics and physics. Robin Le Poidevin, *Travels in Four Dimensions: The Enigmas of Space and Time* (New York: Oxford, 2003). A much older, 1884, but continually published because it is easy to read and understand, is Edwin Abbott's *Flatland: A Romance of Many Dimensions* (New York: Paw Prints, 2010). Most, if not all, spiritualities developed within the era of four dimensions. If there are more than four, they would be included in the "world" category. See also Bernard Carr, ed. *Universe or Multiverse?* (New York: Cambridge University Press, 2007).

4   I realize that spiritual authorities claim to have otherworldly guarantees regarding their promises and their promotion of transformation and transcendence, but these are all based on this-worldly experience. It is impossible to be totally in the other world and this world at the same time. These revelations are always in this-worldly language based on this-worldly experience. This is a paradox, perhaps worthy of inclusion in the list found below.

5   These signposts are found, for example, in the religion or spirituality's writing, art, music, and rituals.

6   Choice and habit are many times in need of support from one's close associates for both understanding and performance. Without them one needs a strong conviction and a need to overcome past habits. See Sheena Lyengar, *The Art of Choosing* (New York: Twelve Publishers, 2010).

7   Patrick Hughes and George Brecht, *Vicious Circles and Infinity: A Panoply of Paradoxes* (New York: Knopf, Doubleday, 1975).

8   This absurdity is many times evidenced by the psycho-social ego defense reaction of denial among many experiencing the death.

9   See http://www.psychotherapy.com.au/TheDoubleBindTheory.pdf

10 Ernest Becker , *The Denial of Death* (New York: The Free Press, 1973).

11 For how discipline, not genes, gives us direction in life see David Shenk, *The Genius In All of Us: Why Everything You've Been Told About Genetics, Talent, and IQ Is Wrong* (New York: Doubleday, 2010).

12 For a summary of these views see Joel J. Kupperman, *Theories of Human Nature* (New York: Hackett Publishing Co, 2011).

13 See W.W. Meissner, "The Ignatian Paradox," in *The Way*, 42/3 (July, 2003), 33-46.

14 Although a half century old, the following is the best review of what follows: Paul Tillich's *Dynamics of Faith* (New York: Harper & Row, 1957).

15 Is a form of psychic or existential distress caused by environmental change, such as mining or climate change. See Albrecht, G., Sartore, G-M., Connor, L., Higginbotham, N., Freeman, S., Kelly, B., Stain, H., Tonna, A., & Pollard, G. (2007). "Solastalgia: the distress caused by environmental change." *Australasian Psychiatry* 15 (1): S95-S98.

16 See   http://witcombe.sbc.edu/sacredplaces/sacredplacesintro.html; http://www.sacredsites.com/; http://www.sacred-destinations.com/

17 See Martin, Laura, "Eskimo Words for Snow: A case study in the genesis and decay of an anthropological example" in *American Anthropologist* 88 (2:1986), 418-23. Geoffrey K. Pullum, *The Great Eskimo Vocabulary Hoax and other Irreverent Essays on the Study of Language* (Chicago: University of Chicago Press, 991). Andrew Spencer Andrew, *Morphological Theory*. (New York: Blackwell Publishers, 1991).

18 See Bruce M. Metzger and Michael D. Coogan, eds., *The Oxford Companion to the Bible* (N.Y.: Oxford University Press, 1993), 295-96 (Human Person).

19 Slightly over 25 percent of Americans believe in astrology. See http://pewforum.org/Other-Beliefs-and-Practices/Many-Americans-Mix-Multiple-Faiths.aspx

20 See http://allaboutfrogs.org/froglnd.shtml

21 See Julia Corbett Hemeyer, *Religion in America* (Upper Saddle River, NJ: Prentice Hall, 2006), Chapter Two.

22 To claim a spirituality with "no place" is to claim one that cannot be spoken about nor imagined, if lived. Remember that essential dimensions to this world are height, depth, and width; in other words, "place." No religion or spirituality exists without place in it in some way. This world is always a starting point of every spirituality and the next world

is always spoken or imagined in pictures, words, or ideas that reflect this world.

23   The idea of what has happened in the past is somehow always present is foundational for understanding how humans are connected from one generation to another. "Conserved core processes" is the phrase used by those who elevate this connection to an evolutionary bond with those who have gone before us. For such a connection in religions and spirituality see Robert N. Bellah, *Religion in Human Evolution: From the Paleolithic to the Axial Age*, (Cambridge, Mass: Harvard U. Press, 2011).

24   Some spiritual directors expand this simple statement by accepting Carl Jung's theories of communal archetypes. See the theories associated with Transpersonal Psychology. Also Patricia Sermabeikian, "Our Clients, Ourselves: The Spiritual Perspective and Social Work Practice" in Social Work, Mar 1994 (v39 n2), 178-83, and David John Tracey, *Remaking Men: Jung, Spirituality And Social Change* (New York: Routlege, 1997) .

25   Although the philosopher Karl Jaspers misframed the time periods, his description of the early development was accurate. He titled the early developmental epoch the Axial Age (*Achsenzeit*) and placed it between 800 BCE and 200 BCE. See Karl Jaspers; Michael Bullock (Tr.), *The Origin and Goal of History* (London: Routledge and Keegan Paul. 1953) from the original Karl Jaspers, *Vom Ursprung und Ziel der Geschichte* (München: Piper Verlag, 1949. There is not universal acceptance of Jaspers's theory and conclusions. What I present here is generally agreed upon by the majority of historians.

26   The development of human culture is based upon Jared Diamond, *Guns, Germs, and Steel: The Fates of Human Societies* (N.Y.: W.W. Norton, 1999).

27   These were usually listed as twelve, but both the number and the members of the pantheon varied throughout the ages.

28   The Texas textbook controversy during 2010 and 2011 is only one example of such strongly held beliefs. See *Recommended: Creationism controversy again slips into Texas textbook debate* http://www.believeme-whenitellu.com/2011/07/21/recommended-creationism-controversy-again-slips-into-texas-textbook-debate/ Also See also Ian Buruma, *Taming the Gods: Religion and Democracy on Three Continents* (Princeton, NY: Princeton University Press, 2010).

29   One of the earliest investigators, who possibly may have coined the word, is Mircea Eliade, Shamanism, Archaic Techniques of Ecstacy, (New York: Pantheon Books, 1964). The Bollingen Series LXXVI

30 The current view of mysticism that emphasizes the irrational and paranormal seems to have its origins in the late 17h century. See Michel de Certeau, *The Mystic Fable* (Chicago: U. of Chicago Press, 1992).

31 See Khaled Anatolios, *Retrieving Nicea: The Development and Meaning of Trinitarian Doctrine* (Grand Rapids, MI: Baker Academic, 2011).

32 Much of what follows is dependent upon Aime Solignac, "L'apparition du mot 'spiritualitas' au moyen age," *Archivum Latinitatis Medii Aevi* 44-45 (1983-85): 185-206.

33 For the first usage of "religions" in English see P. Harrison, *"Religion" and the Religions in the English Enlightenment* (Cambridge, 1990), 39.

34 Although dependent upon Dobbelaere in the following discussion, I am interpreting his work with the intention of applying it to our discussion about spirituality. This intention may give a meaning beyond the author's intent. See Karel Dobbelaere, "Secularization: A Multi-dimensional Concept." *Current Sociology* 29 (1981):3-213. This is a summary and analysis of the literature until 1980.

_____, "Secularization Theories and Sociological paradigms: Convergences and Divergences." *Social Compass* 31(1984)199-219. He develops his previous work by providing us with a synthesis, through the use of paradigms, of the much larger analytical piece.

_____, 1990. "From Pillar to Postmodernity: The Changing Situation of Religion in Belgium." *Sociological Analysis* 51(1990)S1-S13. Here he returns to the use of secularization and secularization in general by refining his previous definitions.

35 Dobbelaere (1981), 9.

36 An excellent example of where the sacred may be found in the secular see Theodore Ziolkowski, *Modes of Faith: Secular Surrogates for Lost Religious Belief* (Chicago: University of Chicago Press, 2009).

37 Foundational to the scientific endeavor is an ability to measure objectively. At present we are still striving for an absolute system of measurement. See Robert P. Crease, *World in the Balance: The Historic Quest for an Absolute System of Measurement* (New York: W. W. Norton, 2011).

38 The middle decades of the twentieth century witnessed a strong and ultimately devastating argument against ideas of the supernatural as developed after the beginning of the modern age. These ideas set the supernatural as totally beyond what was titled "pure nature." The arguments against this position favored the older and longer tradition that grace, or super nature, while totally free, was constitutive to human nature as it now exists. See any of the works by Henru de Lubac especially *The Mystery of the Supernatural* (New York: Herder & Herder, 1967).

39 An interesting parallel development was slow but growing interest in the meaning and consequence of resurrection among Christians during the twentieth century. A heaven without a resurrected body neglects an essential part of the Christian creed. See Colleen McDannell & Bernhand Lang, *Heaven: A History* (New Haven, Conn: Yale University, 1988)

40 Christian evangelical fundamentalism accepts many aspects of secular fundamentalism while verbally rejecting modernism. It is reductionist, word oriented, and literal in mentioning some shared characteristics. See my "Secular Fundamentalism and Secular Humanism: Value Sets for the Twenty-First Century" in *Studies in Formative Spirituality* XIX (May, 1993).

41 I have offered three choices here. There are many other ways for a religion to respond to its surrounding environment; see my "The End and The Future," in *Rising From History*, Robert J. Daly editor (Lanham Md., University Press of America, 1987), 12.

42 See Inglehart-Welzel Cultural Map of the World Written by Ronald Inglehart, which is best found at http://www.worldvaluessurvey.org/wvs/articles/folder_published/article_base_54

43 Joan Ringelheim, "The Strange and the Familiar," in Michael A. Signer's *Humanity at the Limit: The Impact of the Holocaust Experience on Jews and Christians* (Bloomington: Indiana: Indiana University Press, 2000), p. 37

44 This in between time is well described by Zbigniew Brzezinski in *Strategic Vision America And The Crisis Of Global Power* (New York: Basic Books, 2012).

45 See "Passages, Margins, Poverty," in his *Dramas, Fields, and Metaphors: Symbolic Action in Human So*ciety (Ithaca: Cornell University Press, 1974).

46 Many mystics also have this time of inbetweeness when it seems all of the past has been for nothing and the future holds no promise. The God they have been so close to is no more. The words of Jesus on the cross, "My God, my God, why have you forsaken me," rumble through every moment of their existence. It is called "Noche obscura del alma," or, the dark night of the soul. See St. John of the Cross, *The Dark Night of the Soul* (New York: Image Books, 1990). Allison Peers translator and editor.

47 For a description of what happens within each of these dialectical events, see N. Kollar, "The Death of National Symbols: Roman Catholicism in Quebec," in *Ethnicity,Nationality, and Religious Experience*. Peter C. Phan ed. (Lanham, MD: University Press of America, 1995).

48 See *Generations at Work* (N.Y.: AMACOM, American Management Association, 2000).

49 A book that describes how to educate these subcultures, although it is not intended to do so, is Judith Berling's *Understanding Other Religious Worlds: A Guide for Interreligious Education* (Maryknoll, NY: Orbis Books, 2004). She describes the learning theories and views of one's own and other religions that are necessary to live in a pluralistic universe.

50 A summary of the research dealing with technological change may be found in "Old Fogies by Their 20s" in Ideas and Trends, *The New York Times*, Sunday, January 10, 2010, 5.

51 There are many sources for affirming the fact that most people affirm their membership in some religion. The best for diverse comparisons is *Association of Religion Data Base Archives* (http://www.thearda.com/)

52 These are 1 Cor 11:23-25, Matt. 16:26-29, MK 14:22-25, LK 22:15-20.

53 Although not using my categories, the best source for thinking about the evolution of religion is Robert Bellah, *Religion in Human Evolution: From the Paleolithic to the Axial Age* (Cambridge, MA: Harvard University Press, 2011).

54 The completeness of this description and its consistent applicability among both hard and soft sciences is, as always, a matter of argument. This topic may be seen in all its intricacy in V. V. Raman, *Truth and Tension In Science and Religion* (Center Ossipee, New Hampshire: Beech River Books, 2009).

55 The scientific method does not rule out what today would be called a singular event. This would have ramifications for what I am calling "here and now." For our explicit purposes the book by Nassim Taleb, *The Black Swan: The Impact of the Highly Improbable* (New York: Random House, 2010), 2nd ed., would be more helpful. Briefly put, the Black Swan is something or event that happens but has never happened before. Once it happens we develop all kinds of explanations for its happening. The reason for doing so is that this is an extraordinary event. Although it is not Taleb's purpose to discuss religion, obviously religious truths, when first discovered, might fit the description of the Black Swan.

56 What follows is dependent upon Monk et. al, *Exploring Religious Meaning* (Englewood Cliffs, NJ: Prentice-Hall, 1980), 2nd ed., 303-4.

57 If we speak of intuition rather than feeling, an excellent discussion of how we think deductively and intuitively may be found in Daniel Kahneman, *Thinking, Fast and Slow* (New York: Farrar, Straus & Giroux, 2011).

58 Two articles are a good summary of scientific illiteracy: "American Adults Flunk Basic Science" in *ScienceDaily* (Mar 13, 2009) and "Scientific Literacy: How Do Americans Stack Up?" in *ScienceDaily* (Feb 17, 2007). For religious illiteracy See Stephen Prothero, *Religious Literacy: What Every American Needs to Know – and Doesn't* (New York: HarperOne, 2008).

59 What follows is dependent upon but identical to Paul Tillich's *Dynamics of Faith* (New York: Harper and Row, 1957), 18-20.

60 What follows is dependent upon Nathan R. Kollar's *Defending Religious Diversity in Public Schools* (Denver CO: Praeger, 2009).

61 Lawrence Kohlberg, *The Philosophy of Moral Development : Moral Stages and the Idea of Justice* (San Francisco: Harper & Row, 1981); Sohan Modgil, Celia Modgil, and Lawrence Kohlberg, *Lawrence Kohlberg, Consensus and Controversy* (Philadelphia: Falmer Press, 1986); and Lawrence Kohlberg and Dawn Schrader, *The Legacy of Lawrence Kohlberg* (San Francisco: Jossey-Bass, 1990).

62 This is a controversial claim. Some contemporary researchers would say it is a male oriented one; others, suggest that it neglects the significance of a sacred community such as a church.

63 William G. Perry Jr., *Forms of Intellectual and Ethical Development in the College Years: A Scheme.* (New York: Holt, Rinehart, and Winston, 1970); William G. Perry Jr. (1981), "Cognitive and Ethical Growth: The Making of Meaning," in Arthur W. Chickering and Associates, *The Modern American College* (San Francisco: Jossey-Bass, 1981), pp. 76–116. Also see S. Parks, *Big Questions, Worthy Dreams: Mentoring Young Adults in Their Search for Meaning, Purpose and Faith* (San Francisco: Jossey-Bass, 2000); Patrick G. Love, "Comparing Spiritual Development and Cognitive Development," in *Journal of College Student Development* 43:3 (May/June, 2002), 357-373.

64 William Stringfellow, *Imposters of God: Inquiries into Favorite Idols* (Dayton, Ohio: Pflaum, 1969).

65 See Harold R. Isaacs, *Idols of the Tribe: Group Identity and Political Change* (New York: Harper and Row, 1975). Hans J. Mol, *Identity and the Sacred* (New York: Macmillan, 1976). Amartya Sen, *Identity and Violence* (New York: Norton, 2006).

66 Jaroslav Pelikan, *The Vindication of Tradition* (New Haven, Con: Yale, U. Press, 1986) said it best: "Tradition is the living faith of the dead; traditionalism is the dead faith of the living. Tradition lives in conversation with the past, while remembering where we are and when we are and that it is we who have to decide. Traditionalism supposes that nothing should ever be done for the first time, so all that is needed to

solve any problem is to arrive at the supposedly unanimous testimony of this homogenized tradition." The term traditioning, as I am using it, is equivalent to his term "tradition."

67   As found in Finest Quotes http://www.finestquotes.com/select_quote-category-Knowing%20Yourself-page-0.htm

68   An excellent overview of this development is Jared Diamond, *Guns, Germs, and Steel: The Fates of Human Societies* (New York: W.W. Norton, 1997).

69   See under the heading "word" and "word of God": Bruce Metzger & Michael Coogan, *The Oxford Companion to the Bible* (New York: Oxford University Press, 1993) and John McKenzie, *Dictionary of the Bible* (Milwaukee, WI: Bruce, 1965).

70   I realize that some Christian theologians argue that each religion has a unique aspect of God's word. At this writing the dominant majority view is still that Christianity is God's unique and final revelation. The other Abrahamic religions also hold that they possess God's unique and final revelation.

71   This information is from 2005 as found in *The Association of Religion Data Archives* at http://www.thearda.com/Archive/browse.asp.

72   An excellent historical timeline with the events of all three of these religions listed may be found in J. Corrigan, F. Denny, C. Eire, M. Jafee, *Jews, Christians, Muslims: A Comparative Introduction to Monotheistic Religions* (Upper Saddle River, NJ: Prentice Hall, 1998), pp.514-524.

73   Ronald L Eisenberg, *The 613 Mitzvot: A Contemporary Guide to the Commandments of Judaism* (New York: Schreiber Publishing, 2005.

74   The focus here is upon spirituality. The Holocaust also included the death of many Christians as well as those murdered for other reasons than religion.

75   See the necessary constant vigilance of the Anti-Defamation League at http://www.adl.org/Anti_semitism/anti-semitism_global.asp

76   Since we are looking at contemporary Judaism, "tradition" here is in reference to Rabbinic Judaism, which was the dominant formative force over Judaism beginning with the destruction of the Temple in 70 C.E. and almost certainly the sole force since the sixth century C.E. See Jacob Neusner, *The Four Stages of Rabbinic Judaism* (London: Routledge, 1999).

77   See William A. Young, *The World's Religions: Worldviews and Contemporary Issues* (Englewood Cliffs, NJ: Prentice Hall, 1995), 277-300.

78   For at least a century there has been an ongoing argument as to whether and how much physiological communality there is among Jews. For a summation and development of the argument see Gil Atzmon, Harry

Ostrer, et al. "Abraham's Children in the Genome Era: Major Jewish Diaspora Populations Comprise Distinct Genetic Clusters with Shared Middle Eastern Ancestry," *The American Journal of Human Genetics*, 03 June 2010.

79 The Central Bureau of Statistics for the state of Israel reported that 8 percent of Israel's Jewish population defines itself as *haredi*, 12 percent as religious, 13 percent as traditional-religious, 25 percent as traditional, and 42 percent as secular. See *Jewish World* at http://www.ynet.co.il/english/articles/0,7340,L-3890330,00.html

80 The word *Tanakh* is actually an acronym composed of the first letters of the current division into Torah (law), Prophets (**Nevi'im**) and writings (**Ketuvim**). See Lee Martin McDonald; James A Sanders, eds. *The Canon Debate* (Peabody, Mass: Hendrickson, 2002. "Canon" here refers to the normative collection of writings for Judaism. The number and composition of books has been debated over the centuries as well as the norms for including holy writings into the religions list of authoritative books.

81 See David Halivini Weiss, *Peshat and Derash: Plain and Applied Meaning in Rabbinic Exegesis* (New York: Oxford University Press, 1990).

82 The foundational statement of Deuteronomy 16:18 is amplified and applied by these prophets. See Amos 8:4; Amos 6:7, 8:11-12; Jeremiah 5:26-29; Jeremiah 27:8, 32:1-5; Jeremiah 27:8, 32:1-5; 22:1-9, 37:16-21, 38:14-28; Isaiah 1:13-17, 10:1-4; and Isaiah 57-58.

83 Jews are currently free to practice their religion in all the Western nations. They, as well as everyone else, are not free to practice their religion in most other nations. One must recognize that there may be constitutional freedom of religion but societal restrictions and hostility. Brazil and Japan rate the most free in both categories. The Pew Research Center's Forum on Religion & Public Life did an extensive study on this topic in 2009. They found, among other things, that over 90 percent of the world's population lives in countries with little or no religious freedom. See http://pewforum.org/newassets/images/reports/restrictions/restrictionsfullreport.pdf

84 This is an approximation dating from Jerome's Latin vulgate translation in 383 CE to the beginning of the Protestant Reformation in 1517.

85 See Gerhard Podhradsky, *New Dictionary of the Liturgy* (London: Alba House, 1966) for a description of its various uses over the centuries.

86 The first publication of what is called the King James Translation in the United States and the Authorized Version in England was in 1611. It, along with the *Book of Common Prayer*, had a formative influence on the English Language.

87   This translation is found in the *Good News for Modern Man* (1970) published by the American Bible Society. It is used by many Christians in English-speaking countries.

88   This translation may be found in *The New English Bible with Apocrypha* Oxford Study Edition (New York: Oxford, 1976). It is used as a text by many studying the Bible in our colleges and universities.

89   For the multitude of interpretations and usage of this prayer see Kenneth W. Stevenson, *The Lord's Prayer: A Text in Tradition* (Minneapolis, MN: Fortress Press, 2004), 250.

90   See, James F. Childress & John Macquarrie, eds. *The Westminster Dictionary of Christian Ethics* (Philadelphia: Westminster Press, 1986), 222-24.

91   The phrase used for this by Jesus is *Kingdom of God* which is now but still to come; a time of vindication by the poor, the persecuted, those in need (Luke 6:20; Matthew 5:10); entered through sacrifice and following Jesus's way of life. Current translations used by many are "Reign of God" and "Kingdom of Heaven."

92   These names are found in the book of *Acts* in the Christian *New Testament*. If you are interested, see Acts 1:16; 2:4; 11:26).

93   An excellent review of the writings dealing with the term Messiah in the Bible and early Christian and Jewish literature may be found in Joseph A. Fitzmyer. *The One Who Is to Come* (Grand Rapids, Michigan: Eerdmans, 2007).

94   The Kingdom of God image is one of God's reign rather than realm. It is an intimate covenant with Our Father rather than God giving us a land. Jesus's teaching is filled with stories describing this kingdom; sermons that provide its commands; actions that initiate it such as healings and other miracles. It is described as "here" but coming in the future. Some contemporary prayers and translations of the bible will not use the term kingdom but instead either realm or reign depending upon the context.

95   Adherents.com/Religions_By_Adherents

96   Frank Mead, Samuel Hill, *Handbook of Denominations in the United States* 12th edition. (Nashville, Tenn.: Abingdon, 2005).

97   An excellent breakdown of major categories of Christian membership may be found in: http://www.religioustolerance.org/chr_deno.htm; U.S. religious statistics: http://lermanet.com/cisar/usa/040101.htm; http://www.adherents.com/rel_USA.html.

98   These are terms I have created to reflect the present emphasis among the diverse Christian churches.

99   See http://plato.stanford.edu/entries/natural-law-ethics/

100 The *New Testament* is composed of the following books: *Gospels, Acts, Letters (epistles), and the Book of Revelation (Apocalypse in some Bibles.).*

101 Catholics call the disputed books Deuterocanonical and consider them to be inspired. Bible-believing Christians call them apocryphal and consider them to be spurious. For a quick easy to read review See http:// en.wikipedia.org/wiki/Books_of_the_Bible

102 There are some who say they are Christian who do not hold a Trinitarian concept of God. Most commentators, however, demand some adherence to historical Christianity to designate a church or religion as Christian.

103 This translation is the one used by most traditional Christians today. Other versions and a short commentary may be found at http://www. creeds.net/ancient/nicene.htm. Also, for a list of Christian churches that use this creed, see http://en.wikipedia.org/wiki/Nicene_Creed.

104 These comments are in response to the many questions asked from students over the years.

105 Christians use this word a great deal. It is their way of confirming what was just said: "So be it!"

106 The use of this Greek term is on one hand a rejection of some bishops' claim that Jesus is similar to God and acceptance of the fact that this human is God. A summary and explanation of the development of this belief may be found at Khaled Anatolios, *Retrieving Nicaea: The Development and Meaning of Trinitarian Doctrine* (Grand Rapids, MI, Baker Academic, 2011).

107 An excellent demonstration of the diversity of interpretations of who Jesus is today may be found in Stephen Prothero, *American Jesus: How the Son of God Became a National Icon.* (New York: Farrar, Straus, Giroux, 2003).

108 It may be helpful to remember that Jews understood these practices to be commanded and revealed by God as part of their covenant with God.

109 A good overview of the development of monasticism is Juan Maria Laboa (ed.), *The Historical Atlas of Eastern and Western Christian Monasticism* (Collegeville, MN: Liturgical Press, 2003). Francis Kline, *Lovers of the Place: Monasticism Loose in the Church* (Collegeville, MN: Liturgical Press, 1997) provides an telling of the same story while calling for its necessary adaptation to contemporary life.

111 Different Christians number the ten commands differently. This is the "old" listing. The Lutherans and Catholics favor the old listing, and the Greek Orthodox and remaining Protestants split the First Commandment. Thus the prohibition against false images (Exodus 20:3-6) stands out as the second commandment (Protestant) rather than remaining hidden with the first forbidding the worship of false gods (Catholic).

The emphasis, of course, fits in with the Protestant distain of statues and other ornaments in the churches.

112   See *Catechism of the Catholic Church* (Washington, DC: United States Catholic Conference, 1994), #2258-2330.

113   Notice I am not saying mystics are always on the edge of society. I am making this claim, in this instance, only when their writings seem to claim that humans are God. See Lawrence S. Cunningham, "Nearer to God: Demystifying Mysticism," *Commonwealth* (Oct 7, 2011) 21-23 for the necessary distinctions.

114   Pentecostalism is best seen as a movement rather than an established church. It is present in many Traditional and Bible-believing churches. In Catholicism, for example, it is known as charismatic Catholicism. For what happens when Pentecostalism becomes institutionalized, see Michael Wilkinson, ed., *Canadian Pentecostalism: Transition and Transformation* (Montreal: McGill-Queen's University Press, 2009).

115   The list of gifts are found in several places in the New Testament, especially 1 Corinthians 12:4-14 and 1 Corinthians 12:27-30. There is a great deal of theological and scientific literature on healing, predicting the future, seeing spirits, and talking in tongues. Some of this will be reviewed in subsequent chapters. It should also be noted that other gifts are included in these lists but do not gain the same notoriety in contemporary times such as wisdom, teaching, and administration.

116   Deuteronomy 23:20-22.

117   This is found in many places; the two most important are III Lateran, Canon 25 and the Law of the Catholic Church, especially the Decree of Gratian, q. 3, C. IV; q. 4, C. IV; and in the *Decretals*, cpts 2, 5, 7, 9, 10, and 13.

118   See especially Mark 12:33 and Luke 10:29-37.

119   For further expansion on these ideas see Paul F Knitter, *Without Buddha I Could Not Be a Christian* (Oxford : Oneworld, 2009). Paul F Knitter, *The Myth of Religious Superiority : Multifaith Explorations of Religious Pluralism* (Maryknoll, N.Y. : Orbis Books, 2004). Peter C Phan, *Being Religious Interreligiously : Asian Perspectives on Interfaith Dialogue* (Maryknoll, N.Y. : Orbis Books, 2004).

120   Since Arabic is the sacred and sole language of both the Quran and this prayer, the transliteration of prayers into Roman letters differs by author. The same can be said of translating both prayer and Quran into English. This particular transliteration and translation is from The *Canadian Society of Muslims* Website, http://muslim-canada.org/salaat.html.

121   http://www.jannah.org/qurantrans/

122   Literally the word Muslim means one who submits to God.

123   "The recitation" is the translation of the word Quran (Koran, Qur'an, Al-Qur'an). Mohammad the prophet heard what the angel Gabriel (*Jibrīl*) said to him between 610-632 CE and recited what he heard for his followers. They in turn memorized what he recited and wrote it down. When it was compiled into one book is a matter of argument. That it is the actual word of God is not contested among Muslims. They believe that to hear the recitation is to hear God, that God has not spoken since, and that the Quran is God's final revelation. It contains 114 surahs (chapters) and, except for the first, the surahs are arranged according to length.

124   A *hadith* is a report of an action and/or saying of Mohammad provided by his followers. There are continual arguments over which are authentic. See Fred McGraw Donner, *Narratives of Islamic Origins: The Beginnings of Islamic Historical Writing* (Princeton, NJ: Darwin Press, 1998).

125   Contrary to contemporary usage, a prophet in the Jewish, Christian, and Muslim traditions is one who speaks for God. See B. Metzger, M. Coogan, *The Oxford Companion to the Bible* (New York: Oxford U. Press, 1995), 620-623.

126   This formula is known as the *Shahada* or witnessing to the core of Islamic belief.

127   William A. Young, *The World's Religions: Worldviews and Contemporary Issues* (Englewood Cliffs, NJ: Prentice Hall, 1995), op. cit., 253

128   These are condensations of examples portrayed in Clifford Geertz, *Islam Observed* (Chicago: University of Chicago Press, 1968) and offered in Carmody and Carmody, op. cit., 380-382.

129   N.J. Dawood, trans., *The Koran* (Baltimore, MD: Penguin, 1968), 10.

130   An excellent introduction to these early years is Fred M. Donner, *Mohammad and the Believers: At the Origins of Islam* (New York: Harvard University Press, 2010). It is a revisionist view of the beginnings using critical historical methods to arrive at his conclusions.

131   See *Jews, Christians, Muslims*, op. cit., cpt. 9, for a description of the origins of such movements.

132   Shia's view of the Imam is one who is a direct descendant of Muhammad and Ali. He is sinless in deportment and infallible in application of Shira. He also intercedes on behalf of Muslims in the afterlife. For further descriptions and explanation see John L. Esposito, *Islam – The Straight Path* (New York: Oxford University Press, 1991), 45 -47). Allamah Tabatabai, *Shiite Islam* (Albany: State University of New York Press, 1975).

133   Martin Lings, *What is Sufism?* (Berkeley: University of California Press, 1977), 45-46.

134 Videos, pictures, and music associated with *Dhikr* and whirling dervishes can easily be obtained on the web.

135 For Sufism and other mystical aspects of Islam see Annemarie Schimmel, *Mystical Dimensions of Islam* (Chapel Hill, North Carolina: University of North Carolina Press, 1978), William Harmless, *Mystics* (New York: Oxford University Press, 2008); Nagendra Kr Singh, *Global Encyclopaedia Of Islamic Mystics And Mysticism:2* (New Delhi: Global Vision, 2009).

136 The Sunni, and much introductory literature on Islam, will usually refer to these as the Pillars of Islam. The Shi'a will add five more to these such as *Tawhid* (profession of God's singularity), *Qiyamah* (Judgment Day), *Nubuwwah* (God's provision of prophets to convey his will), Imamah (the prophets' perfection, including infallibility, of the Twelve Imams), *Adl* (Divine Justice/human honor).

137 See *Jews, Christians, Muslims*, op. cit., 150.

138 See Dr. Umar Sulaiman Al-Ashqar, (1998). *The World of the Jinn and Devils* (Boulder, CO: Al-Basheer Company, 1998).

139 See USC *Compendium of Islamic Texts, at* http: //www. usc.edu/ dept/ MSA/fundamentals/hadithsunnah/muslim/002.smt.html#002.0502

140 One may easily obtain a video or audio of the entire salat prayer on the Internet and from many book stores.

141 Water is usually used for this ritual washing. When it is not available sand or dirt may be used.

142 3:95-97.

143 For an excellent example of the experience and how it changes one's life, see Malcom X, *The Autobiography of Malcolm X,* with the assistance of Alex Haley (New York: Grove Press, 1965), 388-393.

144 http://www.jannah.org/qurantrans/quran17.html

145 An obvious example is that the handbooks dealing with Catholic morality in the late middle ages had five times as much material on usury than on sexual morality.

146 Firm dates are lost in the record keeping of the diverse religions. What I give here are from D. L. Carmody, J.T. Carmody, *Ways to the Center* (Belmont, CA: Wadsworth, 1989) and B. Grun, *The Timetables of History* (New York: Simon and Schuster, 1991). The timeline offered by W.A. Young, *The World's Religions* (Englewood Cliffs, NJ: Prentice Hall, 1995) was used for Shinto. All dates presented here were the same among these three texts.

147 The numbers were rounded up. Percentages are exact. These are statistics from 2005. Remember that although such numbers may be very low, they have had a profound influence upon their cultures of origin.

See *The Association of Religion Data Archives* at http://www.thearda.com/ Archive/browse.asp.

[148] As found in *Katha Upanishad* 1.2.15-7. For another translation see: http://www.hinduwebsite.com/sacredscripts/hinduism/upanishads/ katha.asp.

[149] This is found in literary form in the *Bhagavad Gita* and in contemporary life in the International Society for Krishna Consciousness.

[150] Stephen Prothero, *American Jesus: How the Son of God Became a National Icon* (New York: Farrar, Straus, and Giroux, 2003).

[151] See David Chidester, *Patterns of Transcendence* (Belmont, CA: Wadsworth, 2002), 76.

[152] Op. cit., 76-77.

[153] *The Brihadaranyaka Upanishad*, with the commentary of Shankaracharya, translated by Swami Madhavananda, (Mayavati, Almora: Advaita Ashrama, 1935).

[154] http://www.iloveindia.com/spirituality/sloka/ganesha-sloka.html

[155] N. K. Das sees such deep diversity as a challenge to a clear synthesis of Indian culture when he says that Indian cultural pluralism and syncretism encompasses ethnic diversity and admixture, linguistic heterogeneity as well as fusion, and variations as well as synthesis in customs, behavioral patterns, beliefs, and rituals. See N. K. Das, "Cultural Diversity, Religious Syncretism and People of India: An Anthropological Interpretation". *Bangladesh e-Journal of Sociology* 3(July 2006) 2nd. http://www.bangladeshsociology.org/Content.htm.

[156] Eugene M Makar, *An American's Guide to Doing Business in India : A Practical Guide to Achieving Success in the Indian Market* (Avon, MA : Adams Business, 2008).

[157] See A. L. Basham, *The Wonder That Was India* (New York: Grove Press, 1959) 153.

[158] See Nilufer Medora, "Mate selection in contemporary India: Love marriages versus arranged marriages" in Raeann R Hamon; Bron B *Mate Selection Across Cultures (*Thousand Oaks : Sage Publications, 2003), 209-230.

[159] Carmody and Carmody, op. cit., 78.

[160] The laws were understood to be formulated by Brahma and stated by his son Manu who uses them to teach his students, who, in turn write them down in the Manu Smriti. See Patrick Olivelle, *Manu's Code of Law: A Critical Edition and Translation of the Mānava-Dharmaśāstra* (Oxford: Oxford U. Press, 2005).

[161] Patrick Olivelle, *The Samnyasa Upanisads: Hindu Scriptures on Asceticism and Renunciation* (Oxford: Oxford U. Press, 1992).

162   The Internet is filled with mantras for every issue: health, wealth, and love. Finding one's mantra in this grocery store of mantras is not at all what is suggested in Indian spirituality. One's director of your spirit designs an individual mantra meant to meet your *spiritual* needs.

163   The Indian government website: http://india.gov.in/knowindia/literacy.php

164   See the discussion of this at the Smithsonian, Freer Gallery of Art at: http://www.asia.si.edu/education/pujaonline/puja/start.htm

165   The sacrifices consist of *ghee* (clarified butter), cakes, milk, types of grain, and soma.

166   For more information on Tantra, see D. Brooks, *The Secret of the Three Cities: An Introduction to Hindu ŚāKta Tantrism* (Chicago: University of Chicago Press, 1990). Swami Agehananda Bharati, *The Tantric Tradition / Agehananda Bharati* (New York, Doubleday, 1970).

167   See High Urban, *Tantra: Sex, Secrecy, Politics and Power in the Study of Religions* (Berkeley, CA: University of California Press, 2003), 204-05.

168   See *The Secret of Three Cities*, op. cit.

169   B.K.S Iyengar, *Light on the Yoga Sūtras of Patañjali* (Hammersmith, London, UK: Thorsons, 1966/2002), 246. The Concise Srimad Bhagavatam, trans. Swami Venkatesananda, (New York: SUNY Press 1989).

170   I am accepting Adi Sankara as the author of *The Crest Jewel*. I am using John Richard's translation. See http://www.visionaire.org/advaitavedant/vivekachudamani.htm

171   Its composition may have taken place over centuries. This dating refers to the present copy. See Juan Mascaro, The *Bhagavad Gita* (Baltimore, MD: Penguin, 1969).

172   Patrick Olivelle, *Upaniṣads*, Oxford University Press, 1998).   Ariel Glucklich, *The Strides of Vishnu: Hindu Culture in Historical Perspective*, (New York: Oxford University Press, 2008).

173   See Natubhai Shah, *Jainism: The World of Conquerors* (Sussex, England: Sussex Academic Press, 1998).

174   In Hinduism, *jiva* is one's life principle.

175   See Vijay Singh: *The River Goddess* (London: Moonlight Publishing, 1994).

176   Edward Conze, *Buddhist Texts Through the Ages* (New York: Harper Torchbook, 1964), 48-49.

177   These are what is known as the Three Jewels that are generally recognized as a way of proclaiming one's adherence to Buddhism. It has many variations. This is a Pali chant of the Theravada Buddhists. See Thanisaro Bhikkhu, *Refuge: An Introduction to Buddha, Dhamma and Sangha* (third edition, revised 2001). This and other materials by

Thanisaro Bhikku may be obtained at *Metta Forest Monastery* P.O. Box 1409. Valley Center, CA 92082.

[178] Translation as found in: Elgiriye Indaratana Maha Thera (2002). *Vandanā: The Album of Pāḷi Devotional Chanting & Hymns*. Penang, Malaysia: Mahindarama Dhamma Publication. Retrieved 2008-02-16 from "Buddha Dharma Education Association" at http://www.buddhanet.net/pdf_file/vandana02.pdf.

[179] These techniques are found in the Pali Canon, in which at least fifty are described. See Joseph Goldstein, *One Dharma: The Emerging Western Buddhism* (New York: HarperCollins, 2003).

[180] Michael K. Jerryson and Mark Juergensmeyer, editors , *Buddhist Warfare* (New York: Oxford University Press, 2006). Dale S. Wright, *The Six Perfections: Buddhism and the Cultivation of Character* (New York: Oxford University Press, 2010). For a Tibetan view of the Six Perfections see http://bodhihut.17.forumer.com/a/the-six-perfections-in-tibetan-buddhism_post992.html. For a Chinese view (remember to press the English option) see http://www.paramita6.org/en/index.html

[181] A helpful commentary with understanding the difficulty of translating this into English is http://www.sacred-texts.com/bud/mcb/mcb10.htm. This translation is from the Pure Land perspective.

[182] *Layman P'ang (740-808)* As found at: http://viewonbuddhism.org/resources/zen_poems.html

[183] A Chinese version of the above can be found on the wall of Sun Yatsen Hall St. John's University, Jamaica, New York. This English translation is by Dr. Shih-shun Liu.

[184] *The Book of Mencius*, 7A: 4

[185] From *Tao Te Ching* by Lao-tzu J. Legge, G. Translator. See http://www.sacred-texts.com/tao/taote.htm

[186] This work is claimed to be written between 350-275 BCE. Lost in history is who the author is and what the mutual dates are for both ancient claims to authorship (Lao Tzu) and the writing of this most important spiritual text.

[187] This is an interpretation of a description found in the Chuang Tzu. For various levels of interpretation, including the image I am using here, see Holmes Welch, *Taoism: The Parting of the Way* (Boston: Beacon Press, 1966), 35-49.

[188] The "Five Classics" said to be authored by Confucius are said, by most authorities, not to be so. However, since they did exist in some form during his time, he may have edited them. These classics are: *Shu Ching* (the Book of History), *Shih Ching* (the Book of Poetry), the *Li Ch* (the Book of Rites), the *I Ching* (the Book of Changes) and the the *Ch'un Ch'iu*

(The Annals of Spring and Summer). the *Hsiao-Chin* was added to these by his disciples.

189   For a discussion about the value of these cultures of the past and present for classical spiritualities, see both Avind Sharma, *A Primal Perspective on the Philosophy of Religion* (Dordrecht, Netherlands: Springer, 2006) and the subsequent discussion in *Journal of the American Academy of Religion* 79(4:Dec., 2011), 749-849. Whether to call these cultures primitive, primal, indigenous, or aboriginal is of continual interest throughout the discussion.

190   A reminder of how our seeking for immortality is essential to our survival is found in Stephen Cave, *Immortality: The Quest to Live Forever and How It Drives Civilization* (New York; Random House, 2012).

191   For our purposes these three present the basis for what follows. This is an application of Lifton's ideas. Robert Jay Lifton, *The Broken Connection: On Death and the Continuity of Life* (New York : Simon and Schuster, 1979). Robert Jay Lifton, *The Protean Self : Human Resilience in an Age of Fragmentation* (New York, NY : Basic Books, 1993). Robert Jay Lifton, *Death in Life: Survivors of Hiroshima* (New York, Random House, 1967).

192   See Peter Berger, *The Sacred Canopy: Elements of a Sociological Theory of Religion* (New York: Garden City, 1969).

193   See Lifton, *Broken Connection*, op. cit., p. 101 ff.

194   The following exemplify this diversity: Jordan Paper, *Native North American Religious Traditions: Dancing for Life* (Santa Barbara, CA: Greenwood Publishing Group, 2007). Lawrence Eugene Sullivan, *Native Religions and Cultures of North America: Anthropology of the Sacred* (New York: Continuum International Publishing Group, 2003). Lee Irwin, *Native American Spirituality: A Critical Reader* (Lincoln NB: U of Nebraska Press, 2000).

195   There are two ways to discover Japanese beginnings: The quick historical timeline found at: http://www.history-timelines.org.uk/places-timelines/29-timeline-of-ancient-japan.htm and the archeological materials found at About.com. Begin with Fukui Cave and Jomon, at http://archaeology.about.com/od/fterms/g/fukui_cave.htm. Texts may be found in Frederick Victor Dickins, *Primitive and Mediaeval Japanese Texts Translated Into English with Introductions, Notes, and Glossaries* (New York: Design Books, 2010).

196   This, *The Great Purification Ritual*, may be found at: http://tvv.proboards.com/index.cgi?action=display&board=Homer&thread=1010&page=

197   See, William A. Young, op. cit., 234-35.

198   See *Ontario Consultants on Religious Tolerance* at http:// www.religious tolerance.org/shinto.htm

199   Carmody and Carmody, op. cit. 207.

200   William Scott Wilson an Gregory Lee, *Ideals of the Samurai: Writings of Japanese Warriors* (Burgank, CA: Ohara Publications, 1982).

201   An excellent and comprehensive site for Buddhism is: http://www. onmarkproductions.com/html/dainichi.shtml

202   See Kenji Matsuo, *A History of Japanese Buddhism.* (Kent: Global Oriental, 2007) and Oscar Ratti and Adele Westbrook. *Secrets of the Samurai: The Martial Arts of Feudal Japan.* (Japan: Tuttle, 1973).

203   Daisetz T. Suzuki, *Zen and Japanese Culture.* (Princeton: Princeton University Press, 1993), 93.

204   Aside from those already mentioned an excellent source dealing with the Samurai is *The Samurai Archives Japanese History Page* at www.samurai-archives.com/

205   See N. Kollar, "Religious Perspectives on Economics and Poverty: Perspectives of Roman Catholicism in North America" in *Explorations* 14 (Fall, 1995).

206   See Levine, Adam Seth, Frank, Robert H. and Dijk, Oege, *Expenditure Cascades* (September 13, 2010). Available at SSRN: http://ssrn.com/ abstract=1690612

207   There are no true and false answers. Each set is composed of four identical signposts: belief, ritual, moral norms, community. If you answer "true" to all the questions in a set, that suggests you are liminal, first set; or modern, second set.

208   Alice Belle Garrigus was a central figure in the Pentecostal movement beginning in Newfoundland, Canada. The history of Pentecostals in Newfoundland is exemplary for demonstrating how a movement becomes an essential part of the culture and continues to grow in the process. Dr. Hans Rollman's work is particularly helpful for understanding the transition of Pentecostalism from the edge of society to an essential ingredient in it. For the quote see: http://www.mun.ca/rels/ pent/texts/essay/essay2.html

209   Bellah's book provides many examples of how Americans have little awareness of the economic and political forces outside their niche that influence their daily life. Robert Neelly Bellah, et al, *Habits of the Heart : Individualism And Commitment In American Life* (Berkeley: University of California Press, 1985).

210   By Sam Meekings (New York: Thomas Dunne Books/St. Martin's Press, 2010).

211   Part of what follows as well as an essential bibliography dealing with Fundamentalism may be found in my "Secular Fundamentalism and Secular Humanism: Value Sets For the Twenty-First Century," in *Studies in Formative Spirituality* XIV (May, 1993) 2:233-46.

212   Cf. Milton Yinger's many works but especially his *Scientific Study of Religion* (New York: Macmillan, 1970) also of importance is Hans J. Mol, *Identity and the Sacred* (N.Y.: Macmillan, 1976).

213   The origin of the term "fundamentalist" is usually credited to the *The Fundamentals*, a collection of twelve books on five subjects published in 1910 and funded by Milton and Lyman Stewart. The reduction of Christian belief to a few dogmatic statements began much earlier (one might suggest with the first Christians saying "Jesus is Lord," or the early baptismal creeds).

214   Christopher Lasch, *The Culture Of Narcissism: American Life in an Age of Diminishing Expectations* (New York: Norton, 1979).

215   William G McLoughlin, *Revivals, Awakenings, And Reform : An Essay on Religion and Social Change in America, 1607-1977*, (Chicago : The Univ. of Chicago Press, 1978).

216   Fifty-nine percent of Christian churches in the United States have fewer than one hundred members. Ninety-four percent of Christian churches have a membership of fewer than five hundred. See Hartford Institute for Religion Research website http://hirr.hartsem.edu/research/fastfacts/fast_facts.html#sizecong

217   The entire statement came to be known as the "Niagara Creed." David O. Beale *In Pursuit of Purity: American Fundamentalism Since 1850* (Greenville, SC: Unusual Publications, 1986), 275-79. Ernest Robert Sandeen, *The Roots of Fundamentalism: British and American Millenarianism, 1800-1930* (Chicago: University of Chicago Press, 1970), 273-77.

218   The formulation of American fundamentalist beliefs can be traced to the Niagara Bible Conference and, in 1910, to the *General Assembly of the Presbyterian Church*, which distilled these into what became known as the "five fundamentals."

219   See Sandeen, op. cit., 273-77.

220   See http://www.the-churchofchrist.com/morality/is_dancing_a_sin.htm

221   See http://pewforum.org/Christian/Evangelical-Protestant-Churches/Spirit-and-Power.aspx

222   The touchstone of discussions concerning contemporary, or what some call classic, Pentecostalism is the continuous Azusa Street revival led by Charles Parham in Los Angeles between 1906 and 1909.

223   I am using the *New English Bible* translation while placing the common Pentecostal/Charismatic phrases within brackets.

224   See "Living Up to God's Expectations 101" by Mrs. Gaulsted at the Klan's website: http://kkk.bz/main/?page_id=578. Chester L Quarles, *The Ku Klux Klan And Related American Racialist And Anti-Semitic Organizations : A History And Analysis.* (Jefferson, NC : McFarland, 2008). Bruce Hoffman, *Inside Terrorism* (New York : Columbia University Press, 1998).

225   Lee was not antagonistic to the fundamentalists. On the contrary, he was an editor of a Baptist newspaper. See Sandeeen, op. cit., 188.

226   For the entire series of texts see: http://www.xmission.com/~fidelis/

227   There are many who reject the applicability of this term to contemporary Muslim anti-Western movements. A quick check with Wikipedia provides a review of such statements.

228   The basis for what follows may be found in Bernard Lewis, *The Political Language of Islam* (Chicago: University of Chicago Press, 1988) and John Esposito, *Voices of Resurgent Islam* (New York: Oxford, 1986).

229   For a list of these rights as found in the United Nations declaration, see this site for language and other commentary. http://www.ohchr.org/EN/UDHR/Pages/Introduction.aspx

230   The general theory and process of this search may be found in my "The Death of National Symbols: Roman Catholicism in Quebec," in *Ethnicity, Nationality, and Religious Experience.* Peter C. Phan ed. (Lanham, MD: University Press of America, 1995).

231   See John Esposito, *Voices of Resurgent Islam*, op. cit.

232   See *Voices of Resurgent Islam*, op. cit., Lawrence Davidson, *Islamic Fundamentalism* (Westport, Conn: Greenwood Press, 1998) Ann Elizabeth Mayer, "Islamic Law and Human Rights: Conundrums and Equivocations," in Carrie Gustafson, Peter H. Juviler (eds.), *Religion And Human Rights: Competing Claims?*, (New York: Columbia University Press, 1999). Changes in Egypt during 2011 may bring about changes in the Muslim Brotherhood.

233   The most famous list and explanation of these "fundamentalisms" may be found in the series of books known as the *Fundamentalism Project*, eds. Marty E. Marty and R. Scott Appleby, editors, University of Chicago Press (1994-2003).

234   One must remember that a "nation" and its consequent "nationalism" are part of the modern era. To find it in the past is truly finding a pattern of life that does not exist. See Liah Greenfiled, *Nationalism: Five Roads to Modernity* (Cambridge: Harvard University Press, 1992). Sinisa Malesevic, *Identity as Ideology: Understanding Ethnicity and National-*

ism, (New York: Palgrave, 2006). Umut Ozkirimli, *Theories of Nationalism: A Critical Introduction*, (New York: Palgrave, 2010).

235   It was said that the conservative churches are growing. It was found that many of the same people go to different conservative churches. For a discussion of ways that people are searching in these churches for something that one church does not seem able to provide, see Reginald W. Bibby, especially his *Restless Gods: The Renaissance of Religion in Canada* (Toronto: Stoddart, 2003). The mere increase in size as well as accompanying multiplicity of Fundamentalist and Pentecostal churches may be found in the various editions of *Handbook of Denominations in the United States,* the most recent of which is the 13th edition (Nashville, TN: Abingdon Press, 2010) by Craig D Atwood, Frank Spencer Mead, and Samuel S Hill.

236   Although I use Paul Ricoeur's phrase, it is meant to include all the discussions that usually go under the title "modern hermeneutics" and "postmodern hermeneutics." Some of the central discussants are Paul Ricoeur (1913-2005), Jacques Derrida (b. 1930-2004), Jean-Francois Lyotard (1924-1998), Michel Foucault (1926- 1984), Stanley Eugene Fish (1938), and Richard McKay Rorty (1931- 2007).

237   *Tous les jours à tous points de vue je vais de mieux en mieux,* for a bibliography and further discussion of Coue see http://emilecoue.wwwhubs.com/

238   See the introductory quote in C Alan Anderson and Deborah G Whitehouse, *New Thought: A Practical American Spirituality* (New York: Crossroad, 1995).

239   See Mitch Horowitz, *Occult America: The History of How Mysticism Shaped Our Nation* (New York: Bantam Books, 2009), chapters 3-6.

240   This may be found at www.sacred-texts.com/eso/som/index.htm

241   For an elaboration of these and other principles of *Science of the Mind* see Holmes, op. cit., 63-105, 108-111, 137-162, 266-293, and 357-389.

242   *The Power of Positive Thinking*, (New York: Ballantine Books, Reissue edition August 1, 1996). *Guide to Confident Living*, NY: Ballantine Books; Reissue edition, September 1, 1996. Others may be found at NormanVincentPeale.wwwhubs.com.

243   *Moral Re-Armament* (MRA) is a modern, nondenominational evangelical movement founded by American churchman Frank ND Buchman (1878–1961). In 2001, the MRA movement changed its name to *Initiatives of Change* . See Daniel Sack, *Moral Re-Armament: The Reinventions of an American Religious Movement* (New York: Palgrave Macmillan, 2009) and http://www.iofc.org/

244   These are the original Twelve Steps as published by Alcoholics Anonymous. See Alcoholics Anonymous (June 2001). "Chapter 5: How It Works" (.pdf). Alcoholics Anonymous (4th ed.). Alcoholics Anonymous World Services http://www.aa.org/bigbookonline/en_bigbook_chapt5.pdf.

245   The American Psychological Association has condensed these steps into a secular, scientific language see: Gary VandenBos, (2007). *APA Dictionary of Psychology* (1st ed.), (Washington, DC: American Psychological Association, 2007).

246   An excellent description of Scientology is Janet Reitman, *Inside Scientology: The Story of America's Most Secretive Religion* (New York: Houghton Mifflin Harcourt, 2011).

247   See Melton, J. Gordon, *The Church of Scientology* (Salt Lake City: Signature Press, 2000).

248   David G. Bromley, "Making Sense of Scientology" as found in Lewis, James R., *Scientology* (New York, NY: Oxford University Press, 2009), 170-71.

249   Joseph Campbell, *The Power of Myth*, (New York: Doubleday, 1988), 22-23.

250   This description is dependent upon Robert Bellah who coined the term "American Civil Religion" to summarize this total dedication. He does not make nationalism and Civil Religion identical. It may be found at http://www.robertbellah.com/articles_5.htm

251   Michael Mann has described the transcendence of fascism, for example, as creating a pure nation of Aryans and the means to do so paramilitarism and a classless society. See Michael Mann, *Fascists* (New York: Cambridge University Press, 2004).

252   See Liah Greenfeld, *Nationalism: Five Roads to Modernity* (Cambridge: Harvard University Press, 1992). Eric J. Hobsbawm, *Nations and Nationalism Since 1780: Programme, Myth, Reality* 2nd ed. (Cambridge: Cambridge University Press, 1992). Gregory Jusdanis, *The Necessary Nation* (Princeton, NJ: Princeton University Press, 2001). Sinisa Malesevic, *Identity as Ideology: Understanding Ethnicity and Nationalism* (New York: Palgrave, 2006). Umut Ozkirimli, *Theories of Nationalism: A Critical Introduction* (New York: Palgrave. 2010). http://www.nationalismproject.org/about.htm

253   Fifty-one percent of scientists say they believe in God or a higher power. For more detail, see the research of the Pew Form, for example: http://pewforum.org/Science-and-Bioethics/Scientists-and-Belief.aspx. Metanexus is an organization dedicated to showing how science and

religion support each other in developing a wholistic spirituality. http://www.metanexus.net/faq.asp

254 See Wallace K. Ferguson, *The Renaissance in Historical Thought. Five Centuries of Interpretation* (Boston: Mifflin, 1948)

255 see Tony Davies, *Humanism* (New York: Routledge, 1997).

256 http://www.americanhumanist.org/

257 http://www.iheu.org/minimumstatement

258 *http://www.uua.org/visitors/6798.shtml*

259 Anton Szandor LaVey, *The Satanic Bible* ((New York: Avon Books, 1969), 180.

260 Sybil Leek, *Reincarnation: The Second Chance* (New York: Stein and Day, 1974), 14.

261 As found in Julia Mitchell Corbett, *Religion in America*, 4th ed. (Upper Saddle River, NJ: Prentice Hall, 2000), 248, quoting Sandy Boucher (ed.), *Turning the Wheel: American Women Creating the New Buddhism* (Boston: Beacons Press, 1993), 1-2.

262 Mara Freeman, *Kindling of the Celtic Spirit* (San Francisco, CA: Harper San Francisco, 2001), 1.

263 As found in John L. Reynolds, *Secret Societies* (New York: Arcade, 2006), 4.

264 See Henry Steel Olcott , *Buddhist Catechism*, p. 27. http://www.gutenberg.org/ebooks/30216.

265 H. P. Blavatsky, *Isis Unveiled: A Master-Key to the Mysteries of Ancient and Modern Science and Theology* (Pasadena, CA: Theosophical University Press, 1972).

266 The lists used were from Amazon: Religion and Spirituality; Spirituality and Healing; *New York Times* Best Seller list : Paperback Nonfiction Best Sellers, Advice, How-To, and Miscellaneous bestsellers both hardcover and paperback; Library Journal staff picks 2-8-11; Top Ten Books in Religion and Spirituality Booklist, American Library Association, Nov. 15, 2010; Adult: Spotlight on Religion and Spirituality, Ibid.

267 (New York: Penguin, 2006).

268 (New York: Hay House, 2010), 312. Also did *The Age of Miracles* (NY: Read How You Want, 2009).

269 (Nashville, TN: Thomas Nelson, 2004).

270 (Nashville, TN: Thomas Nelson, 2010).

271 (Chicago, IL: Northfield Publishing, 2010).

272 (Novato, CA: New World Library, 2004).

273 (New York: Harper Collins, 2010).

274 (Berkeley, CA: Parallax, 1998).

275   Ahlstrom, Sydney, *A Religious History of the American People*, v. 1, chapter 10 (New Haven, CT: Yale Press, 1965).

276   Robert D. Putnam and David E. Campbell, *American Grace: How Religion Divides and Unites Us* (New York: Simon and Schuster, 2010).

277   The series by Jeffrey Burton Russell has not been matched over the years for comprehensiveness, depth, and originality. They are all published by Cornell University, Ithaca, NY: *The Devil: Perceptions of Evil from Antiquity to Primitive Christianity* (1977); *Satan: The Early Christian Tradition* (1981); *Lucifer: The Devil In the Middle Ages* (1984); *Mephistopheles: The Devil in the Modern World* (1986).

278   See Neil Forsyth, *The Old Enemy: Satan & the Combat Myth* (NJ: Princeton University Press, 1987).

279   (New York: Avon Books, 1969).

280   See Stephen Flowers, *Lords of the Left Hand Path: A History of Spiritual Dissent* (Runa Raven Press, 1997). Richard Sutcliffe, "Left-Hand Path Ritual Magick: An Historical and Philosophical Overview," in G. Harvey & C. Hardman (eds.), *Paganism Today*. (New York: Harper Collins, 1996), 109-37.

281   Anton Szandor LaVey, *The Satanic Rituals* (New York: HarperCollins; Maidstone: Amalgamated Book Services, 2002), 129-140. See also Anton Szandor LaVey, *The Satanic Bible* (New York: Avon Books, 1976).

282   This was translated as *The Damned* by Terry Hale (New York: Penguin Classics, 2001). Previously many other authors such as Marquis de Sade (1740-1814) had placed the elements of the Mass such as the bread and wine in sexual contexts similar to what Huysman's describes. In 1987, *La-bas* was a popular duet by Jean-Jacques Godman and Sirima. The American musical group Coven included a recording of a Satanic Mass in their 1969 album *Witchcraft Destroys Minds and Reaps Souls.*

283   The reader should also be reminded that the spate of satanic ritual abuse cases put forth by some child counselors during the late twentieth century were demonstrated to be artificial constructs drawn up by the desires of the counselors more than the reality of the children's interaction with adults.

284   Hans Holzer, *The Supernatural: Explaining the Unexplained* (Franklin Lakes, NJ: New Page Books, 2003). James Houran, *Hauntings and Poltergeists: Multidisciplinary Perspectives* (New York: McFarland & Company, 2001). Harvey J. Irwin and Caroline A. Watt, *An Introduction to Parapsychology* (New York: McFarland &Company, 2007).

285   *The Satanic Bible*, op. cit., 81.

286   See Edward Evans-Pritchard, *Witchcraft, Oracles and Magic Among the Azande* (Oxford: Oxford University Press, 1937), pages 8-9 for this definition of witchcraft. It came to be used by many anthropologists. It did not, however, seem to describe the European experience. See Keith Thomas, *Religion and the Decline of Magic* (Oxford: Oxford University Press, 1997), 464-5 ; Bengt Ankarloo and Gustav Henningsen, *Early Modern European Witchcraft: Centres and Peripheries* (Oxford: Oxford University Press, 1990), 1, 14.

287   Gerald B Gardner, *Witchcraft Today* (London: Rider, 1954).

288   Originally published in 1948 from a series of articles he wrote and corrected and edited four times since the final edition is that of Grevel Llindop (ed.), *The White Goddess : A Historical Grammar of Poetic Myth* (Manchester: Carcanet, 1997).

289   For authors who disagree with these founders of Wicca see: Ronald Hutton, *The Pagan Religions of the Ancient British Isles: Their Nature and Legacy* (Oxford: Blackwell, 1991). Ronald Hutton, *The Triumph of the Moon: A History of Modern Pagan Witchcraft* (New York: Oxford University Press, 1999). "Margaret Murray: Who Believed Her and Why?" by Jacqueline Simpson. *Folklore* #105 (1994), 89-96. Richard Kieckhefer, "Foreword" to *A Razor for a Goat: A Discussion of Certain Problems in Witchcraft and Diabolism* (Toronto: Toronto University Press, 2003).

290   Carol P. Christ, "Why Women Need the Goddess: Phenomenology, Psychological, and Political Reflections" in *Womanspirit Rising: A Feminist Reader in Religion*, ed. Carol P. Christ and Judith Plaskow (San Francisco: Harper and Row, 1979), 279-285. See also Hallie Inglehart, *Womanspirit: A Guide to Women's Wisdom* (San Francisco: Harper and Row, 1983), 97.

291   See *Religion in America*, op. cit., 291-292.

292   For a sense of how one part of the Wicca movement would celebrate the year, see Mara Freeman, *Kindling the Celtic Spirit: Ancient Traditions to Illumine Your Life Throughout the Seasons* (San Francisco: Harper and Row, 2001).

293   This will have diverse spellings depending on the historical roots of the wicca/witchcraft/craft/old religion coven.

294   Before this time (fifteenth, sixteenth, and seventeenth century Europe and the colonies), the term "witch" could refer to cunning folk, unbinding witches, blessers, wizards, sorcerers, folk magicians, and healers. See Alan Macfarlane, *Witchcraft in Tudor and Stuart England* (London: Routledge, 1979), 130; also Appendix 2.

295   In 1993, The United States Supreme Court ruled in *Church of Lukumi Babalu Aye v. City of Hialeah* that laws passed to prevent these types of sacrifices were illegal.

296   For magic, Santeria, and Vodoun see Rosemary Ellen Guiley, *Harper's Encyclopedia of Mystical and Paranormal Experience* (New York: HarperCollins, 2001).

297   Mircea Eliade, *Shamanism* (Princeton, NJ: Princeton University, 1951/1964).

298   Much contemporary writing takes a more anti-authoritarian, radical feminist, and antinomian view of Gnosticism. For both sides of the argument and their respective bibliography see Diarmaid Macculloch, *Christianity: The First Three Thousand Years* (New York: Viking, 2010), 119-124.

299   See "Gematria" in Gully, op. cit., 230-31.

300   See "Kabbalah" in Gully, pp. 306-09, as well as Yehuda Liebes, *Studies in the Zohar* (New York: SUNY Press, SUNY series in Judaica: Hermeneutics, Mysticism, and Religion, 1993). Micha Odenheimer, "Challenging the Master: Moshe Idel's critique of Gershom Scholem," as found in Michael Berenbaum and Fred Skolnik, *Encyclopaedia Judaica* (Detroit, Michigan: Macmillan, 2007), 2nd ed. This is also a good source for discussions about Kabbalah and Mysticism.

301   For more detail on recent Western developments see John Lawrence Reynolds, *Secret Societies* (New York: Arcade, 2006), 124-135.

302   Two websites may be helpful in your investigations: For a translation of some of the books see the Alchemy website: http://www.levity.com/alchemy/corpherm.html; for a collection of other commentators on the texts and developers of the tradition see *The Hermetic Library* at http://hermetic.com/. Two books are helpful. For the actual texts, see P. Brian, ed., *Hermetica: The Greek Corpus Hermeticum and the Latin Asclepius in a New English Translation, with Notes and Introduction* (London: Cambridge, 1992). For a sense of where they come from, see Garth Fowden, *The Egyptian Hermes: A Historical Approach to the Late Pagan Mind* (Cambridge/New York: Cambridge University Press, 1986).

303   Gulley, op. cit., 259-62; 518-522. Reynolds, op. cit., 139-155.

304   For bibliographical information see Mitch Horowitz, *Occult America* (New York: Bantam, 2009), 42-49. Guiley, op. cit., 64-66; 611-16.

305   See, for example, Peter Washington, *Madame Blavatsky's Baboon: Theosophy and the Emergence of the Western Guru* (London: Secker & Warburg, 1993).

306   As far as I know, she makes no allusions to Gottfried Wilhelm Leibniz (1646-1716)'s famous theory of monads.

307   See Helena Blavatsky, *The Key to Theosophy* and *The Secret Doctrine: The Synthesis of Science, Religion, and Philosophy*. All texts may be obtained on the Internet at: http://www.theosociety.org/pasadena/ts/tup.htm

308   See J. Krishnamurti 1968, para. 57 at J. Krishnamurti online, the official repository of his teaching, http://www.jkrishnamurti.org/krishnamurti-teachings/view-text.php?tid=3&chid=3

309   http://religions.pewforum.org/

310   See Statistics Canada: *Religions in Canada—Census 2001. 2.statcan.ca. 2010-03-09.*

311   Rita Gross, "Buddhism after Patriarchy?" in *After Patriarchy: Feminist Transformations of the World Religions*, ed. Paula M. Cooey, William R. Eakin and Jay B. McDaniel (Maryknoll, NY: Orbis Books, 1991), 65-68. Sandy Bourcher (ed.), 2nd ed., *Turning the Wheel: American Women Creating the New Buddhism* (Boston: Beacon Press, 1993).

312   While this is a more esoteric form of Buddhism, the Naropa University and the headquarters itself do not necessarily focus on this aspect of Vajradhatu Buddhism, which is also called Tantric Buddhism, Tantrayāna, Mantrayāna, Secret Mantra, Esoteric Buddhism, and the Diamond Vehicle.

313   Douglas E. Cowan and David G. Bromley, *Cults and New Religions: A Brief History* in Blackwell Brief Histories of Religion Series (New York: Wiley-Blackwell, 2007), 48–71.

314   See the following site for history: The *Sikhism Home Page: History of Sri Guru Granth Sahib* at http://www.sikhs.org/granth1.htm; for a complete English version, see http://adigranth.greenspot.fi/

315   This phrase, the *Mul Mantar*, is prayed in the Punjabi language. Thus, in the original, there are no verbs or pronouns, and it is said that many of the words we read in English here are only rough approximations to the original Punjabi. See Eleanor M. Nesbitt, *Sikhism: a very short introduction.* (Oxford: Oxford University Press, 2005), 22–24, and Dr. Santokh Singh, Dr. Santokh, *English Transliteration and Interpretation of Nitnaym Baanees, Sikh Prayers for English Speaking Sikh Youth* (Amristsar (Punjab), India: Sikh Resource Centre, 1990). http://www.csjs.com

316   Robert D. Putnam and David E. Campbell, *American Grace: How Religion Divides and Unites Us* (New York: Simon and Schuster, 2010).

317   See especially http://pewresearch.org/pubs/1780/poll-global-warming-scientists-energy-policies-offshore-drilling-tea-party

318   Ibid. 71.

319   Ibid. 4-5.

320   "...the most highly religious Americans are likely to be Republicans." Ibid., 369.

321   The authors use the term "devotion" rather than spirituality. Ibid., 35. The description of the spirituality is the typical one for a current defini-

tion of a highly religious person, p. 18, and current religious conservative, p. 11.

322   Ibid., 5-6, 114-15, 133.

323   The original critiques are found among Lynn White, Jr., "The Historical Roots of Our Ecological Crisis" in *Science* 155 (1967): 1203-07; Roderick Nash, *The Rights of Nature: A History of Environmental Ethics* (Madison: The University of Wisconsin Press, 1989); J. Baird Callicott and Roger T. Ames, eds. *Nature in Asian Traditions of Thought: Essays in Philosophy* (Albany: State University of New York, 1989).

324   An excellent example of this is Lester R. Brown, *World on the Edge: How to Prevent Environmental and Economic Collapse* (New York: W.W. Norton, 2011). This small compact book is written by a leader of the environmental movement. It provides an up-to-date diagnosis along with solutions to what is diagnosed. Religion is not mentioned.

325   Eileen Holland, *The Wicca Handbook* (San Francisco: Wiser Books, 2008), 7.

326   For a detailed discussion of this and the challenge of discovering the religion of a lost oral tradition, see N. Kollar, "Religion" in *Ready Reference: American Indians*, Harvey Markowitz, Ed., (Pasadena, CA: Salem Press, 1995).

327   *The Encyclopedia of Catholicism* summarizes salvation as "…the ultimate restoration and fulfillment of humanity and all creation…" Richard McBrien, ed., (New York: HarperCollins, 1995), 1158.

328   See, for example, anything referring to the biblical green movement and sites such as http://www.christianecology.org

329   Most of these responses were to White's 1967 article, op. cit. that blamed all of Christianity for the ecological crisis. Although scientific dating has been constant to the present, the response of the religions were primarily in the 1980s with little updating of the arguments, but a great deal of amplification of these until the present.

330   Young, op. cit., 288-91.

331   Isma'l Al Faruqi, "Islamic Ethics," in *World Religions and Global Ethics*, ed. S. Cromwell Crawford (New York: Paragon House, 1989), 120-22.

332   http://www.gits4u.com/envo/envo4.htm.

333   This equates to 2.63 gallons per liter, thus approximately 26 billion gallons of sewage.

334   Robert Monk, et al, *Exploring Religious Meaning*, 6th ed. (Upper Saddle River, NJ: Prentice Hall, 2003), 303-09.

335   Brown, op. cit., p. x. The changes in nature are exponential, not arithmetic.

336   The Way, The Truth, The Life (John 14:6)

337 "Truth Force" used by Mohandas K. Gandhi to describe the necessity of bringing together within oneself both "truth" and "love" in order to deal with social injustices. The way of life necessary for Satyagraha to become reality in life and society was also advocated by Martin Luther King and Nelson Mandela. See Mahatma Gandhi; Kumarappa Bharatan, *Non-Violent Resistance (Satyagraha)* (New York: Schocken Books, 1961), 37.

338 From Jon Courtenay Grimwood, *9Tail Fox* (San Francisco: Night Shade Books, 2007), 230.

339 This is, of course, the thesis of Ernest Becker found in his Pulitzer Prize-winning book *The Denial of Death* (New York: The Free Press, 1973). We dealt with some of this in Chapter One.

340 Nathan Kollar, "Challenges to Theories of Grief," *Human Development* 11(Winter, 1990) 4.

341 Becker, op. cit., 42.

342 "The Pornography of Death" *Encounter* Vol. V: No. 4, (October 1955), 49-52.

343 For an extended discussion of this topic, see Nathan Kollar, "Death: Is It Ever Natural?" *New Directions in Death Education and Counseling*, R. Pacholski, ed. (Ag Press, 1981).

344 There are many polls dealing with people's understanding of the after-life. A good place to begin is at the site provided by Ontario Consultants on Religious Tolerance. http://www.religioustolerance.org/chr_poll3.htm

345 Much of what follows is based on my entry "Afterlife" as found in *New World Encyclopedia* (Paragon Press, 2008).

346 The idea of individual survival after death is rather recent in human history. See J. Hick, *Death and Eternal Life* (San Francisco: Harper and Row, 1976).

347 Paul Theroux, "Why We Travel," *The New York Times*, Travel, Sunday, April 3, 2011, p. 1.

348 Such need of others at every level is demonstrated mathematically and described in detail in Martin A. Nowak with Roger Highfield, *Superco-operators: Altruism, Evolution, and Why We Need Each Other to Succeed* (New York: Free Press, 2011).

349 Aside from the inhumanity of using numbers alone for decision making, when dealing with humans they can also be very inaccurate and misleading. See Jonah Lehrer, *How We Decide* (Houghton Mifflin Harcourt, 2009); Jonah Lehrer, *How We Decide* (Houghton Mifflin Harcourt, 2009); Gardner, *Truth, Beauty and Goodness Reframed* (Basic Books, 2011).

350   Much of what follows was originally published in *Explorations* 17(Spring) 3:43-58.

351   Arnold Pacey, *A Culture of Technology* (Cambridge, Mass: MIT Press, 1983), 8-10. Authors making the same point are Robert Pirsig, *Zen and the Art of Motorcycle Maintenance* (New York: Bantam, 1975), 163, 194, 238, 280; William Lowrance, *Modern Science and Human Values* (New York: Oxford, 1986), 3-21.

352   The application and development of these ideas may be found in my "Secular Fundamentalism or Secular Humanism: Continuing a Tradition," in *Humanities in the South* 72 (Fall, 1990), 6-12.

353   Victor Frankel, *Man's Search For Meaning: An Introduction to Logotherapy* (Boston: Beacon Press, 1962).

354   The following is adapted from M. Rokeach, *The Nature of Human Values* (New York: Free Press, 1973) and James P. Shaver and William Strong , *Facing Value Decisions* 2nd ed. (New York: Teachers College Press, 1982),.

355   For the test see: http://faculty.fortlewis.edu/burke_b/Personality/PIL. pdf. For discussion of its validity see. James C. Crumbaugh, "Cross-Validation of Purpose-In-Life Test Based on Frankl's Concepts" as found in *Journal of Individual Psychology*, Vol. 24(1), 1968, 74-81.

356   This is dependent upon but not in advocacy of Sidney Simon and L. Howe, *Values Clarification: A Handbook of Practical Strategies for Teachers and Students* (New York: Hart, 1972).

357   For just how much our community and the ends of the task influence our sense of justice, see Max H. Bazerman and Ann E. Tenbrunsel, *Blind Spots: Why We Fail to Do What's Right and What to Do About It* (Princeton NJ: Princeton University Press, 2011).

358   See for the following material Erik Erikson, Joan Erikson, *The Life Cycle Completed* (New York: W.W. Norton, 1998).

359   This is an adaption from information found in *Blind Spots*, ibid.

360   Much of what follows was originally part of an article titled "Choice" that may be found in *Ready Reference: Ethics*. John Roth, ed., (Pasadena, CA: Salem Press, 1994). Roy F. Baumeister and John Tierney have written a book that helps us carry through on the choices we make. See *Willpower: Rediscovering the Greatest Human Strength* (New York: Penguin Press, 2011).

361   If determinism is true, wouldn't we be able to predict what will happen? Dan Gardner, a retired professor of business, psychology, and political science, traced 27 predictions of 451 experts over 25 years. They could not do so with any consistency. See Dan Gardner, *Future Babble: Why Expert Predictions Are Next to Worthless and You Can Do Better* (New York: Dutton, 2011).

362   Stage theories are good for clearly providing what usually happens to most people. However, they are weak as to the final stage or stages because these seldom happen to most people. The researchers, then, are usually imposing their own values upon the data to suggest their ideal of the process's goal.

363   Twenty-five percent of U.S. households were mixed-faith marriages in 2010. The influence of mutual spiritualities or religions on the family usually results in the more strongly held spirituality providing direction for both the couple and their children, when present. For statistics on both Canada and the United States, see Ontario Consultants on Religious Tolerance at http://www.religioustolerance.org/ifm_fact.htm. An excellent article that reviews both models of marital health in the context of spirituality is Paul Giblin's "Marital Health and Spirituality" in *Journal of Pastoral Counseling* 43(2004) 45-87.

364   This process is demonstrated in detail for Quebec society in my "The Death of National Symbols: Roman Catholicism in Quebec," in *Ethnicity, Nationality, and Religious Experience*. Peter C. Phan, ed. (Lanham, MD: University Press of America, 1995). Since that time, the same events have occurred in Poland and Ireland with devastating results for the Roman Catholic Church. More detail to the process is provided in my "Pivotal Cultural Turning Points: Examples, Processes, and Signposts: The Religious Canary's Role in the Mining of Cultural Signposts," As found in *Humanity at the Turning Point: Rethinking Nature, Culture and Freedom,* Soja Servomas, ed. (Helsinki: Renvall Institute Publications 23, University of Helsinki Press, 2006).

365   One can press the discussion about sameness further by asking if we understand "the same" today as they did a thousand years ago. Before the perfection of mirrors, processes of duplication, and machine parts, nothing was exactly the same as another thing. One could hold up two books, the Bible for example, in the year 700 CE and say they were the same even though they did not contain identical words, types of writing, and pagination. Sameness too may be in the eye of the beholder.

366   I realize that Kohlberg's work dealt with ethics, but it also applies to the answers to the question of truth as they are being developed in our contemporary philosophy and the social sciences.

INDEX

Animism, 28-30

Answers to life's questions, 278-84

Apophatic transcendence, 17

Apostles, 101-02

Apostolic church, 101

Astrology, 236-37

Aum (om), 133

Authority and spirituality, 63-64

Beginning of every spirituality, 5

Belief and faith, 56-63

Bhagavad gita 141-42

Bhakti yoga, 134, 134, 137, 139, 141

Bible and spirituality, 96-99

Bible believing Christians, 94

Bible believing christians, 94

Body and soul, description of 22

Body, mind, soul, and spirit, 22, 298

Book of changes, 154

Buddha nature, 148

Buddhism, Mahayana, 148-50

Buddhism, Theravada, 146-147

Buddhist churches of America, 149, 242

Buddhist spirituality and signposts 143-145; death 275

Buddhists spiritualities, 146-151

Challenges to contemporary Christian spirituality, 110-12

Change and spirituality,11

Changing values, 316

Charismatics, 192-94

Ch'i, 158

Chinese spirituality, signposts 153 -155; death 276

Choosing your spiritual values 311-23

Christian fundamentalist spirituality and signposts 187-191

Christian fundamentalist spirituality, 187-91

Christian identity groups and militias, 192

Christian spirituality 90-113; signposts 96-110; challenges to 110-112; death 269

Classical spiritualities and afterlife, 268-276

Classical spiritualities, 81-83

Community and spirituality, 10

Community, 70-71

Compassionate beings, 146

Confucian spirituality, 155-156 and see Chinese spirituality

Contemporalist spirituality, 199-209

Conversion, 5, 74, 188, 220, 315

Co-temporalist spirituality, 210-

Culture and spirituality, 20-22; foundational values of, 20; feelings indicative of disintegration, 20.

Death and spirituality, 259-268

Death as spiritual or secular, 259-61

Discovering your spirituality see chapter nine

Doubt and spirituality, 61-63

Emptiness, 148

Environmental movement and spirituality, 244-253

Exorcism, 223,225-26

Faith, 10, 13, 39, 41, 43, 56
Feminist movement and spirituality, 253-55
Feng-shui, 154-55
Fundamentalist spiritualities, 183-199; Christian, 187-91; Muslim, 196-97; non-Christian, 194-95
Gnosticism, 232-33
God, ix,5,6,17,31,33,81-2
God's word, 81
Habits and spirituality, 5-7
Here and now: culture, 20-1; the cosmos, 23;
Hermetic order of the golden dawn, 236
Hermetica, 236
Hindu spirituality, 134-140; signposts, 133-139; death 274-5
Home, 21
I Ching, 156-57
Idols, 74-75
Immortality and spirituality, 9
Immortality, 165, 265-66
Indigenous and survival spiritualities, 160-163
International Buddhist meditation center, 242
Ise shrine, 170
Islam, see Muslim
Jainist spirituality, 142-143
Jewish spirituality, 83-90; signposts 85-90; death 271; environment
Jnana yoga, 134, 139
Kabbalah, 234-37
Kami., 167-68
Kataphatic transcendence, 17
Key facts for understanding any spirituality 75; for Buddhist spirituality 146; 151;

for Christian spirituality 113; for Confucian spirituality 156; for Hindu spirituality 140; for Jewish spirituality 90; for Muslim spirituality 129; for Taoist spirituality 159.
Krishna consciousness (iskcon/ hare krishna movement, 241
Lazy values, 314-16
Liminal as postmodern, 44-47
Listening to the suffering of the other, 284-287
Magic, 26, 75, 137, 150, 154, 158, 222, 227
Mantra, 150,142,130-7
Marginal spiritualities, see chapter seven
Medieval culture and spirituality, 35
Middle way, 143
Modern culture and spirituality, 37-43
Modern spiritualities, see contemporalists
Modern world, 38-41,
Morals and ethics, 66-9
Muslim fundamentalists, 196-98
Muslim spirituality 113-129; signposts 121-128; death 272
Mutual responsibility, 299
Mystery of life, 4-5, 19,32,38,140
Mystery religion, 33
Mystics and spirituality, 34-36
Nationalism as spirituality, 203-4
Niche, vii
Non-Christian fundamentalism 193-94
Non-violence, 142,252
Om, 133
Other worldly spirituality, 6
Paradox and spirituality, 7-
Pentecostal spirituality, 192-193

Poverty and spirituality, 253-55

Prayer, 83

Prayers, Jewish 83;
    Christian 90-01;
    Muslim 113-91;
    Hindu, 113, 134-114;
    Jain, 113, 142-43;
    Buddhist, 133, 145, 148;
    Shinto, 169

Presence, remembered and embodied, 52

Presuppositions of the book, ix

Puja, 137, 334

Pure land spirituality, 148 -149

Quran, 116-118; 120

Ritual, 64-65

Sacred, 14-16

Salafi spirituality, 119-21

Santeria, 231-2

Satanic spirituality & signposts 223-227

Science as spirituality, 205

Secular fundamentalism, 184 -187

Secularization, 40-42

Self and identity in the classical spiritualities, 295-298

Self help movements as spirituality, 201-203

Seven deadly sins, 107

Shakti, 138, 336

Shamans, 232

Shiite spirituality, 117-119

Shinto (kami-no-michi) spirituality 167-174; death 276

Signposts of the spiritual life 55- 72, 164 ; belief and faith 56-63; ritual 64-65; morals/ethics 66-9; community 70-71; transcendence 71.

Signposts, symbolic immortality, and spirituality, 165-167

Sikh spirituality, 243

Socialization into a spiritual life, 53, 71, 73, 314-6.

Soul searching, vi

Sources of the spiritual life, 52-54

Spirit baptism, 192

Spiritual compass, 71-73

Spiritual development, 69-70; 71-73; 299-301; 310

Spiritual doubt, 61-63

Spiritual emotions, 14-15

Spiritual gifts, Christianity, 192-93

Spiritual illiteracy, 61

Spiritual life, definitions of, see glossary of key terms

Spiritual maturity 299 -301; 310

Spiritual paradoxes, 8-13

Spiritual values and maturity 301-311

Spiritual views of the self, its choices, and ultimate transcendence, 295-97

Spirituality & the Holy Spirit, 36-38

Spirituality and authorities, 63-4

Spirituality and contemplation, 38

Spirituality and evil, 290-93

Spirituality and liminality, 48-49; 178-79;

Spirituality and mutual responsibility, 299-301

Spirituality and mystery, 4-5

Spirituality and others, 298-99

Spirituality and transcendence, 16-17

Spirituality and value choices, 305-08

Spirituality of nature, basic approaches, 252-53

Spirituality of New Thought, 201, 333

Spirituality of Positive Thinking, 201

Spirituality today: themes and trends, 217-223

Spirituality, 50-51

Spirituality, foundations of 3-

Spirituality: past, present, and future 26-

Stories and spirituality, viii, 16, 26-27, 29, 31, 161, 164, 220, 227

Suffering and classical spiritualities, 281-84

Suffering and spirituality, 276-83

Sufi spirituality, 119-21

Sufism, 119

Sunni spirituality, 119-21

Supernatural, 14, 40, 43

Survival spiritualities, see indigenous spiritualities

Symbolic immortality, 221

Tantrism, 138

Tao, see Chinese spirituality

Taoist spirituality 157-159 and see Chinese spirituality

Ten commandments, 107-08; 191

The Christian bible, 97-98

The International Society for Krishna Consciousness, 241

The Kabbalah Center, 236-37

The Order of Buddhist contemplatives, 242

The Vedanta center, 241

The way of devotion, 137, 140, 275

The way of knowledge, 134, 139

Theosophy, 238-39

Tibetan Buddhism, 150-51

Torah, 88, 89

Traditional Christians, 94

Traditionalist spirituality 183-

Transcendence and spirituality 16-17

Transcendence, 16-17; ultimate, 16; desire 46, 58, 74, 76, 128, 227, 301l; as extraordinary, 21

Transcendence, touchstones of, 52-54

Transcendental meditation, 242

Transcending place 27

Tree of life, 225

Triple goddess, 228

Twelve step spirituality, 201-3

Values, 302-5

Vishnu, 138, 141

Vodoun (voodoo), 231

Western and Eastern spirituality, 22

Wicca spirituality, 227-230

Witch, 225, 227-9

Witches, 230

Zen spirituality, 148-149; 172-5

*Professor Kollar has set an ambitious goal with **Spiritualities** and delivers the goods. Anyone interested in his or her own spirituality or in the spiritualities of other cultures, past and present, will find this carefully researched and highly readable volume to be a stimulating companion.*

As a recognized scholar, he provides both depth and breadth in his treatment of the major traditions of spirituality which provide new insights even to those well versed in theology and the history of spirituality. He brings into the conversation many of the contemporary spiritualities which are often overlooked or devalued by mainstream theologians and shows how they are related to the classical traditions and the ways in which they respond to the demands of our age. This history is particularly important in what he calls our "liminal age." We are on the threshold of a future that is unknown and perhaps unknowable. Never has spirituality been more important but never have the traditional ones been so wanting in their responses.

Professor Kollar is not satisfied with providing intellectual and historical insights into these traditions. He is committed to provided help and guideposts to each of his readers and he or she struggles to find paths of meaning and significance. He provides highly practical methodologies that anyone can use to discover an apt spirituality or to deepen one already embrace.

*It is rare to find both scholarly discipline and pastoral concern in a single work but **Spiritualities** is one of those. It deserves to be in everyone's library.*

William L. Pickett, Ph.D.
Former President, St. John Fisher College
Retired Director of Pastoral Planning, Roman Catholic Diocese, Rochester, NY

Dr. Kollar's book presents the world of spirituality in a clear, concise, easy-to-understand over view. His view of spirituality is perfect for the novice or the person who is well-schooled in the study of spirituality. The reader is led through the history of the world's great spiritualities as well as his own relationship to those spiritual awaken-

ings. The novice finds as easy-to-understand summary of traditional spiritualities as well as a path to personal spiritual development. The well-versed finds a deeper understanding of the world of spirituality as well as a deeper understanding of himself. Both the novice and the learned can profit greatly from Dr. Kollar's book.

Lola Carol Thomas, MA
Chairperson of the English department
Teacher of Advanced Placement English
Chatfield High School
Littleton, CO

Dr. Kollar's book on Spiritualities is designed for those seeking information on those spiritualities embedded in the world religions. His scholarly analysis of contemporary spiritualities and his unique wholistic approach to spirituality distinguishes this book from others. Spiritualities: Past, Present, and Future contains important information about spirituality for World Religions teachers and necessary things to keep in mind for interfaith leaders charged with guiding those on an interfaith spiritual journey.

Muhammad Shafiq, PhD
IIIT Chair in Interfaith Studies
Executive Director
The Hickey Center for Interfaith Studies and Dialogue
Nazareth College

For the handbook ***Soul Searching: A Handbook for Discovering, Developing, and Talking About Your Spirituality***

Dr. Kollar has devised an unbiased method of discernment for today's serious soul searcher. This book will provoke the seeker to examine his or her journey thus far, in order to explore that deep call for awareness and response that can inspire profound change. In today's world of secular drives and religious division, Soul Searching: A Handbook for Discovering, Developing, and Talking About Your Spirituality offers a much needed tool for understanding the value of the many paths toward spiritual growth, enabling conscious choice. Indeed, it is in that realm of spiritual growth that healing happens.

Elizabeth Campbell, Spiritual Director
Episcopal Lay Minister
Associate, Shalem Institute for Spiritual Formation
Member, Spiritual Directors International